Contemporary Russian Politics

For Maura, Sáoirse and Mani, and in memoriam:
Frank Robinson and Peter Frank

Contemporary Russian Politics

An Introduction

NEIL ROBINSON

polity

First published in 2018 by Polity Press

Polity Press
65 Bridge Street
Cambridge CB2 1UR, UK

Polity Press
101 Station Landing
Suite 300
Medford, MA 02155, USA

ISBN-13: 978-0-7456-3136-3
ISBN-13: 978-0-7456-3137-0 (pb)

A catalogue record for this book is available from the British Library.
Names: Robinson, Neil, 1964- author.
Title: Contemporary Russian politics : an introduction / Neil Robinson.
Description: 1 | Cambridge, UK ; Medford, MA : Polity, 2018. | Includes
    bibliographical references and index.
Identifiers: LCCN 2017057445 (print) | LCCN 2018012665 (ebook) | ISBN
    9781509525188 (Epub) | ISBN 9780745631363 (hardback) | ISBN 9780745631370
    (paperback)
Subjects: LCSH: Russia (Federation)–Politics and government–1991- |
    Post-communism–Russia (Federation) | BISAC: POLITICAL SCIENCE /
    International Relations / General.
Classification: LCC JN6695 (ebook) | LCC JN6695 .R62 2018 (print) | DDC
    320.947–dc23
LC record available at https://lccn.loc.gov/2017057445

Typeset in 9.5 on 13 pt Swift Light
by Fakenham Prepress Solutions, Fakenham, Norfolk NR21 8NN
Printed and bound in the UK by CPI Group (UK) Ltd, Croydon, CR0 4YY

For further information on Polity, visit our website: politybooks.com

Contents

Tables and Figures

Tables

Figures

Glossary

autonomous republics	One of the three names for the large territorial units that made up the Union republics of the USSR and make up the Russian Federation. Now known as republics in Russia (see the entry 'krai' below).
CIS	Commonwealth of Independent States
colour revolutions	Protest movements that overthrew established rulers or their designated successors in Serbia (2000), Georgia (2003), Ukraine (2004–5) and Kyrgyzstan (2005). The term comes from the names given the Georgian and Ukrainian revolutions, which were labelled 'Rose' and 'Orange', respectively.
CPRF	Communist Party of the Russian Federation
CPSU	Communist Party of the Soviet Union
Duma	The lower house of Russian parliament from 1993
EU	European Union
federal districts	Eight administrative units established by Putin in 2000 as a new layer of regional administration
glasnost'	'Openness': the media management policy adopted by Gorbachev
krai, *oblast'*, *okrug*, republics	The large territorial-administrative units that made up the Union republics of the USSR and now the names for Russia's provinces (federal subjects).
LDPR	Liberal Democratic Party of Russia
NGO	Non-governmental organization
perestroika	'Restructuring': the collective name for reform policies launched in 1985–6 by Gorbachev.

Politburo	The permanent standing committee of the CPSU's Central Committee, chaired by the general secretary (also known as the first secretary), and the highest decision-making body in the USSR.
polpredy	Presidential representatives, first appointed by Yeltsin to each of the constituent units of the Russian Federation in 1991, replaced by heads of the federal districts under Putin in 2000.
RSFSR	Russian Soviet Federal Socialist Republic
Supreme Soviet	The legislature of the USSR and Russia (until 1993)
Union republic	The fifteen main constituent parts of the USSR, named after their dominant ethnic group, each of which became an independent state in 1991.
USSR	Union of Soviet Socialist Republics

Acknowledgements

As usual there are too many people to thank and not enough space in which to do it. My colleagues at the University of Limerick's Department of Politics and Public Administration are owed thanks for putting up with my frequent lapses in attention to their needs while I have been diverted by this book and for the help that they have given me along the way. I have had a lot of advice about its content, both directly and indirectly, from other Russian and post-Soviet specialists. It is unfair to single people out since so many different conversations and e-mails have helped me towards its completion, but (and in no particular order) David White, Richard Sakwa, Cameron Ross, Vladimir Gel'man, Paul Chaisty, Sarah Milne, Stephen White, Rico Isaacs and Derek Hutcheson have all left a mark in some way. They have my thanks and apologies for not always heeding what they have tried to teach me. My thanks and apologies, too, to Louise Knight and Nekane Tanaka Galdos from Polity, who have been exemplary in their professionalism and diligence and saintly in their tolerance of my lack of either of those virtues.

The people who really keep my show on the road are family and friends. The 'Cheetahs', Stephen McNamara and Sinead Lee, Katie Shishani, Natália Ferracin and Rafa Rossignoli have provided help and support in so many ways that they have blurred the line between family and friends to a point where you wouldn't know there was one. Maura, Sáoirse and Mani are the three pillars on which everything rests, as always, but it is great that they have been joined of late by Adam, Somjai and Pitcha. I need all of the familial support I can get.

Illustration Acknowledgements

p. 21: 'Raise the Banner of Marx, Engels, Lenin and Stalin': Soviet propaganda poster from 1933: https://commons.wikimedia.org/wiki/File:Marx,_Engels,_Lenin,_Stalin_(1933).jpg

p. 27: 'Chimney smoke is the breath of Soviet Russia': Soviet propaganda poster promoting industrial growth: https://commons.wikimedia.org/wiki/File:Smoke_of_chimneys_is_the_breath_of_Soviet_Russia.jpg

p. 49: Gorbachev addressing the CPSU Central Committee: https://en.wikipedia.org/wiki/Mikhail_Gorbachev#/media/File:RIAN_archive_850809_General_Secretary_of_the_CPSU_CC_M._Gorbachev_(close-up).jpg

p. 57: Boris Yeltsin rallying opposition to the August 1991 coup: Wikimedia Commons

p. 86: Putin meeting Mikhail Khodorkovsky, the owner of Yukos, in 2002; Khodorkovsky was arrested for economic crimes in 2003 and lost control of Yukos: https://commons.wikimedia.org/w/index.php?curid=5398658

p. 89: Some of the victims of the Beslan school siege: https://commons.wikimedia.org/w/index.php?title=Special:Search&profile=images&search=beslan+&fulltext=1&searchToken=92ibc0ib9f8y1y05wyqtyikql#/media/File:Beslan_foto_pogibshih.jpg

p. 98: Putin and Medvedev at the military parade marking the sixty-ninth anniversary of victory in the Great Patriotic War: https://commons.wikimedia.org/wiki/File:Sergey_Shoigu,_Vladimir_Putin,_Dmitry_Medvedev,_May_9,_2014.jpg

p. 114: The Duma building, Moscow: https://commons.wikimedia.org/w/index.php?title=Special:Search&profile=images&search=Russian+Duma&fulltext=1&searchToken=55c4qpf7t7lkcv99g2tswbukw#/media/File:Russian_Duma_1.jpg

p. 123: Leader as action man: Putin submerges on board a mini-submarine to explore a shipwreck in the Black Sea: http://en.kremlin.ru/events/president/news/50147

p. 136: Chechen fighters with a downed Russian helicopter, 1994: https://commons.wikimedia.org/w/index.php?title=Special:Search&profile=images&search=Chechen+war&fulltext=1&searchToken=5qsv7xuzrxejd5guzdlfldg3t#/media/File:Evstafiev-helicopter-shot-down.jpg

p. 148: Alexei Navalny at a protest rally, Moscow, 2013: https://commons.wikimedia.org/wiki/File:Alexey_Navalny_at_Moscow_rally_2013-06-12_3.JPG

p. 155: CPRF leader Gennady Zyuganov and supporters in Red Square celebrate the 130th anniversary of Lenin's birth: https://commons.wikimedia.org/w/index.php?title=Special:Search&profile=images&search=CPRF&fulltext=1&searchToken=eyqvl8vqsr3z5yn4dw39t64sk#/media/File:RIAN_archive_783695_The_leader_of_the_CPRF_Gennady_Zyuganov_at_the_Red_Square.jpg

p. 162: A United Russia campaign poster for the 2007 Duma election: 'Moscow votes for Putin!': https://commons.wikimedia.org/w/index.php?curid=17665177

p. 188: 'I didn't vote for these bastards' (the United Russia logo adapted by Alexei Navalny to show the United Russia bear with a bag of swag), 'I voted for some other bastards' (logos of Yabloko, A Just Russia and the CPRF). 'I demand a recount!': https://commons.wikimedia.org/w/index.php?curid=17665177

p. 191: The late Boris Nemtsov at the December 2011 For Fair elections rally: https://commons.wikimedia.org/w/index.php?curid=59977710

p. 211: Putin's tears in oil: graffiti in Perm satirizing Russia's oil dependency: https://www.flickr.com/photos/centralasian/7180754004/in/photostream/

p. 212: 'If Russia has oil, I'm shopping in Milan': https://youtube/bnyBwNAdTu0

p. 224: Bill Clinton and Boris Yeltsin: https://commons.wikimedia.org/wiki/File:Bill_Clinton_and_Boris_Yeltsin_1994.jpg

p. 237: The EuroMaidan protest, Kiev, 2014: https://commons.wikimedia.org/w/index.php?curid=33132150

p. 252: The cult of leadership: Putin, Lenin and Stalin impersonators outside Red Square: https://pixabay.com/en/putin-lenin-stalin-policy-1453504/

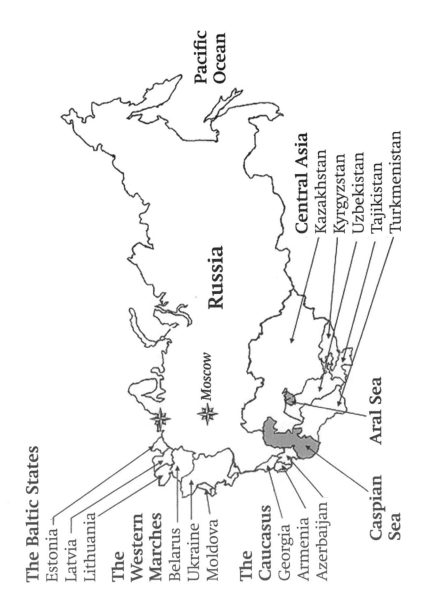

The Baltic States
Estonia
Latvia
Lithuania

The Western Marches
Belarus
Ukraine
Moldova

The Caucasus
Georgia
Armenia
Azerbaijan

Caspian Sea

Aral Sea

Central Asia
Kazakhstan
Kyrgyzstan
Uzbekistan
Tajikistan
Turkmenistan

Russia

*Moscow

Pacific Ocean

Map 1 *The USSR and its republics*

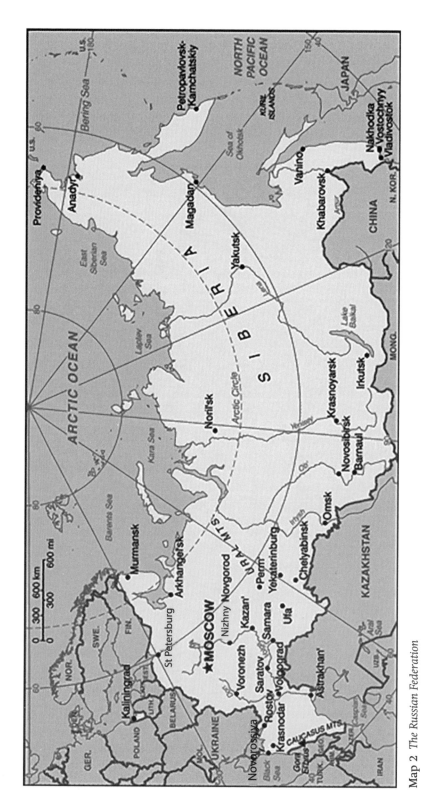

Map 2 *The Russian Federation*

1
Change and Continuity in Russian Politics

Introduction

Russia has experienced massive shifts in its political and economic organization over the last hundred years. In 1917, the tsarist system of autocratic monarchy fell as the Romanov dynasty was deposed. The Soviet system that replaced it was supposed to usher in an era of equality and social freedom, to lead the global liberation of humanity from economic oppression. The higher goals of the revolution never came to pass, but Russia, and the rest of the tsarist empire that fell under the rule of the Bolsheviks, was transformed. Economic backwardness was attacked head-on by Stalinist modernization policies. Agriculture, which was the main activity of the mass of the Soviet population in the 1920s, was reorganized, and industrialization and urbanization transformed a peasant society into a version of modern society. Although the political system remained a form of dictatorship, the social basis of the Soviet regime was vastly different to that of the tsars. Aristocracy was replaced by rule through a mass party and bureaucracy, which together formed a party-state. The power of Soviet leaders was greater than that of the tsars, since they commanded huge apparatuses of coercion and ideological control which destroyed organized opposition to the Soviet system. The Soviet system rebuilt Russia and competed for power globally with the United States and the 'West', but it collapsed under the strains of competition and because of its systemic intractability, which made it slow to adapt and reform.

The post-Soviet Russian political system was supposed to develop liberal market democracy but has become increasingly dictatorial and illiberal. A form of capitalism has been built in which the market plays a role in the distribution of resources, but this is a political capitalism in which the economy is dominated by elite political interests, which take 'rent' – essentially unearned profits – from the economy and use them to buy support. In some respects, this system resembles its Soviet predecessor. The Soviet system also gathered rents, and the direction of its economy was also set politically. However, the new authoritarianism in Russia is as different to that of the Soviet past as the Soviet system was to its tsarist predecessor. The ruling mass Communist Party of the Soviet Union (CPSU) has been replaced by United Russia, but this is a highly personalized party loyal to President

Vladimir Putin; it is not a political force in its own right. Repression still exists but is less systematic than it was for most of the Soviet era. The last few years have seen an increasingly ideological politics developing based on what Putin calls 'traditional Russian values' (respect for family, patriotism, intolerance for social difference, Orthodox Christianity, and hostility to liberalism). This worldview infuses media commentary in Russia on its politics and relations with the outside world, but it is not (yet) an official ideology in the way that Marxism-Leninism was. Large parts of the Russian population are sceptical of 'traditional Russian values' and are able to express their scepticism (mostly on the internet). A weak opposition exists and protests. Russians enjoy some freedoms of speech, association, belief and movement which were denied them in the recent past.

A central problem in the study of Russian politics, which is fundamental to how we see Russia developing in the future, is how to account for these changes and for the continuities that we can see in the midst of change. Describing change and continuity involves identifying the key factors, forces and institutions that we believe have acted as agents of and obstacles to change in the past and that will shape political development in the future. This chapter sets out the problems encountered in building states and regimes, Russia's place in the world under the tsars and the Soviets, and how the country is placed following the fall of the USSR.

Political development: the problem of building states and regimes

Day-to-day politics involves a lot of change, much of which is ephemeral. Decisions to remove some minister or other, to alter economic policy by raising tax rates, or to modify social welfare spending impact on people's lives but they rarely transform a political system fundamentally except as they add to the accretion of many changes that take place over time. Looking at political development involves looking at fundamental changes both in political systems and in the nature of political institutions through which day-to-day policy decisions and political manoeuvres are made. Political development concerns how institutions are built and how their construction influences who can access power and decision-making. It is about how rule over people by politicians evolves, what constrains or enables how that rule is exercised, and what shapes the ends to which rule should aspire. It is about the establishment of 'political order', involving two related political phenomena: the development of states as institutional ensembles that seek sovereignty over territory and endeavour to monopolize decision-making and the legitimate use of violence in that territory; and the development of political regimes, the rules that govern how power in and over the institutions of the state is organized and the rules that determine who can access that power and what they can use it for.

The distinction between state and regime is a fundamental one for this book. Practically, state and regime development often overlap, and the actors involved, if they even think about the relationship between them, will probably not see a distinction between the two. Analytically, however, we can see that they are different processes and that they therefore have different criteria for success and failure and need not be complementary, even if, and as, they affect one another.

Political science recognizes many regime types – democracy, autocracy, oligarchy, monarchy, pornocracy (really, look it up) – to name but a few. No matter what labels we choose to characterize individual regimes, they all describe who may make decisions and how they come to occupy decision-making positions, together with the relationship of society to power and resources that exist within the state. The creation of any regime is a process that centres on elite groups and their struggles. Elite groups may represent wider society, but agreeing the rules (regime) that govern access to power is generally the preserve of different elites as they try to achieve dominance over each other. Regime building is brought to a conclusion – a regime emerges – when such groups achieve a set of political rules that they cannot change without at least some fraction of the elite incurring a high cost to themselves. Regimes seek stability once constructed; they try to reproduce themselves and the particular patterns of access to decision-making and resources that they contain. Initiating regime change and restarting competition over the rules that determine rights to make decisions creates uncertainty for elite groups about their future prospects. It is thus something that they will try to avoid for fear that it will lead to a loss of access to positions of political power.

State building is a much more complex process than regime building. States have functions, the most basic of which is providing security to their populations by protecting them from external predation and enforcing some common standards of behaviour among them. Developing this ability entails creating both institutions (such as armies and police forces) to provide security and institutions (such as tax collection agencies) to finance them. Achieving even a basic level of state formation can be hard to achieve where a state faces security threats externally or has to develop extensive mechanisms to manage internal order – for example, because of the difficulties of regulating relations between different ethnic communities. As provision of security and order become more complex, state building has to develop to ensure continued functionality. If security threats can be dealt with only by the development of larger, better equipped and organized military forces, states have to regulate more of their economies to fund such militaries, create industries to arm them, develop education systems so that soldiers can use advanced armaments, etc. The more complex the functions a state has to fulfil, the more it needs its institutional development to create state 'capacity' and to be based on 'organizational integrity'. Capacity means the proliferation of agencies that can make and implement public policy, while organizational integrity means that these agencies have clear lines of authority and accountability based on functional specialism and common standards of administrative practice, as well as mechanisms for arbitrating and resolving disputes between them. Success in state building is a moving target. Basic state functions will need to be supplemented over time by other state welfare functions, such as the active promotion of economic growth and the delivery of a broad range of public goods – education, health care, etc. Because the functions required of a state are always changing, state building is never actually completed.

The different criteria for success in regime and state building mean that the relationship between them is complex. The consolidation of state formation is far more difficult to achieve than the consolidation of a regime. A regime may be stabilized before the development of a state that can easily fulfil a state's classic functions, let alone carry out an expanded repertoire of tasks. If this occurs, the question before a regime is whether it can contain and ameliorate the problems of maintaining social order and national security in such a way that it can survive ruling through a 'weak' state. If it cannot do so (for example, by gaining aid or security guarantees from other states), it will come under pressure to develop the state, and, if it doesn't respond to this pressure, its long-term viability will be open to question. It may be called to question from below – that is, from society at large concerned about its security and future – or from within, as pressure to take action grows from state officials who cannot maintain order and security. Failure to perform these functions threatens the state's ability to reproduce itself, and hence the interests of state officials who draw their living and privileges from its existence.

Regime building may involve state building, since an elite may try to prop up its preferred regime by delivering greater state capacity and public goods. Alternatively, regime building might substitute for state building, which involves building up regime strength rather than state capacity to deal with the relevant functions. A strengthened regime might suppress calls for increased state functionality so that it appears to have resolved state-building dilemmas. This suppression may be coercive or through consensus building, or it may combine both approaches. Coercion can limit the range of demands made of a polity from within or from society, so that the regime can claim that the level of state formation is adequate to the tasks at hand. Consensus building can be used to try to persuade people that demands for higher state functionality are illegitimate or to limit the range of demands that can be made. Substitution of regime strength for state development can give the impression of a strong state. Indeed, political actors who build up the former as a substitute for the latter may well believe that there is no difference between regime and state strength, and that development of one automatically delivers the other. This may occasionally be true, since a strong regime that secures both high degrees of loyalty from officials within the state and social compliance will be able to shape people's notions of security, order and welfare and persuade them that it has delivered these things. However, such strong regimes can face problems when the state needs to be reformed to continue to deliver welfare and security. Where regime strength has been built up as a substitute for state formation, reform can threaten regime stability. State reform will often involve changes in the balance of power between elite groups, not least as it means the redistribution of resources between policy areas. It can therefore look like an attempt to change the regime in ways that threaten the members' future access to power. Trying to build up the state's capacity in this situation is thus fraught with danger: it may be resisted, with struggles over reform endangering regime stability; or it might be delayed as members fear its consequences, but this delay might then eat away at regime stability as state functionality remains low over the longer term.

This brief discussion shows that a basic issue of political development is whether or not regime building supports, or substitutes for, state development. Both strategies can be successful in the short to medium term (Robinson, 2008). However, over the longer term, the better developed a state, the more likely there is to be government stability, and hence regime stability, since continuity of governments – or at least their regularized replacement – is less likely to call in to question the basis on which power is accessed and used. How long the 'long term' is depends on the pressures that a country has to deal with. Where pressures are great, supplanting state for regime building will be dangerous, especially if a state has low capacity to begin with. A regime in a state with high capacity has more resources to deploy, better chances of extracting extra resources to deal with problems, and potentially more and broader reserves of political loyalty to fall back on because it is able to deliver a wide range of public goods through the state. Moreover, there is less chance of political fragmentation if the delivery of these goods is not delivered directly by some elite faction of a regime but is filtered through the capacity of a state. Where states deliver public goods, they can be rationed in times of crisis or shortage; where delivery is personalized through connection to the regime, there is more chance of political contestation. This is because power within a regime depends on the ability to deliver resources, which then become objects of struggle between different factions or are unevenly distributed so that regime legitimacy declines.

Long-term stable political development therefore generally depends on finding a regime form that supports continual state development through reform that responds to new pressures and demands as they emerge. Finding such a regime form is never easy, but democracy has historically been better at supporting continual state development than other regime types. This is probably because elite members in democratic regimes have agreed to be democratic citizens and 'subject their interests to uncertainty' (Przeworski, 1986: 58) – i.e., elite members do not expect that the arrangement of politics and policy will always work to their advantage. Democratic citizens should not expect to get their own way all of the time, so they are more tolerant of reform that could threaten their interests. Losers from change and reform in a democratic regime know that they have mechanisms available to them – political participation and organization at elections – that can be used to readjust the balance of interests back in their favour; democratic politics is not a zero-sum game in which losses are permanent. Consequently, while democracies are not necessarily efficient in adjusting the state to deal with the problems that confront them, some have, historically at least, been able to 'muddle through' and endure over time (Runciman, 2015).

These means of dealing with the need to reform the state and its capacity are not necessarily features of non-democratic polities. Elite members that lose power or status as a result of reform have no chance of recouping these through regular elections. Even if elections are held, they will not be free or fair. Loss of access to political office and the resources that come with it, or the weakening of such access or of the rewards of office holding, may well be permanent. This incentivises resistance to change if reform is enacted and also makes enactment less likely: would-be reformers, if they have any realistic appreciation of what change entails, know that embarking on reform will create enemies and resistance which will undermine their chance of success, and that such resistance and failure may lead to their being ejected from office. Reform, and the adjustment of the state that it entails, may well, therefore, be delayed, perhaps until it is so late that the dysfunctions of prioritizing regime building and maintenance over state development overwhelm a regime.

The complex relationship between state and regime development makes the course of political development difficult to predict. The range of factors and forces that might influence it is vast and includes unexpected events, both natural and man-made. Political development – change in how political order is constructed – can only rarely be analysed as the outcome of a single cause, or even of a few causes. Most often it is the result of a combination of a wide range of structural factors – i.e., circumstances and phenomena that are the products of the natural world, the long-term development of society and economy, the organization of power within global systems of international relations and economy, and how political actors and agents read (or misread) and react to those factors.

Political development: state, regime and Russia's place in the world under the tsars and the Soviets

Russia's experience of political development over the last hundred years has been marked by a high degree of instability. The radical changes that have occurred were not preordained in either their outcomes or their timing. The highly unpredictable shifts have been the result of a combination of structural and contingent factors (the latter including such things as the personalities and choices of the political actors involved) and external events. Recognizing the importance of contingency and the incidental, whether it is the character of political actors and their choices or the intrusion of external events such as war, does not mean that there are no enduring factors, problems or patterns in the development of Russian politics, state and regime. Regime development has generally taken precedence over state building and has substituted for the development of state capacity and organizational integrity. Because strong regimes have been able to control access to political institutions and force economic development through coercion, this has sometimes given the impression that the state has become powerful and capable of achieving economic and social change and providing security. Appearances, however, have been deceptive. Over time, regime stability, and the security of elite groups and their access to power brought by regime consolidation, has made Russia's political regimes both too rigid to adapt and deal with new pressures and increasingly ineffective at providing development. This has created conditions that have weakened the state, eroded regime legitimacy, and led to radical shifts in Russian political development.

This pattern has repeated itself because Russia has never been able to deal with its state-building tasks through sustainable state formation. There has always been pressure on regimes to build up the state – pressure that has only, and generally only for a short time, been alleviated by the substitution of regime consolidation for state building.

Pressure to build up the state is high because of Russia's political and economic geography. The country has a lot of territory to protect, and permeable borders, and it has often had unstable and hostile neighbours. Economic development is spread out across huge distances that add to its costs and mean that state action is necessary. The Greek philosopher Heraclitus is supposed to have said that 'geography is fate'. This is stretching things a bit and is a little too deterministic, since institutions and political choices also play a significant role in shaping development and the political possibilities that it creates, but the idea still contains a kernel of truth. To adapt Marx's famous dictum a little, people make their own history but they do not make it as they please; they do not make it under self-selected geographic circumstances. You can't change your geography, no matter how much you might wish to be somewhere else. The 'Subtropical Party', which campaigned in the 1990s under the slogan 'Bananas should grow in a Banana Republic' and wanted Russia to have a permanent temperature of 25° Celsius, was never going to fulfil its campaign promises. Borders might change, but unless it disappears through conquest or total dissolution, or expands massively through imperialism, a state will stay in the same place and have access to the same physical resources. Geography – where you are and what you have – shapes economic structures, trade and international competition, and therefore shapes some of the pressures that have to be dealt with by the construction and development of the state.

Where you are influences both how close you are to major markets and historical centres of development and what you have to sell on these markets. It also determines which other states you have to compete with and what resources you have to dedicate to competition. Competition with others creates a further constant pressure on states and regime: pressure to modernize in order to compete. Competition is economic and military, involves changing levels of technology and economic organization, and brings about, and in turn is stimulated by, social change, the rise of new status and occupation groups and new social classes and forces, which have to be managed or accommodated to secure stable political order. The type of competition in which a polity engages can vary over time as its society and relations with the outside world change, and as it reacts to the alterations that are taking place, both in its neighbours and globally. Economic development can be more important than military competition at times, and vice versa, although generally they are linked, since effective military competition demands treasure from economic development and technological advancement to keep pace with rivals. All polities are therefore engaged in a balancing act as they seek to find the optimal equilibrium between economic development, security – which must be addressed through state development – and the stability of their political orders. Social change complicates this balancing act. Social groups' demands for access to the fruits of economic development for consumption challenge traditional patterns of economic redistribution and inequalities.

The tremendous and fundamental changes that Russia has experienced and suffered over the last hundred years are a result of the difficulties that it has experienced in dealing with its geography and the problems that this poses for state and regime in the form of economic and military competition and modernization. The geographic core of economic development in Europe was centred in the past, first, on the Mediterranean and the Baltic and, later, on the Atlantic. Russia's access to trade and markets was thus more limited historically than that of its competitors. It was not a major power in the Baltic region until the eighteenth century, by which time the centre of economic development had shifted to favour the Atlantic maritime economies.

Russia's great size compounded the economic problems caused by its relative isolation from the main centres of economic growth. Even early in its history, before its expansion into Siberia and Central Asia, this meant that it had smaller domestic markets than its more compact competitors because of the dispersal of its population, the distances between its urban centres, and the distance between Russia and the major urban centres driving economic development in Western Europe. Great size meant that diffusion of new technology in the economy was slower: it took decades for technological innovation from the more advanced markets and economies in

Western Europe to move across the continent and into Russia, and once these technologies arrived it was not always economic to adopt them because of the relative smallness of Russian markets.

Size also increased security costs. Russia had to police a large territory and extensive borders open to the south, west and east. This openness made expansion easy for the tsarist empire from the sixteenth century through to the end of the nineteenth century, but at the same time expansion increased the territory that the state had to administer and defend and brought Russia into competition with other states. Size, access to markets, constraints on internal market development, and security costs meant that Russia was increasingly challenged by international political and economic competition as its rivals progressed and developed.

These problems became particularly marked from the late eighteenth century onwards as the growth of the Atlantic economy combined with the intellectual revolutions that had taken place in Europe to start the Industrial Revolution and transform the power of Western European states. As the latter's power grew in the nineteenth century, Russia's went into relative decline. The country remained a military power for some time, but the base of this power, its economic infrastructure, lagged behind that of its rivals. As a result, from quite early on in the nineteenth century, Russia was well on its way to becoming a one-dimensional power. It had a large army but, without an economy to back up this armed force, remained uncertain what it could do with its military power. Some observers, such as the Duke of Wellington, recognized this even as Russia's military prowess was at its height following the defeat of Napoleon. The Russians, the duke pointed out, 'have neither wealth nor commerce nor anything that is desirable to anybody excepting 400,000 men, about which they make more noise than they deserve' (quoted in Zamoyski, 2007: 461).

Russia's problem in dealing with the issues of economic and military competition has often been labelled as a problem of 'backwardness' or of late or semi-peripheral development (Gerschenkron, 1962; Bradshaw and Lynn, 1994). These labels should not be taken as claims for the moral or cultural superiority of more 'advanced', less 'peripheral' developers and polities, nor should they be used to accuse Russia of some moral or cultural inferiority (although unfortunately this is sometimes the case). Rather, they describe how Russia has fit into the global system of states and show the necessity of its developing state institutions and policies that can overcome the structural conditions that have made it weaker and less economically developed than its rivals.

A perceived need to develop state institutions and policy to achieve modernization and parity with other states militarily and economically has been a constant in Russian political discourse since the reign of Peter the Great (1682–1725). The 'great debate' of Russian social and political thought between 'Westernizers' and 'Slavophiles' that began in the nineteenth century was an argument over what form state and regime development, and hence modernization, should take to achieve parity with other powers and create conditions for stable and durable political order: should Russia follow its own developmental path, as the Slavophiles proposed, or copy those of more advanced European powers, as argued by Westernizers?

It is not really surprising that this debate became so heated in the nineteenth century, as Russia became relatively weaker in international terms. As other polities developed their states and economies, Russia's ambitions came increasingly to be at odds with its power and place in the international system. It was unable to achieve the parity with other European states that it desired. Sergei Witte, the reformist tsarist minister of finance at the end of the nineteenth century, explained:

> The economic relations of Russia with western Europe are fully comparable to the relations of colonial countries with their metropolises. The latter consider their colonies as advantageous markets in which they can freely sell the products of their labor and of their industry and from which they can draw with a powerful hand the raw materials necessary for them. This is the basis of the economic power of the governments of western Europe, and chiefly for that end do they guard their existing colonies or acquire new ones. Russia was, and to a considerable extent still is, such a hospitable colony for all industrially developed states, generously providing them with the cheap products of her soil and buying dearly the products of their labor. But there is a radical difference between Russia and a colony: Russia is an independent and strong power. She has the right and the strength not to want to be the eternal handmaiden of states which are more developed economically … She wants to be a metropolis herself. (Quoted in von Laue, 1954: 66)

Reform was needed to eradicate this discrepancy between ambition and power. However, recognizing Russia's need to modernize, as did the intellectual debates of the nineteenth century and politicians such as Witte, and achieving it while maintaining social order were two different things. Russia's efforts to keep pace with changes elsewhere in the world began to tear at its social fabric and undermine the tsarist autocratic regime.

A late developing economy, as the émigré Russian economic historian Alexander Gerschenkron (1962) pointed out, expands by using the machinery of the state to shift resources from consumption (people using resources to satisfy their personal desires) to investment that will secure future economic growth and prosperity for the country as a whole. The tsarist system was only partially successful in achieving this, since there were limits to how far it could encroach on the consumption of the elites that were its core support and personnel. The economic change encouraged by politicians such as Witte at the turn of the twentieth century was both dramatic and inadequate. New social forces were created: an industrial working class, the intelligentsia (a social stratum of educated citizens drawn from across the social spectrum and created by the expansion of the education system) and a middle class. But the size and social power of these new social groups was not great enough to force the transformation of politics by breaking the hold of the tsar and aristocracy on political power and decision-making. New social groups could protest for change, and often did so violently as their desires for change were frustrated. But political change, when it did take place from within the tsarist regime, was often partial and hesitant, even after the revolutionary crisis of 1905–7, which threatened to engulf the tsarist political order totally. The regime sought to perpetuate itself and the rules that governed access to power rather than change to facilitate state development. The result, as Tim McDaniel (1991: 227–8) has argued, was that autocratic modernization divided regime and state internally. Reformers and conservatives were brought into conflict with one another: no 'coherent administrative apparatus c[ould] develop, and competing ideas … deepen[ed] political cleavages and administrative conflicts within the bureaucracy.' Worse, this political confusion within the polity was mirrored by divisions that occurred in society over change, so that regime legitimacy was compromised. Groups desirous of change were alienated by its compromised nature; opposition groups were alienated by the threats they saw in reform and in calls to extend it. The end result was that the tsarist autocratic regime proved unable to secure a state strong enough to support its ambitions and weakened its legitimacy. When the state as a coercive apparatus began to fail in the course of the First World War as a result of military losses and declining legitimacy, the autocracy could not perpetuate itself; the regime fell as social protest at the ineptitude of regime and state in the war became uncontrollable.

The end of tsarism initiated a violent search for a new regime that could start and carry through a new state-building project. The Soviet regime that was consolidated through the Civil War of 1917–21 faced the same problems of economic development and security as its tsarist predecessor. Witte's 1899 argument that change was needed for Russia to catch up with other states – to become a colonial 'metropolis herself' – was repeated in slightly different form thirty years later by Joseph Stalin:

> Whoever falls behind gets beaten … The history of old Russia was … a history of the continual beatings she suffered because of her backwardness. Beaten by the Mongol khans. Beaten by the Turkish beys. Beaten by the Swedish feudal lords. Beaten by the Polish and Lithuanian gentry. Beaten by the Anglo-French capitalists. Beaten by the Japanese barons. Everyone beat her because of her backwardness: her military backwardness, cultural backwardness, administrative backwardness, industrial backwardness, and agricultural backwardness. They beat her because it was profitable and would go unpunished. … This is why we must no longer lag behind. … There is no other way. That is why on the eve of the October Revolution Lenin said: 'Either perish, or overtake and outstrip the leading capitalist countries.' We are 50 or 100 years behind the leading countries. We must make good this distance in 10 years. Either we do it, or they will crush us. (1952 [1931]: 361–2)

The Soviet system was better at both regime consolidation and mobilization than the tsarist system had been, largely through ideological control and its ability to mobilize the population using extreme violence. This enabled the Soviet regime both to move large numbers of people around the territory of the USSR in a way that had never been possible before and to control them politically through police control and terror to suppress their economic demands. The coercive capacity of the Soviet state, backed up by ideological control, overrode both popular and elite resistance to change. This enabled the Soviet system to use the state as a vehicle of economic transformation to a far greater extent than had its tsarist predecessor. The Soviet Union had fewer constraints on moving resources from consumption to investment and reallocated resources more harshly and thoroughly than any previous political system through the collectivization of agriculture and a programme of rapid industrialization. Wages – the means of funding consumption for most people – were kept low, giving the regime more to invest. Lower wages also enabled the greater mobilization of the population into the labour force by driving larger numbers of women out of the home and into the 'productive' economy (in practice, it meant that most women worked what came to be known as the 'double shift' – a shift in factory, office, shop, school or hospital followed by another shift of domestic labour). Resources were also forced into investment and away from consumption by the political prioritization of heavy industry and 'capital goods' in the centrally directed planned economy. The production of these capital goods – products used to produce other goods – was supposed to be the basis of future economic growth and meant that consumer goods were kept in short supply.

The USSR was able to achieve this high level of mobilization of human and physical resources through violence and because it effected a merger of regime and state via the intertwining of the Communist Party of the Soviet Union (CPSU) with the state bureaucracy, something that will be discussed at greater length in the next chapter. Formally, the merger of regime and state was a success. Regime goals – that is, the policies decided at the apex of the political system by the Soviet leadership in the Politburo, the decision-making body at the apex of the CPSU – could not be questioned either by society or by any functional part of the state. Practically, political control was less than complete; the high demands made on Soviet officials led them to reinterpret the orders they received from above and to protect themselves from political sanction. This changed the way that state and regime interacted in practice. In theory, the Soviet state was supposed to fulfil orders transmitted from the regime, from the CPSU and its leadership; the state's aims were supposed to be those of the regime. In practice, and increasingly as the system developed, officials' particular interests became important factors motivating their actions and behaviours to the detriment of regime goals. Coercion meant that there were no challenges to the regime until near the end of the Soviet system, but the Soviet state was never as strong in its capacity to deliver regime goals as the regime wished or as organizationally integrated as Soviet propaganda would have had us believe (Urban, 1985; Robinson, 2002). Soviet political history is in many ways a tale of the regime's efforts to try to develop state capacity and organizational integrity to be able to fulfil its goals, the continuing shortfall of these efforts, and their eventual failure.

A key part of this failure was that, by the late 1960s, the USSR had caught up with its rivals, the leading capitalist countries, only militarily – that is, in only one dimension of politics. The promise of economic abundance for the Soviet population was never achieved. Living standards did improve for the bulk of the Soviet people over time, as they enjoyed high levels of welfare in education, health and housing relative to most citizens of other developing economies. But consumption levels overall remained below those of other leading economies, and the USSR was unable to reform itself, its economy and its political-administrative systems to match the consumption levels of its rivals. One reason for this is that the means – the policies and institutions – which a polity uses to catch up with its rivals are not necessarily the best instruments to keep pace with them once they have drawn level. Institutions and polices created in the race to catch up, if they are too deeply embedded (as Soviet institutions were), can eventually constrain adaptation to new patterns of growth, suck up resources that people would prefer to see spent on consumption, and in the end lead a polity to fall behind rivals that are more flexible. This is especially the case when the regime's capacity to use violence declines, as was the case in Russia after Stalin's death. Elite interests cannot be broken down to force reform through, and social complaint becomes more possible.

The USSR fell behind the West almost as soon as it had partially matched it. Catching up again meant reform, but, just like the tsarist autocracy, the Soviet autocracy struggled to achieve this. Changes made after the death of Stalin were constantly stymied by bureaucratic intransigence, so that they were often more cosmetic than substantive. Pressure for radical reform grew within the Soviet system as the post-Stalin generation of leaders saw the need for change (Gel'man et al., 2014). The reformist generation's rise to power was delayed, however, by the slow turnover of elite members and leaders in the Soviet system. While reform was delayed, or half-hearted, the regime sustained itself by boosting its prestige, domestically, by spending on consumption that it could barely afford and, internationally, by spending on arms and financially shoring up Soviet client states in Eastern Europe and the developing world. By the mid-1980s, when a younger generation of the reformers led by Mikhail Gorbachev came to power, the circumstances for the launch of reform were inauspicious. The investment needed for economic modernization was colossal, far in excess of the resources that the USSR had available. Nor was the Soviet leadership's desire for reform matched by popular or bureaucratic willingness to bear the cost of change. Calls for reform, and the experience of reform, divided political and economic elites just as they had during the end of the nineteenth century. Political reform allowed these divisions out into the open so that the self-declared political uniformity of the Soviet system broke down. Social discontent with the Soviet system grew as suppressed political identities such as nationalism took the opportunities presented by reform to organize and press for political alternatives and were not repressed as they would have been earlier in the Soviet era. Elite adherence to the political rules that had bound them to the Soviet regime, and subsequently the integrity of the Soviet state, collapsed between 1989 and 1991. Again, unwillingness and/or inability to coerce the elite into line behind reform played a part in the breakdown of the already weak Soviet party and state organizational integrity.

Political development: state and regime and Russia's place in the world after the USSR

The failure of the Soviet model of state building mirrored the failure of tsarism, although the process of change that followed the collapse of the Soviet Union was very different to the violence of the end of tsarism. Neither tsarist nor Soviet autocracy was able to overcome the interests of its elites to reform soon enough, quickly enough, or as thoroughly as was needed to deliver security and development. The chaos of Soviet collapse and the failure of economic reconstruction in its wake deepened the distance between Russia and its rivals even further. Again, Russian leaders, first Boris Yeltsin and subsequently Vladimir Putin and Dmitry Medvedev, recognized the problem of relative backwardness and called for reform and modernization. The language that Russia's post-Soviet leaders have used to talk about modernization has varied, as have the means by which they sought to achieve it. There have been some striking continuities with the past, however. Modernization was supposed to be the main goal of the Medvedev presidency, for example, and the language Medvedev (2009a) used bore a close resemblance to that of Witte. Medvedev recognized 'centuries of economic backwardness' as one of the ills that beset Russia, 'its humiliating dependence on raw materials' for economic growth, its lack of global influence economically, and the negative effect that this had on the country's international political power.

We will discuss the post-Soviet efforts at state building at greater length in chapters 4 and 5. For now, we will just note that the pattern of state building and its relationship to regime building have not been broken. The first effort at state building under Yeltsin was based on economic reform but was compromised by Yeltsin's struggle to remain in office, a struggle that led him to build up the power of the presidency and to co-opt potential opposition forces. This expanded the political base of the regime but undermined constitutionality and formal politics. Influence peddling, patronage politics and informal politics grew to be more important than legality and transparency. The pressure to build up the state remained high, however, even as Yeltsin was sacrificing state development for regime stability. Russia's security was threatened by regionalism within the country and instability within the former Soviet space, and it had lost international influence and prestige (see chapters 7 and 10). Economically it struggled to get out of the recession that came with the move from planned to market economy. Living standards dropped, economic inequality grew unchecked, and the state was faced with a permanent fiscal crisis throughout the 1990s.

Russia's leaders have all been aware of these problems and the need to rebuild the state to check decline and to provide security and welfare for their people. Yeltsin, for example, identified the problem of state weakness as a key reason for the country's economic problems in his 1997 'state of the union' address to the Russian parliament. His successor, Putin, made the same assessment in his first speeches and statements when he took office in 2000. The problem that beset earlier Russian and Soviet leaders persisted, however. Maintaining power and at the same time conducting reform is no easier now than it has been in the past. Reform brings risks to the maintenance of regime stability. Faced with this problem, Russia's rulers have engaged with reform half-heartedly and have compromised by trying to accommodate reform to the maintenance of regime stability.

A simple illustration of this can be seen in Figure 1.1, which shows the World Bank's governance indicators for Russia from 1996 to 2015. The indicators were composed biannually from 1996 to 2002 and have been produced annually since then. The bank scores countries on a scale of roughly +2.5 to -2.5 on six indicators, which describe control of corruption; the rule of law; voice and accountability (essentially how far citizens are able to hold government to account through political processes and the media); political stability and the absence of violence/terrorism; government effectiveness (the quality of public services and the bureaucracy and how independent it is from political pressure); and regulatory quality (whether the government is able to formulate and implement good policies and regulations to develop the private sector). The higher the score, the better the quality of governance in a country is perceived to be. A score of +2.5 for political stability and absence of violence/terrorism would, for example, mean that a polity is stable and faces no threats from terror. Russia's scores are all negative. For comparison, most consolidated European democracies have scores of around +1.5; East European post-communist states have scores around +1. Russia's scores are good, of course, in comparison with states such as Sudan, Syria or Libya, but they are poor for a major developed industrialized nation. Moreover, as Figure 1.1 shows, Russia's governance has been relatively consistent over time as well as relatively poor. Some indicators have gone up, but mostly where this has happened – as with most of the indicators after 2000, when Yeltsin's departure from office seemed to offer the prospect of improved governance – they soon regressed to Russia's post-communist mean. In other words, despite commitments to reform – from Yeltsin in the early 1990s and again in 1997, and from Putin and Medvedev more or less continually since 2000 – the quality of Russian governance has not budged: the state has not developed any greater capacity (hence the poor effectiveness and regulatory quality scores), and it lacks organizational integrity, one sign of which is an inability to stem corruption.

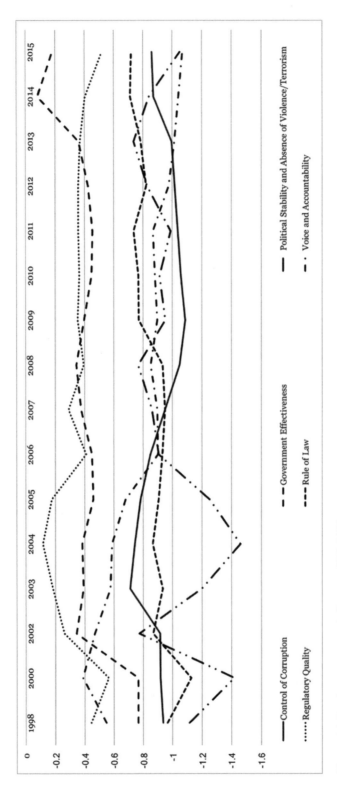

Figure 1.1 *Russian governance indicators, 1996–2015*
Source: World Bank, 2017a.

The growth in political authority that we have seen in Russia since 1991, whether in the power of the presidency as an institution (as under Yeltsin) or in the personal authority of the president (as under Putin), has been to stabilize regime politics and elite access to power rather than to use that power for the development of a state that can deal with the problems faced by the country. This probably looks rational to a Russian leader confronted with the need to reform but wanting to hold on to power; they get to protect their position and at the same time make an effort to develop the state to deal with issues that might threaten that position in the longer term. But the result has been consistent with past patterns of political development: the elite groups that rule Russia have tried to mobilize the country to gather the resources necessary for a strong state and have consolidated political power within the regime to achieve this. Where this consolidation of political power has been contested – by elite groups and sometimes by wider society – but not resolved, as under Yeltsin, the regime has been ineffective both as a regime – i.e., often unable to consolidate itself and secure its replication – and as a state builder – i.e., unable to develop systems of administration capable of providing security and welfare and adapting to face new challenges. Where the contestation of power consolidation has been successfully overcome, as under Putin, but has not delivered reform of the state, the outcome has been politically more stable but at the cost of the strength of the regime standing in for state development.

Conclusion

Political development in Russia has been shaped by a wide range of international and geographic factors as well as the choices made about, and possibilities for, regime stabilization and state development. The consolidation of a political regime under Vladimir Putin, who will be in power until at least 2024, does not mean that the process of political development has reached an end. As we argued earlier, it is questionable if the substitution of regime stability and power for state development can be a long-term solution to security problems and developmental tasks. Certainly, putting regime stability above state development has never helped Russia over the longer term in the past. This does not mean that the failure of a regime-based political strategy for stability is necessarily going to collapse rapidly and/or violently. What it does mean is that how we think about Russia's future needs to allow for a range of political possibilities. We will return to this issue in the last chapter, when we consider what type of political system Russia has and how we might conceptualize its nature in a way that helps us think about the range of future developmental possibilities in the country.

2
The Soviet System

Introduction

The Soviet political system was founded through revolution in the hope of giving political and economic shape to the noblest aspirations of humankind. Its founders sought to achieve social equality by ending economic exploitation together with the political systems that protect and perpetuate it. This would lead to history reaching its terminal point; as communism was built, the state and organized politics would wither as human suffering was eradicated and humanity achieved mastery over nature. However, the USSR ended in political ignominy, a political and economic failure, morally and economically bankrupt and unable to sustain economic and military competition with its rival socio-political system, liberal capitalism.

The Soviet system's high initial aspirations and its final and miserable demise are related. In the pursuit of its ideologically inspired transformation of society, it fused economy and political system together. This fusion, which was supposed to ensure the correct development of society towards communism through the merger of the intellectual energy and guidance of the Communist Party of the Soviet Union (CPSU) – the party – with the physical might of the people, lapsed into bureaucratic self-interest and dictatorship. The result was not a rationally organized and smoothly functioning society progressing inexorably towards a perfect, harmonious order, but a chaotic one in which there developed a 'gap between words and deeds', as Mikhail Gorbachev, the last general secretary of the CPSU Central Committee, put it; the claim of the Soviet system that it was morally superior, politically more just, and economically more efficient than the best of the capitalist world was increasingly at odds with the lived reality of Soviet citizens.

In this chapter, we will examine how the Soviet system was supposed to work towards its developmental goals under the tutelage of the CPSU and how it operated in practice. Until the 1980s and the Gorbachev reforms, the self-image of the Soviet system was of relentless economic progress under the benevolent and wise guidance of the party. According to its own propaganda, the party both represented the Soviet people and drew them into the political system so that their productive energies were developed and enhanced in the service of socialist construction. It did this by monitoring the political and economic system as a whole, ensuring that their operation was efficient and directed towards the resolution of tasks that were 'objectively' and 'scientifically' defined by the party as necessary to building socialism, the first stage of communism. The self-image was thus one of a stable, well-organized and strong state. In practice, the CPSU struggled to link up effectively with its citizens and draw on their energies to advance socio-economic development. The political system did not serve the collective interest of the Soviet people but was infested with multiple bureaucratic interests, which developed into networks of corruption and bureaucratic mutual protection from the vagaries of Soviet political life. Such networks were present in the Soviet system from the outset. Over time, and especially after the end of the Stalinist terror, they stabilized and became increasingly parasitic in their corruption (Jowitt, 1992: 121–58) and inhibited reform of the state.

The intellectual origins of the Soviet system

The origin of the Soviet system's problems lies in its aspiration to effect a total change in the organization and purpose of human society. This desire led the CPSU to create a political system between the revolution of October 1917 and the late 1930s in which there was no place for independent political or economic activity, at least officially. This system was based on the interpenetration of the CPSU as the USSR's ruling party with organs of the state, both representative and executive, and through the control of the state – and, by implication, the party – of all major productive economic activity. The intention behind this union of political power in the party-state and the merging of economy and politics was to create an efficient and effective political machine that could connect the individual Soviet citizen to the great project of social transformation in which the CPSU was engaged. The individual would be empowered through this connection, becoming conscious that their best interest was realized only through the party's ability to direct society as a whole towards communism. The absence of political and economic freedoms as they are understood in liberal democracies was supposed to lead to a deeper form of liberty. Individual and collective interests would not be in conflict as they often are in liberal democracies, but would be reconciled to the advantage of both. The lynchpin in this system was the CPSU and its self-proclaimed capacity to represent the general social interest throughout the Soviet political system and into economic planning. The party claimed this position because of its command of Marxist-Leninist political theory – its ideology – which, it was argued, made it a vanguard organization uniquely suited to lead the Soviet people.

The ideology of the CPSU was that history was leading inexorably towards communism through an unfolding process of class struggle. This view was common to other variants of Marxism at the turn of the twentieth century, but the innovation of the CPSU was to try to give this process a helping hand.

It was an innovation born of the peculiar circumstances that prevailed in Russia before the revolution.

Marx and Engels's theory of history as a process of class struggle foresaw the development of socialism and communism as the product of deepening crises in the capitalist system. As it developed and spread, capitalism would make an ever greater number of people members of the industrial working class, the proletariat. The common experience of dehumanizing work in factories would develop social solidarity in the working class, giving it a singular identity and consciousness of itself as a class. Socialism would not develop until capitalism had created a large class-conscious proletariat that would not need leadership: the 'proletarian movement is the self-conscious, independent movement of the immense majority, in the interest of the immense majority', as Marx and Engels (1967 [1848]: 92) put it in *The Communist Manifesto*.

The descriptions by Marx and Engels of how socialism would be created and organized were very different to the sociological reality that Russian revolutionaries faced at the turn of the twentieth century. Industrial capitalism had begun to grow rapidly in the late nineteenth century, but Russia was still a predominately rural, agrarian economy, ruled by an autocrat, the tsar, and dominated politically by the aristocracy. The key task that Russian Marxists set themselves at the end of the nineteenth century was to agitate among the working class to help force the replacement of tsarist autocracy with bourgeois democracy. This would then open the way for socialist revolution by liberating capitalist development from the constraints placed upon it by the tsarist system and the landed aristocracy.

While Russian Marxists agreed on the strategic objective of needing to bring down tsarism, they were divided both on tactical matters and on the question of how quickly a socialist revolution could be brought about. The radical position was espoused by Vladimir Lenin, who argued, first, that political struggle, rather than economic agitation over wages or working conditions, should be at the forefront of revolutionary activity and, subsequently, that it was possible by creating a strong political movement that drew in workers and some of the peasantry to shorten the time between the demise of tsarism and the triumph of socialism. Lenin stated that political agitation, and the revolutionary possibilities that it created, required a dedicated professional, revolutionary organization. Nowhere, he argued in *What is to be done?* (1949 [1902]: 31–2), had workers managed to develop on their own beyond a 'trade union consciousness' 'the conviction that it is necessary to combine in unions, fight the employers, and strive to compel the government to pass necessary labour legislation etc.' Lenin maintained that the leadership of full-time revolutionaries, who could teach the working class the political dimensions of its struggle and organize its members to respond to them, was required so that the proletariat could draw the correct political conclusions from their clashes with authority. In tsarist Russia, a repressive police state, this meant a secret, highly dedicated organization rather than a mass movement with a large, open

'Raise the banner of Marx, Engels, Lenin and Stalin': Soviet propaganda poster from 1933

membership. Such mass movements were possible in capitalist democracies, Lenin said, but in Russia they would lead to the weakening of the revolutionary movement, since its work would be disrupted by arrests and imprisonment.

The immediate result of Lenin's ideas was to split the Russian Social Democratic Labour Party (RSDLP) in two, with Lenin's supporters organizing as the Bolsheviks (majority). Lenin's proposals in *What is to be done?* laid the theoretical and organizational framework for what was to be a new type of political party, the 'vanguard party', which would not just agitate among, and educate, workers; it would also have a duty to lead them through the revolution to socialism. The revolutionary party's leadership role was a product of its command of Marxism (or Marxism-Leninism, as it was termed by Stalin after Lenin's death). Having a command of Marxism(-Leninism) equalled a high class consciousness and signified an ability to lead the revolution, to create it and socialism, rather than just to protest the injustices of the world unsystematically.

The idea of the vanguard party as political leader and guide at the centre of all political action in the USSR was to become a constant in Soviet political discourse. The clearest expression of it was in Article 6 of the 1977 Soviet Constitution:

> The leading and guiding force of the Soviet society and the nucleus of its political system, of all state organizations and public organizations, is the Communist Party of the Soviet Union. The CPSU exists for the people and serves the people.
>
> The Communist Party, armed with Marxism-Leninism, determines the general perspectives of the development of society and the course of the home and foreign policy of the USSR, directs the great constructive work of the Soviet people, and imparts a planned, systematic and theoretically substantiated character to their struggle for the victory of communism. (Constitution, 1977: 16)

The final sentence of Article 6 is important. The party's leading role was not granted to it simply because Marxism-Leninism possessed a vision of a better, fairer society in which people were free of need and hence of social oppression. Marxism-Leninism was not just a set of beliefs about a just society but a *scientific* body of thought that provided the means to analyse society objectively and develop policies and institutions that could lead society to the best possible form of social organization – communism. It alone could deduce where society should go next in terms of development towards communism and break this down into a set of objectives for the political system and the Soviet people to achieve. As explained in the *History of the Communist Party of the Soviet Union (Bolsheviks) (Short Course)*, a Stalinist primer on the party's history and ideology:

> The power of Marxist-Leninist theory lies in the fact that it enables the party to find the right orientation in any situation, to understand the inner connection of current events, to foresee their course and to perceive not only how and in what direction they are developing, but how and in what direction they are bound to develop in the future. (Short Course, 1941: 355)

The CPSU's vanguard status led it to justify its power in a radically different way to that of other political systems. The Soviet system demonstrated its worth to its citizens not simply because it gave them increasing material wealth, something that came with the building of communism, but because it translated general social betterment into a series of 'goals' for society to achieve. Only the party could define goals that would bring society from the present to the future, communism. This view of the party and the claims that it made about itself were, as Jowitt (1992) has pointed out, 'heroic'; the party, and sometimes its leaders, had a charismatic quality because of a unique ability to transform the world in a correct manner. This charisma made the CPSU unchallengeable politically: society was supposed to follow rather than influence, or object to, party instructions and policies. However, this was also one source of the USSR's later problems. The party could not always set aside its heroic self-image and its charismatic claim to power to deal with change effectively.

The CPSU in the Soviet political system

The CPSU's role as the leader of scientifically managed social change demanded that it be a hierarchical, disciplined and omnipresent organization, linking all Soviet institutions together in a common cause. The hierarchical nature of the party was necessary to ensure that ideology was developed correctly. Party leaders were supposed to be better able to see what needed to be done to advance socialism, so after the Tenth Party Congress in 1921 instructions and policy flowed from the centre of the party down. Before that, party meetings were lively and combative. However, faced with rebuilding Russia after revolution and civil war, the Bolsheviks decided to ban any factional activity at the congress. Discussion within the party became ritualized, since criticism of proposals emanating from higher bodies came to be tantamount to criticism of the party as a whole and, indeed, of the project of socialist construction.

The changes put in place in 1921 meant that effective political communication, which would have questioned how policy was arrived at or its purpose, was suppressed within the USSR. In its place, the party sought to police and educate itself and to ensure that it was disciplined and united in promoting the right policies. Party membership was deemed to be an honour that could be given only to people who had proved themselves worthy of joining the vanguard and who would uphold the high moral and intellectual status of party membership (Hill and Frank, 1986: 20–30). Joining the party required going through a stage as candidate. Once accepted, party members were supposed to show practical leadership by being exemplary members of socialist society: hard-working, selfless, sober, responsible, and supportive of the party's political line. Members who did not live up to these ideals could be censured by their colleagues.

The CPSU's role as vanguard charged with leading the total transformation of the USSR meant that it had to gather information from across Soviet society and ensure that the correct course was being followed. The basic unit of the party was the primary party organization (PPO). All party members were in a PPO, and most PPOs were located in workplaces: enterprises (as Soviet factories were called), offices, shops, newspaper offices, all collective and state farms, schools and educational establishments, police and military units, and throughout the bureaucracy of the Soviet state. The CPSU's presence was ensured by its size, which varied over time. By the later Soviet period, membership ran at about 10 per cent of the USSR's adult population (Hill and Frank, 1986: 19–46) – by the 1980s, over 19 million people. PPOs were supposed to channel information up to higher party bodies and ensure compliance with party policy and thinking.

PPOs 'elected' (voted on the approved list of candidates given them by their superiors) representatives to local (district) party conferences. These conferences in turn 'elected' representatives to city, regional, republican (the USSR was made up of fifteen republics, of which Russia was the largest) and all-USSR conferences and congresses. These conferences and congresses discussed policy, but real power lay with the permanent bureaucracy of the party, its committees, headed by a party secretary (who would be the top party official in the area) and the administrative departments that he oversaw. At all-Union level, there were two of these executive bodies: the Central Committee, which had representatives from across the USSR, served as a kind of party 'parliament' and met about twice a year, and the Politburo, a smaller body of top officials and party leaders, which met weekly. The general secretary of the Central Committee headed the Central Committee and chaired Politburo meetings. This post was held by all Soviet leaders except Lenin, who dominated the party and the Politburo thanks to his authority as the party's founder. Later leaders used the power that being general secretary gave them to ensure that they became politically dominant.

The party's full-time bureaucracy was organized along functional lines. For example, the work of the Central Committee Secretariat was directed by the general secretary of the Central Committee, and it had, at various times, departments (sometimes more than one) overseeing party affairs, ideology, the media and propaganda, foreign relations, agriculture, various branches of industry, the military and security apparatus, relations with foreign communist parties, consumer affairs and social welfare. Lower down the system, party bureaux were concerned less with foreign affairs and strategic issues, and their departmental composition and supervisory activities would reflect this; they would concentrate on economic matters, public order, education and propaganda.

Because CPSU members and organizations were present throughout the Soviet system and the party's full-time bureaucracy oversaw all the functions of other branches of the Soviet political system: the popularly elected Soviets (councils) and the executive branch of government, which comprised the Council of Ministers (head by a chairman who was in effect the Soviet prime minister), ministries (defence, interior, foreign affairs, plus a galaxy of economic ministries dealing with manufacturing, energy, transport, trade and agriculture, social welfare, education, health, etc.) and committees (such as the State Committee for Security – the KGB – and committees concerned with economic planning). The party's control over these bodies was in theory all-encompassing. It had branches within all of them through the system of PPOs, and the secretary of each PPO was supposed to oversee management at their place of work.

The presence of the party at all levels was supposed to enable it to fulfil its vanguard role by facilitating social engagement with party policy as well as ensuring oversight of policy implementation. It should also have created a high degree of organizational integrity, as every public body was to be working from the party's hymn sheet, and of state capacity, as the energies of all public bodies and the Soviet people should have been directed to meeting party-defined goals.

Social transformation not only required the right party line, it also meant the mobilization of the people. First and foremost, this meant political socialization and ideological work. The party lay at the heart of a whole network of organizations that propagated the correctness of the party's general theoretical approach (Marxism-Leninism) and its practical inter-pretation, the day-to-day party line. These social organizations included associations to indoctrinate children and youth as well as trade unions, which were to act as what Lenin called 'transmission belts', conveying the party's instructions and ideas to the workforce for their enlightenment and imple-mentation. Other bodies, whether cultural, sporting or social, could not be established without the party's permission, so that even where they did not perform overt ideological tasks they could not provide an escape from the party's worldview. Political socialization also meant that the party oversaw censorship of all media and the design of educational curricula.

Ideological work and political socialization were, however, often compromised by administrative practice. One reason for this was the complexity of the planned economy, which we will deal with below, and the demands that it made of the party. Another is that the party's monitoring and control of the whole Soviet political system meant that there was a tension between its vanguard role and the fact that the party offered a career structure. The CPSU controlled access to all positions of responsibility (and hence to privilege) within the USSR through the *nomenklatura* system. This consisted of two lists – one of key posts at every level of the Soviet political system, whether in the Soviets, the government, or the party itself, which were given out by the party leadership, and one of people suitable to fill these jobs. At the level of the Politburo and the Central Committee, the jobs on the *nomenklatura* list were the top jobs in ministries, the military, the media, key strategic enterprises, top positions in the party around the country, and the like. The people who made up the *nomenklatura* at this level have sometimes been called the Soviet ruling class, and appointment to a job on the *nomenklatura* of the Central Committee brought with it material privileges – better housing, health care and access to consumer goods. Lower down the political system, jobs on the lists held by local party organizations were less important and the privileges attached to them less extensive.

The *nomenklatura* system meant that the party had enormous powers of patronage, whether it was deciding on the Soviet Army's next chief of staff or who should be in charge of a local hospital, school or shop. One other effect of the system was that there was always a political dimension to advancement in the USSR. This created problems as the party had to strive to find a balance between appointing people who were politically orthodox and those who were competent. The tension between 'red' and 'expert' was particularly marked during the early years of Soviet rule, when experts were in short supply; most had been trained under tsarism and were hence politically suspect. Over time, and as the Soviets trained their own specialists, the tension was resolved somewhat, but at a cost. The *nomenklatura* system and the fact that political criteria affected life chances made party membership a necessary qualification for social advancement. Many people joined the party not out of ideological conviction but because they had to in order to progress professionally. This increased party control over certain institutions because certain types of post – those that had administrative responsibilities, such as heads of schools, factories, etc., or access to coercive power, such as military officers and police commanders – became 'saturated' with party members (Hough and Fainsod, 1979: 347–51). However, it also meant the party was increasingly less ideologically minded and socially more white-collar than proletarian. As a result, it came to be less revolutionary, less committed to

change, and more wedded to a status quo that benefited many of the administrators who were its most important members. The Soviet system was to
struggle with this tension between officialdom with a vested interest in the
status quo and the imperative to transform the world that it had as a revolutionary polity. Violence was one way of overcoming this tension, by coercing
or scaring recalcitrant bureaucrats into pursuing change. However, this was
a costly strategy and one that leaders less secure in power than Stalin did not
use, fearing that it might lead to their own suppression.

The centrally planned economy

The CPSU's direction of political life also involved direction of economic
activity through the planned economy, meaning that the party had to take
on a wide range of bureaucratic functions that compromised its vanguard
political role and helped to make the Soviet system dysfunctional. The
USSR's planned economy was also dysfunctional in its own right, however.
Although it enabled the country to develop rapidly at first, it was inefficient
and wasteful in the longer run.

There was no specific blueprint for the creation of a planned economy
in Marx or Lenin's thought. It was created at the end of the 1920s because
the party, Stalin argued, had to force the development of 'socialism in one
country' as a means of protecting the revolution from hostile domestic social
forces and ending its international vulnerability (see the quotation from Stalin
in chapter 1, p. 11). To this end, the party began campaigns in the late 1920s
to collectivize agriculture and increase the rate of industrial development by
forcing production to fulfil state orders rather than satisfying private ends for
private profit. This meant the nationalization of all industrial and agricultural
production, apart from some small plots of land on which peasants were able
to produce food for their own consumption and for limited sale.

This created a system in which economic activity responded not to demand
from society as expressed through the market but to political directives. In
theory, this meant that Soviet collective interest, as determined by the party,
replaced private, individual economic interests as the motor force behind
economic development. It supposedly meant that the party had greater
control over the use of wealth generated by the Soviet people and could use
it in their best interest – for their welfare and security, for further economic
development, or for any combination of these deemed in the interest of
moving most effectively towards communism. Planning meant that the party
could command growth in certain sectors to bring about social engineering
and to force the pace of social development. In practice, this meant that
the Soviet economy favoured heavy industry and armaments production.
Armaments were seen as necessary to defend the USSR first from capitalist
encirclement in the 1930s and later from the threat of the 'West' in the Cold
War. Heavy industry was seen as the foundation for the further development

ДЫМ ТРУБ

ДЫХАНЬЕ СОВЕТСКОЙ РОССИИ

'Chimney smoke is the breath of Soviet Russia': Soviet propaganda poster promoting industrial growth

of the economy and as the best way to develop towards a materially rich, technologically advanced society with a socially dominant industrial working class.

The party's control over the economy was both direct and indirect. From the 1930s all Soviet production was guided by the need to fulfil plan targets. These targets were both general, for the economy as a whole, and specific, for individual economic enterprises. The general economic targets – issues such as which industrial sectors would be prioritized for investment in the next five-year plan period or what share of wealth would be allocated to social welfare and public consumption – were decided politically and centrally by the party's Politburo. These were broken down into specific targets for industrial enterprises by the central agencies charged with drawing up plans, particularly Gosplan (the State Planning Committee), and by the Council of Ministers and the sectoral ministries involved in economic production (the number of ministries increased over time as they became more specialized, and in the end there were about seventy concerned with economic production) (Hewett, 1988: 108–9). The plans were then sent down to enterprises, which were told what they should produce (their plan target), what material inputs they would have to fulfil their plan, whence they would receive these inputs, the price of inputs, who their customers were, and what price they would receive for the goods produced. The process of drawing up plans at each stage would be monitored by the party, both directly through bodies such as the Central Committee Secretariat and indirectly through the PPOs in ministries and enterprises. Local bodies, particularly the full-time party bureaucracy, also had responsibility for checking that plan targets in their districts were being fulfilled, so that the party in one way or another monitored all aspects of economic activity.

The party's control through setting economic objectives and its monitoring of performance meant that the Soviet economy had a different dynamic to capitalist market economies and created different socio-political relations. Although governments in capitalist economies intervene in markets to provide assistance to uneconomic firms and to subsidize goods that they wish to make available to their people regardless of cost, most economic activity has to take account of the costs of production and the price that consumers are willing to pay. Failure to be relatively efficient and to produce goods that consumers demand and are willing to pay for will entail making a loss; making a loss in a market economy will mean bankruptcy and closure, so that firms work under 'hard budget constraints'. Such concerns, if they existed at all for many enterprises, were secondary in the Soviet planned economy, where production was politically directed. Enterprises operated not under 'hard budget constraints' – break even or go under – but under 'soft budget constraints'. Losses were written off through subsidies, tax breaks, credits from the state, or administrative price adjustment, because producing a quantity of goods decreed by the party at the price set by authorities was more important than economic efficiency and breaking even or making a profit (Kornai, 1992: 140–5).

Soft budget constraints meant that Soviet production was wasteful and economically inefficient. This made it difficult for the USSR to move from extensive to intensive growth. The economy expanded through increasing factor growth rather than increasing factor productivity. In other words, rather than getting more out of existing labour and plant to step up productivity, the country increased the amount of labour, the quantity of raw materials, and the amount of capital invested in production. The complexities of the planning process exacerbated this problem of efficiency and developing productivity. Planning was a haphazard process. The amount of information needed to plan the manufacture of the 24 million products made by the 100,000 enterprises and collective farms in the Soviet economy was too great for any agency to manage. Detailed planning by Gosplan was undertaken only for 2,000 or so products deemed to be strategically important (Hewett, 1988: 183, 112–13). For the rest, plan targets were often set arbitrarily. Producers were generally set a crude gross output target; enterprises were told to manufacture so much of a good rather than a good of a certain quality at an economically efficient cost in terms of labour, capital and raw materials. This meant that much Soviet production was of poor quality and went to waste. It was easier to fulfil the plan by producing shoes in one size and colour than to ensure that there was a wide range of shoe sizes sufficient to satisfy all consumers. Consequently, there would be gluts of one type of product – a vast amount of general purpose stainless steel, or XL men's black boots, for example – but little of another – no steel with lower carbon content for welding, no shoes for men with small feet, etc. It was hard to finish jobs, given the scarcity of some products and the erratic nature of their supply. Workers rushed to fulfil their enterprise's plan on time (and earn their bonus for its fulfilment) heedless of the quality of what they produced. Factory managers hoarded labour so as to be able to throw workers at production problems when they occurred. This meant that many Soviet factories were overstaffed: in comparison with factories in capitalist economies, they had higher wage bills, and productivity per worker was generally lower.

Growth was planned in an equally crude fashion. For the most part, enterprises were told to produce what they had produced in the previous year plus a percentage increase. The call for growth was more or less automatic and did not take account of the actual capacity of an enterprise to increase production. To guard against unrealistic demands, enterprises tended to underestimate their capacity and to overestimate the resources, capital and labour that they needed. Where they could get away with this – and the CPSU was supposed to make sure that they did not – enterprises had a buffer against both demands for growth and any breakdown in the system that might occur when suppliers failed to deliver the required inputs. The cost, of course, was more inefficiency, as producers hoarded goods and demanded more investment than they provided a return for (a point to which we shall return below).

Inefficiency and soft budget constraints were, however, politically useful, since they facilitated the party's use of the economy as a means of extra social control. The party could use planning to mobilize people to fulfil the goals that it chose to prioritize regardless of cost. Moreover, people and economic enterprises had limited autonomy as economic actors, at least officially. The goods available through official channels were limited to what the party decreed should be produced as socially useful. This meant that consumers had limited choices. Many items were always in short supply, since the party decided that the collective good of the Soviet people required investment in heavy industry and arms. As a result, access to some things – accommodation for example – was controlled by the party, and denial of access could be used as a means of disciplining individuals and groups. Cultural goods – books, media and means of entertainment – were produced and priced according to political criteria rather than to meet demand. Since economic management was political and administrative, individuals and enterprises could not easily change their circumstances. In market economies, monetary reward for hard work or corporate success can be reinvested or used to change living conditions by buying a new house, consumer goods, a holiday, private medical care or education. This was not the case in the USSR. What could be invested and where was determined by the plan, not by the economically efficient or successful; money could not be used easily to purchase property, consumer goods which the party had not provided, or a service such as health care that was provided by the state, except illegally on the black market. The party thus determined both what people 'wanted' and what they could have access to. This made the Soviet system a 'dictatorship over needs', in which citizens were told what their needs were and were then supplicants to political authorities for access to the relevant goods (Fehér et al., 1983). Escaping this dictatorship by purchasing things on the black market was possible for some items, such as books, records, food and clothing, and for preferential access to some services, for example health care and education. Recourse to the black market left Soviet citizens vulnerable to police action, however, and at the same time it increased the economic inequalities that the party was supposed to eradicate and diverted resources from the already dysfunctional official economy.

The dysfunctions of the Soviet system

The party's vanguardism and control over the economy through the planning process meant that there was no meaningful separation of politics from other spheres of life in the USSR: the party strove to control cultural, economic and social practices. Any distinction between public and private was negated by the CPSU. There was also no meaningful distinction between political arenas as there is in democracies, where a ruling party is not the same thing as either the government or the state. In a democracy, members of a ruling party can dissent from the government's position, and the ruling party should change sooner or later; not all bureaucrats owe their position exclusively to party patronage, most of them do not regard party and collective interests as one and the same, and all operate under legal constraint. These differences and the implications of the party's vanguardism meant that the USSR's political system was a *party-state* rather than one in which the party competed for power and influence and in which both it and the state bureaucracy were subject to legal scrutiny. Ideology and the CPSU displaced the legal regulation of political life until virtually the end of the Soviet Union. The Soviet system was supposed to be an administrative and social seamless whole, directed and committed to one vision of social progress.

In theory, this should have meant that the Soviet Union had an effective political system, able to draw on the energies of its people and direct them much more systematically than any other political system: it should have meant high state capacity and organizational integrity. The CPSU was supposed to define the collective interest of society scientifically and explain to the population how it was acting in its interest. This should have enabled the USSR to draw on the social energy of its people and direct their activity to its developmental ends without recourse to coercion. In practice, the Soviet Union was, of course, extremely despotic and violent, though the nature of its power changed over time. In its early years and under Stalin, coercion was frequently arbitrary and applied against millions for a wide range of social and political 'crimes'. After Stalin there was still political persecution, but for the most part Soviet citizens were repressed by the petty tyranny of shortages and the 'dictatorship over needs', as well as by the omniscience of the party, which subjected all Soviet citizens to some form of surveillance, even if this was frequently passive.

The despotism of mass coercion under Stalin and the petty invasiveness of the later administrations show that the Soviet system never worked as a seamless, progressive order guided by the CPSU towards communism. From the onset, it was not neatly ordered under the party but relied on a chaotic informal arrangement to keep going. As time progressed, this arrangement bedded in as a social phenomenon and became less effective in dealing with the management of Soviet society. Indeed, in many ways violence such as that perpetrated by Stalin was a response to informality in the system, an attempt to contain it and have people work to the demands of the central party leadership rather than deviate from those orders.

The informal Soviet polity

The informal system developed in tandem with the official party-state system. From early on, oversight of all economic and political activity stretched the administrative capacity of the CPSU. Party workers were forced to improvise administration and decide which orders from the centre they would implement and which they would pay lip-service to. At the foundation of the Soviet state, and in the years after the revolution, there was a lack of trustworthy personnel, and the motives and abilities of many of the new party members were untested. Moreover, the Soviet state was isolated from the bulk of its population, who had not supported the takeover of October 1917, and it also had to deal with the destruction of infrastructure caused by the fighting in the First World War and the Civil War of 1917–21. With a deficit of personnel and resources, party-state officials had to find ways of bypassing the bureaucratic hierarchy when it stood in the way of fulfilling important central demands and to ensure that there were people they could call on to help them when they needed to switch resources from one task to another to fulfil an assignment from the centre. In short, and despite the fact that they were supposed to work uniformly, party workers adapted policy to local conditions, which were diverse in the ethnically mixed and geographically highly varied territory of the USSR. They improvised to close the gap between the party's actual administrative capacity and that needed, first, to win the Civil War and, later, to implement Stalin's economic reforms. They often did this by building on the personal connections developed during their years of underground struggle against the tsarist regime (Gill, 1990: 37–9). The implementation of policy frequently took place not through bureaucratic hierarchies but through the delegation of tasks to 'trustworthy and reliable personal associates' (Easter, 2000: 33).

The informal system was cemented in place with the development of the planned economy from the late 1920s onwards. The demands made of party workers with the introduction of planning were immense and were generally impossible to fulfil. Officials had to ensure that the areas under their control met plan targets that required more skilled labour, more investment and more time than they had at their disposal. Failure in some policy area was inevitable, and there was no possibility of objecting to orders and the demands made by the centre because internal party democracy had been destroyed by the changes made at the Tenth Party Congress in 1921. Moreover, challenging orders would have meant challenging the party, since it was claimed that the orders it issued were rational responses to social needs based on an objective assessment of the situation and created the best possible way towards communism (Urban, 1985). Party-state officials were therefore always in a position where the centre, if it desired, could review their activities, find fault with them and punish them. To ward off this threat, they improvised administration, reinterpreted policy to their own ends, and built informal links to facilitate this, which meant diverting resources and activities to those policy areas that were most important to the centre, since these were the ones where plan fulfilment would be checked. This increased the tendency to be economically wasteful and exacerbated the plan's uneven distribution of resources. Party-state officials robbed low-priority projects – generally social welfare projects and consumer goods industries – to over-invest in and ensure the completion of high-priority ones – military and heavy industrial production.

This reallocation was, of course, illegal, since it was not provided for by the plan. However, party officials could interfere freely in the economy to ensure that resources were delivered to high-priority projects. They also protected those who lost resources and could not meet their plans by covering for them, and in turn were protected by their superiors, who were interested in reporting success in important areas rather than failure in unimportant ones. Consequently, 'both controlled and controllers not infrequently cover[ed] up for each other's sins and omissions in discharging tasks for which they [were] held jointly responsible'; in this way, administrators tried to ensure that they had a 'collective guarantee' that their mistakes were not punished (Fainsod, 1963: 388–9).

The reinterpretation of policy and the cover-ups it entailed were often facilitated by corruption and were always possible because resources could be redistributed around the Soviet system without consideration of their economic value: no one had to make a profit under the plan, so resources could be freely used without the fear of being declared bankrupt. Soviet officials often saw corruption and misuse of office as necessary for the system to work. The dangers that flowed from this for the system as a whole were that corruption increased the identification of the party with private interests and weakened the party-state's capacity and organizational integrity. Corruption and the reinterpretation of policy meant that sections of the party acted independently of the centre, so that the party as a whole lacked a common purpose (Jowitt, 1992). Capacity was diminished because the centre, by virtue of demanding so much, did not see all its instructions fulfilled. Consequently, it was not able to redistribute resources as it wished; its main priorities were met, but there was a constant shortfall in some area of economic growth. As time progressed, the diminution of the official system's organizational integrity meant that it was harder to get officials to go along with policies that were designed to reverse this fall in capacity. There was a terrible circular irony to this. The centre demanded too much of its cadres, which led to the creation of informal political relations that were flexible and capable of delivering some of the policy outcomes desired by the central leadership. Cadres involved in these relations were guilty in the eyes of the leadership of failing to work as required and of acting autonomously in picking out which of its policies to fulfil. The centre tried to correct such tendencies by issuing more orders and increasing pressure on its cadres, thus re-creating the incentives to improvise administration, work informally, and concentrate effort and resources on what were regarded as central priorities.

The Soviet system forced its cadres to be adaptable by trying to restrict flexibility. Gradually this led to the spread of what Soviet leaders were to condemn as 'formalism': both the leadership and local party organs 'went through the motions', pretending to honour central policies but implementing only part of them. By the mid-1930s Stalin was complaining that 'bureaucrats and red-tapists long ago became skilled hands at demonstrating their loyalty to party and government decisions in words while in practice pigeonholing them', and placed particular blame on regional leaders, 'those people who have given great service in the past, who have become magnates and who consider that party and Soviet laws are not written for them but for idiots' (Stalin, 1952 [1934]: 515, 517). The purges under Stalin were designed to break down resistance to 'party and Soviet laws', either directly through the suppression of the 'guilty' or indirectly by cowing officials into compliance. Later Soviet political leaders complained about the 'substitution' (*podmena*) of the party for the state, claiming that the party had become tainted by a bureaucratic mind-set and had lost its revolutionary purity and drive (Hill and Frank, 1986: 21–4). What they meant by this was that many party officials were unable to see themselves as political leaders separate from the state bureaucracy and so could not, or would not, take action that went against the interests of bureaucracy even where directed to by the central leadership. Instead the party compromised itself politically in order to administer Soviet society with and through the state bureaucracy and paid only formal lip-service to the large political goals of the party leadership. As a result, dissident Marxists such as Trotsky, after his exile from the USSR in 1929, described the party-state bureaucracy as having developed into a distinct social stratum (some even said as a class) with interests that overrode the cause of revolutionary development (Robinson, 1999a).

Whether the party-state ever did develop a social stratum or class that ruled is open to debate. However, the development of the informal Soviet system and the identification of the party with bureaucracy and corruption bred popular cynicism about the official order. The party commanded its subjects to build socialism and claimed this was in their interest, but people could see that socialism was undermined by the very forces of the party-state that were supposed to be developing it. This could only be confusing: What was proper political and administrative practice and what was not? What parts of the Soviet system should a citizen trust and actively obey and what should they scorn? In the Stalin period this confusion can be seen in the rapid rise and fall of some political leaders, one day praised as exemplars of socialist construction and the next day cast down as 'enemies of the people'. Confusion and the risk of being wrong to which it led bred passivity. People accepted the Soviet system because there was nothing else: it looked permanent; it was a unique 'civilization' that would endure. But this was far from the active engagement in the process of socialist construction that the party was supposed to create and lead. As a form of 'civilization' it was strong not in its own right but because it allowed no competition.

Modernization and stagnation

Modernization made these problems worse. Between the 1930s and the 1980s Soviet society changed dramatically. In the 1930s, the USSR made a dramatic shift towards becoming a more urbanized and industrialized country. This shift was then deepened in the period after the Second World War as population movements to the towns continued and the economy diversified with the growth of service sectors (see table 2.1). These processes confronted the Soviet system with a wider range of issues to manage and created more demands for resources that had to be satisfied. Economic development meant dealing with new technologies and processes. Experts in these areas had to be accommodated in decision-making structures and resources allocated to pursue new technological development. At the same time new urban communities had to be provided with services and new forms of social interaction and problems created by growing urbanization had to be managed by the party. Development also added an extra dimension to the Soviet system: it limited the range of acceptable actions that party leaders could take. Progress was not simply a material fact for which the party could take credit in the same way that a politician in a capitalist democracy might claim credit for economic growth and improved living standards. Soviet leaders were happy to proclaim growth and its benefits when it occurred, but economic development in the Soviet system also had to be explained and interpreted as progress on the road to communism. Economic development and change could not just bring benefit to people materially; development was also supposed to change the relationship of the people to the system. Legitimacy depended on developing the ability of the population to 'participate' through their identification with the system as well as on improvements in standards of living.

The problems this presented for the CPSU pushed the party in contradictory directions. In theory, as participation increased and people developed socialist

TABLE 2.1   The modernization of Soviet society

	Population (millions)		% of population	
	Urban	Rural	Urban	Rural
1917	29.1	133.9	17.9	82.1
1940	63.1	131.0	32.5	67.5
1981	168.9	97.7	63.4	36.6

	Employment by economic sector (%)	
	1940	1980
Industry and construction	23	39
Agriculture	54	20
Trade	5	8
Transport and communications	5	9
Health care, education and science	6	17
Administration	3	2
Other	4	5

Source: Goskomstat SSSR, 1987: 168, 181–2.

consciousness, the necessity for party guidance should have lessened and the distance between ordinary citizen and vanguard party member should have narrowed. In practice, the party tended to mobilize the population half-heartedly and to guard its privileges and hence its ability to intervene in the administration of the economy. This enabled party managers to get on with day-to-day administration, but it meant that new skills and potentialities created by modernization were never efficiently incorporated into the political system or fully put to its service. As a result, and as Soviet society became more complex, and participation and mass mobilization became ever more ritualized and formal in content and meaning and divorced from the interests of the people.

Post-Stalinist leaders struggled to deal with this problem. Under Stalin, coercion had meant that mobilization took place under threat. At the same time, terror disciplined party-state officials. Mobilization under these conditions did not have to be meaningful to be effective: the danger of avoiding it was potentially fatal. People may not have given their all when pressed to be involved in some production or political campaign, but individual effort was compensated for by numbers.

From the mid-1950s onwards, the potential for mobilization and for pressure on party-state officials to comply with policy were weakened as terror lessened. Khrushchev tried to invigorate the system by launching campaigns to increase grain production and to combat religion, by proclaiming the full-scale construction of communism, and by introducing reforms to administration. These measures, he hoped, would increase pressure on cadres to implement policy from below and make mobilization more meaningful and effective, since the population would have better access to political structures and officials. It was not Khrushchev's intention that these policies should lead to a collapse of party authority. However, his reforms were viewed as a threat to the interests of the party and the state, both because they impinged on bureaucratic prerogatives and because they threatened the party's position of political privilege. Consequently they helped bring about Khrushchev's downfall in 1964. His successor, Leonid Brezhnev, relaxed pressure on party-state officials. Brezhnev proclaimed a policy of 'stability of cadres', enabling high party-state officials to stay in post without fear of removal through purge or old age and infirmity, and he argued that progress towards communism would take a long time. It would involve perfecting the existing system of 'developed socialism' above all else, and this, Brezhnev claimed, meant not transforming society as a whole but correcting individual behaviour and developing existing institutions (Robinson, 1995a: 88–9). In effect, this let Soviet officials off the ideological hook. They had no longer even to pretend that they were struggling to build socialism on all fronts. Instead, they could settle back into routine and mouth platitudes. The USSR, like its leader Brezhnev, began to subside into physical decline and decrepitude. The needs of the regime and the rule and privileges of the party-state bureaucracy became more important practically than the development of the Soviet system and state to create economic development. Occasionally Brezhnev and other leaders protested the system's lack of vigour, pointing out that the USSR was falling behind the West as it underwent what Soviet analysts called a 'scientific-technical revolution' (essentially the birth of the computer age and the development of ever more mechanized production) (Hoffman and Laird, 1982). But Brezhnev and the system as a whole lacked the strength of body and will to take corrective action.

The result of these changes was that informal political practices became more widespread. The USSR developed a 'neo-traditional' system where the party's traditional, ideological claim to power persisted but was a cover for personal enrichment (Jowitt, 1992: 142–4). Corruption became systemic under Brezhnev as resources were moved around to compensate for break-downs and as people took advantage of the leader's policies to take personal profit. Huge amounts were siphoned away from the state budget during this time, and the networks of corruption reached into the upper echelons of the party and state. Corruption in the top of the party-state under Brezhnev was matched by the growth of a 'second economy', which involved most Russian citizens, and petty influence peddling (*blat'*) throughout the political system (Ledeneva, 1998). By the early 1980s it was estimated that the 'second economy' accounted for about 25 per cent of Soviet GDP, that it involved between 17 and 20 million workers (many part-time) or 15 per cent of the labour force, and that it was a vital source of services such as home and automobile maintenance (Hewett, 1988: 180).

TABLE 2.2 Soviet economic performance, 1965–85 (average annual growth, comparable prices, %)

	1961–5	1966–70	1971–5	1976–80	1981–5
Official statistics	6.5	7.8	5.7	4.3	3.6
Unofficial recalculation	4.4	4.1	3.2	1.0	0.6

Source: Adapted from Åslund, 1989: 15.

The growth of corruption and the weakening of the party's ability to mobilize the population had detrimental effects on the economy. The decline in the economy is recorded in table 2.2. Two sets of figures are provided: the official statistics and the figures as recalculated by two independent Soviet economists in the late 1980s. Both show that the general rate of economic growth slowed. On its own this means little. Many economies have high growth when they begin to industrialize and then slow down to a steadier rate. This was not the case in the USSR, where the decline was symptomatic of larger problems. Soviet economic slowdown was caused by its having exhausted the possibilities of extensive growth. Both labour and raw materials supply began to decline or became expensive under Brezhnev. The increase in labour fell from 6 per cent in the five-year plan period

1971–5 to 2 per cent in 1981–5, while the increase in production of fuels and raw materials fell from 25 per cent to 7 per cent (Åslund, 1989: 16). These changes were caused by a slowing down of population growth, as family sizes shrank in response to housing shortages and other pressures of urban life, and because the wastefulness of Soviet industry had exhausted many easily available and cheap sources of raw materials. Moving to intensive growth could have compensated for this, but the USSR was unable to squeeze much more out of its labour force or plant. Labour productivity rose in the 1970s, but it did so at a declining rate, while capital productivity fell consistently under Brezhnev, by 1.9 per cent during 1966–70, 3.8 per cent in 1971–5 and 2.9 per cent in 1976–9 (Keep, 1995: 222). This meant that, although output from Soviet industry grew, it did so at increased cost: the USSR was using more raw materials to obtain less than other economies. Excess demand for investment meant that, although the rate of investment as a percentage of GDP was high, there was a general shortage as resources were spread thinly between competing interests, especially after military production and prestige projects such as the space programme had taken their large cut from the budget. The effect of this was to delay the completion of projects for roughly twice as long as was the norm in capitalist economies (Hewett, 1988: 89–90). To try to cope with this, investment levels were raised at a far greater rate than in the West and outstripped general economic growth (Kornai, 1992: 167–8). In short, and in the absence of the political will to reform, the material wealth of the USSR had been eaten away to support inefficient economic growth. As we shall see in the next chapter, this situation was kept going in the 1970s only because high oil prices propped up the Soviet economy. These high prices, the inefficiencies that they promoted and the relative economic backwardness that they protected could not last for ever, however, and their exposure by the start of the 1980s was one source of the Gorbachev reforms.

Conclusion

Many of the USSR's problems originated in its particular vision of social progress and the CPSU's role in securing this progress. However, its problems cannot be reduced to a single source. Some originated in the political system that was established haphazardly following the October revolution of 1917 and some with the system of planned economy introduced to manage the industrialization drive under Stalin in the late 1920s. Others came with success. Demands made of the political and economic system became more complex as the Soviet economy developed an industrial base and society became urbanized, but administration did not change sufficiently to meet these needs or to incorporate new interests in the political system. The development of the Soviet system was thus far from well ordered or managed. In the end, it was a long way from a perfect embodiment of progress towards the eradication of human suffering. The USSR depended on its leaders to initiate change. However, the party leadership increasingly became a hostage to its own bureaucracy, as Khrushchev's fate showed. Change threatened party-state officials' ability to manage society; it created new goals for them, and they were already overburdened by their duties as political and economic managers. When faced with change they were forced to choose between implementing new policies and practices with the scarce resources that they had at their disposal or carrying on as before, honouring change in name only. By the late 1970s, the combination of bureaucratic intransigence and reliance on the top leadership to initiate reform led to what Mikhail Gorbachev was later to call 'stagnation'. The Brezhnev leadership's physical and mental decrepitude combined with bureaucratic self-interest to stultifying effect. Gorbachev aimed to reinvigorate the Soviet system with his reforms. The problem that he faced, however, was not a new one. Like other leaders before him, he had to try to get the party-state to embrace change and engage the Soviet population in order to implement his policies. While Gorbachev was no more successful than his predecessors at making the Soviet system work, he was not defeated by conservative opposition either. As a result, his reforms had a novel outcome – the destruction of the USSR – as we shall see in the next chapter.

3

Perestroika and the Fall of the USSR

Introduction

The demise of the USSR in December 1991 was the unintentional result of Mikhail Gorbachev's *perestroika* (restructuring) reforms. Gorbachev had hoped to revive the USSR, not destroy it. The problem that he faced in trying to revive the Soviet system was how to get the party-state to comply with his instructions and engage with the Soviet people. This, as we saw at the end of the last chapter, was not a new problem, but Gorbachev went further in his efforts to resolve it than other Soviet leaders, and in doing so he unwittingly revealed that the party could not connect with the Soviet people; it could only dictate to them. In bringing this to light, Gorbachev undermined the party, exposing it to questioning and fragmenting it. As the CPSU declined, other forces were able to enter politics. The party had no way of controlling or countering these new forces, especially since their appearance coincided with an economic downturn, which was itself partly caused by Gorbachev's reforms and was accelerated by the political fragmentation of the USSR. This made a common political response to economic crisis impossible.

Economic collapse and the emergence of new political actors prevented Gorbachev from saving some version of the Soviet Union. The new forces that had been created by *perestroika* were not able to overthrow the USSR: they were not recognized internationally, they were often fearful of the consequences of a complete break, and the Soviet state appeared to be holding together because its coercive apparatus – the army and most of the security and police forces – was still Soviet rather than Russian, Ukrainian, Kazakh, etc. The result by the summer of 1991 was a stalemate. Gorbachev and most of the Soviet republics had agreed that new political structures for a reformed multinational state should be created, but it was not clear what kind of political system would emerge. The stalemate was broken in August 1991 by an attempt by conservative Soviet state loyalists to roll back change. This coup exposed the hollowness of the Soviet state's power. Its unity as a coercive organization was shown to be a fiction when the plotters failed to rally coercive forces to their side, and the rapid unravelling of the coup changed the balance of power. Soviet republics broke away from the USSR, and the Russian government under President Boris Yeltsin forced through policies that destroyed the Soviet Union as a single political space. In December 1991 Gorbachev bowed to the inevitable and agreed its dissolution. This chapter will look at the development of *perestroika* and the political struggles that led to the collapse of the USSR rather than at broader arguments about whether collapse was inevitable and its nature (see Robinson, 2017a, for a discussion of the latter). While the nature of collapse is an interesting question, we can see from the events of the Gorbachev era that disintegration was prompted by changes from the apex of the Soviet system, and that popular involvement was sporadic and geographically dispersed (there was more popular action in the Baltic states and Moscow, for example, than across Russia as a whole). The implications of this for post-Soviet Russian politics will be discussed in the next chapter.

The origins of *perestroika*: economic trials, international tribulations and social crisis

Reform was not a new phenomenon in the USSR. Previous efforts had either ended in the removal of a leader, as with Khrushchev's fall in 1964, or been undermined or neutralized by party-state officials, as had happened with the moderate reforms that Brezhnev had attempted in the late 1960s and early 1970s. The fact that Gorbachev's reforms went further and did not lead to his removal but instead ended in the demise of the Soviet system requires some explanation. Part of the reason is that there was a constituency for change – the younger generation of Soviet officials whose advancement had been held back under Brezhnev's policy of 'stability of cadres'. This constituency was divided between conservative and radical wings, which were themselves then split into smaller factions. Gorbachev sat between these camps, and none of the factions in the party felt confident of removing him for fear of the others. The other reason that Gorbachev's reforms went further without his removal, and indeed one of the factors that helped produce the reform constituency that he headed, was because, by the mid-1980s, there could be no arguing with the need for change of some sort. The USSR was politically stagnant, facing economic and social crisis, and losing its ability to compete internationally.

The political stagnation under Brezhnev had led to corruption (see chapter 2), a gerontocracy as the Soviet leadership aged in post under the 'stability of cadres' policy, and a routinized administration of society unable to tackle the underlying problems of the system. Regime stability had triumphed over state reform and development. The result of this in economics was not just that growth rates declined (see table 2.2) but that the USSR began to lag behind the rest of the developed world so that it became relatively backward in comparison to its rivals. The country was unable to shift from the production of industrial and military goods dictated by the state to a balance of industrial and consumer goods production or to secure a moderate and constant overall rate of growth after its initial developmental spurt. Permanent international competition and arms expenditure combined with the bureaucratic power of industrial ministries to prioritize industrial goods production. Investment in these sectors remained high and crowded out the development of consumer goods and services. Moreover, the predilection of Soviet planners was to specialize so that vast industrial complexes with a small number of economic functions and requiring equally vast amounts of investment were created. At the start of the 1990s, Soviet and Russian industry was on average five times more monopolized than West European industry, and in some sectors, such as machine-building, monopoly levels were up to fourteen times higher. The creation of these industrial behemoths made for powerful lobbies which worked against a switch from industrial to consumer goods production. The structure of economic power and its favouring of military and industrial production meant declines in both labour productivity and investment returns. Workers, with no access to consumer goods or services, had no incentive to produce and earn more, since money could not be used to improve lifestyle. Excess demand for labour and ideologically guaranteed full employment meant that there was no sanction of unemployment for unproductive labour. As we saw in the last chapter, excess demand for investment meant that, although the rate of investment as a percentage of GDP was high, there was a general shortage of investment as resources were spread thinly because of high demand.

These problems were cumulative and exacerbated by the contradictory nature of change after Stalin. The political structures that had overseen high initial levels of development became a drag on progress in the post-Stalin era. Institutional structures, systems of management and lines of responsibility were tinkered with rather than fundamentally amended. As the economy became more complex, the party became less efficient and useful when interfering, and it became an impediment to change. From the 1970s, Soviet leaders relied on energy exports to maintain investment and living standards instead of forcing change through the rigid political system. The USSR took advantage of high oil prices after 1973 to reap huge profits. By the mid-1980s, energy sales accounted for 80 per cent of Soviet foreign currency earnings (Gustafson, 1989: 263–4). The revenue generated went a considerable way towards subsidizing industrial production and increases in living standards at a time when the rest of the industrialized world was closing down inefficient plants and seeking to rationalize production through job cuts, efficiency drives and technological modernization (Kotkin, 2001). Energy sales perpetuated rather than ameliorated Soviet tendencies to backwardness and briefly created 'an illusion of salvation' for the economy in the 1970s (Gaidar, 2007: 100). Soviet industry did not, for example, have to take account of the rising costs of energy in that decade, and their profligacy imposed significant costs on the central state in terms of subsidies.

The end result was that, by the 1980s, the USSR had an advanced industrial structure that demanded huge amounts of investment, with low productivity and poor quality production. As a result, and apart from in the energy sector, the country began to lose comparative advantage relative to other industrial economies. Although trade expanded as time passed, the USSR was peripheral in the world economy. In 1990 it accounted for only 2.1 per cent of exports and 2.3 per cent of imports – less than Belgium, the Netherlands and Italy, and a long way behind the USA and Japan. The USSR had the foreign trade structure of an industrially undeveloped state; it exported raw materials rather than manufactured goods. By 1987, 46 per cent of Soviet exports were from the energy sector. Poor quality meant that industrial and consumer goods were unsaleable on world markets: much Soviet production consisted of 'negative value added goods', manufactured objects worth less on world markets than the raw materials used to produce them (McKinnon, 1993). Technological developments in the rest of the world had simply left the USSR behind, and by 1991 only 4 per cent of Soviet plant met world standards.

Economic backwardness relative to its competitors strained the one area in which the USSR was strong – its military. The amount taken out of the economy by the party leadership to fund defence, and thus diverted from consumption and investment, did not decrease as the economy declined. Since the economy was smaller and less efficient than those of other countries, the amount spent by the USSR to keep up with its rivals was far larger relative to its economic strength. By 1987, US defence spending was about 7 per cent of GNP, while Soviet defence spending accounted for about 40 per cent of GNP. The defence burden was also growing as the Soviet economy slowed down. Relations with the West, which had improved gradually under Khrushchev and in the early 1970s during the period of détente, were upset in the late 1970s. Changes in the balance of power in the developing world, the coming to power of Ronald Reagan in the USA and Margaret Thatcher in the United Kingdom, the Soviet invasion of Afghanistan in 1979, and the deployment of intermediate nuclear forces in Eastern Europe led to the outbreak of the 'second Cold War' in the early 1980s, and a new, expensive round of the arms race began.

Finally, the decline in the Soviet economy weakened its hold on Eastern Europe. Maintaining is 'empire' was increasingly costly to the USSR since it subsidized the inefficient economies of its neighbours, as well as Cuba and Vietnam (Bunce, 1985). This strained its budget and brought only poor returns, as shown by Polish protest over Soviet influence and for independent trade unions in the early 1980s. The USSR's ability to cope with these changes and to maintain its superpower status was in doubt. Although (thanks to the nuclear balance of power and Mutually Assured Destruction) no state was likely to challenge it militarily, it was losing position and influence in the world and would not be able to maintain its military might relative to the USA without economic reform.

The defence burden of being in superpower competition with the more prosperous USA and its European allies deprived the USSR of vital resources that it could have used to stimulate production in other areas and to fund social services. This contributed to what Gorbachev described as the 'pre-crisis situation' that was created by the 'stagnation' of political and economic life under Brezhnev. The party had allowed what Gorbachev called a 'gap between words and deeds' to grow up: 'the world of day-to-day realities and the world of feigned prosperity were diverging more and more' (Gorbachev, 1987: 22). While the CPSU leadership talked of equality and social progress and used the slogans of socialism to proclaim their right to rule, 'social justice', defined by Gorbachev as equality of access to services, education and the wealth produced by society, had declined and social problems had grown. The difference between the party's 'words' and its 'deeds' was, Gorbachev argued, eroding the moral base of socialist society. The signs of this were to be seen not just in the corruption of the political system in the late Brezhnev era. In many ways the USSR was undergoing a hidden social crisis caused by the combination of political malaise and its economic development model. The most obvious sign of this social crisis was rampant alcoholism. By the early 1980s, about 15 per cent of the Soviet population could be classified as alcoholic (White, 1996: 40). Together with diet, smoking and work practices, alcohol consumption led to a decline in average life expectancy for men, an almost unique occurrence in an industrialized country: life expectancy for men in the USSR had risen to 64.5 years by 1972, but by 1984 had fallen to 62.6. Alcoholism also caused economic problems, contributing to the high rate of absenteeism from work that plagued the Soviet economy.

Yuri Andropov, a former head of the KGB, Gorbachev's patron, and Brezhnev's successor following the latter's death in November 1982, began to try and curb some of the excesses of corruption and improve social and labour discipline more generally by clamping down on absenteeism and drinking. Andropov's campaigns ended when he himself died in February 1984; he had been seriously ill for much of his tenure as general secretary. Andropov's reforms were rolled back by his successor, Konstantin Chernenko; but Chernenko too was ill and died in March 1985, enabling Gorbachev to come to office.

This procession of deaths in the Politburo was illustrative of a generational change that was to lock in reform. Brezhnev's 'stability of cadres' policy had created an aged leadership in the Politburo, the centre of the political system, where key reform decisions had to be taken. However, there was no such sclerosis in other parts of the system. Regional leaders, particularly party secretaries in the many *oblast'* and *krai* (large district administrative units) that made up the larger republics of the USSR (such as the Russian Soviet Federal Socialist Republic, Ukraine or Kazakhstan), were significantly younger than Brezhnev, Andropov and Chernenko, who had begun their ascent to the top leadership around the time of the great purge of 1937–8. Regional leaders towards the end of the Brezhnev period had mostly begun their careers during the Khrushchev era and were on average fourteen years younger than members of the top leadership (Hough, 1980: 69–78). Many of these officials were waiting for change.

Gorbachev was typical of the generation of politicians waiting to take power at the start of the 1980s – men in their early fifties for the most part who had been held back by the gerontocracy in Moscow. These individuals had practical experience of the problems that were building in the Soviet system because of their recent experience of hands-on administration in the provinces. They included Yegor Ligachev and Boris Yeltsin, who had been regional party secretaries and whom Gorbachev was to appoint to important party positions, and Nikolai Ryzhkov, Gorbachev's chair of the Council of Ministers – prime minister – from September 1985 to November 1990, who came from industry. By the time of Chernenko's death in 1985, this new generation of leaders were 'increasingly determined not to let the Politburo juggle another, old, sick or weak person into the top position again', as Gorbachev (1996: 165) put it in his memoirs. Thanks to Andropov's patronage, Gorbachev had the support of some of this new generation within the Central Committee and Central Committee Secretariat, where the question of leadership succession was decided, and where the battles to remove the last of the old guard would have to be fought once the succession was settled.

Finally, there was also a wider constituency for change that was a useful support for Gorbachev, the community of policy-orientated intellectuals that had developed a relative independence under Brezhnev in research institutes and in parts of the party apparatus, and which had begun to consider aspects of reform policy in the 1970s. This community, which was not a large or unified one, was to be important in several ways for Gorbachev (Brown, 2007: 157–90). Discussions with some of its members before he took power helped to reinforce Gorbachev's belief that change was needed. Several key individuals were later to become Gorbachev's advisors and helped to provide some of the ideas that were grouped together as 'new thinking'.

Gorbachev's contact with this community did not mean that he had a blueprint for change or concrete goals for reform before his accession to the general secretaryship. However, he was clear that change was needed, and when at the end of 1984 he made a speech critical of the economic slowdown, and calling for politics to be directed to ensuring 'social justice', he used many of the phrases and ideas that had been developed within the community of policy intellectuals. Gorbachev's familiarity with and his use of these ideas was a signal to those who wanted change to support him when Chernenko died. When he came to power the following year and began the first steps to reform, the wider constituency interested in reform were important proselytizers for change through the liberalization of the media that he introduced with his policy of *glasnost'* (openness). While their arguments helped to build popular support for Gorbachev, they did not make reform any easier to implement.

Reform begins

Gorbachev's aims on coming to power in March 1985 were relatively vague. Insofar as he had grand goals, he wished, as he was to later put it, to reform the economy so that by 2000 the USSR would attain 'the highest levels of social productivity in the world'. This would mean that Soviet citizens would enjoy living standards comparable with those of the wealthy industrial states. Moreover, he wanted the party to act as a vanguard, leading and guiding the Soviet people rather than administering them. However, policy developed slowly to address problems. First, Gorbachev needed to consolidate his power. This he did relatively quickly in 1985 and early 1986, removing the most obdurate remnants of the Brezhnev leadership from the Politburo and from major positions in the republican parties of the USSR.

Consolidation of power brought with it its own problems, however: Gorbachev had to feel out what policies the new leadership that he appointed would support. Many of the policies enacted in 1985 and the first months of 1986 were relatively traditional and continued Andropov's policies from 1982 to 1984. Chief among them were efforts to tighten labour discipline and raise the quality of Soviet production. Andropov had tried to improve labour discipline by cutting down on absenteeism from work by having the police raid shops, bars and other public places to round up absent workers. In May 1985, this was extended into a full-scale campaign against alcohol consumption, which was blamed for absenteeism as well as for many of the USSR's social problems. Another campaign was launched to 'accelerate socio-economic progress' (a twist on Brezhnev's claim that 'scientific-technical progress' needed to be speeded up) by investing in new technology and creating 'state quality control' auditors in factories to force up the quality of production, and there was a crusade against 'unearned income' – in other words, against the second economy and corruption.

At the same time Gorbachev began to explore how he might move beyond these traditional themes. To this end he began the policy of *glasnost'* (openness), appointed Yeltsin head of the Moscow city party apparatus, and criticized Soviet ideology at the XXVII Party Congress in the spring of 1986. *Glasnost'* was a media management policy aimed at encouraging both officialdom and people to take up reform by publicizing problems – such as drug abuse and prostitution, as well as some aspects of official maladministration – that had not been discussed previously and which had therefore contributed to the 'gap between words and deeds'. In 1985–6 this was far from the creation of press freedom, let alone general freedom of belief and expression. Elements of these freedoms would develop later and often autonomously of Gorbachev. However, even at that time they created space for novel critiques of the CPSU, such as the complaints about party privilege that appeared in the press before the XXVII Party Congress. The arguments over this showed there were differences in the leadership over how far and fast change should progress. Yeltsin's appointment as head of the Moscow city party added to these divisions. Yeltsin's leadership style was brash and populist, as he confronted the status quo in the capital and tried to root out petty corruption. He supported the extension of *glasnost'* and clashed with Ligachev over this at the XXVII Party Congress. Finally, Gorbachev himself at the congress criticized Brezhnev's idea that the USSR had entered the stage of 'developed socialism', which was defined as a prolonged stage of communist construction during which the country would develop incrementally. This, Gorbachev argued, had become an excuse for inaction and had led the USSR into a period of 'stagnation' during which the CPSU had lost sight of its role as political vanguard and inspiration of the Soviet people.

The mixture of new policy elements such as *glasnost'* and criticisms of the recent past (as yet Stalin and Lenin were not criticized) with more traditional policy elements such as the anti-alcohol campaign sent mixed messages about reform and created uncertainty about its depth and purpose. This pattern was to be repeated over the years of *perestroika*, sometimes because of attempts by leaders such as Ligachev to roll back reform, sometimes because Gorbachev did not see the contradictions between what he was trying to preserve in the Soviet system and elements of his reform programme. This meant not only that reform developed in fits and starts but also that it was implemented piecemeal. Officials put into effect those parts of the programme that suited them. This made the situation dynamic, as Gorbachev moved to try to get reform implemented. However, this generally introduced new contradictions in policy so that his efforts were never successful. There was nothing unusual in this: Soviet politics, as we saw in chapter 2, had always been characterized by officials selecting what parts of policy to implement and then being pressed by the party leadership to do more. What was novel under Gorbachev was not that this pattern of pressure–subversion–more pressure was repeated, but that the increased pressure to reform put on officials led to the alienation of sections of the party-state so that they began to act autonomously, taking advantage of the growing political chaos to secure their positions materially or politically, or both. This, coupled with the growth of popular politics and nationalism, was to doom the USSR in the end.

The first signs of this pattern developing came after the XXVII Party Congress in 1986. The traditional policies that Gorbachev had introduced in 1985 were not working. The results of the anti-alcohol campaign were less than impressive. Russians kept on drinking. Alcohol production went underground and deprived the state of tax income. Local party branches initially reported impressive figures for the closure of shops selling alcohol, sanctions against party members who drank excessively, and membership of temperance societies, etc., but once the attention of the centre shifted slightly the campaign was put on the backburner. The fate of the anti-alcohol campaign demonstrated that the party's style of administration was a problem, while the fate of other campaigns showed that the economic system was too rigid to create growth or improve quality.

The economic policies of 1985 and early 1986 also had disappointing results. Changes in investment priorities to emphasize technology caused confusion, increased waste, as some existing projects were abandoned for lack of funds, and achieved only modest returns: a 15 per cent rise in investment in machine-building led to an increase of only 3 per cent in new assets. The move to increase the quality of production caused a slump because large amounts of industrial output were condemned as sub-standard. This in turn hit the pay packets of workers, because they were penalized for failing to fulfil plan targets, but didn't lead to any rise in quality because defective supplies were the cause of most problems.

A further sign that change was needed came in April 1986, when an accident at the nuclear reactor at Chernobyl' in Ukraine spread radioactive material over large parts of the western USSR, Scandinavia and Eastern Europe. Gorbachev was embarrassed by this international demonstration of the faults of Soviet industry and by the fact that the Soviet Union had not been able to react to the accident effectively because of the culture of official secrecy. Chernobyl', Gorbachev (1996: 189) wrote in his memoirs, 'was graphic evidence, not only of how obsolete our technology was, but also of the failure of the old system.' After Chernobyl', Gorbachev began to change tack and talk more and more of *perestroika* (restructuring). Reform, he proposed, needed to involve radical change and had to be directed not just at the economy and public morals but also at the political system. Gorbachev argued that the USSR would solve its economic problems only when the political system became more flexible and able to secure popular support for its policies.

Reform spreads

From mid-1986 onwards, *glasnost'* began to tackle more substantial political issues to build support for reform and demonstrate why it was needed. Greater tolerance of discussion was signalled by the release from internal exile of the dissident Andrei Sakharov in December 1986. The real start of *perestroika* came in 1987 with the January and June plenums of the CPSU Central Committee. At these two meetings, Gorbachev turned his attention to the party and the role that it played and the related success in economic reform to changes in the party's role. Gorbachev argued that Soviet socialism had lost its way and degenerated into a bureaucratic maze because the party spent too long on administration and not enough time on political work with the people. It was necessary, he claimed, to separate the party and the state and for each to play its own role properly without interference from the other.

Gorbachev addressing the CPSU Central Committee

These were not new themes in Soviet political discourse, but the solutions that Gorbachev proposed were different. A new 'Law on Enterprises' proposed that businesses should have more independence from both the party and ministries and should operate according to calculations of profit and loss, and that workers should have the right to elect their factory managers. This was not full industrial democracy, since elections had to be approved by higher authorities, but Gorbachev was trying to break down barriers to economic reform and innovation. Independence from party and state ministries, and the need to take account of losses, was supposed to do away with inefficient work practices and waste. It would also create incentives because factories would have the right to dispose of profits and could pay their workers if they did well. Party branches in factories were to work as political leaders, supporting political educational work among the labour force and convincing them of the need to work in line with national party policy. This would increase party activism at grassroots level.

Gorbachev also proposed that party members should play a greater part in the administration of the CPSU to break down its internal bureaucratic mind-set. Party management should be democratized, he argued, with the leaders of local party organs and the central committees of the republican communist parties elected by secret ballot. The democratization of party life, Gorbachev maintained, would serve as an example to the rest of society, remove party workers who were not capable of implementing reform policies from office, and make party leaders focus on political leadership to support the ordinary party member. Gorbachev hoped that these changes would be consolidated by the convention of a party conference in 1988 (the first since the 1940s) to develop political reform further.

The problem with these ideas was a simple one: How to get them to work? Both political authorities and economic managers were being asked to take steps into the dark. A factory manager, for example, might think that more independence was a good thing and try to implement the policy line. However, if he or she did so and broke away from the local party and the relevant ministry, to whom would the factory turn for help if things went wrong, if suppliers failed to deliver necessary raw materials and components, or if payments were not made for goods delivered? The USSR had no effective system of commercial law to which a manager could turn for redress. In the absence of an administrative system designed to support managerial independence, it was better to keep working with the ministry in Moscow and asking for assistance from the local party. Party work thus did not change greatly because economic administration was done elsewhere all of a sudden. Party leaders continued to see themselves as responsible for economic management, and there was still a demand from enterprises for them to help out.

The reforms were thus blunted in their effectiveness because of the preference for traditional ways of administration. Gorbachev's hope was that agitation 'from below', from ordinary party members, would break down some of this bureaucratic resistance. However, party work changed only slowly because democratization was opposed by parts of the leadership and because of mixed signals about reform. Gorbachev did not set specific goals for the party to achieve; he wanted it to find the answers to Soviet problems through its own political work so as to close the 'gap between words and deeds'. The party, Gorbachev believed, had to make its ideological message real by demonstrating that it reflected the interests of the people; in the process, it would discover on its own the best way of implementing reform and would be able to renew its political leadership by drawing on the support of the people. The key to success for Gorbachev was not to command the party to fulfil specific tasks but to get it interact with the Soviet people, to learn from this interaction where the Soviet system was failing, to work out how to mend failure and to lead the people in the resolution of problems. *Perestroika* as Gorbachev conceived it was not about setting out specific targets for the CPSU to strive to fulfil: if set firm goals, the party would simply formally obey orders as it had done in the past and declare that it had success-fully done what it had been charged to do, and no one would be able to protest that this was not the case. To be successful, *perestroika* had to increase pressure on the party to limit its role to political activity and to create mecha-nisms through which party and people could interact. Gorbachev's vision was of the CPSU continually engaged with the Soviet people, of it working with them to develop and implement new policies so that the Soviet system would become efficient and productive.

Putting pressure on the party: political reform and the failure of *perestroika*

There were several problems with this vision: party leaders were unsure of what they were to do in practice. Divisions in the leadership came to a head and compounded this problem in October 1987, when Yeltsin attacked party conservatives at a Central Committee plenum. His speech was a political mistake. The plenum had been called to discuss (i.e., approve) Gorbachev's speech commemorating the seventieth anniversary of the 1917 revolution and was supposed to be a celebratory event. Instead of rallying support for his work, Yeltsin found himself abandoned by Gorbachev and attacked on all sides, first at the Central Committee and then at a meeting of the Moscow city party committee, which removed him from his post as head of the Moscow party (Colton, 2008: 130–50).

The 'Yeltsin affair' unleashed a personal animosity between Yeltsin and Gorbachev that was to fester over the coming years and to make it difficult for the two to cooperate. It lessened Russia's commitment to the union when Yeltsin became Russian leader, and this helped seal the USSR's fate. More immediately, the affair highlighted the extent to which change in the party had shallow roots and the fear that existed that Gorbachev's reforms could easily be pushed back. With hindsight it can be argued that the latter fear was ungrounded. Conservative forces were always a threat to Gorbachev, but they never came close to removing him from office. Their power was almost entirely negative: they blocked the progress of reform but could not stop it from being promulgated. The limits to conservative power were not apparent in 1987, however. People feared that reform would be halted in the same way that Khrushchev's ejection had stopped post-Stalinist reform in 1964.

The Yeltsin affair encouraged party workers to adopt a 'wait and see' attitude to reform. Gorbachev needed a means of pushing them to change their way of working. The solution that he announced at a CPSU conference in June 1988 was an ambitious set of political reforms that were supposed to force the party to work with the Soviet people, but which created the possi-bility of organized opposition to party rule. At the conference, Gorbachev announced the creation of a new two-tier parliamentary structure. The

Supreme Soviet, previously a large and ineffective body that rubber-stamped party directives, would in the future be a smaller, full-time legislature with 542 deputies. Instead of being directly elected by the people, it would be elected by a new parliamentary body, the Congress of People's Deputies, which would have 2,250 members. This new body – which would be elected in part by multi-candidate elections – would meet twice a year and set out the strategic goals of policy, and the Supreme Soviet would transform these goals into legislation. An election for the new Congress of People's Deputies was set for March 1989, and the new Supreme Soviet would be elected when the congress met in June 1989. Gorbachev saw the Congress of People's Deputies as representing two things: it would be a symbol of what he called the 'socialist pluralism of opinions', and it would be the pinnacle of a new 'socialist law-based state' (Robinson, 1992). The CPSU, through the election campaign scheduled for March 1989, would illustrate to the people that, although there were different opinions in Soviet society, it represented all of them. It would thus demonstrate that there was a rough unity that underpinned pluralism in the USSR based on support for socialism. By inter-acting with the people, the CPSU would also learn about how the different approaches to socialism could be strengthened through developing policies to integrate them further and perfect the unity of citizens in support of the party. The creation of a 'socialist law-based state' would help party workers concentrate on political work. The Congress of People's Deputies was legally charged with the determination of state policy. Party workers would have to secure their control over politics by winning election to the congress. This would automatically turn them away from administrative to political work (in the form of electioneering) and demonstrate to the party how it could control politics through elected representative institutions (Robinson, 1995b).

Gorbachev labelled these new initiatives *demokratizatsiya*, 'democratization'. His vision of democratization did not foresee the CPSU losing power; the intent was for it to exercise power in a new way. The party, however, did not prove equal to the task. Gorbachev was partly at fault for this failure as – again – he sent the party contradictory messages. He both insisted that the CPSU needed to interact with the people *and* told the party that it alone repre-sented the unity at the heart of the 'socialist pluralism of opinions' and had to ensure this unity was represented in the new Congress of People's Deputies and Supreme Soviet. Gorbachev was thus asking the party to change the way that it worked but, at the same time, ordering it to intervene in politics and produce a parliament that reflected a particular 'socialist' point of view. The CPSU could not do both; it could not change and at the same time secure a parliament in which a particular set of political views dominated. The election in March 1989 made the CPSU's deficiency public, and as it failed the myth of party power would begin to be exposed. The election demonstrated that the CPSU was actually an unrepresentative body and allowed people to begin to argue that its rule was the cause of Soviet problems, not the solution to them.

Gorbachev was caught in a trap, and he exposed *demokratizatsiya* to criticism when it publicly failed. Two-thirds of the deputies to the congress were elected by popular vote in single-mandate constituencies, while the rest were nominated by 'public organizations' such as the party and trade unions. The nominations from public organizations caused a scandal as they failed to respect the wishes of ordinary members: deputies were chosen by the central plenary meetings rather than by popular vote. In the CPSU, 31,500 nominations were received for the party's hundred seats from the grassroots membership. However, only a hundred nominations were voted on by the party's Central Committee for those seats. Gorbachev himself was elected to the congress in this way. Direct elections were marred by the actions of electoral commissions, which sought to ensure that many party leaders stood unopposed and, where possible, to bar candidates that the party saw as too troublesome. Over two-thirds of the names put forward by public meetings for the post of deputy never made it onto the ballot sheets. Despite these efforts at limiting competition, many party leaders failed to get the necessary 50 per cent of the vote needed to secure election, and 'troublemakers' such as Yeltsin who made it on to the ballot paper scored striking successes against officially approved candidates (Henderson and Robinson, 1997: 46–8).

The elections proved a moral defeat for the party and for Gorbachev. Gorbachev argued that the party leaders who had lost had deserved to lose because they had not changed the way that they worked. Conservatives blamed the losses on him and became further entrenched in their scepticism about reform. Radicals, on the other hand, were disappointed that Gorbachev did not see that the party was an obstacle to change and were alienated from him at the meeting of the new parliament in May–June 1989. Efforts to marginalize radical voices at the parliamentary sessions failed. Gorbachev was elected as chair of the new Supreme Soviet, but an opposition parliamentary caucus, the Inter-Regional Deputies Group (IRDG), emerged and began putting forward alternative political proposals. This new group was the first organized opposition group inside the Soviet state since the 1920s, and its membership included Yeltsin, who was emerging as the popular figurehead of anti-CPSU protest, and Andrei Sakharov (who was to die in December 1989). The formation of a parliamentary opposition meant that the unity of a 'socialist pluralism of opinions' that Gorbachev had hoped the CPSU would summon forth dissolved into ineffective parliamentary politics. Gorbachev did not receive unanimous support for *perestroika*, and the opposition saw their proposals rejected by the CPSU majority (Robinson, 1993). Worse, the first convocation of the Congress of People's Deputies was followed by miners' strikes in Russia and Ukraine that rapidly developed from protests about economic and welfare issues to address political issues, including calls for the revocation of Article 6 of the 1977 Constitution which enshrined the CPSU's 'leading and guiding' role. The revolt of the miners was symbolically damaging. Miners had been held up in Soviet iconography as exemplary 'elite' socialist workers. That this supposed mainstay of socialist construction was prepared openly to oppose the CPSU's central place in the Soviet political system showed how far the distance was between the reality of CPSU activity and Gorbachev's talk of it being a vanguard party.

Endgame

The election and meeting of the Congress of People's Deputies marked a turning point in the development of *perestroika*, but not in the fashion that Gorbachev had hoped. Before the election, Gorbachev had been subject to some criticism from below from the 'informal groups' (independent political organizations) that had begun to emerge with the liberalization of *glasnost'*. However, by and large he had been free to develop policy as he saw fit, constrained only by opposition from within the party leadership and by his own unwillingness to be specific about *perestroika* in the hope that this would lead party members to take up the reins of political leadership.

After the elections to the congress, Gorbachev began to lose control over the political agenda at home and abroad. The rejection of communist party rule in Eastern Europe in the latter half of 1989 laid him open to charges of betraying the gains that the USSR had made in the past in international politics. The loss of Eastern Europe also encouraged nationalists to think about breaking away from the Union; events in Eastern Europe showed the Soviet leadership was unwilling to use violence to prop up its power. Radicals and nationalists began to go well beyond Gorbachev's vision of reform over the last few months of 1989 and early in 1990, slowly at first but then with greater intensity as it became apparent that Gorbachev could not stop them.

Gorbachev continued his efforts to force the CPSU to act as a political leader, but the party was beginning to fragment. Membership declined as individuals quit and the flow of new entrants dried up. In January 1990, those members associated with the IRDG formed the 'Democratic Platform' to argue that the CPSU should be transformed into a political party that had no other function but to fight elections and no other means of ruling except via elected assemblies. Republican communist parties increasingly began to ignore the orders that emanated from Moscow. CPSU finances dried up or were appropriated, and the party began to divide along republican lines (Gill, 1994). In June 1990, a Russian communist party organization was established. Previously party organizations in the Russian Federation had been subordinated to central all-Union party bodies. The establishment of a party organization for Russia was a move by conservatives to take control of some of the resources of the CPSU as the Soviet Union began to disintegrate. Nationalist movements in the republics – sometimes emerging from within the ranks of the party – began to push for greater autonomy from Moscow, especially in the Baltic republics of Latvia, Lithuania and Estonia and in Ukraine and the Caucasus (Beissinger, 2002).

Gorbachev tried to reassert his control over domestic politics in early 1990. In March he was elected as president of the USSR (a new post) by the Congress of People's Deputies. This new position gave Gorbachev strong executive powers that he hoped to use to push reform forward. By taking on these powers and more responsibility for reform, he also hoped that the CPSU would be freed of bureaucratic activity and would be able to concentrate on political work. As the new presidential post was established, Article 6 of the 1977 Constitution was revised to remove the legal guarantee of the party's right to rule. Gorbachev was not thereby abandoning the CPSU, but he was recognizing that, at least in the near future, the party could not reform itself quickly enough in order to deal with the USSR's problems nor deal with these problems on its own.

The new reforms came just before the March 1990 elections to parliaments in the republics and Gorbachev hoped that they would signal to the population that there was no need to support radical forces since there was reformist life in the party yet. If this signal got through, it did so only weakly, and the disintegration of the Soviet political space sped up with the election of republican legislatures. In Russia, the experience of the 1989 elections and the fate of radical proposals at the Congress of People's Deputies prompted the organization of an umbrella group, Democratic Russia, to support candidates who were pro-democracy and in favour of both limiting CPSU power and economic reform. Although Democratic Russia was founded only in January 1990 and never managed to develop a mass membership, local party organizations or a discrete political platform, candidates aligned with it managed to take enough seats in March 1990 to control the city councils of Moscow and Leningrad and to elect Boris Yeltsin as chairman of the Russian Supreme Soviet (White et al., 1997: 31–4). Yeltsin's grasp on power was slight, since Democratic Russia didn't command a majority in either of the two chambers of the new Russian parliament (like the USSR, Russia had a directly elected Congress of People's Deputies, which was a part-time body and which elected a smaller, full-time chamber, the Supreme Soviet). This, as we shall see in chapter 4, was to have a profound effect on post-Soviet Russian politics. Nonetheless, under Yeltsin's leadership Russia was able to declare its 'sovereignty' in June 1990. This meant that the Russian parliament and government under Yeltsin's general leadership considered that their own laws took precedence over those issued by the parliament and government of the USSR. Other republics quickly followed suit. Republican leaders were often not true nationalists but were more than happy to expand their power to give themselves room to manoeuvre politically. Conservative and pro-Soviet forces supported votes for sovereignty since they saw it as weakening Gorbachev.

The proclamations of 'sovereignty' started a 'war of laws' as Gorbachev and the central Soviet government struggled to assert their authority over Russia and the other republics (Dunlop, 1993). The result was administrative chaos. The Soviet and Russian governments, and below them other regional authorities, issued contradictory instructions, and economic reform plans were caught up in squabbles over authority. In the absence of effective administration, economic decay became economic collapse. Prices rocketed as industrial production slumped because of the breakdown in the system of state orders. The absence of effective administration enabled something else too: spontaneous privatization. As controls over party workers and economic administrators weakened, and as the contest for control in Moscow between the Russian and Soviet governments grew, local authorities and economic managers began to use state and party property as if it was their own. The economic *nomenklatura* did not seize resources collectively as a social group aware of its interests. Individuals and groups simply took advantage of opportunities as they presented themselves and as they faced the challenge of economic disintegration in the last years of Soviet power. Other privatizations occurred as ministries were broken up in efforts to reduce economic bureaucracy, only to re-emerge as giant corporations and 'concerns' (such as the Gazprom company that replaced the Ministry of Gas) under the control of former ministers (Barnes, 2006: 43–67). Many officials transferred party resources to themselves by setting up companies that took over party property and resources (McAuley, 1992). In a sense, the Soviet state began to disappear in many areas of life as its resources were 'stolen' from it by its officials when they realized that Gorbachev and the central authorities no longer had the power to prevent them from using property as they wanted (Solnick, 1998).

The collapse of the economy, the fight with the republics, the quickening disintegration of the CPSU, and the weakening of the state as resources were transferred into private hands reduced the chances of Gorbachev pressing forward with reform. From the end of 1990 onwards, he was concerned to survive politically and to preserve some vestiges of the collapsing Soviet state. In the winter of 1990–1, he allied himself with conservatives in the Soviet state and promoted them to positions of responsibility in the hope that their loyalty to the USSR would halt the flow of power to the republics. This period has been labelled Gorbachev's 'drift to the right' – i.e., to conservatism. The drift did not last long. Gorbachev changed tack and drifted 'back to the left' after the failure of attacks on the pro-independence governments of the Baltic republics and moves against Yeltsin in Russia initiated by the recently promoted conservatives. He called a referendum in March 1991 that asked whether or not people thought it necessary to 'preserve the Union of Soviet Socialist Republics as a renewed federation of equal and sovereign republics'. The Russian authorities under Yeltsin added a question to the ballot paper in the Russian Federation asking if people thought it necessary to introduce a new office of Russian president. Both questions were supported by about 70 per cent of voters (White et al., 1997: 73–7). People didn't want to lose the USSR entirely, but they wanted more effective and local leadership from a president of the Russian republic to tackle economic and social collapse.

The division of opinion among the people reflected the political stalemate between Gorbachev and Yeltsin. The central state was not powerful enough to remove Yeltsin. However, it was powerful enough to prevent the Russian authorities from taking action to halt economic collapse. Yeltsin was able to extend his personal power by securing election to the new post of Russian president in June 1991 with 59.7 per cent of the vote, but he was not able to rule Russia while Soviet institutions still existed and sovereignty was divided. Faced with stalemate, Gorbachev and Yeltsin put aside their differences, and with other republican leaders negotiated a new treaty to replace the 1922 Union treaty.

The treaty broke the stalemate, but in a way that neither Gorbachev nor Yeltsin expected. Faced with the transfer of some powers away from the central state to the republics, the conservatives whom Gorbachev had appointed turned on him and launched a coup attempt on the day before the new treaty was signed in August 1991. The plotters, who formed a State Committee for the State of Emergency (SCSE), imprisoned Gorbachev in his holiday home in Ukraine but failed to arrest Yeltsin or fully to mobilize the Soviet security forces behind them. SCSE incompetence and drunkenness, and popular resistance around the Russian parliament building, the White House, brought the downfall of the SCSE within three days.

The plotters also brought down the USSR with them. What Yeltsin, the Russian democratic movement and the nationalist movements of the other

Boris Yeltsin rallying opposition to the August 1991 coup

Soviet republics could not manage on their own was achieved for them by the Soviet state itself, which ceased to exist in practice after August 1991. The Baltics led the way, declaring independence and securing international recognition, something that had been denied them before the August coup. Russia took control of its economy in September and announced economic reform would begin in January 1992. With Russia going its own way economically, there was no connecting tissue to hold the remaining republics together. The last nails in the coffin of the Soviet state were hammered home after Ukraine voted for independence in a referendum on 1 December 1991. On 8 December, Yeltsin, Leonid Kravchuk, the new president of Ukraine, and the chairman of the Belarusian parliament, Stanislau Shuskevich, met and agreed to exit the USSR and replace it with a new organization, the Commonwealth of Independent States (CIS). A week later the former Soviet republics in Central Asia joined. As its name suggests, the CIS was not a new federal state but an international organization created by sovereign states as a forum to discuss issues of common concern; many of its founders did not want to pool their sovereignty, and the CIS was to struggle to reach and honour collective agreements (see also chapter 10). But in the short term, and since it was not a new federal arrangement, the CIS was effective at drawing a line under the existence of the Soviet Union. With its creation the USSR was finished; Gorbachev resigned as president and left the Kremlin on 25 December 1991 and the Soviet Union was formally wound up on 31 December. Yeltsin and the Russian government stepped into the vacuum to try to create a new Russia.

Conclusion

Gorbachev's attempt to reinvigorate the Soviet Union destroyed the Soviet system as a political regime, and this then led to the destruction of the Soviet Union as a state. His decision to begin political reform in 1986–7, and then to radicalize reform in 1988–9, recognized that it was impossible to improve the functioning of the state apparatus of the USSR without changing the party's role and the terms on which it held power. For the political system as a whole to adapt to deal with its problems, the regime of the USSR and the political rules that regulated access to power had to change. Gorbachev's misfortune was that there was a great deal of reluctance to alter how power was accessed on the part of many Soviet officials. Some were reluctant because of their conservatism. Some were reluctant because they didn't know how to operate the Soviet system in a new way. And some didn't have a clear idea of what Gorbachev was asking of them. This lack of clarity was Gorbachev's fault. He saw the need for change but didn't want that change to be formalist, change in name only, made at the command of the party leadership and not actually carried through. But his desire for party officials to discover change for themselves made many uncertain and hesitant. Consequently, they carried on claiming their authority as representatives of the CPSU, an authority that Gorbachev licensed them to claim because of his faith in the party. This created a contradiction at the heart of political reform. The CPSU's centrality to the Soviet system was affirmed and at the same time exposed as hollow. This contradiction created space for opposition to protest the limits of reform centred on the party changing its way of working. This led to an even greater crisis of trust in the party, and within it, so that the Soviet system began to disintegrate. Once it had disintegrated, once political forces were created that argued for new political rules and new political regimes, the Soviet state as a territorial entity began to collapse too. The particular fusion of regime and state in the USSR meant that one could not continue without the other: when the Soviet regime fell, the Soviet state fell too.

4
Yeltsin and the Politics of Crisis

Introduction

Post-Soviet Russian politics was born in crisis and has developed through crisis. Each Russian leader, first Boris Yeltsin and then Vladimir Putin and Dmitri Medvedev, and now Putin again, has been struggling with the same set of problems. Each has been trying to develop the post-Soviet Russian state, to put in place a system of administration that is adequate to managing Russian society. This means developing political structures that can support economic development so that the state has resources sufficient to cover both the welfare needs and the security of its people.

Rebuilding the state is a task that is revolutionary in scale and involves reshaping society and economy so that the state is able to develop on a new, more secure financial footing. However, the means to accomplish changes of revolutionary scope and depth were not available, since the collapse of the Soviet Union was an incomplete revolution at best. The destruction of old elites and of old patterns of behaviour was far from exhaustive. Social struggle was muted during the demise of the USSR; social patterns of power and privilege did not change as rapidly as the political institutions that had given birth to them. Political activity had been, and was to continue to be, a struggle between different elite factions, between Gorbachevian reformers (although these now disappear from the historical scene), new political actors such as Yeltsin and his supporters, and resisters of reform, who opposed it for a combination of ideological and personal reasons. Thanks to the need to reconstruct the state and its foundations, the problems of change were too great for these elite groups to deal with on a consensual basis. This meant that there was little chance of agreeing on the form that a political regime should take. Questions about how the state should be reformed bled into disputes about how a new political regime should be constructed and on what terms power should be accessed, by whom and to what ends. Crisis provided opportunities for leaders to try to force through change to rebuild state and economy, but political struggle over the nature of the regime soon helped create other crises, which meant that state development was compromised and no resolution to Russia's deeper problems was reached. Instead Russia's leaders made concessions over state development in return for agreement over regime stability. Elite factions agreed to mute their challenges to Yeltsin's leadership in return for privileged access to wealth and power. Rough, ready, unstable and weak agreements over the rules governing access to power were reached at the cost of political and economic renewal. Regime building – arriving at an agreement over how power should be divided up – was favoured over state building – developing new forms of governance and the economic structures that could support them.

This chapter and the next examine these questions in the two 'periods' of post-Soviet Russian politics, the Yeltsin era of 1991–9 and the Putin era of 2000 to the present day. There are differences between these two stretches of time caused by changes in circumstance and by the fact that Yeltsin and Putin are very different in character. But there are also powerful continuities and commonalities between the two periods. Not least among these is the struggle to combine regime stability with deeper changes that meet the challenges that arose as the USSR collapsed. Dealing with this issue has been the common thread that has driven much of the institutional development that is the focus of later chapters of this book.

The Yeltsin reform project

The failure of the August 1991 coup and the unravelling of the USSR that followed it helped create a *de jure* state as Russia was recognized as the main successor state to the Soviet Union. This, however, gave Yeltsin responsibility without power. Russian governmental structures did not really exist. The Russian government inherited Soviet institutions plus the Russian parliament of the Congress of People's Deputies and the Supreme Soviet. The loyalty of neither the inherited institutions nor parliament could be taken for granted. Yeltsin's already weak parliamentary base frayed since it was no longer held together by opposition to Gorbachev and the Soviet system, and there was little that he could do to force institutions inherited from the USSR to follow his orders. Power was for the most part held by regional political and economic leaders and was based on the mutual support that they provided for one another. This had helped them keep their positions during *perestroika*, and they had begun to convert their bureaucratic and personal power into personal wealth. The weakening of party control and central planning in the last years of *perestroika* had been accompanied by 'spontaneous privatization' as factory directors and other officials converted official assets into personal ones, thus giving the elite members sources of patronage. Patronage is a great source of power and influence in a collapsing economy in which resources and goods are in short supply.

Soviet disintegration did, however, give Yeltsin an opportunity to try to balance out the power of the old elite. He was able to control the political agenda in Russia for a short time as president and victor over the coup plotters, an advantage he used to press forward with radical economic reform, often referred to as 'shock therapy'. This was as much for political as economic reasons. First, adopting radical economic reform also solved Yeltsin's problems with government formation. Gennadii Burbulis, the secretary of his State Council and an ally from his hometown of Sverdlovsk, pressed on him the radical reform package, which came with a team of young reform economists headed by Yegor Gaidar, who were ready to implement it in government. Reform was to be introduced by decree, with parliament granting Yeltsin powers for a year to enact it. Yeltsin became prime minister, with Burbulis as first deputy prime minister, in charge of day-to-day administration. Gaidar became minister for finance and a deputy prime minister in 1991 (he was later acting prime minister for the last six months of 1992, before entering government again briefly between late 1993 and early 1994). Elections for regional administration heads were cancelled. Presidential representatives to the regions were appointed by Yeltsin as the August coup fell apart. These representatives were supposed to ensure compliance with Russian government laws and decrees to ensure the implementation of economic reform (Clark, 1998: 30–1, 37). In rapid order, therefore, and using economic reform as a pretext, Yeltsin created what is often called the 'executive' or 'presidential' 'vertical', a hierarchy of administrative bodies responsible to the president and supposed to ensure the implementation of government policy throughout Russia. Whether or not this 'vertical' was strong was to prove another matter.

Radical economic reform was more than a solution to immediate issues with the organization of government, however. It was a state-building strategy as well as a package of economic measures which promised to deliver socio-economic transformation to match, and underpin, the political transformation that Yeltsin had helped bring about against the CPSU and the Soviet state since 1989–91. This economic transformation would change the relationship of state to society by creating new means of socio-economic regulation and developing a resource base for the state to regulate social and economic activity. This promise resonated with the Russian leadership at the end of 1991 because Yeltsin occupied a position at the apex of a state that barely existed. Although the Russian government began to appropriate the functions and resources of some parts of the USSR after August 1991, the state had little capacity, few resources and small means to collect them. The new regime was committed to democracy and could not appropriate resources from society by force. Potential opponents of both Yeltsin and political and economic reform from the old Soviet *nomenklatura*, on the other hand, had considerable resources because of 'spontaneous privatization'.

At the end of 1991, the new Russian state did not have the personnel or the means (that is, the capacity or the resources) to tackle the legacies of the Soviet system head-on. But economic reformers argued it did not need to. 'Shock therapy' promised that the legacies of the Soviet era could be dealt with through economic policy without building up a new administrative system to implement reform. It was thus administratively 'cheap', in that its implementation did not require great bureaucratic capacity, only political will. Compliance with government policy depended on persuading people that the government had a 'credible commitment' to reform, that it was dedicated to reform and would pursue it no matter what, that evading its implementation would only lead to the pursuit of more reformist policies to keep reform on track. Once people were convinced of its credibility, Soviet legacies would be diluted as reform provided incentives to act differently and empowered the state and new economic groups relative to the old *nomenklatura*.

Reform, as conceived by Gaidar and his team, would take place in two stages. Stage one, which was supposed to last between January 1992 and early 1993, was concerned with macro-economic stabilization – that is, financial and monetary stabilization – and would involve controlling inflation and stabilizing the rouble and the budget deficit by liberalizing prices and commercializing economic activity as subsidies were cut and state spending reduced. Stage two, which was to occur between early 1993 and 1995, would consolidate financial and monetary stabilization and see the restructuring of property rights, as mass privatization would pass the bulk of industry and commercial activity into private hands.

The key to success was the successful completion of stage one, when policies to effect price liberalization and financial stabilization were supposed to be mutually reinforcing. The reasoning behind the policy went as follows. Central government would end subsidies to industry and consumption by liberalizing prices. Without subsidies, enterprises would be dependent on private investment and credit to cover their economic activity. Acquiring private investment would require transparency in corporate governance, which would be detrimental to the semi-legal control of enterprises by the *nomenklatura*, and a commercial response to market opportunities. Where managers did not respond to the market or open up their books to outsiders they would push their enterprises to the brink of bankruptcy and would be driven from office by workers whose livelihoods would be threatened. Ending subsidies and price liberalization would create accurate information about costs and demands so that managers would have ample information about how to commercialize economic activity. Ending subsidies and liberalizing prices would also create the incentive to make profit. Money as a means of accounting and measuring success, and as a common unit of exchange, would thus be re-created across Russia. The need to commercialize and the ability to make profits would also ensure a flow of goods to consumers. As demand would be satisfied, prices would be brought down after an initial rise, caused by too much money pursuing too few goods. Inflation would thus be controlled and money would become a stable store of value and a universal means of exchange.

Cutting subsidies and freeing prices would thus create a virtuous circle. They would establish both an incentive – profit – to change behaviour and a threat – loss of control over enterprises – to those who might ignore this incentive. As this circle was completed and behaviour, or management, changed, old forms of economic activity would be replaced by monetized exchange, which the state could tax and regulate through its control of fiscal policy, credit emissions from the Central Bank of Russia and taxation policy. The completion of the virtuous circle would be helped by the entry of Russia into global markets. Controlling inflation by cutting the state budget and liberalizing prices would help to facilitate the arrival in Russia of foreign capital and an expansion of foreign trade by creating a stable, convertible rouble. Imports would introduce market prices in the form of a ready-made price system used to trade goods in the rest of the world. Competition with importers would force the restructuring of production to ensure competitiveness and prevent monopolies from raising prices once they were freed by providing more consumer choice. Without major restructuring effort and commercialization, Russian industry could not compete with foreign industries that might enter the country or sell their products to it. Russian industry at the end of the Soviet period was outdated technologically, and concentrated in monopolies, and made goods of low quality that were unsaleable on world markets. Many were 'negative value added' – that is, the products were worth less than could have been achieved by selling the raw materials used to make them. Trade would thus support the commercialization of economic activity by setting domestic prices at levels comparable to those on world markets and forcing competition onto Russian industry; any enterprise that might hope to access foreign capital would have to restructure and open up its management to the detriment of elite power (Robinson, 1999b).

'Shock therapy' thus sought to remove 'soft budget constraints' and restore value to money in the first stage of reform before the semi-legal control over enterprises enjoyed by the *nomenklatura* could be legalized through privatization; privatization would occur only in stage two of reform. It would balance out the power of the *nomenklatura* by destroying part of it and by creating new economic actors who would have an interest in promoting and supporting the market rather than the Soviet old-boy network. Finally, and in some ways most importantly, it would help secure both the Yeltsin regime and a democratic state. Yeltsin would have the support of new actors in the economy and of a population with greater economic freedoms that was able to purchase goods. The state – with Yeltsin at its head – would be empowered over old elites since it would be able to raise resources by taxing economic activity that would now be transparent. This would give it the financial means to develop its capacity. It would be empowered further by its control of money through fiscal policy and taxation. This would enable the state to shape economic activity, and hence the balance of power in society. The state, by setting interest rates to contain access to credit, by regulating the amount of money going into the economy from state-managed printing presses, and by setting tax rates and customs tariffs, would control the amount of money people and firms could spend and on what they could buy. Since money and market exchange would be national, it would be able to do this across the whole of Russia. New economic agents and an economically liberated population enjoying the public goods of reform would support the state, so that the exercise of state power would be enforced by social demand. New groups would endorse the state and its activities so as to safeguard property rights, enjoy public goods such as protection from criminality and stable money, and facilitate profit maximization rather than rent-seeking. Making money sound and requiring all economic transactions to be monetary were thus central components of the building of state power (Woodruff, 1999: 12–13).

The project comes unstuck

Radical economic reform needed centralized power to work. As one foreign advisor was to put it, 'reconstitut[ing] a state capable of representing common national interests … required a centralization of decision making on such essential matters as basic legislation, monetary policy, and fiscal policy' (Åslund, 1995: 75). In the absence of strong state capacity to implement it or of a social movement to support it, reform relied on what is called 'credible commitment': it would work if people were persuaded that the government was stable and would not deviate from its chosen course – if people accepted that its policies would be implemented.

Such a commitment was not possible. Yeltsin was not even able to ensure unity behind economic reform within the executive branch of government, let alone get parliamentary support. Vice President Aleksandr Rutskoi soon emerged as a critic of the new government and its economic policies, and the chair of the Supreme Soviet, Ruslan Khasbulatov, felt excluded from decision-making and began to drift towards opposition. Rutskoi and Khasbulatov's dissent would soon develop into a complete break between them and Yeltsin and lead to the tragedy of October 1993 and the physical destruction of the parliamentary cause, but in the short term Khasbulatov's stance helped unify parliamentary opposition to the government. Less visible, but equally important, were the growing divisions between the presidential administration and government. There was no broad agreement between the two over economic reform, and the consolidation of the government posed questions of how resources seized by the presidential administration from the Soviet party-state would be distributed and how the administration would manage access to Yeltsin as prime minister/president. As intra-executive competition grew in the first few months of 1992, there was little policy coordination. Policies that would always have been difficult, perhaps impossible, to implement were weakened as 'lobbying' became an integral part of government and a successful means of altering policy. As Yeltsin (1994: 258) noted in his autobiography, 'lobbying in Russia is quite easy.' Lobbyists came through the presidential administration in early 1992, and their influence on policy was facilitated by Yeltsin's predisposition to listen to 'energetic representatives of the body of factory directors': 'if some middle-aged industrialist comes to me and ... says "I've been in Gazprom* for forty years, what's your [minister] doing ..." my heart, it goes without saying, cannot stand it.'

For Yeltsin personally, lobbying was not all bad. It gave him political options, enabling him to trade policy implementation for political support as the conflict between president and parliament over economic policy developed into a full-scale contest for power in the spring of 1992. Yeltsin also built up his political support by changing the way that power was balanced within the government and presidential administration. Together these enabled him to counter his low support in parliament; he constructed alliances with parliamentary forces at second hand, by favouring groups that had influence in parliament and dividing his opponents. This allowed him to survive politically, but at a cost to policy. He began to play reformers and political allies off against one another to maintain his position as the arbitrator between them. Coalitions were built that made it look as if one side had gained the upper hand over policy and were then subtly changed to balance forces within government and enable Yeltsin to dominate and choose between policy options. In effect, this meant that Yeltsin was putting support for his regime above state development and reform.

This coalition building began in April 1992, when Viktor Chernomyrdin (from Gazprom and then in late middle age) and two other industrialists came into government and Burbulis resigned as first deputy prime minister. In June, Yeltsin balanced this change in the government by making Gaidar acting prime minister and another reformer, Anatolii Chubais (who had been in charge of privatization), a deputy prime minister. In the autumn of 1992, the pendulum swung back away from the reformers, as Yeltsin sought an alliance with the industrialist and centrist forces that were a part of 'Civic Union' (a powerful association of industrialists and some political forces, such as Rutskoi's People's Party of Free Russia), before the December 1992 meeting of the Congress of People's Deputies. To do this, he distanced himself from the government's economic policy and in October 1992 attacked the government's performance in a speech to the Supreme Soviet. Gaidar was not confirmed as prime minister at the seventh convocation of the Russian Congress of People's Deputies in December, and Chernomyrdin was brought in to replace him. The elevation of Chernomyrdin and the perceived change in economic policy brought by Gaidar's removal split Civic Union in the

* The gas monopoly and successor to the USSR Ministry of the Gas Industry. Gazprom is owned by the Russian state, but throughout the 1990s it was able to act with a great deal of freedom; it was often behind in its payments to the government and was a major source of unofficial subsidies to unreformed industries.

spring of 1993 as its economic lobbies and politicians such as Rutskoi parted ways over the issue of a referendum on the constitution. Industrial groups (particularly the energy sector where Chernomyrdin had made his career) no longer needed a grand political alliance of parties and social movements to influence policy; struggle over economic policy was internalized in a government to which lobbies had ready access. In turn, Chernomyrdin's promotion in December 1992 was matched by the appointment of another economic reformer, Boris Fedorov, as minister for finance in January 1993. Yeltsin thus ensured that no single interest gained too much power in government, but also that coalitions were not stable. The basic pattern of Yeltsin's 'pick and mix' policy of appointing conservatives and then balancing them with economic liberals, and vice versa, was to continue after 1993 and the introduction of the new constitution.

The dispersal of power at the centre between competing groups, and the compromising of state authority and reform, was complemented by a diffusion of power from the centre to the regions and republics (territorial units in which there is a sizeable, titular ethnic minority) of the Russian Federation. This meant that the state's power over its territory, one of the basic characteristics of a state, was compromised. Although Yeltsin created the 'presidential vertical' in 1991, getting the provinces to abide by central policies was difficult. Many regional governments were under the control of old elites, and ethnic elites in the republics pressed for greater independence from Moscow. These groups often had links with industrialists opposed to government policy and sought to maintain their own power by isolating themselves and their peoples from the effects of economic reform. They were helped in this by the fact that the relationship among the president, the government and the republics and regions was not adequately codified after the fall of the USSR. A Federal Treaty was signed in March 1992 by most of the republics and all of the regions (Chechnya, which had declared itself independent in September 1991, and Tatarstan, which wanted greater autonomy, refused to sign). The treaty recognized all as having equal rights and obligations but allowed the republics the trappings of statehood – constitutions, parliaments, presidents, etc. However, it was too vague to regulate properly the relationship between centre and periphery for long. Both republics and regions tried to negotiate concessions for themselves: the regions complained that the rights enjoyed by the republics were unjust and threatened to proclaim themselves republics, while the republics threatened to secede from the federation unless they were granted greater concessions and economic autonomy. Eventually, many of the rights that regional leaders gained were codified in 'bilateral' treaties between the central government and the regions, most of them signed between 1994 and 1996 as Yeltsin bartered for support from regional leaders before the 1996 presidential election. These treaties let regions out of tax obligations and allowed regional leaders to control local political development, frequently in violation of the national constitution, so that Russia as a unified political and economic space fractured (Hughes, 1996; see also chapter 7).

The power struggle in Moscow between Yeltsin and the parliament made this administrative mess worse. Local elites took advantage of the weakness of central government to do what they pleased. President and parliament were played off against each other, and the power of local elites and industrialists over the regions and republics was strengthened at the expense of central government. The most visible outward sign of this was the compromise, and then the loss of control, over the appointment of governors. Yeltsin was forced to concede that governors should only be appointed with the agreement of local Soviets, which had been elected in 1990 and were often under the control of old elites, and relented on some of the appointments he had already made. As a result, the majority of governors were chairmen of Soviets and members of the *nomenklatura* (Slider, 1994: 256–7) who had little sympathy with the reformers in Moscow. Taxes and contributions to the federal budget went unpaid, and government economic policy was flaunted as elites cushioned their populations from the effects of reform by subverting the market and by aiding the takeover of their enterprises by local industrialists.

Yeltsin's style of rule was successful in one thing: it enabled him to survive and defeat his political rivals in the Russian parliament. Parliamentary leaders had less to offer in the way of patronage to potential allies from either the old *nomenklatura* or the new commercial elites that were emerging to dominate finance and media. The natural allies of the anti-Yeltsin forces were communists and nationalists; both disliked economic reform because they saw it as betraying the country to the alien capitalist 'West', and neither could forgive Yeltsin his role in the destruction of the Soviet Union. Although Yeltsin and the governments that he headed, either directly when he was prime minister or indirectly as arbitrator between government factions, lost popularity as economic reform stalled and popular dissatisfaction with the political impasse in Moscow grew, the parliamentary cause was not able to gather sufficient support from these extremist sources to defeat him. An attempt to solve the constitutional battle between parliament and president by a referendum in April 1993 saw Yeltsin victorious: 58 per cent of voters (or 37 per cent of the whole electorate) expressed confidence in him, 53 per cent (34 per cent of the electorate) approved of the executive's socio-economic policies, and 67 per cent (43 per cent of the electorate) thought it necessary to hold early parliamentary elections. Only 49 per cent (31 per cent of the electorate) thought it necessary to hold early presidential elections (Henderson and Robinson, 1997: 193). This was not a strong enough victory for Yeltsin to settle the constitutional question peacefully, but it meant that the population broadly preferred him to the parliament. The crunch came when relations between president and parliament broke down in violence in September–October 1993. Yeltsin, in violation of the constitution, dissolved the parliament. Appeals by Rutskoi and Khasbulatov for popular revolt were ignored, and Yeltsin was able to organize the military suppression of the parliament. The threat of civil war fizzled out in shocking, but localized, bloodshed around the parliament building and Moscow's main television studio, in which over one hundred people were killed.

Regime consolidation and reform compromise after 1993

Yeltsin's victory over the parliament did not complete any of the processes of change under way in Russia, revolutionary or democratic transitional. Parliament's defeat was followed by a referendum on a new constitution and elections to a new parliament. The new constitution invested power in the presidency and weakened parliament (these powers are discussed in chapter 6). The new presidency was not, however, an institution that would see through the economic reforms that had been introduced in 1991–2 and complete Russia's economic revolution. The elections to the new Duma (the lower house of parliament) and Federation Council (the upper house) (the elections are described in chapter 9) did not create constitutional checks on power, a new political legitimacy, or the means of reconciling competing political forces to give new life to Russian democracy.

The new constitutional settlement locked in place the political rules that had developed between the collapse of the USSR and the defeat of parliament. In formal institutional terms, the December 1993 Constitution introduced a measure of stability (McFaul, 2001a) and ended some of the fragmentation of power so that open political struggle became less destructive and more concentrated on elections. The big events of the rest of Yeltsin's presidency were his endeavours to secure his re-election in 1996 and to secure a successor in 1998–9. These events were influenced by governmental failures, most notably by the ongoing crisis in the economy in 1995–6 and the war in Chechnya and by the economic collapse in 1998.

Political passions around these events were intense, but they did not lead to the same kind of institutional conflict that had marked the end of the USSR and the presidential–parliamentary struggle of 1992–3. While overall there was considerable change in the electoral fortune of political parties, there was a large degree of electoral stability for the main ones. The Communist Party of the Russian Federation (CPRF), the Liberal Democratic Party of Russia (LDPR, the party headed by the maverick nationalist Vladimir Zhirinovsky, which is neither liberal nor democratic and is not really much of a party), the liberal Yabloko party, and whatever 'party of power' the government sponsored (different government parties competed in the 1993, 1995 and 1999 elections) repeatedly won the bulk of parliamentary seats. This meant that, although there was considerable disagreement between Yeltsin and the parliamentary opposition, particularly the CPRF, the opposition had incentives to preserve the post-1993 constitutional order. They had a guaranteed political place and role in the post-1993 settlement because they were electorally successful, and in both 1996 and 1999 they had aspirations to take the presidency.

This formal stability was matched, however, by a subterranean factional politics. Struggle over policy and resources, over the continued division of Russia's wealth, took place between blocs in government. The competition was for Yeltsin's ear, and the presidency became an arbitrator between competing factions. As in the pre-December 1993 period, Yeltsin maintained a broad coalition, favouring different groups according to how he perceived his political advantage and pursuing policies that were frequently either unclear, since they tried to satisfy too many different preferences among elite groups, or contradictory of one another. The new constitution thus brought little change in the sense that it led to new reform efforts from Yeltsin. Yeltsin's press secretary from this time argued that the president had 'no ideology of his own except the ideology of power'. Yeltsin preserved his influence by playing off institutions and forces against one another. What was a problem in the early days of post-communist governance in Russia became almost an art form after 1993 as Yeltsin balanced institutions and competing and shifting policy coalitions. During this period, he managed what was at least a three-way divide at the apex of government: Viktor Chernomyrdin and his colleagues from Gazprom who were now in government, together with industrial and agricultural interests; Chubais and economic liberals; and conservatives such as Aleksandr Korzhakov, Yeltsin's bodyguard and close companion, and other figures from the 'power ministries' – the armed and security forces – who were keener on state control over the economy than on the development of market economics.

The choices that Yeltsin made from among these competing groups in the executive were influenced by the electoral cycle. In 1994 the pendulum seemed to swing to conservatives such as Korzhakov. Yeltsin was also less than able – witness his drunkenness on a visit to Berlin and failure to get off the plane at Shannon Airport to meet the Irish prime minister at this time – and reliant on such cronies. The decision to invade Chechnya in November 1994 and the subsequent invasion in December is generally regarded as evidence of this. This can also be described as having an electoral dimension: Yeltsin was posing as a strong national leader, the defender of the territorial integrity of the Russian Federation, to distinguish himself from his competitors in the 1996 presidential election. The decision to go to war in Chechnya showed that the government could not be constrained from arbitrary, despotic acts by the new constitution and the Duma.

However, Chechnya and electoral considerations weakened the conservative interest quite rapidly. Chechnya was a political and military disaster. There were also fundamental issues of economic redistribution to be settled that were of greater importance to the presidential campaign of 1996, since they involved financial interests that could supply media and monetary support for re-election. These questions underlay the development of another major alliance of 1994–7, the political linkage of economic liberals in the government and presidential administration with commercial banks and financial-industrial groups. Government policy and mutual advantage promoted this linkage. The banks gained from the government's move to financing the budget deficit through the sale of short-term treasury bills and developed their industrial holdings though the 'loans for shares' programme, described by one Russian media commentator at the time as 'a transition from shapeless cooperation [between Yeltsin and business] without fixed rules to highly formalized cooperation', in which vast swathes of valuable assets still held by the state were transferred to the banks at knockdown prices (see chapter 10).

Once the basic relationship was established between the banks and the government, electoral factors shaped its fuller development into an alliance. Chechnya, the lack of a clear and effective economic policy, and Yeltsin's health problems wore down the president's popularity over the course of 1994 and 1995. The pro-government party 'Our Home is Russia', formed to compete in the 1995 parliamentary election to test the waters for the 1996 presidential election, captured only 10 per cent of the vote, while the CPRF took 22 per cent (White, Rose and McAllister, 1997: 197–239). Yeltsin panicked at the Duma election results. At first he blamed the economic liberals and promoted conservatives to try to recapture support. This surge in the fortunes of the conservative faction was short-lived. To win the 1996 presidential election, Yeltsin needed money, media support and backing from Russia's regions. Money and media support could only come from the banks, which were cash rich and had extensive media interests. Dismayed at the rise of the conservatives, a group of bankers (popularly known as oligarchs from this point onwards) decided to finance Yeltsin's campaign and restore some balance by placing Chubais in his campaign team as a first step towards pushing the conservatives to one side.

His relationship with the banks saved the election for Yeltsin, as they bankrolled his campaign and their media outlets promoted him to the virtual exclusion of other candidates. At Chubais's direction, and using media controlled by the banks, the campaign developed into a referendum on the communist past. The effect was startling. The battle was to persuade people that only Yeltsin was a credible opponent to the CPRF candidate, Gennady Zyuganov. At the start of the campaigning season in January 1996, only 8 per cent of people considered voting for Yeltsin; 14 per cent thought he might win, but a plurality (43 per cent) did not want him re-elected under any circumstances. Gradually, the media coverage of Yeltsin's campaign, the scorn poured on the CPRF, Zyuganov's lacklustre performance, and Yeltsin's use of his office to make lavish promises to ordinary voters on the campaign trail and to do deals with regional leaders and sign 'bilateral treaties' began to have an effect. None of the other candidates could break through the media's barrage of pro-Yeltsin propaganda to present themselves as serious alternatives. Gradually, people began to believe that Yeltsin would win the election; the anti-communist tenor of the campaign made them turn against Zyuganov and consider Yeltsin's re-election necessary. This was vital, since it meant that Yeltsin stood more chance of winning a second-round contest against Zyuganov if he did not win a first-round victory by securing 50 per cent of the vote; only firm CPRF voters and a small proportion of the rest of the population were totally against him. Yeltsin topped the first ballot in June 1996, with Zyuganov second. Believing that Yeltsin could win, and persuaded of the danger of a CPRF victory, more voters transferred their votes to Yeltsin in the second round than to Zyuganov; people who could not bring themselves to opt for Yeltsin either did not vote (turnout fell between the two rounds) or voted against both candidates (White et al., 1997: 241–70).

In the aftermath of the 1996 election, Yeltsin paid off his debts. Chubais became head of the presidential administration, and two oligarchs, Vladimir Potanin (a banker and industrialist) and Boris Berezovsky (a financier with wide media and industrial holdings), entered the government as, respectively, first deputy prime minister with responsibility for economic policy and a deputy secretary of the Security Council.

The triumph of the economic liberals and their business allies could not last, however. Yeltsin's securing of, first, a presidential constitution and, second, his re-election to the presidency had created a more stable political regime in that elite groups knew that access to power nationally had to be negotiated with him. Nothing had been done to address reform of the state, however, and it was on the point of financial collapse. The costs of short-term borrowing to cover basic government expenditure were too high to be sustained, and the borrowing needs of the state were too great for the oligarchs and their pet banks (Robinson, 1999b: 551). Money had to be borrowed from abroad. Accessing this meant putting the state's finances in better order. Tax collection in particular had to be improved, which meant ending the 'virtual economy' – i.e., barter (Gaddy and Ickes, 2002; see chapter 10). Local deals where firms paid their taxes in kind to local authorities had to be terminated. It was all very well for a local authority to accept construction firms extending their public transportation network in lieu of tax owed, as happened in Chelyabinsk for example, but this did nothing for the national federal government budget; central government could not spend a metro line in Chelyabinsk on pensions in Moscow or soldiers' salaries in Vladivostok (Gaddy and Ickes, 2002: 171–2). Vast swathes of the economy had to be 'remonetized', including workers' wages. The non-payment or payment in kind of wages meant that much of the population was unable to pay tax; payment in kind meant that people were not active as consumers and could not pay sales taxes, for example. If, as the Anglo-Irish political philosopher Edmund Burke put it in the eighteenth century, the 'revenue of the state is the state', and in effect 'all depends upon it, whether for support or reformation', the Russian state was almost non-existent. It was certainly incapable of either support for its people or reformation of its economy and society.

The largest tax defaulters were financial-industrial groups owned by oligarchs. These were the target of a new wave of reforms aimed at developing the power of the state anew which were launched in 1997. The state, Yeltsin noted in his annual address to parliament that year, was too often at the service of a narrow set of private interests and as a consequence post-communist transformation was stymied. Potanin was removed from office in a government reshuffle in March 1997. Chubais and Boris Nemtsov (the ex-governor of Nizhny Novgorod region, an economic liberal and, until his assassination in 2015, one of the leaders of the opposition to Putin) were brought into government as deputy prime ministers with responsibility, respectively, for economic reform and the Ministry of Finance and for energy monopolies (the biggest tax defaulters and the centrepiece of the oligarch economy). Reform, particularly a tightening of tax collection, was necessary to counter a possible further devolution of power to Russia's regions. Yeltsin's re-election as president was to be followed by the election of regional heads of administration from late 1996 onwards, who would be less reliant on the central administration for their positions. The relationship between centre and periphery thus shifted further from an administrative one to become one of 'political interaction' (Gel'man, 2000: 101). This increased the amount of bargaining between centre and regions over tax payments and concessions, and the amount of tax paid to the centre declined as more independent regional leaders appropriated tax due to the centre or colluded with local enterprises to evade federal tax payments (Shleifer and Treisman, 2000: 113). One of the central planks of reform in 1997 was a presidential decree aimed at curtailing the independent taxation powers of regions, and the appointment of a more reform-minded government after March 1997 was supposed to signal the centre's commitment to tax collection and central state sovereignty.

Promoting the economic liberals and some reform policies was also a way of strengthening the dependency of the government on Yeltsin. The issue of who would succeed him had been forced onto the political agenda early in the second term, when his victory was almost immediately followed by his hospitalization for a quintuple heart bypass operation. Reform was supposed to help Yeltsin control the rest of the contenders. The promotion of Chubais to the government weakened the hold of Chernomyrdin over economic policy, the main potential area of policy activity for the prime minister. If Chernomyrdin did not have control over economic policy, then his potential to act as heir apparent to Yeltsin was that much lessened. Chernomyrdin was the big loser in the cabinet reshuffle in March 1997: he lost control of the Ministry of Energy to Nemtsov, and some of his associates were removed from their posts. Chubais and the economic liberals were dependent on Yeltsin: they had no national political base of their own and were unpopular because of the failed reforms of the early 1990s.

The reform measures taken from late 1996 onwards were an attempt to restore state autonomy, by weakening its connection with private interests, and state capacity, by generating resources that the state could use to increase its effectiveness. However, in trying to reform, Chubais, Nemtsov and their supporters rediscovered the vicious irony involved. The state needed resources to build up its capacity, but to obtain resources required capacity: the state needed organizations and administrators capable of collecting taxes and resisting corruption and legal tools to punish defaulters, but it needed resources to develop such institutions and personnel. As the Russian state lacked such institutions and bureaucrats, especially after the years of corruption, lobbying and compromise, reform was going to be difficult. In the absence of institutions to do their bidding, the reformers relied once more on their ability to convince people that they were serious about reform and that compliance with the government's orders was ultimately going to be unavoidable. Reform, therefore, depended once again on 'credible commitment': it would work if people were persuaded that the government was stable and would not deviate from its chosen course.

Credible commitment to reform proved no easier to maintain in 1997 than it had in 1992. The government rapidly became embroiled in a conflict with the banks, and the structural weaknesses of the Russian economy meant that its attempts to extract more tax revenue were only partially successful. The banks' loss of influence over economic policy led to the outbreak of the so-called bank wars in the summer of 1997. The 'bank wars' showed that the oligarchs did not make up an oligarchy: when faced with loss of influence and some economic sacrifice to support the state, their natural inclination was to fight one another rather than to compromise and secure some joint advantage that would have protected an oligarchic system. Berezovksy, who was still a deputy secretary of the Security Council and close to Yeltsin's daughter and advisor, Tatyana Dyachenko, accused Chubais of favouring Potanin. Yeltsin first tried to calm the media storm that accompanied the bank wars; the dispute was in many ways a squabble in what was becoming known as his 'family' – the web of officials, advisors and businessmen connected to him through Dyachenko. When his efforts at mediation failed, Yeltsin acted on the advice of Chubais and Nemtsov to remove Berezovsky from the Security Council. Materials were released that implicated Chubais and some of his closest aides in corrupt practices (they had taken a huge advance for a book on privatization from a company owned by Oneksimbank). Yeltsin was forced to discipline Chubais and fire his aides. Chubais was fortunate to stay in office and was saved in part because of the growing financial crisis in Asia, which was beginning to impact on Russia and which would be one of the causes of the country's financial collapse in August 1998. The fortunes of Chubais and Nemtsov waned further in January 1998, when Chernomyrdin took responsibility for overseeing the security services and the ministries of Finance, Energy, Foreign Affairs and Defence. This, however, was too much for Yeltsin, since Chernomyrdin's increased powers made him look too much like a successor. Yeltsin faced a loss of authority as the impetus for reform would be slowed with Chernomyrdin's increased power and as the latter became more confident of the succession. Yeltsin's reaction was to try to restore the balance in his favour. On 23 March 1998 he removed Chernomyrdin and Chubais and proposed a relative unknown, Sergei Kiriyenko, as the new prime minister.

Kiriyenko's nomination showed that Yeltsin was committed to continuing the reform started in 1997 as a means of controlling the succession as much as an end in itself. However, a credible commitment to reform still did not develop. Kiriyenko had to be forced on the Duma, which rejected him twice before approving him when Yeltsin nominated him a third time and signalled he was prepared to dissolve it if the vote went against his nominee for a third time. Kiriyenko could not stop the economic rot, however. As the economic downturn continued, the Duma attacked the government and stalled the full passage of its anti-crisis package. Consequently, the International Monetary Fund (IMF) held back some of the extra aid that it had granted Russia to support the rouble. The actions of the Duma and the IMF were precipitating factors in the debt default and rouble devaluation in August 1998 that brought down the Kiriyenko government.

Securing the Yeltsin succession

The fall of the Kiriyenko government and the economic shock of devaluation halted any further possibility for Yeltsin of trying to control his succession and maintain his influence as president through the promotion of reforms. He tried to put the clock back and nominated Chernomyrdin to be prime minister once more, but the Duma rejected him, and Yeltsin was forced to find a compromise candidate, the foreign minister Yevgeny Primakov. Primakov began to take on 'presidential' tasks, such as representing Russia overseas, as Yeltsin partially withdrew from public life due to a fresh bout of illness. Primakov's cabinet was formed with less presidential interference than previously and was relatively consensual, containing figures more acceptable to the Duma such as a former head of Gosplan, the Soviet central planning agency. Primakov also developed links with regional leaders. This effort at creating a kind of a coalition government found favour with the Duma, and as a result the political initiative passed to the government under Primakov and to the Duma. It was even mooted either that Yeltsin might retire or that he might rule as a figurehead president, passing his executive powers to Primakov. Primakov attacked Berezovsky as a means of putting pressure on Yeltsin through his daughter and of giving more credence to claims that Yeltsin's family had taken bribes.

Yeltsin fought back. He had to rely solely on the powers of the presidency to try to place himself back at the centre of political life. The result was a political mess. Primakov, who, like Chernomyrdin before him, was being touted as a successor to Yeltsin, was censured for his inability to deal with Russia's economic crisis and removed from office by presidential decree. This only improved his reputation, and he joined the Fatherland–All Russia electoral bloc that was organized by the mayor of Moscow, Yurii Luzhkov. Neither Yeltsin nor Primakov's successor, Sergei Stepashin, was capable of halting the political advance of Fatherland–All Russia. Regional leaders rallied around the bloc, and its popularity in the polls at the end of the summer was high. In October 1999, 21 per cent of voters polled said they would vote for it. This meant that Fatherland–All Russia would be the second biggest party in the Duma (after the CPRF) and that Primakov would probably be regarded as the strongest non-communist presidential candidate. This would mean that, like Yeltsin in 1996, he would be the candidate to face Zyuganov in a second round and would therefore win, as many voters would rally to him to veto a return to communist government.

Yeltsin therefore rolled the dice once more. Stepashin's failure to head off Primakov and the challenge of Fatherland–All Russia led to his removal by yet another presidential decree. His replacement as prime minister, Vladimir Putin, admitted that the change in prime ministers 'reflected the desire of the president to alter the arrangement of politics in the country on the eve of the State Duma and presidential elections' (*Rossiiskaya gazeta*, 10 August 1999). In other words, Yeltsin was using his office proprietarily to handpick a successor and try to change the outcome of the parliamentary elections.

At first, Putin looked no more likely to facilitate an orderly succession than his predecessors. However, Putin had luck on his side. The economy began to improve over the course of 1999, not because of any government action but because rising oil prices raised government revenues and because the August 1998 crisis bounced the economy back. Things did not improve dramatically for the average citizen, but they didn't get worse, and the general drift of economic news was good. More importantly, Chechen rebels tried to take advantage of Moscow's troubles to launch raids into neighbouring Dagestan. Then, in the autumn of 1999, a series of bomb attacks occurred on apartment buildings in Moscow causing great loss of life and popular anger. These attacks were blamed on the Chechens, although claims were also made against the Russian security services. It has been argued that the FSB (Federal'naya Sluzhba Bezopasnosti, Federal Security Service, the domestic successor to the KGB), which had been headed by Putin between July 1998 and August 1999, planted the bombs to restart the conflict in Chechnya and enable Putin to ride a nationalist wave to the presidency (Dunlop, 2012). Whoever was responsible for the bombings, the war duly escalated. Russian troops crossed the border once more into Chechnya.

The 1999 Chechnya campaign was a boon for Putin. The attacks on Russian civilians made it popular and, as the campaign was not as badly handled as in 1994–6, Putin was seen as competent. His relative youth and emergence from obscurity to take the post of prime minister also helped: he bore less responsibility for the political mistakes and fudges of the Yeltsin years. The rise in Putin's approval ratings at the end of 1999 was astounding and had a knock-on effect on Fatherland–All Russia, whose poll rating fell by nearly half in the run-up to the election. Medved-Unity, the party set up to counter Fatherland by the government and now perceived to be Putin's party, enjoyed a commensurate increase in popularity, and the broadly pro-Putin Union of Right Forces, headed by former prime minister Kiriyenko, also began to pick up some support. In the December election, the CPRF took first place in the proportional representation vote as usual because of the loyalty of its core supporters – the elderly and the impoverished. The Fatherland–All Russia electoral challenge faded as it captured only 13 per cent of the vote, and with it went Primakov and Luzhkov's hopes of being strong presidential contenders. Other presidential hopefuls such as Chernomyrdin, Zhirinovsky, and Grigory Yavlinsky from Yabloko saw their party's vote share decline from 1995. Putin, buoyed by the success of Medved-Unity at the polls, became the leading contender for the presidency. Yeltsin seized the moment by stepping down as president on New Year's Eve 1999. As prime minister, Putin took over as acting president, and elections were brought forward to March 2000. One of Putin's first acts as acting president was to grant Yeltsin immunity from prosecution for himself and his family. Yeltsin had thus won his last political battle in the same way that he had won so many others. He had used his office and its powers to secure a short-term political outcome favourable to himself.

Conclusion

Russian political development throughout the 1990s was driven by the continued tension between establishing a stable political regime and completing the rebuilding of the state, which was a task of revolutionary proportions that involved changing the socio-economic foundations on which the state rested. Yeltsin's rule was punctuated by a series of rolling crises. These were caused by his inability to bring to an end both to Russia's democratic transition, which would have meant the establishment of democratic rules governing access to power, and to the reconstruction of state power. The country lurched between regime crisis, when there was conflict concerning who should rule and on what basis, and state crisis because of the existential, and generally economic, threat to the state's ability to reproduce itself and to maintain its basic functions. Yeltsin survived by navigating between these two crises but saw little sustainable progress in either regime or state construction. The one point of stability was the 1993 Constitution, which set the bar to institutional change high and gave much of the political elite a stake in the system. This institutional stability was, however, dependent on the crisis of the state being held in check. Russia could not compromise on state building indefinitely. It had to deal itself with its socio-economic and security problems. Reform had to return to the political agenda even after its failure in the early 1990s. But reform and state building were politically disruptive and showed the fragility of the compromises upon which regime politics were built, as events after 1996 showed. The ensuing struggles over reform and the political fallout after August 1998 showed that the alliances that Yeltsin had built could shatter and threaten the president's ability to rule. In the end, Yeltsin's ability to control his succession was down to luck – he found the right man at the right time, and (mis)fortune smiled on them in Chechnya – and the brute power of the presidency.

5
Putinism, Reform and Retrenchment

Introduction

Putin learnt from Yeltsin's problems. Yeltsin's presidency showed that there was no avoiding the dilemma of reforming the state and its socio-economic foundations in the long run. Russia needed a reformed state administration if it was to provide its citizens with security, both domestically and internationally. Putin also learnt that securing change needed a stable political base. Such a platform could not be founded on too great a set of political compromises: as Yeltsin's misfortunes had shown, such compromises were liable to fracture and undermine reform efforts.

Learning the lessons of the Yeltsin years was not, however, the same as solving the inherited problems. Putin was remarkably successful in dealing with the problems of regime building, but he was less successful at reforming the state – partly because of his success at regime building. Political stability became an end in itself, something that Putin is loath to risk in the cause of reform. State building was deferred partly because it could be. Economic circumstances favoured Putin, at least initially, as they had never favoured Yeltsin. Russia reaped huge economic rewards from the high prices of hydrocarbon fuels in the 2000s, so that the fiscal crisis of the state that had dogged Yeltsin disappeared until 2008. Rebuilding the Russian state as a complex institutional ensemble became 'avoidable' since Putin was able to build a simpler means of extracting resources from the economy to sustain the state by recapturing control of the energy sector.

This simpler, politically risk-averse form of state building was not without its own problems. It gave Putin huge political power and considerable political authority, but it didn't raise Russia to the status of a great power. The country's dependence on oil and gas exports made it appear a mere appendage to the global economy, the source of raw materials for more advanced and prestigious states, a problem that Russian leaders have complained about since the nineteenth century (as we saw in chapter 1). There are also questions about the sustainability of a model of state development and economic growth based on energy sales. Although it is not irrational to focus on maximizing gains from its energy resources, depending on these alone leaves Russia vulnerable to changing global demand, as the country's experience of the international financial crisis of the late 2000s was to demonstrate. Russia also needs investment and technology transfers from abroad to access its oil reserves (Gustafson, 2012: 449–79). Securing investment and technology transfers requires reform of public administration.

Finally, the system of politics built by Putin on the back of his electoral success in 2000 and energy revenues was institutionally weak and highly dependent on his personal power and authority. Democratic institutions, parliament, political parties and local representative institutions were not developed or saw their already weak development halted. This leaves open many questions: How robust is the Russian political system if something should happen to Putin? Can it adapt to face new challenges? What social support does it have to draw on to adapt and what institutions within the Russian polity could drive adaptation? How can Putin and the political system accommodate political opposition when it occurs? These questions were brought to the fore between 2008 and 2012, when Putin left the presidency to become prime minister and Russia dealt with an economic downturn. Eventually Putin oversaw this by returning to the presidency in 2012. This both stabilized and destabilized Russian politics at the same time. It ended discussion of who was in charge of the country but highlighted the personalized nature of Russian politics, the frailty of alternatives to the status quo, and the inability of the political system to build consensus by incorporating alternatives into it in a democratic manner.

Building Putinism

The general expectation at the end of Yeltsin's term was that little would alter. Powerful social groups were against change and had a monopoly over effective political action on account of their economic power or control over the regions. Russia's new leader would, just like Yeltsin before him, be a 'leader–arbiter' of a regime that it 'was impossible to consolidate because doing so would deprive the leader–arbiter of the manoeuvring room that is essential for the regime's survival' (Shevtsova, 2000: 37; Treisman, 1999). Putin escaped this fate because he had four advantages on taking office that gave him freedom of manoeuvre against Russia's elites.

First, since he had been elected to the presidency with 52.9 per cent of the vote, he had an uncompromised personal mandate. Putin had not had to make any deals, either with Russia's oligarchs, who controlled the mass media, or with any regional leaders to win in round one. His government's actions had been broadly popular before the election, when he was prime minister and acting president, and he had strong personal approval ratings because of popular confidence in him and support for his actions against Chechnya. War restarted in Chechnya in October 1999 after a series of terrorist attacks on apartment buildings – in which the Russian security services may have been complicit (Dunlop, 2012). This second Chechen war was prosecuted more successfully and was popular since the apartment bombings made it appear to have a just cause. Putin thus came to power without any significant debts to powerful elite groups. These groups were divided. As we saw in the last chapter, the oligarchs had failed to act to protect their collective interests, to act in an oligarchic fashion, in the run-up to the 1998 crisis and could not cohere after it to force Putin to compromise. Regional leaders who had sought to provide an alternative successor to Yeltsin's choice had stumbled when their electoral vehicle, Fatherland–All Russia, came in behind Putin's Unity party in the 1999 Duma election. Putin had support in the election from some because it was obvious that he was going to win. Others, like Vladimir Gusinsky's NTV television station, criticized him quite fulsomely, but the tide was running against them and their reach was not as great as the national media that supported Putin.

Second, Putin's popularity meant that he had Duma support (see chapter 6). As his popularity grew in the autumn of 1999, Unity managed to overtake rivals such as the Fatherland–All Russia movement and gained 23 per cent of the proportional representation vote in the December election (only 1 per cent less than the CPRF) and nine seats in the single-mandate constituency election. In December 2001, Unity and Fatherland–All Russia merged to form United Russia to create the first government party that managed both to last longer than one electoral cycle and to secure a series of electoral 'victories' (see chapter 9). This merger and the growth of United Russia gave Putin control over the Duma's agenda.

Third, Putin was able to rebalance power among factions within the executive to bolster his personal authority. His administration contained some members of Yeltsin's circle as he paid off his debts to his patron. Their power was counteracted by the renewed influence for officials associated with the 'power ministries' (the armed forces, the agencies of the former KGB and the Ministry of the Interior, which controls the police service). These officials formed the faction of *siloviki* (men from the power ministries). By 2006, and the end of Putin's first presidential term, the proportion of *siloviki* in government had risen to 25 per cent, and by early 2008 this figure had grown to 42 per cent (Kryshtanovskaya, 2008: 595). Putin also introduced into government a new tranche of economic liberals and former colleagues from the St Petersburg mayor's office (often labelled the *Pitersy*, St Petersburgers), where he had worked after leaving the KGB in 1990 until Yeltsin appointed him deputy chief of the presidential administration in 1996.

There was nothing inevitable about Putin's ability to control these factions and factionalism, and he has never managed to do away with them totally. Ultimately, as Richard Sakwa (2008: 72) put it, Putin 'reforged the elite structure while not fundamentally repudiating the old system'. But he did manage to control factions to a considerable degree, even during the discussions over who should succeed him as president in 2007–8, when he had to stand down because of the two-term limit. In part Putin could achieve this control because elite factions were divided. In many ways the label of factions is a false one, imposing order on what are often very fluid alliances and cross-cutting groups. People frequently hold different views within rival camps, and allegiances shift over time and frequently towards more dependency on Putin. The *siloviki* have not always acted as a unified bloc any more than the oligarchs before them. Not all security officials' past service was formative of their political attitudes, and even where there was a rise to prominence of security issues it has not always been driven by the *siloviki* or been a sign of their political dominance (Renz, 2006; Bacon et al., 2006). The remains of Yeltsin's 'family' were also divided politically and economically, and many of them were politically opportunistic. Some stuck with Putin or were forced to resign when he turned on their business patrons, starting with Berezovsky. The economic liberals were probably never anything but dependent on Putin, and many were outsiders brought to Moscow by him. The *Pitersy* have among them both *siloviki* and economic liberals, so they have not always been a cohesive group.

Finally, Putin's election to the presidency coincided with a period of economic growth. The cause of this was the August 1998 rouble crisis. Devaluation of the rouble resulted in imports becoming expensive and domestic industry becoming competitive without having to reform. The recession of the 1990s meant that there was spare industrial capacity to meet increased domestic demand, as people bought local rather than imported goods. Investment, which would have been hard to come by because of the financial crisis, was thus not needed to stimulate increased output. Gross domestic product and industrial output expanded in 1999, and the fiscal deficit shrank to a post-Soviet low before entering a period of surpluses that lasted until the international crisis impacted Russia in late 2008. Private consumption also dipped in 1999 as the crisis hit household budgets, but it soon rose again, and rose quite dramatically. The state's stronger fiscal position further enabled it to expand its spending, albeit cautiously so as not to be inflationary, leading to a rise in public consumption (Robinson, 2009).

In 2000 Putin used these advantages to consolidate his authority by attacking the power of the oligarchs and regional leaders. Vladimir Gusinsky's Most Bank lost control over NTV, Russia's most independent television station and one of the few that had criticized Putin. Media-Most was taken over by Gazprom, the gas monopoly under government control, in lieu of debts owed to it by the media group, and Gusinsky was forced into exile. Boris Berezovsky tried to organize opposition to Putin in the Duma (he had won a seat in the 1999 election) and then resigned in protest against Putin's authoritarianism. He was forced out of ORT, the main television broadcaster in Russia, which he had controlled. In November 2000 Berezovsky went into exile in London, whence he tried to organize opposition to Putin.

Putin did not destroy the oligarchs 'as a class', as he had claimed he would in the election campaign (the phrase echoed Stalin's promise from the late

1920s to 'destroy the kulaks [rich peasants] as a class'). His actions against the economic elite were, in the end, the same as against the political elite; once again he 'reforged the elite structure while not fundamentally repudiating the old system.' Putin explained his intentions in a meeting with leading businessmen in late July 2000 at which he laid out the terms of a new social contract. There would be no reversal of privatization of industry, but businessmen should stay out of politics. Significantly, Putin did not promise an amnesty for illegal actions during the privatization drives of the 1990s or for tax evasion. In other words, there was to be no mass roll-back of privatization, but, should people stray into politics, the state was retaining the option of looking at how they had made their fortunes. The Kremlin had the power to punish anyone it decided had crossed the vague line in the sand that Putin had drawn because of the changes he was initiating more generally (Tompson, 2005: 194–5). Many of the most powerful businessmen in Russia – Oleg Derispaska, Vladimir Potanin, Vagit Alekperov and Mikhail Fridman – had made their fortunes in the economic chaos of the 1990s, and many of them had links to Yeltsin and the 'family'. They now largely abandoned political activity, and their economic power was balanced by the creation of new strata of so-called state oligarchs – businessmen whose fortunes were built under Putin's leadership and who have depended on the direct support of the state for their wealth (Rutland 2003). Putin was to refer to this new relationship as a policy of maintaining 'equidistance' from economic elites (Sakwa, 2011: 79). In practice, 'equidistance' was more about rendering economic elites subservient to the presidency than of separating the structures of political power and economic inequality. Such a separation is an aspiration of many democracies, something to be achieved so that the interests of the rich are not mirrored in the division of political power. Putin curbed the wilder excesses of the Yeltsin era by disciplining economic elites, but this was not the same as developing political structures and official behaviour that gave all citizens equal access to political power; nor was it the same as creating equal access to state resources and economic advancement for all. Powerful economic interests have continued to use political connections to appropriate wealth by overturning the property rights of the less powerful (Sakwa, 2012).

Putin's moves to curtail the independence of regional leaders also began in May 2000 (see chapter 7 for details). Like the moves made against the oligarchs, these were disciplining measures rather than a full reform of relations between the centre and the regions. Overall, the actions taken by Putin limited the freedom of manoeuvre of regional leaders. The 'bilateral' treaties that had been signed under Yeltsin were revoked (with a few exceptions) and a greater institutional uniformity between regions was created. However, the powers of regional leaders within their own territories were not placed under any greater democratic scrutiny by the measures. Indeed, local representative institutions generally withered under the combined blows of recentralization and as United Russia's national electoral success was repeated locally (Golosov, 2011a). There was turnover among regional leaders, but generally the Kremlin preferred to keep loyal incumbents in office where it could. Putin's powers over regional leaders often remained a threat, though most were reappointed even after he cancelled the elections of regional executives and moved to an appointment system (Blakkisrud, 2011: 369).

The consolidation of Putinism

On taking power in 2000, Putin put in place the foundations of a system of controlling access to politics and economic resources – in other words, the foundations of a political regime. At first there were high hopes that his actions would lead to democratic renewal. The weakness of the Russian state was widely seen as a reason for the failure of democracy in the 1990s. In addressing the issue of the power of the state relative to the powers of regional leaders and economic elite groups, Putin was – arguably – restoring a necessary balance. He was certainly aware of the need to restore the state's authority and to have it take the lead in political and economic recon-struction. Putin (2000 [1999]) released a manifesto on 'Russia at the turn of the millennium' just as Yeltsin resigned to let him take over as acting president. This document argued both that Russians expected the state to play a far greater role in national life than did citizens in other parts of the world and that the development of Russia required a stronger state: 'a country like Russia can live and develop within its existing borders only if it is a powerful state.' That the necessary adjustments were being made to the balance of power between public authorities and private interests was summed up in the idea that the moves made by Putin constituted a 'normalization' of Russian politics.

'Normalization' meant an end to the upheaval, to the cycles of revolu-tionary change and revolutionary failure that had marked Russia for most of the previous hundred years. Change, Putin (2001) argued in April 2001:

> should be justified by the circumstances ... there will be neither revolution nor counter-revolution. State stability built on a solid economic foundation is a blessing for Russia and for its people. It is high time now to start living according to normal human logic and realize that we have long and hard work ahead of us. Our main problems are too far-reaching and require not a policy of jumps forward here and there but qualified, daily work.

The promise of normalization was welcome to many Russians after the turmoil of the Yeltsin years and was one of the reasons that Putin's popularity was consistently high in his first two terms as president. But the move from 'system transformation to system management', as Richard Sakwa (2004: 19) has defined it, promised by normalization was the management of an imperfect and incomplete democratic system. 'System management' was not founded on an institutional arrangement in which 'circumstances' or 'the framework of everyday human life' were defined by representative politics or subject to checks and balances. The 'system' that was being managed was the system of elite politics that Putin had inherited from Yeltsin. The actions that Putin had taken against the oligarchs and regional leaders after his election restored one element of the constitutional order, the power of the presidency, without breathing new life into other parts that could have balanced that power. Normalization was consequently not a new round of democratization. Stability of the system, with all of its inherited imperfections, became an end in itself rather than the foundation upon which change was based. Change that came from outside, even if it was only a possibility, became something to be feared and countered. This meant that there was little positive about the consolidation of Putinism that followed the initial moves against the oligarchs and regional leaders. Although Putin talked of developing Russia, the emphasis on stability meant that the consolidation of Putinism was largely opportunistic and reactive and based on his popularity, which in turn was based on economic growth and state economic power and his skill at transforming this popularity into electoral success for himself and for United Russia in the 2003–4 elections.

Economic growth was not the product of reform but the result of the ongoing positive side effects of the 1998 crisis and the high price of energy. The export value of oil, gas and metals nearly doubled in dollar terms between 1998 and 2002. In 2000, oil exports were 171.5 per cent of what they had been the previous year; this level of output was maintained in 2001, expanded again in 2002, and accounted for about a quarter of Russia's growth between 2001 and 2004 (Robinson, 2009: 442). Russia had a resource windfall of a sort, therefore, even before the better-known spike in energy prices between 2005 and 2008, and both booms provided the means to transfer resources from the energy sectors to the rest of the economy. The Russian state became cash rich: the budget deficits of the 1990s were replaced by budget surpluses, and Putin was able to pay off the country's debts in 2006. Overall, the energy boom and the boost that it gave to other sectors of the Russian economy led to average GDP growth of about 7 per cent a year during Putin's first two presidential terms. Per capita income began to rise and by 2006 had recovered to the late Soviet levels (OECD, 2009: 21).

Economic growth helped to control elite conflict and boost Putin's popularity. Much of that conflict had been over the distribution of resources under Yeltsin, as during the 'bank wars' in 1996–7. The economic boom caused by high energy prices meant that there was more to share so less to fight over. The political costs of going against the Kremlin – costs that had been paid by Gusinsky and Berezovsky – were shown even more plainly by the Yukos affair, which sealed Putin's dominance over Russia's economic elite (Sakwa, 2009).

Putin meeting Mikhail Khodorkovsky, the owner of Yukos, in 2002; Khodorkovsky was arrested for economic crimes in 2003 and lost control of Yukos.

Yukos was one of Russia's largest oil firms. The company and its boss, Mikhail Khodorkovsky, were not very different to other firms and their oligarchs in how they had acquired their wealth. Khodorkovsky made Yukos different, however, by challenging Putin on several fronts. Despite the latter's warning to business leaders in July 2000 to stay out of politics, Khodorkovsky continued to involve himself visibly in Russia's political life. Yukos was active in trying to secure support in the Duma so that it could influence legislation, in particular the setting of tax rates in the oil industry (Gustafson, 2012: 264). Khodorkovsky was also active in financing Russian political parties and opposition groups, an involvement that was a mixture of self-interest and altruism, of 'cynical ruthlessness … combined with a streak of what can only be called naiveté' (ibid.: 283). He further challenged the state's economic control over the oil industry, entering into negotiations with Exxon over a stake in Yukos, and proposing to build a private oil pipeline to China. The former was against Putin's wishes – he would have preferred another partner for Yukos – and the latter was a direct challenge to the state's monopoly over oil pipelines, one of its major sources of income. These challenges were an affront to the beliefs of Putin and of Igor Sechin – a close associate and *siloviki* from St Petersburg who was deputy chief of Putin's presidential executive, who later worked with him in government when he was prime minister, and who chaired Rosneft's board, which was to gain Yukos's assets. Putin and Sechin had both written doctoral theses in which oil and trade outlets such as pipelines are described as a key resource that the state has to control for the sake of economic development (Balzer, 2005; Gustafson, 2012: 247–9).

Finally, a mixture of personal animosity and covetousness was involved. The chief beneficiaries of Yukos's eventual dismemberment after Khodorkovsky's arrest and conviction for tax avoidance were Sechin and *siloviki* factions. They had been angered by Khodorkovsky's attempts to take over Rosneft, then the last of the state-owned oil firms, and by his independence, brazen political lobbying and tax schemes. Putin had been angered personally by Khodorkovsky's attitude and demeanour. Cumulatively, ideology, personal dislike, politics and economic factors combined to create 'an anti-Yukos "politburo"' within the executive under Putin, which pushed for action against Yukos (Sakwa, 2009: 139). Leading economic liberals in government, such as the finance minister Aleksei Kudrin, were not tied to oligarchs as they had been in the 1990s, but to Putin, and like Putin they were as keen to guarantee the fiscal stability of the state, so they didn't try to protect Yukos (Gustafson, 2012: 257–8).

The sale of Yukos to Rosneft and Khodorkovsky's arrest became a *cause célèbre* among opponents of Putin in Russia and abroad (Sakwa, 2009: 304–21). It has been described as a pivotal moment in the creation of 'state capitalism' in Russia, as it preceded an expansion of the state's role in economic management (see chapter 10). Khodorkovsky's imprisonment transformed him into the country's leading political prisoner, particularly after his second trial in 2009 on embezzlement charges. A notable feature of the anti-United Russia and anti-Putin protests of 2011–12 was the Yukos flags held by many demonstrators. Public opinion on Khodorkovsky and Yukos has recognized the cynicism of the actions against them and the flawed nature of Khodorkovsky's trials. However, at the same time, Putin's actions have been in accord with the popular mood on the role of the state and big business. Surveys by the Levada Centre, for example, have consistently found that around 60 per cent of Russians in the 2000s believe the state's role in the economy was too small. The number of Russians who wanted all of the results of 1990s privatization reviewed fell between 2000 and 2010 from 28 to 22 per cent, but the numbers who wanted the privatization of large firms reviewed increased (from 24 to 36 per cent). Economic growth and Putin's actions against the oligarchs underpinned his personal popularity (Treisman, 2011). This popularity, however, was largely personal. Putin was far more popular than the government as a whole, as shown in figure 5.1 (which gives the approval indexes, where the percentage of people disapproving is subtracted from the number approving). There was some relationship between Putin's popularity and that of the government in that both generally rose and fell together. Government popularity only rose substantially, however, after Putin became prime minister in May 2008.

Putin's popularity transferred more easily at election time to United Russia, which took just under 50 per cent of the seats at the 2003 election. Putin was then easily re-elected to the presidency the following year, winning

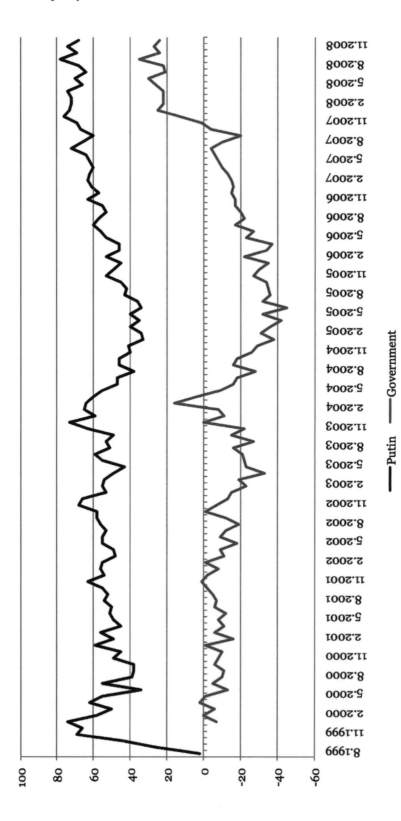

Figure 5.1 *Government and Putin's popularity indexes, 1999–2008*
Source: Adapted from Levada Centre data at www.levada.ru/indeksy.

in the first round with 71.3 per cent of the vote. This mandate and United Russia's success did not lead to a more aggressive reform strategy. Instead Putin concentrated on extending his power in his second term, using crises at home and abroad to deepen his hold over the political system to ensure stability and to extend the economic control of the state.

The main crisis that Putin used to consolidate his power further was the Beslan atrocity in September 2004. He had managed to reassert Russian control over Chechnya following the outbreak of the second Chechen war in 1999. This didn't end the conflict, however; it simply detached it from its original geographical setting. There had been terror attacks in Moscow, most notably on the Dubrovka theatre in 2002 which had left 170 dead after the special forces operation to end a siege went wrong. Conflict had also spread from Chechnya across the North Caucasus region, with attacks on security forces a regular (and continuing) occurrence. Beslan was the worst of these incidents. Chechen separatist forces seized a primary school on the first day of the school year, taking over 1,000 children, parents and teachers hostage. After a three-day siege, for reasons that have never been totally clear, Russian security forces entered the building with catastrophic loss of life: at least 330 hostages were killed, most of whom were children (Philips, 2007).

Putin argued that the tragedy at Beslan showed that the Russian state was weak, and that the 'weak get beaten' (Putin, 2004). To strengthen the state he proposed both ending the direct election of regional governors in favour of presidential appointments and introducing election to the Duma by proportional representation (PR) only (the legislation was passed in late 2004 and early 2005). Both of these measures hit at the powers of regional

Some of the victims of the Beslan school siege

leaders and strengthened the role of United Russia. The official rationale was that the move to PR only would strengthen the role of political parties. Temporary electoral blocs were banned from competing in elections, the rules for party registration were tightened up, and the threshold for securing seats in Duma elections was raised from 5 to 7 per cent of the vote. All of these measures favoured United Russia. The raised threshold squeezed out poorer performing parties, and most of those that applied to stand in the 2007 Duma election were ruled ineligible. United Russia received 64 per cent of the vote, which translated to 70 per cent of the seats (315) (see chapters 9 and 10).

United Russia's importance also rose because of the changes in elections for regional leaders. Gubernatorial elections were abandoned in response to Beslan. At first, provincial leaders were nominated by the president and local assemblies would confirm the appointment. Later this was amended so that the largest party in a region could nominate a candidate. United Russia was the largest party in most regions of Russia, and Putin, by then prime minister, was its chair (Ross, 2012: 149). Putin thus ensured that he had a large say in the appointment of regional leaders both as president and as prime minister.

Further measures to ensure Putin's political dominance followed the Orange Revolution in Ukraine, which developed in response to perceived electoral fraud in the first round of the Ukrainian presidential election in November 2004. Putin's favoured candidate in the election, Viktor Yanukovych, was the beneficiary of this fraud. The results were overturned by the Ukrainian Supreme Court after street protests, and Yanukovych's opponent, Viktor Yushchenko, was elected in a fresh ballot. Putin was personally humiliated because of the support he had given Yanukovych and also alarmed by the way that popular protest had upset what was supposed to be the managed succession of president in Ukraine from Leonid Kuchma to Yanukovych.

The Orange Revolution was ultimately the result of divisions within the ruling Ukrainian elite, but Putin blamed external interference from Western-sponsored democracy promotion programmes for the upset. Elite division was the cause of other 'colour revolutions' in Georgia and Kyrgyzstan. Thanks to his subjugation of the oligarchs and political reforms, Putin had already made sure that such splits were not going to happen in Russia. Prompted by the Orange Revolution, more controls were introduced over parties and voting by the creation in 2006 of an official opposition party, A Just Russia, to take votes away from the CPRF and left-leaning liberals. A Just Russia was the latest in a line of so-called project parties – i.e., parties designed from within the Kremlin to control the vote rather than to work actively for a particular social constituency or ideological goal. A 'street politics project' was now added to the Kremlin's arsenal of political weapons. Puppet non-governmental organizations (NGOs) were created to counter any threat from foreign-funded NGOs, such as human rights organizations and electoral monitoring organizations. Groups such as Nashi (Ours), a Kremlin-backed youth movement, were set up and began to harass regime opponents (Atwal and Bacon, 2012) (see also chapter 8).

The creation of Nashi, as its name suggests, was part of a turn to a politics of divide and rule, of 'us' (and 'ours') against 'them' (and 'theirs'). A law adopted in December 2005 required foreign NGOs to register was seen as a means of closing down any NGOs that angered the Kremlin. But these actions were in many ways overkill. Putin was over-insuring his rule at this point, creating a 'preventative counter-revolution' (Horvarth, 2012) for a threat that barely existed. What opposition there was to his rule was fractured. Control over electoral politics meant that there was little room for the opposition, and there were no incentives for elite factions to break with the regime and provide opposition forces with resources of the kind that had enabled success in the 'colour revolutions' (Gel'man, 2005; Hale, 2005, 2006a).

Opposition and criticism from abroad were further countered by the claim put forward by Putin and his spokesmen that what Russia was developing was a form of democracy that was appropriate to its national traditions and needs and that reflected its 'sovereignty'. This theory of 'sovereign democracy' was the brainchild of Vladislav Surkov, a former public relations man for Yukos and other oil firms, who had worked in the presidential executive from 1999 to 2011 before joining the government until 2013. Surkov was one of Putin's main 'political technologists', in essence a political fixer. He was also one of the creators of United Russia, A Just Russia and Nashi. The theory of 'sovereign democracy' gave rhetorical justification to these actions. Russian democracy, Surkov argued, was like all forms of democracy – unique. This uniqueness was a product of Russian culture and historical experience; in particular it reflected the need for unity in a vast geographic space, a unity expressed in the centralized state that both merged competing forces into a nation and represented them. The idea of 'sovereign democracy' was another 'them and us' explanation of politics: critics of Putin were critics of Russia and its traditions, imposing an alien, rational and divisive view of democracy over Russian idealist and holistic traditions. The point of sovereign democracy, as one Russian critic put it, was not to 'explain': it had 'mobilization objectives … aims to transform … social and political reality' by denying legitimacy to opposition (Okara, 2007: 20). Use of the notion of sovereign democracy waned after the mid-2000s, but it set the tone for dealing with opposition later. When opposition emerged as a more serious threat during the Duma and presidential elections of 2011–12, the regime argued that it was opposed to the will of the Russian people, was in the service of foreign powers, and acted in ways that are alien to Russian values (see below). Sometimes that charge was easy to make. The prosecution of members of Pussy Riot for their 'punk prayer' performance in Moscow's Cathedral of Christ the Saviour was easy to portray as an affront to traditional Russian religious values, and opinion polls have consistently shown that most Russians agreed with their arrest and imprisonment.* Legislation was also passed after 2012 making it compulsory for any non-governmental organization taking money from abroad to register as a 'foreign agent'. Obviously this sinister labelling is intended to deny opposition groups and bodies such as human rights NGOs the ability to claim that they are acting on their own behalf or on the behalf of the Russian people.

Tandemocracy and crisis, 2008–12

'Sovereign democracy', its associated projects, and economic growth gave Putin an unprecedented level of control over Russian political life. Public politics, the contestation for power and office through open forums such as elections, was lifeless by the middle of his second presidential term. Substantive competition for power took place within government and the presidential executive. Some of this was visible to outsiders as the political fortunes of competitors rose and fell and they gained and lost appointments. But this visible political competition was like the tip of an iceberg; its shape and nature could only be guessed at, since most of it was hidden below the surface.

The main bone of contention in these hidden struggles was who would replace Putin when his second presidential term finished (Sakwa, 2011). Constitutionally, Putin was compelled to stand down in 2008 after two consecutive presidential terms. There were rumours that he would have the constitution changed to allow him to serve a third consecutive term, and it may indeed have been seriously considered. *Siloviki* factions were thought to be particularly keen on this option, since it was unlikely that one of their number would be chosen as successor, both because they lacked a credible candidate and because it would have been interpreted negatively by the rest of the world.

Tearing up the constitution, however, was not an attractive idea for Putin and didn't fit with his claim to be a democrat (of any kind) who was 'normalizing' Russian politics. It was the kind of thing that dictators did in other post-Soviet states; Russia was supposed to be better than that. An assault on the constitution was not necessary. Putin had other options, with the Duma and the regions under the control of United Russia, and United Russia dependent on him and his popularity. With a loyal parliamentary majority, Putin could move to the post of prime minister and use that as a base for his rule. Moreover, if he selected the right person to succeed him as president,

---

* The performance can be seen at www.youtube.com/watch?v=ALS92big4TY, among other places. One YouTube link generally leads to another. Those of a delicate disposition may want to take care about watching some of the performance art of the 'Voina' collective from which Pussy Riot emerged. The same goes for anyone not of a delicate disposition who is thinking of having chicken for dinner.

he could also surround that individual with people loyal to him and constrain the new president's field of action. Putin took this option almost immediately after United Russia won its majority in the Duma election of 2 December 2007 and chose Dmitri Medvedev, one of the *Pitersy*, as his (and therefore United Russia's) candidate. In announcing his candidacy at a Kremlin meeting with leaders of the political parties represented in the Duma, Putin made it clear that Medvedev was his personal choice more than United Russia's.

Medvedev's first act of any significance as a presidential candidate was to ask Putin to be prime minister. Thus when Medvedev won the presidency in March 2008 Putin had managed what Yeltsin had been conspicuously unable to achieve: an orderly succession with no open elite contest that threatened to disturb the political peace. The succession was no more democratic than the Yeltsin succession, however. There had been, for a while at least, a possibility that Yeltsin's anointed heir would not win election, but there was no chance of this happening in 2008. There was fraud in Yeltsin-era elections, but now electoral fraud was systematic (see chapter 9). Medvedev and United Russia would have won without fraud taking place, though not as convincingly, and a less convincing victory for United Russia in the Duma would have meant Putin had less authority as prime minister. Fraud did not change who held power, but it did change how it was held, influencing the balance of power within the executive branch of government. The influence of electoral corruption on the arrangement of power then influenced the possibilities for future change in Russia, limiting how reform could be developed.

Medvedev's election showed that Putin had achieved the political stability that had eluded Yeltsin, but it also bore witness to the failure of the Putin era, the failure to rebuild the Russian state. Putin's reforms had been about securing dominance and authority over elite factions, over the political system and, finally, over large parts of society, which was not the same thing as making the Russian state and governance more effective. As we noted in the introduction to this chapter, Putin's lack of success in state building was due in part to his success at regime building. Political stability became an end in itself and there were dangers that reform might upset it. There was much rhetoric from Putin on the need to change public administration, but little action. He complained endlessly, for example, about corruption in the state, but corruption did not decline: if anything, it grew, especially in Putin's second term. Even Putin admitted his failure in this area in his last press conference as president (Holmes, 2008: 1011). As we saw in chapter 1 (see figure 1.1, p. 16) there was some improvement in governance in the first years of Putin's rule as the chaos of the Yeltsin era drew to a close. However, after a time, and especially in his second term, Russia's governance indicators worsened, so that overall the perceived quality was no better, and frequently worse, than it was at the end of the Yeltsin era (Robinson, 2012).

Putin implicitly recognized the failure to change Russian governance and develop the state in the last years of his second presidential term and as he handed over to Medvedev. Medvedev was supposed to 'modernize' Russia. Modernization for both men meant ending dependency on energy sales by strengthening other economic sectors. Putin launched a new state development plan in February 2008, just before Medvedev's election, and admitted that, 'even with the economic situation in our favour at the moment, we are still only making fragmentary attempts to modernize our economy' (Putin, 2008). He therefore introduced modernization as the theme for Medvedev's presidency. The problem, however, was that it was not clear how far Medvedev would be able to push a modernization agenda, partly because it was not obvious who had power in the Medvedev–Putin tandem. Medvedev had a platform as president to launch ideas, while Putin as prime minister had control of the day-to-day running of the government. How Medvedev's ideas would fit with Putin's running of the government was an unknown, not just for outside observers but for many Russian politicians. Were Medvedev's ideas also Putin's? To a degree they were, in that Putin launched modernization as a theme for the Medvedev presidency. But once Medvedev was in post, would they continue to see eye to eye? Some, both in and outside of Russia, wanted Medvedev to develop the modernization agenda beyond what Putin had outlined. Some of those in Russia who wanted this were close to Medvedev, and there were hopes that he would develop a 'team' of his own so that he could become more independent of Putin.

These issues would have dominated and shaped the Medvedev presidency whatever had happened between 2008 and the presidential elections of 2012. But they were given added gravity by the impact on Russia of the international economic crisis.

The crisis had been developing in Western economies before Medvedev's election. Russia was drawn into the circle of crisis-stricken economies in the autumn of 2008 and hit hard. Its economic growth had been spectacular under Putin, but this growth, as the OECD (2009: 21) noted, rested more on 'temporary factors' than on deep-seated structural change and renewal. Chief among these 'temporary factors' was the price of oil, which plummeted, falling by $90 per barrel between July 2008 and the start of 2009, and the Russian economy fell with it. Government revenues were hit as tax and excise duties declined, industrial production decreased, the value of the rouble slumped, construction work stopped, inflation rose, hitting household incomes, and the economy contracted sharply (see chapter 10).

The Russian government dealt with the problems quite well. Large amounts of the oil windfall profits had been set aside to deal with the boom–bust cycles that are associated with dependency on oil exports as a source of government income. This money was now used to stabilize the state's budget to slow the depreciation of the rouble and ease pressures on banks and firms with foreign debts, to support economic sectors hit by recession, and to increase welfare payments and public-sector wages. The amount deployed in the stimulus package was substantial, equivalent to between roughly 12 and 13 per cent of GDP in both 2009 and 2010. Overall, it has been estimated as being the third largest in the world during 2009–10. Russia's plunge into crisis was one of the steepest, but its recovery was also one of the quickest. The upturn in the price of oil in 2009 and 2010 restored the foundations of the country's economic fortunes and, together with the stimulus package, helped the economy to grow again, albeit at a more moderate rate than before 2008.

This success, however, did not mean that the economic crisis was dealt with well politically. It was not simply a result of Russia's oil dependency but also a failure of the Putin system, on account of Putin's inability to deal with the deeper problems that had beset Russia since Soviet times. In this view, Putin had not broken the crisis cycle of Russia's history. His economic 'success' in the 2000s had been a temporary reprieve; crisis was a return to 'normality' and crisis management would not deal with the fundamental problems of the economy. As one Russian economist put it, the country's crisis was 'twenty years older than the global crisis. ... when the leading countries of the world have solved the external signs of crisis Russia risks being left alone with its enduring crisis, which will be deeper than ever' (cited in Robinson, 2013c: 464).

Part of the reason for this criticism was that the main beneficiaries of initial anti-crisis measures were pro-Putin oligarchs, as the government, both directly and indirectly, took over their debts by providing government credit guarantees and interest rate subsidies, stalling tax payments, and setting preferential export and import tariffs. This led to accusations that the response to crisis was perpetuating the very structures that had caused it. As the late Boris Nemtsov (2009) – the former Yeltsin minister and in 2009 an opposition leader – argued, the 'monstrous structure of the Russian economy, based as it is on monopolies and close ties between the authorities and oligarchic groups, is the main reason for the deep financial-economic crisis in Russia. ... Putin's actions amount to supporting oligarchic groups and banks that are close to the government ... it is impossible to explain the social utility of saving the oligarchs.'

This sense of crisis as being more than the fallout of changes in the oil price compounded the tension over strategy within the tandem of Putin and Medvedev and among their followers. Medvedev argued that there could be no success in dealing with the crisis unless there was modernization. The association of modernization with diversification away from energy highlighted the idea that the structure of the economy was the enduring problem that underpinned the crisis. In 2009, Medvedev made modernization central to the government's anti-crisis response. This meant that the standard against which that response was judged was not the reversal of economic downturn but the prevention of crisis in the future. This confused short-term goals of dealing with the crisis with long-term ones of structural reform and tied recovery to things that might well have been difficult, if not impossible, to achieve even under favourable economic circumstances (see chapter 10). The anti-crisis efforts of the government could only be found wanting. Indeed, recovery itself could be regarded as a form of failure, since it was associated more with rises in energy prices rather than with modernization. Such a way out of the crisis, Medvedev argued in December 2009 – as the crisis was ending and growth was returning to the economy – 'leads nowhere. We need to get out of the crisis by reforming our own economy' (Medvedev, 2009c). Over the course of 2009–11, the development of thinking on modernization from within Medvedev's circle and in his own speeches and writings increasingly implicated the political system as the main barrier to tackling crisis in the right way.

From Putin's point of view it was unclear what affect the type of reforms Medvedev proposed would have or where they would stop. There was talk in parts of the press of a 'Medvedev *perestroika*'. This was near-heresy for someone as concerned with political stability as Putin. The result was that although the economy stabilized the political system froze. No consensus emerged from within the executive on what substantive political changes were necessary to deal with the underlying political factors that had helped to cause the crisis. Consequently, it could only look as if the executive was gridlocked on a key issue that Medvedev deemed necessary to solve in order to resolve the crisis once and for all. This probably sent out political signals that supporting reform was a gamble that elite members might not want to take and, more broadly, that the factors that the President recognized as underlying crisis were not going to be dealt with.

This stalemate dragged on throughout 2010 and into the following year. It was made worse by speculation about whether Medvedev would be allowed to stand again for election as president. The stalemate, and the sense that the crisis was not being dealt with at a fundamental level even though the economy was growing again, had an impact on people's assessment of the future and on the popularity of Putin and Medvedev. As figure 5.2 shows, Russians' positive assessment of the country's future development collapsed as crisis hit and did not fully recover: by the Duma election at the end of 2011, roughly as many Russians thought that the country was on the wrong path as believed it on the right one.* Medvedev and Putin were still popular. To an extent, it was the 'system' rather than them personally that took the blame for economic problems. But the overwhelming support that Putin had, and that Medvedev had because of Putin, had dropped away. United Russia's popularity declined too. In the end Putin decided that he needed to return as president to restore order. There is debate over when this decision was made. Medvedev subsequently claimed that it had been the plan all along. However, he looked shell-shocked when he had to make the announcement that Putin would be United Russia's candidate at the party's congress in September 2011, and rumours abound that he was told he would have no second term only moments

---

* Again, figure 5.2 shows the approval indexes, where the percentage of people disapproving is subtracted from the number approving.

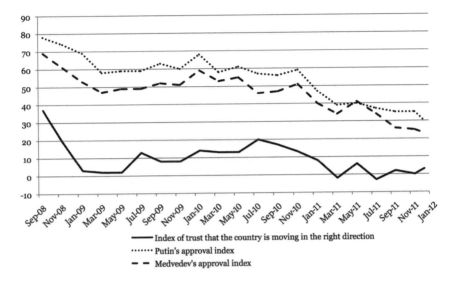

Figure 5.2 *Approval ratings for the tandem and trust in Russia's future, September 2008 to January 2012*
Source: Based on Levada Centre monthly survey data, available at www.levada.ru/indeksy.

before he had to announce that Putin would replace him. Whatever the case, Putin's reinstatement, for what was now going to be six years (the length of a presidential term was extended in 2008), did not solve the problems that United Russia was to face in the December 2011 election. It won, but charges of massive fraud led to mass demonstrations in Moscow and other cities. Some measures were put in place to control fraud for the presidential election in 2012, but their effectiveness was questionable (see chapter 9). Protest continued, and an opposition took shape (see chapter 8) that made the 2011–12 electoral cycle a challenge to Putin. Although he was successfully returned to the presidency, the elections, following the 2008 crisis as they did, highlighted the mismatch that had grown between the stability of Putin's regime, his ability to control access to power, and the lack of success that the Russian political system had in ensuring popular loyalty because of the dysfunctions of the state.

Putin's second term: the 'cultural turn' in Russian politics

Putin's return to the presidency restored his undisputed personal dominance over the political system but was not a means either of rebuilding trust in the state as a provider of welfare or security or of developing its functionality. Putin could have chosen to take up the Medvedev modernization variant after 2011 and developed it as his own political project to try to reform politics and create a sustainable path to economic growth that was not dependent on energy. This, however, would have meant the redistribution of political power and changing the rules on which his regime rested. Such an undertaking would have been to risk alienating parts of the elite that would have lost out in any such redistribution. Consequently, Putin rejected reform in favour of what has been called his 'cultural turn' (Sakwa, 2013a). This created a state project for Russia without actually doing anything about the state as a functional bureaucratic order. Rather, it shifted what counted as success in state building from issues of functionality – administrative reform to provide welfare and security – towards vague and indeterminate goals based on a cultural conception of the state (Robinson, 2017b).

Starting around 2012, Putin began to argue that Russia is a 'state-civilization'. By this he means that there is a close alignment between the country's ability to exist as a state and as a civilization: each depends on the other; without the state there would be no civilization, and without the civilization there would be no state. The strength of a state is a function of how strong its civilizational identity is. This identity is a resource, one that needs to be protected so that the state can survive. The character of this civilization is essentially a religious one, but it is not totally determined by one religious denomination. Although the main source of Russian civilization is Russian Orthodox Christianity, which it shares with Belarus and Ukraine, its state-civilization is not underpinned by Orthodoxy alone but is formed because Orthodoxy and the other religions that are present in Russia are joined by a common concern for the preservation of traditional moral values such as religiosity, family, heterosexuality, etc. This shared set of values enables Russia to exist as a multi-faith and multi-ethnic society. The dominant values are Orthodox and Russian, but the other faiths fit with Orthodoxy and coexist with it to support the state. There is no need for them to propose state missions of their

Putin and Medvedev at the military parade marking the sixty-ninth anniversary of victory in the Great Patriotic War

own in the form of separatist projects, because their core moral concerns are already addressed in the larger Russian Orthodox faith and the Russian state. As a result, they are subsumed in the greater Russian state-civilization and have not and should not develop state-bearing cultures of their own.

The task of the Russian state, according to Putin (2013a), is to protect Russia as a state-civilization. This, Putin has argued, has never been more necessary than at present. Other state-civilizations are giving up and debasing the traditional values they once had. This is because of globalization, particularly cultural globalization, and because of their abandonment of traditional values. Globalization is different to previous types of interstate competition because it is not just military or economic but also ideational. Population movements and attempts to deal with them have given rise to multiculturalism. This multiculturalism is not based on any organic, native intellectual foundations such as the mixture of religions that underpin Russia's state-civilization. Rather, it is founded on abstract principles, such as the idea of 'tolerance', which, Putin maintains, are 'neutered and barren'. As a result, Putin (2013b) argued in his address to the Federal Assembly in 2013:

> Today, many nations are revising their moral values and ethical norms, eroding ethnic traditions and differences between peoples and cultures. Society is now required not only to recognize everyone's right to the freedom of consciousness, political views and privacy, but also to accept without question the equality of good and evil, strange as it seems, concepts that are opposite in meaning. This destruction of traditional values from above not only leads to negative consequences for society but is also essentially anti-democratic, since it is carried out on the basis of abstract, speculative ideas, contrary to the will of the majority, which does not accept the changes occurring or the proposed revision of values.

The last part of this quotation is important. Putin is not rejecting 'democracy' but claiming to be its truest representative, articulating a populist position that he asserts is more in tune with societal aspirations than anything that can be uncovered through an electoral system, since elections are designed to secure representation of sectional interests – i.e., fractions of the people (Robinson and Milne, 2017). Putin's argument puts him above such elections as president and representative of the majority, which, of course, is opposed to the erosion of traditional values. In this way he sets his version of democracy against the forms of democracy that are most common in Europe. Not surprisingly, Putin also argues that the erosion of traditional values is especially advanced in Europe, which thereby stands in stark contrast to Russia.*

For Putin, Russian state-civilization provides a form of immunity that keeps at bay revolutionary and reformist ideas. Such ideas 'are always

---

* As Putin (2012a) put it, 'Behind the "failure of the multicultural project" is a crisis of the very model of the "national state" – a state that was historically constructed exclusively on the basis of ethnic identity. And that is a serious challenge that both Europe and many other regions of the world will encounter.'

some kind of bacillus that destroys this social or public organism.' When 'immunity decreases … millions already believe that things cannot get any worse, let's change something at any price, we shall destroy everything there, "we shall build our new world, and he who was nothing will become everything." In fact, it did not happen as one wished it to be.' Russia has suffered such 'decreases in immunity' in the past and the change to which they led involved a 'loss of the state self-identity both during the Russian Empire's collapse and during the Soviet Union's breakup [that] was disastrous and destructive.' The chief culprit in 'loss of state self-identity' was the elite, in particular the intelligentsia, who, according to Putin, are always keen to 'emphasize their civility, their level of education; people always want to be guided by the best examples.' This intellectual arrogance led to a disdain for Russian tradition and attempts to copy foreign social, economic and political practices, which in practice amounted to betraying Russia (Putin, 2013c).

Equally as dangerous and perverse as copying from abroad is the threat of 'mono-ethnicism', which, for Putin, is any attempt to put the interests of ethnic Russians above those of the broad set of religious traditional values that join different ethnicities and religionists in the Russian state-civilization. Putting one nationality above another, Putin argues, 'was the formula used by those who paved the way to the collapse of the Soviet Union' and stands in contrast to the longer-established cultural values of Russia that have been reaffirmed over the centuries. Promoting 'Russia first' simply opens up the floodgates to competing claims to sovereignty as occurred when the USSR collapsed. Claims made about mono-ethnic rights and aspirations is also a Western idea, since it is based on 'the notorious concept of self-determination, a slogan used by all kinds of politicians who have fought for power and geopolitical dividends, from Vladimir Lenin to Woodrow Wilson' (Putin, 2012c). Although many nationalists and liberals would see themselves as poles apart in Russian politics, they are, Putin argues, essentially the same. They both work from abstractions, and as a result the differences between them 'cancel each other out insofar as they are used to express something identical underlying them all', namely their opposition to the true values of Russia's state-civilization.

Russia, Putin maintains, was lucky to survive previous attempts at change through revolution and reform. The dangers to the country from reform, however, are greater than ever before. In the past, competition between cultures was not as intense as it is now and did not so clearly involve the transfer of 'ways of life' from one place to another. The signs of this for Putin (2012b, 2013a) are many: 'global development is becoming increasingly contradictory and dynamic'; the very idea of 'soft power' 'implies a matrix of tools and methods to reach foreign policy goals by exerting information and other levers of influence' that uses 'illegal instruments' 'to manipulate the public and to conduct direct interference in the domestic policy of sovereign countries.' The cultural ties that bind Russian people are, for Putin (2013a), weaker than they have been before, as shown by Russian's tolerance of 'corruption, brazen greed, manifestations of extremism and offensive behaviour'. Traditional values can no longer be relied on to renew themselves as they have in the past, because they are not a finite resource in the current global order. This, Putin has argued on several occasions, is the lesson that has been learnt over the course of Russia's post-communist history and as the country has dealt with competition from abroad: 'we eventually came to the conclusion that there are no inexhaustible resources and we must always maintain them. The most important resource for Russia's strength and future is our historical memory' (Putin, 2013d). The fact that the 'Russian people are state builders, as evidenced by the existence of Russia', remains true, but the 'cultural code' that has historically under-pinned state building 'has been attacked ever more often over the past few years; hostile forces have been trying to break it, and yet it has survived. It needs to be supported, strengthened and protected' (Putin, 2012a).

Even from this brief survey we can see that Putin's cultural turn towards conservative traditional values is almost relentlessly negative. The only positive thing that he recommends is the preservation of Russian culture and its increased celebration and use in education. This has led, among other things, to calls for new school texts, the establishment of a military-historical society with the involvement of the minister for culture, more celebration of Russian feats of arms, including new war memorials and more prominence given to Russia's part in the First World War, and the re-creation in March 2014 of the programme entitled *Gotov k trudu i oborone* (Ready for labour and defence, a physical and ideological fitness programme, originally launched by Stalin in 1931, which ran throughout the rest of the Soviet period), as well as the persecution of those who are clearly defined as not part of Putin's community of values: the 'disparate traitors' of what have been called Russia's 'fifth column' – the liberal intelligentsia, with their tendency to cringe culturally before the West, ethno-nationalists, and, of course, most famously in the West, the LGBT community. It has been easy for entrepre-neurial policy-makers to introduce legislation that reinforced traditional values but hard for the political system to generate policy and legislation on complex economic issues and follow them through. This has led to a lot of symbolic politicking, such as the law banning gay 'propaganda' or the law that decriminalized some forms of domestic abuse. The organization of the state is not brought into question by the cultural turn, and policy, outside education and physical fitness and 'lifestyle' politics, is barely mentioned within the frame of the cultural turn.

Ultimately, the result of the cultural turn is symbolic rather than admin-istrative politics. Negativity is key to the support that the cultural turn gives to Putin. It denies political agency to any group or interest that might seek change. Liberal or nationalist projects are perverse and may lead to the final eradication of the Russian state as the embodiment of a particular 'civilization'. All that stands between this final eradication of Russia as a state-civilization is Putin and the link that he has to the people who share his traditional values. The end result of the cultural turn has been that Putin's personal rule has been revitalized by its association with a particular view of what the country is and should be, and what it should be protected against. This helped to legitimize the repression of anti-government activists and more clampdowns on independent NGOs and civil society. There have been far more arrests of demonstrators since 2012 than there were before that year. Most opposition leaders have spent time in detention or been sentenced to house arrest in attempts to discourage protest or disrupt planned demonstrations. The courts have been used to try to silence critics. Sometimes trials have been for crimes against Orthodox values – the Pussy Riot trial, for example – but there have also been cases involving opponents accused of economic crimes. Alexei Navalny, the opposition leader and anti-corruption blogger and potential presidential candidate for 2018, has been tried twice for embezzlement, and his brother was dragged into one of the cases against him. Navalny was found guilty both times, and this should block him from running for public office. The assassination of Boris Nemtsov in 2015 was a rare case of a murder of an opposition politician, but journalists and human rights workers have been killed or attacked regularly. There is little evidence of direct targeting by state agencies of opposition figures for attack, although they are clearly targeted for arrest, but the cultural turn has created an atmosphere in which violence against Putin's enemies has been normalized.

The negativity of the cultural turn, and the violence that it has helped to create, has rendered it a reactionary moment in Russian politics. Change, or the call for change, has become dangerous by definition unless it comes from the apex of the political system, from Putin. This made it difficult to deal with the problems that had led to protest between 2011 and 2012. Not surprisingly, reactionary rhetoric, with its view of the state as a protector of a spiritual form of civilization, was only partially effective in the first two years of Putin's new presidency. As figure 5.3 shows, there was some stabilization of his popularity in 2012 and 2013, but his overall approval index remained roughly the same as it was when he took over from Medvedev. Re-election and the cultural turn did not restore Putin's popularity, although the latter did provide grounds for taking action against opposition opponents and civil society groups. The discourse of the cultural turn really bit politically only from late 2013 and early 2014, when the Maidan revolution in Ukraine led to the articulation by Putin of a more nationalist foreign policy and the annexation of Crimea. When this occurred, his popularity rose by about 20 points and has consistently remained high, at over 80 per cent. The cultural turn did not, therefore, independently stabilize the Russian political system after the shocks of the 2008 economic crisis and the election campaigns of 2011–12. It

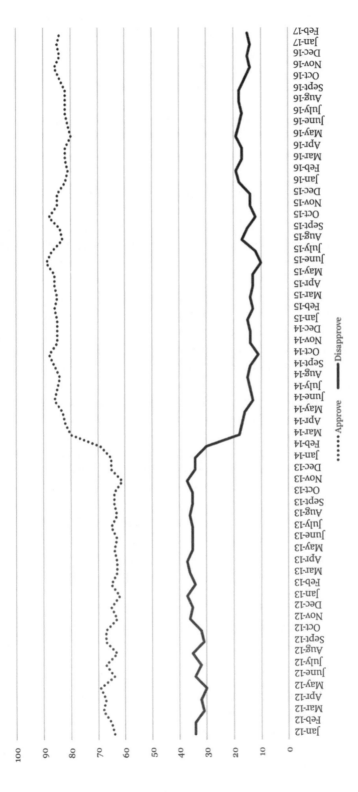

Figure 5.3 *Approval ratings for Putin, January 2012 – February 2017*
Source: Based on Levada Centre monthly survey data, available at www.levada.ru/indikatory/odobrenie-organov-vlasti.

became meaningful for many Russians only when events in Ukraine seemed to confirm that Russia was threatened externally and when there was a cause for national pride as Crimea was reintegrated into Russia. Still, this was enough to compensate for what should have been a loss of popularity as a result of Russia's sluggish economic performance, and, together with changes to electoral rules (see chapter 9) helped to ensure United Russia's dominance in the 2016 election and Putin's re-election to the presidency in 2018.

Conclusion

The feeling of national pride that developed after Putin's Crimean adventure has endured despite several years of economic downturn and sanctions. This has given Russia a form of stability: the regime has become unchallengeable, although protests, such as those that led to the arrests of several hundred anti-corruption demonstrators in March 2017, can still occur and can sometimes draw sizeable crowds. However, this stability is based on avoiding dealing with many problems, and, as we noted in chapter 1, poses a question for any regime: Can it contain and ameliorate the problems of maintaining social order and national security in such a way that it can survive ruling through a 'weak' state – i.e., a state not capable of performing the tasks before it on a long-term basis and adapting to new demands as they are made? As we argued previously, if a regime cannot contain or ameliorate these pressures, it will be constrained to evolve further and to develop the state. This might lead to its viability being called to question from below – that is, from society at large, concerned about its security and future – or from within the state, as demands to take action grow from officials who cannot perform the basic state functions of maintaining order and security. Putin's regime faced such a challenge from below in the demonstrations that occurred in Russia in 2011–12 and, to a lesser extent, in March 2017. The demonstrations showed that there was still a great gap between the achievements of the 2000s and the resolution of all of the transformative tasks that the state had to accomplish (the revolutionary element of post-Soviet change). They also showed that there was an institutional failure to provide avenues for discontented citizens to feel that they had a means of either influencing politics or at least getting a fair hearing (the democratic transitional element of post-Soviet change).

This gap means that, in many ways, the Putin and Medvedev presidencies have been, and continue to be, transitional leaderships rather than the beginning of a new stable political order in Russia in which both the rules governing access to politics were settled and the state was broadly adequate to dealing with the nation's problems. The stability of the regime, of how power was accessed, has been achieved by a combination of force and co-option, but this has not dealt with the state's weaknesses or led to the state becoming dedicated to the collective good. It is still, as Yeltsin had complained in the late 1990s, concerned too much with satisfying the private ends of its bureaucrats and of the economically and politically powerful. These private ends have been disciplined by Putin and put in some sort of order, but that in itself is a problem for many Russians. United Russia, as the party-political symbol of this Putin order, is for many Russians the 'party of crooks and thieves', as the Russian opposition leader Alexei Navalny famously labelled it. Opposition was inevitable when Medvedev's transitional leadership led back to Putin, and the opposition's failure was also inevitable. As we shall see in the next chapter, the institutions of the Russian state had developed over the 1990s and the 2000s in ways that precluded them from serving a democratic purpose or responding to democratic calls.

6
Presidency and Parliaments

Introduction

The presidency is the pivotal institution of the Russian political system, of far greater import than its parliaments. The presidency has shaped the development of the political system and leadership since it and its powers have been at the centre of conflict, and because it has been the main institution from which policies designed to change the country have emerged. For this reason, and because presidencies are generally regarded as more damaging to democracy than other forms of executive power, it has been seen as particularly harmful of Russian democratic development; the 'anaemia of Russian democracy can actually be explained exclusively in terms of a single institutional choice' for presidentialism (Fish, 2001: 237). Alternatively, and while not ignoring some of its negative aspects, a more generous view has argued that the concentration of power within the post of president has helped to control chaos in Russia at some points in its post-communist political development. Moreover, it has been suggested that the problems are not with presidentialism per se but with the lack of checks and balances to presidential power caused by the weakness of other democratic institutions. This chapter will consider both of these positions, looking at the general problems associated with presidentialism, the development of the presidency and political leadership in Russia under Yeltsin, Putin and the tandem of Putin and Medvedev, and at how it has supplanted parliament. The general line of argument is that, although it might be possible to have presidencies that are compatible with democracy, the Russian presidency was flawed from the start, since it was founded in haste and in circumstances that could only lead to conflict. Resolving this conflict was based – as discussed in chapters 4 and 5 – on a shifting blend of compromise and coercion. These created a dysfunctional political system generally, with the presidency both perverting democratic development and being perverted in its turn by democratic failure.

The presidentialism problem

The dangers of presidentialism were first identified by Juan Linz (1990a), who argued that presidential democracies were more likely to collapse or relapse into non-democracy because they were more rigid and less accommodating than parliamentary democracies (Linz, 1990b). Democracy, as we discussed in chapter 3, is a 'contingent outcome of political struggle'. In the struggles around creating democracy it is important to be able to compromise and to accommodate rival interests. Failure to do so may lead some social groups to reject democracy, since there will be nothing in it for them. Presidentialism, because it concentrates executive power on an individual and turns political competition into a zero-sum game, makes compromise less likely than parliamentarism and therefore has a negative effect on democratic consolidation.. Concentrating executive power in a presidency excludes significant groups from decision-making processes to the detriment of democratic representation. Moreover, presidents often contest power with legislatures in a politically destructive fashion. Coalitions that emerge to support a president are likely to be unstable, since they are set up on a president's terms and not negotiated; parliamentary coalitions, on the other hand, are negotiated between political actors who share the spoils of office. Governments and ministers under presidents are less accountable than those answerable to parliaments.

Political crises cannot be resolved easily by the removal of a president and the election of a new government. For the most part it is straightforward to collapse and replace parliamentary coalitions, not least through the holding of fresh elections. Presidents, however, serve fixed terms and cannot readily be removed from office except through impeachment. Impeachment is often difficult to achieve and can ratchet up the level of political conflict in a society. Finally, presidents may suffer delusions of grandeur as they 'conflate … supporters with "the people" as a whole … [and] define [their] policies as reflections of the popular will' (Linz, 1990a: 61). As a result of one or more of these factors, it is argued that presidentialism promotes crisis and democratic breakdown more than parliamentarism. Limited accountability, polarization and frustration on the part of those excluded from power make for less agreement among elite members concerning the rules of politics. The development of democratic citizenship is thus upset, as oppositional elite forces and their supporters do not feel bound to accept the legitimacy of elected executives.

These problems are exacerbated in post-communist states. First, it has been argued that post-communist presidential systems are easy to 'capture' – i.e, post-communist presidents can be suborned easily by private economic interests to serve their narrow agendas. Second, post-communist presidentialism reflects aspects of the communist past that are not conducive to democratic growth. The first of these positions is associated with Joel Hellman

(1998), who argued that presidentialism is associated with stalled economic reform. Economic reform does not take place in a vacuum. Certain groups – 'winners' – are able to take advantage of initial reform moves and use the differences between the old planning system and the emerging market economy to become exceptionally wealthy through the accumulation of high and socially unproductive 'rents' – returns on assets that are in excess of what could be realized if they were used for some wide social benefit (North et al., 2013: 2). There comes a point, Hellman maintains, where the opportunities to take rents of this kind diminish as reform begins to narrow the gap between the old planning system and the emerging market economy. At this point, 'winners' will use their resources to try to stop reform and preserve the circumstances that enable them to accumulate vast wealth. According to Hellman, such moves are easier to achieve in presidential than in parliamentary systems. A president is easier to capture than a parliamentary government. When a president makes a deal for support to limit reform, he gains all the benefits of that deal politically. In parliamentary systems, and in particular where there are coalition governments, deal-making will face opposition and exposure from parties that cannot trade policy compromises for support. Moreover, this opposition to compromise from within parliament can potentially bring down governments over deals done and see the election of a new government. Such a collapse is less likely in a presidential system because of fixed terms and the difficulties of impeachment. Public policy is therefore more likely to be compromised and captured by elite interests under presidents, with a consequent loss of accountability to the public and weakening of democracy.

Another factor that might lead presidents in post-communist polities to favour elite interests is that the choice of presidentialism reflects the elite structure as the old regime collapses. Easter (1997) has shown how post-Soviet polities chose presidentialism either when the elite survived the collapse of communism intact or where there was 'an extrication crisis' from the old regime and a competition between remnants of the old elite and new elite groups. In the former cases – such as in Uzbekistan or Kazakhstan – the intact old elite 'maintained their access, completely or partially, to the state's power resources', and presidentialism was a way of protecting this access (ibid.: 189). In the latter cases, of which Russia was one, presidentialism was favored because, as the crisis of moving from the old system rumbles on, a figurehead offers security of tenure (it is hard to remove presidents) and stable access to the state's resources. In neither case is presidentialism conducive to democratization. Either the presidency will defend the bastions of privilege left over from the past or it will be the centre of political conflict as competing elite factions struggle to use it or contain it. Presidentialism in both cases is 'the preferred strategy of those actors who calculate that they have the most to gain by limiting the access of others to the state's power resources' (ibid.: 211).

Both Hellman and Easter's arguments about the negative impact of presidentialism point out that it is not presidencies alone that lead to an association with poor democratization. Personality, policy choices, and styles of leadership are also important, and so too is parliament and its ability to constrain a president. Generally, presidents construct coalitions to rule, and the stability of such coalitions depends on how the individual uses their formal powers and distributes resources and offices to potential clients (Chaisty et al., 2014). Consequently, the problems may lie not 'just' in the office of president but also in 'the total configuration of institutions' in a country (Horowitz, 1990: 75). In other words, for Russia, as elsewhere, looking at the role and influence of presidentialism means bearing in mind how it interacts with other parts of the political system. Furthermore, its role and influence might change over time as these other parts of the system change and as presidents use their powers and the resources available to them to different effects.

The origins of the Russian presidency and its contest with parliament

The Russian presidency was grafted onto the constitution of the Soviet-era Russian Soviet Federal Socialist Republic (RSFSR) in 1991. As a result, institutions around the presidency and their staffing developed independently of constitutional regulation. Instead of his role being defined by law, the president became an actor in the negotiation of a settlement to fill the constitutional void and secure the transition from one political system to another. The presidency was an addendum to the institutional ensemble of the emerging Russian polity, the main part of which had been the Russian Congress of People's Deputies and Supreme Soviet, which had been elected in 1990.

The Russian presidency was created in this fashion because it was founded expediently as a vehicle for political change, to develop and safeguard the gains made by the newly sovereign Russian state. Yeltsin's position as chairman of the Russian Supreme Soviet was precarious. He was weak in comparison to Gorbachev and had been elected chair of the Russian Supreme Soviet by only a narrow margin. Also his tenure was dependent upon the Russian Congress of People's Deputies. A Russian presidency offered a solution to these problems, countering Gorbachev's powers as president of the USSR and giving Yeltsin some independence from the Russian parliament. The circumstance that led to the creation of a Russian presidency had two effects.

First, it led Yeltsin both to believe his power was based on general popular acclamation, rather than the support of a portion of the electorate, and to assume that his policies were the will of the people. As he put it in his inauguration speech, 'Russia's citizens have made their choice. They not only chose … a president, they above all chose the path that our homeland is to follow … The president is … invested with enormous responsibility for the fate of Russia and his fellow citizens; he is above all the person in whom the people have placed their confidence' (*Izvestiya*, 10 July 1991). This idea of the president as the repository of Russia's popular will has endured into the Putin era.

Second, little attention was paid to the relations between president and parliament. The 'Law on the President of the RSFSR' adopted by parliament in April 1991 was 'a compromise with a pronounced advantage for the presidency' (Biryukov and Sergeyev, 1997: 95). The power of parliament over the formation of the government (it ratified the president's nominee for prime minister) and the ordinary activities of government and president were weak. However, it had the capacity to alter government policy by amending the budget and by voting changes to the structure and powers of the presidency and government, and it had control over some appointments (for example, members of the Constitutional Court). Presidential veto power was weak. The president could return legislation to the Supreme Soviet for reconsideration, but not to the Congress of People's Deputies. A simple majority – the same simple majority that had passed the law in the first place – could override the presidential veto. The Supreme Soviet could override presidential decrees only after a ruling of the Constitutional Court. The president could not dissolve either of the houses of parliament. Mechanisms to resolve conflict between president and the parliament were insubstantial. The Russian Constitutional Court was prohibited by law from dealing with political cases until December 1992, and until July 1994 it could deal only with one case at a time. The weakness of the presidential veto over Supreme Soviet legislation meant that, when drafting laws, parliament had little need to take account of the president's views or the consistency of their legislation with government policy. Moreover, there was no clear demarcation of who was responsible for initiating policy. Both president and parliament saw themselves as the lead institution in policy-making and claimed this role was theirs because they represented the 'people'. Yeltsin, as we have seen, saw the office of president as combining representation of the people with the choice of a 'path that our homeland is to follow'. Parliamentary leaders saw parliament as being more representative because it contained a range of political opinions. In the view of many parliamentary deputies, and constitutionally, the powers of the president were granted by parliament, and what parliament had gifted to the president it could take away. The discrepancy between the lack of day-to-day parliamentary oversight of government activities and the powers of parliament to change the structure and distribution of power within it increased the prospects of conflict between the various branches of government becoming fundamental.

There was little to prevent the conflict between president and parliament because there was no presidential party in parliament or solid support base for Yeltsin. Factions within the Congress of People's Deputies and Supreme Soviet were very unstable as deputies swapped factions and new ones emerged (Chaisty, 2006: 30–2). Yeltsin initially combined the posts of president and prime minister but could not deliver reform in the face of opposition from both parliament and social forces that opposed economic change. As we saw in chapter 4, to survive, Yeltsin had to compromise on reform and build supportive coalitions. Patronage allowed him to appoint people to posts in government, and the lack of a legal definition of the presidency enabled him to expand his position to create more posts that could be handed out to supporters. The presidential entourage became swollen as it developed atop a vast array of new councils and advisory bodies created to incorporate more and more of the people that Yeltsin wanted to co-opt.

These developments created what Eugene Huskey (1995) has called the 'politics of institutional redundancy'. As appointments were made to government and the presidential administration to ensure political support for Yeltsin, the number of agencies with overlapping competencies and their staffs grew. For example, by mid-1993 there were six different analytical centres in the administration providing Yeltsin with information and advice, as well as the Presidential Council, which contained four specialist policy advice groups (Robinson, 2000: 25–6). Other bodies overlapped both other units of the administration and the government. The Security Council, for example, created in 1992, was more or less a parallel government structure reporting to the president and with an unclear relationship to the actual government under the prime minister. Institutional redundancy gave Yeltsin room for manoeuvre and a variety of channels through which he could oversee the work of the executive. It also meant that there were no clear lines of responsibility and that there was competition between overlapping agencies and an incentive for these to make alliances outside of the executive to try to increase their bargaining power and their chances of getting Yeltsin's ear. Huskey (1995 and 1999) has argued that Yeltsin's creation of 'superpresidentialism' blended certain traits of Soviet and Russian organizational culture, combined with what Breslauer (1999, 2002) has called Yeltsin's strong 'personalistic urge'. For Huskey (1999: 7), the growth of the presidential apparatus under Yeltsin was a conscious attempt to re-create an institution similar to the old Communist Party Central Committee that would have oversight over all policy areas and strive to ensure that central decrees were obeyed. However, the efficiency with which it could do this was compromised, Huskey argues, by Yeltsin's Soviet-era belief in the job rights of bureaucrats. This belief, and fear of the destabilization that wholesale purges of personnel might bring, meant that no efforts were made to rationalize the bureaucracy. Administrative problems were resolved not by rationalization but by adding a new layer of bureaucratic structures and developing institutional redundancy as a support for presidentialism.

There are certain similarities between the presidentialism that Yeltsin was constructing and institution building under both the tsars and the CPSU general secretaries, but culture cannot explain everything. Institutional overlap is not uncommon in other countries. Elsewhere in the world, as in Russia, institutional overlap is often useful to political leaders because it allows them to duck responsibility and realign their policy positions quickly and at little cost. This was certainly the case in Russia. Colton (1995: 147) has argued that institutional redundancy meant that Yeltsin could 'invest time and effort in areas that most [caught] his fancy ... and at the same time disclaim responsibility for shortcomings in other areas of administration.' It also allowed Yeltsin to occupy the centre ground politically and increase his chances of political survival. Breslauer (2002: 253) argues that Yeltsin needed to be able to reposition himself politically so as to occupy a centrist position and to avoid marginalization 'at the extreme end of the domestic political spectrum'. To this end, he adopted a policy of 'selective reincorporation', building an 'outsized' coalition as a counterweight to his political insecurity. This did not end the conflict with parliament, but it did give Yeltsin the means to survive and triumph over it. Presidentialism and institutional redundancy was useful in constructing this coalition and enabling Yeltsin to maintain it over time. Ballooning bureaucracy gave him posts within the executive to hand out as patronage. Unclear lines of responsibility and command meant that Yeltsin was able to position himself as the arbiter of policy, the only person able to cut through the maze of redundant institutions and competing interests that inhabited them (Robinson, 2000).

Whatever its source, presidentialism and Yeltsin's politics of patronage weakened the legal accountability of bureaucracy for its actions, subverted bureaucratic hierarchy, and allied the presidency to clientelist interests instead of any general social interest. The expansion of presidential power after the adoption of the 1993 constitution did not change the way that Yeltsin ruled in any remarkable way, but it did safeguard the style of rule that he had developed between 1991 and 1993. Partly this was for electoral reasons; Yeltsin maintained his outsized coalitions in order to give himself as many choices as possible in the run-up to the 1996 presidential election. Partly this continuity reflected the fact that the coalitions that Yeltsin created required constant fine-tuning. They drew together political opposites who were not committed to alliance with one another, or even particularly to Yeltsin, but to influence peddling and building their hold on power (Willerton, 1998).

The 1993 constitution: the consolidation of presidentialism and the weakening of parliament

The way that the presidency developed after its creation in 1991, and in the context of struggles over the constitutional order between 1991 and 1993, established a pattern that was to endure throughout the rest of the Yeltsin years and into the Putin 'eras'. The adoption of the new constitution following Yeltsin's defeat of the parliamentary opposition did not change this. Although the presidency gained considerable powers under the new constitution, the survival of the incumbent depended as much on how these powers were used to maintain coalitions as on the powers of his office.

The president dominates the Russian political process under the 1993 constitution, having vast powers of appointment and the ability to take action against parliament. The constitution established a two-tier parliament, but it was very different to the structure of the old Congress of People's Deputies and Supreme Soviet. The lower house, the Duma, was elected directly through proportional representation and single-mandate districts (this has changed over time; see chapter 8). The upper house, the Federation Council, has two members from each of the units of the Russian Federation. In 1993 the Federation Council was directly elected, but after 1995 its members were *ex officio* the head of the provincial legislature and the head of the provincial executive (the governor or president). Under Putin, members were selected by provincial legislatures and provincial leaders lost their seats (see chapter 7). Both the Duma and the Federation Council were initially elected for a two-year term as transitional bodies; thereafter the parliamentary term was set at four years. Collectively the two houses of parliament are known as the Federal Assembly.

The president, along with the prime minister, can appoint and dismiss ministers and nominates a candidate for prime minister. The Duma cannot reject the president's candidate for prime minister more than twice; a third rejection leads to the dissolution of the Duma, fresh elections, and the appointment of the prime minister by the president. The president also has extensive powers of appointment to the military, judicial and regional posts, as well as the right to initiate legislation – as does the Duma – and referenda and to issue decrees that have the force of law until parliament legislates to supplant them. Legislation is voted on first in the Duma and then by the Federation Council. The Federation Council can reject Duma bills. The Duma must then vote by a two-thirds majority to overcome the Federation Council veto. After passage through the two houses of parliament, the legislation goes to the president for signature. However, the president can veto legislation from the Duma and the Federation Council; to overcome a veto these bodies have to muster two-thirds support for a bill.

There are few checks on presidential powers, which are reinforced by the fact that it is extremely difficult to change the constitution. Changes to those articles of the constitution that define the division of power and the rights of the president and parliament have to be approved by three-quarters of the members of the Federation Council and two-thirds of the State Duma's deputies. However, constitutional amendments come into force only once they have been 'approved by the legislative bodies of power of at least two-thirds of the members of the Russian Federation' (Article 136). There is therefore little prospect of a quick and simple constitutional transfer of power from the president to parliament or government.

Checks on presidential power from the Federal Assembly are weak. The

The Duma building, Moscow

Federation Council ratifies presidential decrees on states of emergency and the deployment of troops outside of the Russian Federation. The Duma can seek a vote of no confidence in the government, but the president can reject its finding. If a second vote is held within three months and goes against the government, the president has a choice: he can disband the government or dissolve the Duma. A vote of no confidence is therefore as much a threat to the Duma as it is to the government. In June 1995, by 241 votes to 72, the Duma declared no confidence in the government over its handling of the hostage crisis in Budyonnovsk (a Chechen group had entered the Russian territory of Stavropol Krai, taken nearly 2,000 people hostage in a hospital, and been allowed to escape). A second vote of no confidence was held in July, but it failed because of the defection of large numbers of deputies to the government side in the interest of preserving their place in parliament (Robinson, 1998: 168), thus clearing the threat that the Duma might be dissolved. Parliament's inability to reject the presidential nominee for prime minister was shown clearly when Yeltsin sacked Primakov in 1998 and forced the Duma to accept Kiriyenko (see chapter 4).

There are some limits to the president's powers vis-à-vis the Duma: it cannot be dissolved until a year after its election if it rejects the candidate for prime minister, or for any reason during the last six months of the president's term of office, a state of emergency or impeachment proceedings. However, impeachment of the president is almost impossible. A charge of treason or some major crime has to be supported by one-third of Duma deputies and be verified by a Duma committee. If the committee's findings are supported by a two-thirds vote of all Duma deputies and the Supreme and Constitutional Courts, a resolution to impeach is put to the Federation Council, where it has to be passed by a two-thirds vote of all deputies. All these procedures have to be brought to a conclusion within three months.

The new Duma was nearly as divided as the old parliament had been. Table 6.1 shows the factions that were formed in the Duma in all seven of its convocations. The number of factions in the earlier convocations was higher than in the latter years. This is because of the chaotic nature of the first elections, when parties were formed quickly to compete. More factions were added after the 1993 and 1995 elections, as independent deputies and defectors from parties that had won seats formed new groupings. The benefit of this was that it gave deputies access to more resources and allowed them to take part in the distribution of committee places, which in turn gave access to yet more resources. All factions had equal rights to take part in the Council of the Duma, the Duma's organizing committee that managed the legislative agenda, and in the deal-making that saw the allocation of committee places and chairs. Places on committees were allocated in 'package' deals: each seat on a committee was ranked according to importance and allocated a number of points. Each faction was allocated a number of points according to how many members it had, which were used by leaders to purchase committee posts. This incentivised faction membership; for example, after the 1995 election many independents joined Our Home is Russia or Russia's Regions, which were created within the Duma. These incentives did not mean that factions were necessarily all that more stable or able to force voting discipline, however. Deputies still changed factions and voted as they thought fit.

What difference did the adoption of the new presidential constitution make to Russian politics? Technically, and in comparative terms, it remained (and remains) an example of a semi-presidential system since responsibility for government formation was divided between the president and parliament, as it had been since 1991 (Huskey, 1995; 1999: 35). While this semi-presidential classification was meaningless before the adoption of the new constitution, it had even less relevance afterwards. Parliament had little control over the government, only occasionally being able to force Yeltsin to change its composition by dropping a minister and able to take any independent action in the legislative arena only when autonomy was ceded by Yeltsin, as it had been in the early reform period, or when there was a contest over power that allowed for some government independence (Morgan-Jones and Schleiter, 2004; Shevchenko, 2004).

This remained true even after the 1995 Duma election and the gains made by the Communist Party of the Russian Federation (CPRF). The CPRF won enough seats to lend some deputies to the Agrarians and People's Power groupings so that they could register as factions, which gave them more control over committee formation and membership and more votes on the Duma Council and brought them close to a simple majority (the three

TABLE 6.1 Factions in the Duma

	Convocation						
	1	*2*	*3*	*4*	*5*	*6*	*7*
	1993–5	*1995–9*	*1999–2003*	*2003–7*	*2007–11*	*2011–16*	*2016–*
Liberal Democratic Party of Russia	64	49	17	30	40	56	39
Russia's Democratic Choice	64	7					
Communist Party of the Russian Federation	43	139	113	47	57	92	42
Agrarian Party	37	35					
Yabloko	27	45	20				
Women of Russia	23						
Party of Russian Unity and Accord	22						
Democratic Party of Russia	14						
Other	21						2
Independents	130	19	34	23			
Our Home is Russia		65					
Regions of Russia		44					
People's Power		41					
Union of Right Forces			29				
United Russia			237	304	315	238	343
A Just Russia				33	38	64	23
Socialist Party–Patriots of Russia				8			
No. of factions	*9*	*9*	*6*	*6*	*4*	*4*	*4*

Source: Adapted from the data at www.duma.gov.ru/about/history.

factions had 218 seats between them; see table 6.1). However, this did not translate into power in parliament. The Duma mostly acquiesced to major bills such as the budget, negotiating with rather than challenging the president. As we shall argue in chapter 8, the CPRF limited its opposition in order to make sure the parliament wasn't disbanded and so that it wouldn't lose its resources. The different electoral systems used to elect parliament and president, especially the fact that the presidential election was in a single national constituency, in which voters were forced to make a choice between the CPRF candidate (generally its leader, Gennady Zyuganov) and a non-communist (Yeltsin), meant that there was a great mismatch between the balance of power in parliament and the interests of the president and the composition of the government (Moser, 1998). Only after the August 1998 economic crisis, when Yevgenii Primakov was prime minister, was there any brief alignment of government and parliament, as Yeltsin briefly lost control of the political agenda, and this was one of the rare and brief occasions where the government gained some autonomy in proposing legislation. There was some hope that this might lead to the assertion of parliamentary power, possibly even parliamentary sovereignty (Troxel, 2003). However, as we saw in chapter 4, Yeltsin restored his control by firing Primakov and forcing his choice of prime minister – first Sergei Stepashin and then Putin – on the Duma. More generally, since he had little control of the Duma, the distance between himself and parliament led to Yeltsin using the decree powers that the new constitution gave him to rule: the government was charged with implementing presidential decrees rather than developing a legislative agenda to be implemented with parliamentary support. At most, Yeltsin was frustrated rather than challenged by the Duma, which, especially after 1995, was only able to delay and create deadlock in the legislative process (Remington, 2001a).

The legal constitutional form of the system was thus less important than the way that power was used by the president, and this was continuous from 1991. Yeltsin's use of patronage and the expansion of the office of the president through the creation of more overlapping departments and agencies associated with it created what has been called a 'superpresidential' system or a 'hegemonic' presidentialism or 'patronal presidency' (Fish, 2000, 2001; Willerton and Shulus, 1995; Hale, 2006a, 2010). McFaul (2001a: 312) is unusual in arguing that the adoption of the 1993 Constitution marks the start of superpresidentialism. For most analysts, Russian presidentialism, is not defined solely by the constitutional powers of the institution. There is little to distinguish between the various different labels that have been attached to it, and the differences are of emphasis rather than substance. The use of the prefix 'super' indicates that the presidency has not been constrained constitutionally by rival political institutions in the way of 'semi-presidentialist' systems. The idea of a 'hegemonic' presidency asserts the primacy of the president and also that the character of the incumbent sets the mood of

Russian politics; it is hegemonic in that it is the only institution capable of organizing effective political alliances (for good or ill) and can break up any efforts to construct 'counter-hegemonic' alliances. The idea of a 'patronal' presidency highlights the importance of personalistic politics, of the use of patronage and informal political ties. None of these labels, however, is mutually exclusive; they all define the powers of the presidency in the Yeltsin period as shaped both by constitutional and formal powers and by the informal powers of patronage that can be used to construct a power base. And all of the various labels attached to the presidency under Yeltsin point to the same problem: it is hard to see what makes Russia's political leader powerful: formal powers, informal powers, the absence of constraints from other institutions, or something else? This problem was to become particularly astute under Putin.

Putin and the presidency

The increase in the formal powers for the presidency did not particularly add to or detract from the quality of democracy in Russia after 1993: it was low before the adoption of the new constitution and remained so afterwards. At most, the president's new constitutional powers could be said to have stabilized a polity that was at best weakly democratic because they resolved some of the ambiguities that existed in the relationship between president and parliament which led to the October 1993 crisis (McFaul, 2001a; Moser, 2001). Yeltsin was unable to do more with the presidency despite the immense formal powers that he had because of the weakness of the Russian state and because of the fragmentation of power at other levels of the political system – most notably the regional level – and in parliament. This led to the bargaining over access to resources between competing economic and political interests noted above and in chapter 4. Yeltsin stood in the middle and tried to bring together enough of these competing interests to ensure his political survival and later to control the succession process. This had left him vulnerable both personally and politically. Changes beyond his control, such as the economic crisis in 1998, broke his hold over the various interest groups and jeopardized his tenure as president (there were threats to impeach him from the Duma in the spring of 1999) and his control over appointing his successor.

Putin's presidency was dedicated to weakening threats to his position and to ensuring that events beyond his control in international politics or economics did not create conditions that threatened his hold on office or his power to control his succession. He did not change the constitution: making the necessary arrangements would have required negotiation both with the Duma, which at this time still had a CPRF plurality, and with regional leaders, and this would have meant compromise and the ceding of power to other institutions. Instead the Putin 'project' called on a combination of the formal powers of the presidency and Putin's own personal image to suppress open political conflict and to make elite participation in the latter less attractive. Once this control was achieved, Putin used it to consolidate his position further by extending his power through United Russia's growing dominance in the Duma and over regional politics. We have already seen in chapter 4 how Putin achieved control. Making use of his personal popularity, he attacked and subdued oligarchs, by weakening their command of the media and threatening their economic interests, and reigned in regional leaders by creating above them a new layer of administration, the seven new federal districts headed by presidential representatives, and then by supervising their appointment. He consolidated relations over the Duma and public politics through the creation of United Russia and other 'project parties' (see also chapter 10).

Regional leaders were compensated in 2000 and 2002 by the creation of the State Council and Legislative Council, which respectively gathered together regional chief executives and the heads of regional legislatures in consultative bodies under the president. These new councils formalized and regularized the types of co-option in which Yeltsin had engaged informally through the politics of institutional redundancy. Two other councils joined them later. In 2005, the Public Chamber was established as a means of linking the president to civil society. Its creation was in part a response to the Orange Revolution in Ukraine, where civil society organizations had been part of the movement that had stopped the incumbent president's anointed successor from taking office, and it was designed to give civil society organizations direct access to the president. As a result, the Public Chamber was also arguably designed to isolate the Duma from such organizations, which would no longer have to lobby political parties (see chapter 8).

Finally, and also in 2005, Putin created a 41-member Presidential Council for Priority Projects, chaired initially by himself (later the post was given to Medvedev as part of the manoeuvrings to set him up as presidential successor). This council was supposed to advise on priority projects in education, health, agriculture and housing and had a dedicated budget and income stream for these projects. It was made up of selected government ministers and the head of the Duma, as well as selected members from business and the administration. Within the areas for which it was given responsibility, it worked in parallel to the government as an alternative source of legislative acts and a means of sending out orders to regional authorities (Oversloot, 2007: 62). Like the other councils and the Public Chamber, it changed the relationship between the president and the government and other political institutions without actually changing the constitution and was an example of what Sakwa (2010a: 192) calls 'para-constitutionalism' (supplemental, existing in tandem, but also false and disordered constitutional development) and innovations that went against the 'spirit of the 1993 constitution, but played important integrative functions'.

Putin's para-constitutional additions to the Russian polity were less about co-opting competing elites and more concerned with filling gaps in the public administration and dealing with problems in other areas of the political system, such as the weak bond between political parties and civil society, which meant that the latter was not integrated into the political system through Putin's supporting party. However, they had something of the same effect as Yeltsin's politics of institutional redundancy. They bound sections of the elite closer to Putin and rendered the conduct of government dependent on the president to the detriment of the constitution (Sakwa, 2010a: 195). Consequently, Putin's actions consolidated the power of the presidency but highlighted the problem that we noted above which goes to the heart of contemporary Russian politics: whether formal or informal powers are the basis of presidential power. What is the relationship between these two sets of power and these two forms of politics? Under Yeltsin it was possible to distinguish to some degree between their use. Presidential power was based on aligning competing groups, but Yeltsin's actions were contested within the constitutional order by other institutions. Formal, constitutional politics was supplemented by informal power. Yeltsin was able to nullify the threat to his tenure from competing institutions by developing informal political alliances and using patronage, but other constitutionally defined institutions still limited his power. Rivals and opponents had access to these other institutions and could use them to contest and question both Yeltsin's constitutional powers and informal practices. The result was something of a stalemate in terms of moving Russia forward economically and politically, but there was a form of pluralism in the system. Yeltsin had to construct support for his positions from elite groups and between the institutions of the presidency, the parliament and regional governors. Although none of these, even in the wake of the August 1998 crisis, was able to remove Yeltsin, they could organize against him and could imagine that they might take power or at least have some small impact, as when parliament was able to influence the composition of the government by pressuring him to drop a minister (Morgan-Jones and Schleiter, 2004).

This competition for power and the pluralism that it allowed was eroded with the containment of the oligarchs (especially the breaking of their hold over the media), the installation of presidential representatives in the regions and the end of elected governorships, and the control of the Duma, which began after 2000 and was completed by the victory of United Russia in the 2004 election. As can be seen in table 6.1, the number of factions in the Duma declined after 1999, when United Russia and the CPRF initially did a deal on the distribution of committee responsibilities. However, the merger of Unity and the Fatherland–All Russia factions to form United Russia, and the defection to it of independent deputies, gave the party a majority of 237 deputies. United Russia overthrew the package agreement that Unity had made with the CPRF and imposed a new arrangement of committee responsibilities. United Russia's dominance continued after subsequent elections. It never lost its majority, even after its poor performance in 2011 (see table 6.1). After the 2003 election, United Russia could also generally rely on support from A Just Russia as well as from the Liberal Democratic Party of Russia (LDPR). This ensured that it took control of the most important committees in the Duma. Opposition parties and the CPRF were not cut out completely but were given less prestigious committee roles (Chaisty, 2012: 94).

The dominance of United Russia in the Duma and changes in the way that the Federation Council was formed meant that parliament became a more passive body that has increasingly seemed to take independent action only insofar as it anticipates Putin's legislative wishes. Early on in the

TABLE 6.2 Control over the legislative process

	Convocation					
	2	*3*	*4*	*5*	*6*	*7*
	1995–9	*1999–2003*	*2003–7*	*2007–11*	*2011–16*	*2016–Oct 2017*
Number of bills submitted to the Duma	4,034	4,323	4,808	4,323	7,129	1,295
Number of bills adopted by the Duma for consideration	3,174	3,355	3,706	3,355	6,098	1,263
Percentage of bills submitted adopted for consideration	78.6	77.6	77.7	77.0	85.5	97.5
Number of laws declined or returned to the Duma:						
Total	441	102	37	102	24	1
By Federation Council	141	61	27	61	23	0
By president	187	31	7	31	1	1
Number of laws adopted by Duma	1,045	781	1,087	781	2,200	457
Number of laws signed by president	734	731	1,076	772	2,196	439

Source: Calculated from data at www.duma.gov.ru/legislative/statistics/.

life of United Russia there was some talk of it taking greater control over parliament and using this to develop policy agendas of its own (Remington, 2001b: 306–7). This talk came to nothing, however, and as it died away the Duma, thanks largely to changes in the party and electoral systems, became just another cog in the government machine – less a check and balance to the executive and more of a handmaiden. Table 6.2 gives some idea of this. The number of bills proposed to the Duma and adopted for consideration (i.e., given a reading) have increased under Putin, especially since 2012. The number that have been rejected by either the Federation Council or the president has decreased, again particularly since 2012. This is in marked contrast to the second convocation of the Duma, when Yeltsin was faced with a CPRF plurality and was forced to reject a large number of bills and delayed signing many others. Putin, by contrast, has rejected few bills, and most of them move quickly through the Federation Council and are signed off by the president.

As the Duma and Federation Council became more integrated into the regime and Putin's power grew in the 2000s, it became harder to see where he was ruling using the formal powers of his office and where informally. The lines between the two became obscured to an even greater extent than under Yeltsin, even though Putin and Medvedev both publicly preached the importance of the rule of law. Putin's immense personal popularity and the image of him projected by the Kremlin as national leader reinforced the blurring of lines. The constraints on intra-elite competition that followed Putin's actions against oligarchs and regional leaders and the evolution of United Russia as a ruling party meant that access to power was simplified and powers of patronage became more concentrated. Where Yeltsin had bargained patronage for support, Putin rewarded loyal supporters. Under Yeltsin, political competition was a means of showing that you were powerful – that you commanded resources and social support – and needed to be incorporated into the presidential team. Under Putin, political competition evolved into a contest to prove that you deserved reward because of your loyalty. The result was that the presidency became more 'patronal', as a transformation was effected from 'a "competing-pyramid" system, where multiple regional and corporate patronage pyramids actively competed for support, to a "single-pyramid" system, where the president has effectively combined the most important lower-level patronal networks into one large nationwide political machine' (Hale, 2010: 35).

Putin's popularity after 2000 was both a source of this transformation and a product of it. His ability to command electoral majorities for himself and for United Russia meant that his position was not open to challenge from any other politician and allowed him to be cast as the only guarantor of political stability and a bulwark against official incompetence and corruption. The most visible aspect of this to Western audiences has been the staged annual displays of machismo: riding horses while stripped to the waist,

Leader as action man: Putin submerges on board a mini-submarine to explore a shipwreck in the Black Sea

tranquillizing 'wild' tigers in Siberia, wreck-diving to 'find' ancient artefacts, catching 'huge' pike, etc. Russian audiences have seen Putin being politically macho as well. He has routinely appeared on TV holding ministers to task or humiliating regional leaders or oligarchs, and he has held an annual phone-in that lasts for hours to display both physical fortitude and command of the details of Russian politics. Cumulatively these displays have created a sense that there is no one else like Putin – 'a strong man, a man who doesn't drink … a man who won't run away', as the dreadful pop song 'Takogo kak Putin' ('[I want] a man like Putin') puts it.* Economic good fortune added to this image of a provider of stability. The popularity of both Putin and United Russia in the polls in 2004 and 2008 was based on economic growth, as Treisman (2011) and McAllister and White (2008b) have shown. Treisman argues that Yeltsin might have enjoyed similar levels of popularity had the economy performed under him at the same level as it did before the 2008 crisis, so we should be careful about ascribing too much to Putin's personality on its own. However, Putin's demeanor – serious, sober, tough, no-nonsense and phlegmatic – and his political opacity – his unwillingness to tie himself to anything but very broad policy positions publicly – made it easy to link his public image to economic success.

The net effect of Putin's popularity and the construction of a national political machine was that it became nearly impossible for elite members to

---

* Available at http://youtu.be/zk_VszbZa_s with English subtitles.

think about defecting from this system and engaging in open political conflict against him: his dominance and the dominance of institutions such as United Russia that supported him would have led to defeat. Putin thus constructed what was (for him) in effect a virtuous political circle: because no one defected from his political machine, Putin and institutions aligned to him continued to dominate and to appear indomitable, so that defection was not an option. This had an effect on the nature of the opposition. Opposition, as we shall see in chapter 8, is generally led or symbolized by figures from the Yeltsin era on the one hand and 'outsiders' on the other. The 'outsiders' were people who had never had a place in the Putin system at all, either because they are too extreme in their views (for example, Pussy Riot) or (at least initially) because they were too junior and insignificant (for example, Alexei Navalny) to be co-opted. Once prominent, these outsiders have been doomed to remain in opposition. Yeltsin-era politicians, such as Mikhail Kasyanov (minister for finance under Yeltsin in 1999 and then Putin's prime minister from 2000 to 2004) or Boris Nemtsov (governor of Nizhny Novgorod in the early 1990s, deputy prime minister in 1997–8, assassinated in Moscow in February 2015), were squeezed out of office by Putin in favour of 'his own' people. In some cases, such as that of Kasyanov, their overthrow came as their allies in other areas fell from grace; Khodorkovsky's demise heralded Kasyanov's removal from office. Under Yeltsin removal from office was not necessarily permanent. A period in opposition could be followed by a return to office and then to opposition once more as Yeltsin's political needs changed. Nemtsov is a case in point. He was a supporter of Yeltsin during the last days of the USSR, a critic in the mid-1990s when he was supported as governor of Nizhny Novgorod by liberal critics of Yeltsin, and then a member of government. This has not been the pattern under Putin: opposing Putin following political loss has been a much harder decision to make as time has gone on, and the tendency has been to praise Putin rather than to oppose him. Vladislav Surkov, the Kremlin ideologue and author of the 'sovereign democracy' thesis (see chapter 5), who 'resigned' as deputy prime minister for economic modernization in May 2013 after being caught up in a battle over economic policy, still insisted after his removal from office that Putin was a 'white knight' sent by God just in time to save Russia (cited in Kolesnikov, 2013).

Cumulatively, the blend of personal popularity, the blurring of the lines between formal and informal politics, and the cowing of elite groups has created the impression that Putin has created a self-perpetuating *sistema* (system; see Ledeneva, 2013). Like the idea of superpresidentialism, the idea of a Putin 'system' is linked to the Soviet past. Where superpresidentialism is supposed to mirror the CPSU's duplication of government administrative structures, the idea of Putin's *sistema* is seen as replicating the informal Soviet polity that existed in parallel to the formal system of the party-state. Like the informal Soviet polity, the *sistema* is based on personal networks and ties and both undermines and is regulated by the formal political system.

The formal system is undermined because (and as we have already seen in chapter 1) the consolidation of power under Putin did not produce any significant improvement in governance by the Russian state. Corruption, the glue that frequently binds together informal networks by ensuring the mutual allegiance of network members, remained a problem under Putin. As with the informal Soviet polity, the parallel informal polity of the *sistema* cannot replace the formal polity, and Putin has a choice about how to use the latter – i.e., the political system and the responsibilities that are defined by the constitution and law – to regulate informal politics. Two sets of rules, two different ways of organizing political life, thus exist in Russian politics (see chapter 12 for more discussion of this).

Managing two sets of rules is a difficult business. This was highlighted as Putin came to the end of his second term as president in 2007–8. There was considerable manoeuvring for position in the run-up to the succession. Putin was able to control this using a combination of his formal and informal powers. However, the fact that he had to stand down still caused problems. The creation of the tandem, with Medvedev as president and Putin as prime minister, never settled into an unambiguous division of powers and responsibilities in either the formal or the informal sphere. Medvedev fulfilled the responsibilities of head of state that are formally those of the president. He attended major state and international events as representative of the Russian people, saw visiting heads of state, and represented Russia at international gatherings such as the G8 summits. However, although Medvedev was 'in office', it was never clear that he was 'in power', in large part because the informal system seemed to deny him substantive power. As a result, speculation was constant between 2008 and Putin's re-election to the presidency in 2012 as to what the relationship was between the two men. There were hopes that Medvedev represented the rise to prominence of a reformist wing from among the Putin factions, and that this rise would be translated into actual power using the office and formal capacity of the presidency. Medvedev's calls for modernization and for the end of 'legal nihilism' reflected Putin's own calls to control corruption, improve government and develop new sectors of the economy, but they were also a challenge to the balance that guaranteed some stability between formal and informal politics. But Medvedev never developed his calls for modernization and 'rule of law' (rather than 'rule by law' – the use of law to punish political disloyalty) into a concrete and comprehensive legislative agenda. That would have required him to take on Putin as prime minister, something he was either unable or unwilling (probably both) to do, and to command the loyalty of United Russia in the Duma. It would also have meant dealing with the tensions that exist between formal and informal politics. The outcome of such a move cannot be foreseen, so it is likely that both Medvedev and Putin were wary of making such a move. Recent historical precedents are not favourable; Putin has on several occasions stated that it was the way that reform developed that caused the collapse of the USSR, in particular that putting political reform ahead of economic reform was a mistake. Medvedev's speeches as president questioned the deferral of political reform in favour of securing economic change, and many of his advisors denied it outright, arguing that the problems of the Russian economy are at least as much political as economic problems. Making an argument is not the same as winning it, although it did some damage to the popularity of both Putin and Medvedev and to the electoral fortunes of United Russia (see chapters 5 and 10). In the end, Putin's retaking the presidency resolved the increasingly public display of the tensions of the 'dual state' that resulted from having a president with formal powers and a prime minister with informal powers. To Russians fearful of the future in the wake of the 2008 economic crisis, this was not a resolution of the contradictions inherent in the Russian polity but a guarantee that they would endure. The 2011 Duma election and the 2012 presidential election were marked by higher levels of public protest than before, protest that served only to highlight the gap that exists between the right to free and fair elections that are supposed to be guaranteed by the constitution and the corrupt practices that the regime uses to ensure 'correct' electoral outcomes (see chapter 8).

Conclusion

The development of the Russian presidency and parliament have shown many of the faults that are associated with presidentialism generally. Both Yeltsin and Putin have portrayed themselves as leaders of the whole nation, with the result that those parts of the population that did not vote for them or see themselves as represented by the elected president became alienated from the political system. Thanks to his popularity, this was less a problem for Putin during his first two terms in office, but it became a problem for him when Medvedev was president and offered what many hoped was an alternative vision of Russia. Coalitions under Yeltsin were unstable, but, again, this was less of a problem for Putin thanks to his actions to control elites. However, this did not support democratic politics; instead it hardened into the *sistema* and made the divide between constitutional norms and actual political practices more pronounced. Putin's actions against elite groups reined in the 'winner' groups who had used their positions and wealth under Yeltsin to weaken reform and transfer state resources to themselves. Putin upset this relationship, but only insofar as it posed a threat to him and presidential power. Those elite members who were loyal to him were not dispossessed and retained access to power and wealth. The position of elites thus became simultaneously more and less secure. The end of open competition meant that loyalty was rewarded, but the capacity of the Kremlin to punish disloyalty was also far greater. Oligarchs and other elite members who fell foul of Putin fell far harder and further than they did under Yeltsin.

Few, if any, of these developments were solely because of some inherent fault in presidentialism, however. Other institutions – the parliament, political parties and regional governments – could not act as a counterweight to the office of president and could not organize effectively either informally or democratically to constrain it. The presidency expanded to fill the vacuum created by the wider institutional failings of the Russian polity so that its parameters extended far beyond those set by any formal governing rules and powers. As an institution it has become something more than an office of state. As one Russian analyst, Viktor Kuvaldin (1998: 15), put it, the Russian presidency 'is at the same time more simple and more complex' than other presidencies; it is 'simpler because it is more primitive, acting in an under-developed political system and a shapeless society ... [and] more complex because it was not established in a firm legal and institutional framework; it is not yet an institution, but a phenomenon.'

7
Russian Federalism

Introduction

The reconstruction of the Russian political system after the collapse of the USSR was complicated by the legacies of Soviet federalism. Post-communist Russia emerged out of a federation, the Soviet Union, and was itself the successor state to one of the latter's federal republics, the Russian Soviet Federal Socialist Republic (RSFSR). This posed several problems for Boris Yeltsin, problems that he did not manage to solve and which he therefore bequeathed to his successor, Vladimir Putin. If Russia was to be democratized in the wake of Soviet collapse, it needed to be kept together as a geographical entity even as centrifugal forces pulled the USSR apart. Lines of authority had to be established so that policy was implemented across Russia and state capacity had to be developed, both through the creation of a national bureaucracy that shared a common culture and through the development of things such as common systems of legal regulation, accountability and taxation. Equal rights needed to be established for citizens living in different parts of the country if a common democratic citizenship was to be established.

These tasks were not accomplished successfully. Reform of Russian federalism and regional politics came to involve a series of trade-offs. Russia was kept together by the development of what came to be called 'asymmetrical federalism', in which its regions and republics possessed different rights and responsibilities to the federation as a whole. As a result, the powers that local elites had varied enormously, and Russia ceased to exist as a single political and economic space as different political and economic regimes were installed across the regions and republics. This inhibited the development of the capacity of the national state, but it also weakened elite interest in secession: why strive for independence from Russia when you could already act independently within it? The preservation of territorial integrity which should have been a precondition for the development of the functionality of the state instead helped to prop up Yeltsin's regime. Since he conceded powers to regional and republican leaders, they supported him, or at least didn't work as actively as they might have done to achieve his demise. The different powers and rights those leaders had also meant that they were often divided as an interest group, so they didn't pose as consolidated a threat to Yeltsin as they might have done. As a result, the organization of post-communist Russian federalism and regional politics worked more to the advantage of regime building and stabilization than it did to state development.

The crisis over his succession weakened Yeltsin's support, as we have discussed in chapter 6. Putin's ascendancy saw reforms of regional politics as the powers of regional leaders were changed to curb their autonomy. Regional and republican leaders' influence over national politics was limited, and they were, for a time, transformed into appointees of the president. A new system of federal districts under presidential representatives was put in place to create an additional layer of administrative oversight and control. On the one hand, these changes were supposed to restore some measure of unity to Russia's political and economic space under the direction of the central state. On the other hand, and increasingly over the 2000s, the changes were a means of ensuring the political loyalty of the regions and the maintenance of the Putin regime. Ensuring loyalty and creating a more functional system of administration were not necessarily compatible aims, and very often the former seems to have been more important than the latter. Consequently, the changes that Putin has put in place have been less impressive in substance than they have been on paper.

Regional politics under Yeltsin

As it disintegrated, the USSR was riven by a clash over who held sovereign power – the Soviet 'centre' or the constituent republics. This clash between republics and centre was replicated in the RSFSR. The RSFSR was made up of both regions (called *oblast'*, *okrug* and *krai*) and republics (when we use the terms 'provinces' or 'provincial' in this chapter we are referring to both regions and republics; for a helpful guide to the terms used to describe units of the Russian Federation and their leaders, see Reisinger, 2013: xxi–xxv). Table 7.1 lists the republics and regions of Russia as they existed in 2016. The most notable changes between 1991 and 2016 were the merging of autonomous regions with the oblasts whose territory they shared under Putin and the addition of Crimea and Sevastopol to the list after their annexation in 2014. Neither of the latter additions is regarded as legitimate by the majority of the international community. Russia's provinces were put into eight federal districts under Putin.

The main difference between a region and a republic is that republics have a titular non-Russian nationality in their population, though this population is in the majority only in the republics marked in bold in table 7.1; elsewhere ethnic Russians predominate or there is a mix of ethnic groups. Republics also have rights to secede from the federation, which regions do not. The Soviet legacy, therefore, was that the subject units of the new Russian Federation were not equal. The republics had more rights than oblasts and a potential source of leverage in that they could press for independence from

TABLE 7.1   Federal districts and subject units of the Russian Federation, 2016 (republics marked in bold have majority titular nationality populations)

Federal district	Subject unit
Central	Belgorod (oblast')
	Bryansk (oblast')
	Ivanovo (oblast')
	Kaluga (oblast')
	Kostroma (oblast')
	Kursk (oblast')
	Lipetsk (oblast')
	Moscow (city)
	Moscow (oblast')
	Oryol (oblast')
	Ryazan (oblast')
	Smolensk (oblast')
	Tambov (oblast')
	Tula (oblast')
	Tver (oblast')
	Vladimir (oblast')
	Voronezh (oblast')
	Yaroslavl (oblast')
Far Eastern	Amur (oblast')
	Chukotka (autonomous okrug)
	Jewish (autonomous oblast')
	Kamchatka (krai)
	Khabarovsk (krai)
	Magadan (oblast')
	Primorskii (krai)
	Sakha (Yakutia) (republic)
	Sakhalin (oblast')
North Caucasian	**Chechen** (republic)
	Dagestan (republic)
	Ingushetia (republic)
	Kabardino-Balkar (republic)
	Karachay-Cherkessia (republic)
	North Ossetia (republic)
	Stavropol (krai)

Federal district	Subject unit
Northwestern	Arkhangelsk (oblast')
	Kaliningrad (oblast')
	Karelia (republic)
	Komi (republic)
	Leningrad (oblast')
	Murmansk (oblast')
	Nenets Autonomous Okrug
	Novgorod (oblast')
	Pskov (oblast')
	St Petersburg (city)
	Vologda (oblast')
Siberian	Altai (krai)
	Altai (republic)
	Buryatia (republic)
	Irkutsk (oblast')
	Kemerovo (oblast')
	Khakassia (republic)
	Krasnoyarsk (krai)
	Novosibirsk (oblast')
	Omsk (oblast')
	Tomsk (oblast')
	Tuva (republic)
	Zabaykalskii (krai)
Southern	Adygea (republic)
	Astrakhan (oblast')
	Crimea (republic)
	Kalmykia (republic)
	Krasnodar (krai)
	Rostov (oblast')
	Sevastopol (city)
	Volgograd (oblast')
Urals	Chelyabinsk (oblast')
	Khanty-Mansi (autonomous okrug)
	Kurgan (oblast')
	Sverdlovsk (oblast')
	Tyumen (oblast')
	Yamalo-Nenets (autonomous okrug)

Federal district	Subject unit
Volga	Bashkortostan (republic)
	Chuvashia (republic)
	Kirov (oblast')
	Mari El (republic)
	Mordovia (republic)
	Nizhny Novgorod (oblast')
	Orenburg (oblast')
	Penza (oblast')
	Perm (krai)
	Samara (oblast')
	Saratov (oblast')
	Tatarstan (republic)
	Udmurtia (republic)
	Ulyanovsk (oblast')

Russia. There was also an expectation that they would be led by the ethnic elite of the titular non-Russian nationality. This expectation, and the idea that the republics within the new Russian Federation had special rights, had been recognized by Yeltsin before the collapse of the Soviet state. As part of his struggle to weaken the central Soviet government and win the support of the leaders of the RSFSR's republics against Gorbachev, Yeltsin had encouraged the constituent Russian republics in 1990 to 'take as much sovereignty as you can swallow' (Ross, 2002: 17–28).

The differences between the regions and republics meant that it was always going to be a political struggle to establish a new constitutional settlement that bound them to a new Russian state. Soviet collapse saw the disintegration of central authority. Local elites in the provinces, where political mobilization was harder to achieve, generally survived and, after a fashion, thrived. Provincial political elites transferred from the CPSU into local council and other administrative structures, and provincial economic elites took part in the 'spontaneous privatization' of state property to ensure their power and status. In the early 1990s most regional governments were under the control of old elites; an estimated 80 to 90 per cent of local officials retained their posts after the fall of communism (White and McAllister, 1996: 107). Political and economic elites were closely interlinked. Due to the nature of the planned economy, they had worked closely with one another under the Soviet system and had a mutual interest in protecting their position against any reform initiatives coming from Moscow that threatened their tenure or dubiously acquired property rights.

Initial efforts at re-creating the Russian federal state

The need to enforce the writ of the central government was not lost on Yeltsin after the failure of the August 1991 coup. One of his first actions was to appoint 'presidential representatives', *polpredy*, to the republics and regions to ensure compliance with Russian government laws and decrees (Clark, 1998: 30–1, 37). This was an attempt to create what is often called the 'executive' or 'presidential' 'vertical', a hierarchy of administrative bodies responsible to the president that is supposed to ensure the implementation of government policy. It didn't work. Presidential representatives lacked administrative capacity and status, and it was unclear how they were to enact oversight. Many of them had no administrative experience or connections with local political and economic elites, who closed ranks against them. They were hamstrung by the fact that the relationship between the president, the government and the republics and regions had not been adequately codified after the fall of the USSR. A federal treaty was signed in March 1992 by most of the republics and all of the regions (Chechnya, which had declared itself independent in September 1991, and Tatarstan, which wanted greater autonomy, refused to sign). Tatarstan, which had a Tatar ethnic majority and a unified ethnic elite under the leadership of President Mintimir Shamiyev, was able to resist pressure from Moscow to a far greater extent than all the other republics and without the open conflict that broke out in Chechnya (see below). The new treaty allowed the republics the trappings of statehood – constitutions, parliaments, presidents, etc. – whereas the regions were headed by governors and had councils and charters. However, the treaty was too vague to regulate properly the relationship between centre and periphery for long. Republics and regions tried to negotiate concessions for themselves; the regions complained that the rights enjoyed by the republics were unjust and threatened to proclaim themselves republics and the republics threatened to secede from the federation unless they were granted greater concessions and economic autonomy.

The power struggle in Moscow between Yeltsin and the parliament made this administrative mess worse. Local elites took advantage of the weakness of central government to do what they pleased. Some regional leaders aped republics and tried to claim sovereignty rights to increase their bargaining powers in these negotiations. President and parliament were played off against each other, and the power of local elites and industrialists over the regions and republics was strengthened at the expense of central government. Yeltsin was forced to concede that governors should only be appointed with the agreement of local Soviets, which had been elected in 1990 and were under the control of old elites. As a result, the majority of governors were chairmen of Soviets and members of the *nomenklatura* (Slider, 1994: 256–7). These governors had little sympathy with the reformers in Moscow. Taxes and contributions to the federal budget went unpaid, and government economic policy was flaunted as elites cushioned their populations from the effects of market reform by subverting the market and by aiding the takeover of their enterprises by local industrialists.

Asymmetrical federalism

The lack of clarity over the legal relationship between the centre and provinces, and the ability of local elites to maintain their influence, weakened efforts to reform the Russian state through economic transformation. The new constitution that was adopted after the destruction of the parliament in 1993 did not alter this fundamentally (Gel'man and Senatova, 1995). New regional representative institutions – dumas and assemblies – were set up, but with fewer powers than the old Soviets. Regional governors and republican presidents were empowered to decide how regional assemblies were to be elected and the number of deputies that were to serve in them; they also had the right to veto any decisions made. Electoral malpractice was rife in the elections to the dumas and assemblies from 1994. Gerrymandering and the distribution of a disproportionate number of seats to rural areas were particularly common. As a result, many regional dumas and assemblies became packed with local officials, or their clients, from local 'parties of power'. Yeltsin buoyed up the power of regional leaders by declaring a moratorium on their re-election until after the presidential election of 1996 so that they might support him. Once secure in office, they did little to promote democracy in the provinces; political parties were weak and local industries and media were suborned.

The new constitution also extended the power of the regions and republics into the national legislatures, as the new upper house of parliament, the Federation Council, was made up of two elected representatives from each of the constituent units of the federation. The deputies elected were closely tied to local political machines. In 1995, elections were replaced by the automatic selection of regional governors and republican presidents and heads of regional and republican legislatures (this has since been changed; see below). This gave provincial leaders a means of negotiating directly with the government and presidential administration over policy.

The hold of private interests over local administration was so great in some places, such as the Republic of Kalmykia under President Kirsan Ilyumzhinov, that boundaries between private interests and political power were eroded completely and provinces were run like fiefdoms. This was the beginning of what is often termed 'sub-national authoritarianism' (Gel'man, 2010, 2011; Gel'man and Ryzhenkov, 2011; Golosov, 2011a; Ross, 2011). The development of sub-national authoritarianism was uneven and depended to a great extent on whether local leaders had resources that they could mobilize to monopolize political development in their province. The more they had these resources, which included access to easily exploitable economic resources such as oil or a non-Russian ethnic group that they could mobilize in their support, the more likely it was that a form of sub-national authoritarianism would develop. The other necessary condition was the weakness of federal authorities and/or their unwillingness to get involved in provincial politics. Where federal authorities were weak, as they often were in the 1990s, or where they tolerated provincial subversion of democracy, as occurred in both the 1990s and later under Putin, sub-national authoritarianism had space to develop. This did not mean that provincial leaders were always powerful, however. Rather than building up local states that were highly functional, they controlled how local regimes developed. In this sense, provincial politics replicated the problems of Russian politics more widely. Nor, as we shall see below, did it mean that provincial politicians had the means to resist encroachments from the centre: their power was limited to management of their relationships with Moscow, not their collective interests, and the management of politics in their own province.

The differences that had been allowed to develop among regions and republics created a system of asymmetrical federalism. Federalism is not supposed to work where the rights and obligations of federal units are mismatched (Ross, 2012). Indeed, asymmetrical federalism is often seen as a recipe for the disintegration of a federation: where differences become too pronounced there will be no incentive for units with fewer rights or more obligations to continue as members.

The Russian example shows that asymmetry will not necessarily lead to collapse. Only Chechnya sought to exit the Russian Federation, and it was a special case. Unlike the situation with many other republics, the majority of Chechnya's population were from the titular ethnic group – i.e., they were Chechens – and, thanks to the collapse of the USSR, it has an international border. These factors combined with a historical grievance and local power struggles to drive the republic towards breaking with Moscow. Chechnya had a history of resistance to the Russian state in the nineteenth century. Moreover, the Chechens had been unfairly charged with collaboration with the Germans and deported at the end of the Second World War to Central Asia. Following their return to the republic after Stalin's death, Chechnya became an ethnically homogeneous republic. This gave the Chechens an historical identity that was antagonistic towards Russia, although that identity alone was probably not enough to make the republic unique in its drive to resist becoming part of the new Russian Federation. Identity became a factor in pushing Chechnya towards secession, as it was a powerful means of mobilizing support in the struggle over who should have power in the republic as Soviet power declined. This struggle was based on divisions within Chechnya between low-lying and mountainous regions, the latter being much less integrated into the wider Soviet economy, and between the old Soviet elite in the republic and new political forces. Chechnya's native party elite was weaker than those in other republics that had been part of

Chechen fighters with a downed Russian helicopter, 1994

the RSFSR and less able to control conflict and marshal secessionist pressures to their own ends – to use them as a means of ensuring their continued domination of the republic's polity as a part of the Russian Federation. Consequently, moves towards political independence began as *perestroika* provided an opportunity for ethnic mobilization and the reassertion of cultural ethnic identity. These fed into a local struggle for power and were radicalized as the republic asserted its right in 1991 to secede from the USSR (Hughes, 2007: 1–38; Evangelista, 2002: 11–20).

The Russian government was unable to prevent Chechnya from achieving a *de facto* independence, despite Yeltsin's declaration of a state of emergency in the republic. Chechnya's leader, Dzhokhar Dudayev, a former Soviet air force general, refused to negotiate with Moscow unless his presidency and the republic's rights to self-determination were recognized. At this stage the Chechen drive for independence was based on a nationalism that was relatively secular, despite the fact that the people are Muslim. Despite the assertion of independence, struggles continued between factions within Chechnya and led to a breakdown of law and order in the republic. Dudayev lacked sufficient control to make negotiations for a settlement with Moscow effective. Criminality – some of which may have been instigated by Russian security forces and which certainly involved Russian organized crime – helped Russia to isolate the republic from international support. The inability to negotiate a settlement, together with encouragement from factions within the Russian government who believed that the suppression of separatism in Chechnya would restore Yeltsin's popularity, led Russia to invade the republic in December 1994 (Hughes, 2007: 76–81). The first war went badly for Russia. It ended in 1996 with a ceasefire that deferred a final settlement on Chechnya's status but recognized its autonomy. Unfortunately, it had also contributed to the radicalization of many of Chechnya's fighters, for whom the conflict had become a religious war. Radical Islam helped to perpetuate the destabilization of Chechnya thereafter and was one of the reasons behind the Russian decision to reinvade in 1999 after the Moscow apartment bombings. This second war brought Chechnya back into the Russian Federation as a republic, albeit at the cost of installing vicious local warlords to the Chechen presidency.

Chechnya aside, 'asymmetrical federalism' provided a means for central government and provincial leaderships to barter with one another, and relations were increasingly codified through bilateral treaties between Moscow and local leaders. These treaties were initially used to avoid conflict with republics, but their use grew in 1995–6 as Yeltsin bid for support before the 1996 presidential election, and they were signed with oblasts and krais. Just over half of the regions and republics had signed treaties with Moscow by the end of 1998. Most of the agreements imposed a cost on the central state, as they frequently included tax exemptions.

The signing of bilateral treaties was a success for Yeltsin in that it ensured his re-election, but it made a mockery of the idea that Russia was a democratic federation under which there was legal equality among federal units. It also made the administration of Russia harder. Tax exemptions contributed to the fiscal crisis that threatened the central government throughout the 1990s and which was to become actual in 1998. The rule of law was diminished as bilateral treaties empowered provincial leaders to arrange local politics to their advantage irrespective of constitutional order. For example, the treaty signed with Sverdlovsk oblast' gave it the right to form an independent civil service, agreed to the governor's authority to hire and fire holders of federal posts, and allowed the oblast' to suspend central government and ministerial acts (Ross, 2002: 42).

The flipside of these negative dimensions of the treaties and asymmetry is that they helped resolve some separatist tensions and provided a structure through which provincial leaders could negotiate with the central government. Russian federalism became asymmetric as relations between centre and provinces varied so greatly, but it was also a form of 'contract federalism' (Ross, 2012: 143–4). Asymmetry was thus both destabilizing, in that it weakened an already weak state and enabled many Russian regional and republican leaders to create authoritarian polities within Russia, and stabilizing, in that it was the means by which central and provincial politicians came to agreement over how the country was to be ruled. Yeltsin's re-election as president in 1996 was followed by the election of regional and republican heads of administration. This made them less reliant on the central administration for their positions, and the relationship between centre and periphery shifted further to one of 'political interaction' (Gel'man, 2000: 101). This was helped by a relatively high degree of competition for governorships and by the fact that voters in regional elections punished poor performance and were able to vote for candidates who opposed Yeltsin (Konitzer, 2005).

Recentralization after Yeltsin: political control versus good governance

Reform of regional politics and of the relationship between the central government and the provinces was clearly necessary by the end of the Yeltsin period if Russian governance was going to be improved. Provincial leaders' freedom of action and bargaining power needed to be curtailed, and a more uniform set of relations between centre and periphery needed to be put in place. The problem was, and remains, getting the balance right between securing Putin's control of the political system and ensuring favourable outcomes for him (re-election and no challenges to his authority) and administrative reform that produces better governance. This is a classic reform dilemma. Compromising with such powerful actors as provincial leaders can mean that they direct their political machines to produce favourable political outcomes for themselves. However, this can mean that good governance suffers, since it can involve allowing local abuses of power and corruption that sustain local political machines and perpetuate variation in regional governance and federal relations. Promoting reform, on the other hand, can weaken the control of local political machines and hence their ability to produce favourable electoral outcomes. Such a loss of control, which would also threaten the status and access to resources for local leaders, may incentivise them to produce unfavourable political outcomes in elections and even lead them to support opposition forces.

Putin's reforms: the roll-back of regional power

Putin has never managed to achieve a balance between reform and political loyalty. Reform of regional politics began in May 2000. The changes that Putin introduced were comprehensive, attacking the autonomy and influence of provincial leaders across the board. His intention, he explained, was to strengthen the 'presidential vertical' that Yeltsin had established in 1991 to ensure the implementation of government policy. The creation of eight new federal districts inserted an additional layer of administration between Russia's regions and republics and the central government (initially there were seven districts, but in 2010 the Southern was divided in two to form the eighth district, the North Caucasian). Central to this new layer of administration was the reformed institution of presidential representatives, the *polpredy*. Putin's decree raised their status by reducing their number to seven (later eight), one for each new federal district (listed in table 7.1). The objective of this was to ensure that presidential representatives did not become dependent on regional authorities as they had under Yeltsin. Being responsible for several provinces would mean that they would not be likely to compromise with any one regional leader. Their status was further raised through being made directly responsible to Putin and promoted as members of the Security Council, which is part of the presidential administration and has a broad remit to discuss domestic and international policy (Hyde, 2001). Putin ensured the loyalty of the new presidential representatives by initially appointing people with backgrounds in the security services, where he had spent his earlier career, rather than those with connections to the regions for which they were responsible, as Yeltsin had done after his initial failures with appointing *polpredy*.

At the same time as raising the status of presidential representatives, and hence central state authority in the regions, Putin sought to diminish the status of regional leaders and their autonomy. First, he proposed that the Federation Council no longer be made up *ex officio* of regional executive and legislative heads. Instead, regional executives and legislatures would each send a representative to work in the Federation Council on a full-time basis. Regional leaders would thus lose their ability to intervene directly in the passage of federal legislation and would no longer enjoy parliamentary immunity from legal prosecution. Not surprisingly, the sitting Federation Council received this proposal unfavourably. However, Duma support for the changes meant that it was passed with only minor changes: Putin had originally proposed that all Federation Council members be replaced by their representatives by April 2001, but the final law replaced existing members as their regional terms of office expired, so that they would not all be replaced until January 2002. Over time the status of regional leaders declined as they lost more autonomy (see below), and by 2014, with the exception of the leader of Tatarstan, they were all called 'heads of administration' rather than presidents and governors.

Second, the centre's ability to intervene in the regions was increased by changes to an existing law 'On the General Principles of the Organization of Legislative (Representative) and Executive Organs of State Power in the Subjects of the Russian Federation'. Putin proposed that this law be changed to permit the president to take action against regional chief executives (their governors or presidents) and legislatures in the event of a court finding that they had passed laws or issued instructions that contradicted the constitution. After the issuing of a presidential warning, he suggested, a second contravention of the constitution would entitle the president to submit a federal law to the Duma on the dissolution of the regional legislature or to dismiss a regional chief executive and appoint a temporary replacement. Again, the Federation Council did not receive these proposals with enthusiasm. Putin's support in the Duma, however, overcame the council's veto of the reformed law with a few amendments. The most significant of these was that the regional legislatures, rather than the president, would appoint a temporary replacement for a suspended executive head. This was an important concession, but it did not stop Putin from suspending a few regional chief executives. Putin didn't make extensive use of these powers; rather, they were a threat that could be used to discipline and manipulate provincial leaders who displeased him. For example, Evgeny Nazdratenko, the governor of Primorskii krai (in the Far East of Russia on the Pacific coast), resigned in 2001 at Putin's request, ostensibly on health grounds but more likely because of energy crises in the krai and his long history of erratic behaviour (see Kirkow, 1995). It was a case of going before he was pushed. Nazdratenko was replaced by another local politician, Sergei Darkin, who had come second in the gubernatorial election earlier in 2001. Nazdratenko was later rewarded for falling on his sword by being made a deputy secretary of the Security Council in 2003.

Third, Putin proposed to restore constitutionality to centre–periphery relations by ending the legal anarchy that had developed in the 1990s when regional charters and republican constitutions had developed independently of the federal constitution. The federal Constitutional Court ruled in the summer of 2000 that republican declarations of their sovereignty were in violation of the constitution. Putin called for the end of the bilateral treaties that Yeltsin had signed with the provinces. Some were voluntarily rescinded and the rest were outlawed by a law passed in 2003. Only Tatarstan was able to get a new bilateral agreement, signed in 2007, that gave it some extra degree of autonomy (Ross, 2012: 147). These changes do not mean that the republics' rights have been fully curtailed: they still retain nominal rights to secede from the Russian Federation, for example. However, the changes that Putin put in place limited their freedom of action and weakened the bargaining power of all the provinces.

Finally, the Federation Council passed a new tax code in 2000 that gave the centre more control over tax collection and the redistribution of tax revenue; it also requires regional authorities to hand over an increased amount of their revenue to the federal government. This limited the financial autonomy of the regions and ended some of the disparities that the bilateral treaties had introduced into the fiscal system. The new law has had a significant effect on the share of total official income that provinces enjoy and made many of the poorer regions dependent on the centre for subventions to their budgets.

The scale and rapidity of the changes that Putin introduced in the years of his first presidential term in federal relations were extraordinary. He was helped partly by the increased power he had in the central Duma, which enabled him to override the Federation Council, where provincial leaders held sway, to get legislative changes through. The reform of the Federal Council itself then gave him even greater control over the regions since it became more of a gathering place for lobbyists for the regions (many of whom are not actually from the regions for which they lobby) than a chamber in which collective action could be organized (Ross and Turovsky, 2013). In some ways this was not surprising. The power of provincial leaders to press for autonomy and to organize regional politics to their own satisfaction during Yeltsin's tenure as president had been the result as much of the latter's weakness as it was on account of the ability of the former to coordinate their actions. Provincial leaders were collectively, in fact, quite weak with regard to the federal centre. Declarations of sovereignty and bilateral treaties were, for the most part, 'defensive' and inward-looking. Provincial leaders used them to protect their positions and manage local competition, as well as to cushion themselves and their constituents from some of the negative effects of Soviet collapse and economic reform. The gains made by many of them during the 1990s were 'limited and temporary', and key elements of economic and political control were not dismantled to guarantee permanent regional autonomy and to create a block on the restoration of central authority (Bahry, 2005, 2013). The fate of the regional effort to 'take over' federal politics that had emerged in 1999 with the creation of Fatherland–All Russia – a rare instance of collective action by some provincial leaders – provides some support for the idea that those leaders were never as strong as they appeared. However, it was also a reaction to what looked like Yeltsin's extreme weakness after the 1998 economic crisis, and it did not bind provincial leaders together permanently or even completely. Fatherland–All Russia was an initiative of the more powerful men, most notably Moscow's mayor Yuri Luzhkov and Tatarstan's Shamiyev, who were among the few leaders who had been able to create an independent power base. In Shamiyev's case this was because he was at the head of a unified Tatar elite and because Yeltsin had conceded to him control of oil revenues in the early 1990s. In Luzhkov's case it was because he was mayor of the most important and wealthy city in Russia. Luzhkov had access to considerable tax revenues and was able to take control of the privatization of Moscow's property and some industry, thus giving him extensive powers of patronage. Fatherland–All Russia was not, however, a project of *all* the regional governors and republican presidents. It represented those who had the most to lose if central authority was reasserted and who had the means to organize some resistance. When this resistance failed and other provincial leaders accommodated themselves to the new administration, Fatherland–All Russia was dissolved and became a part of Putin's United Russia party (see chapter 8).

Finally, Putin was able to change centre–periphery relations because the recentralization of power that he championed was an idea whose time had come, and provincial leaders had no meaningful counter-argument around which they could organize or use to mobilize popular support. Proclamations of sovereignty in the early 1990s had been a part of the national move to end Soviet power and democratize Russia. Federalism and decentralization, even in the particular asymmetrical form that these took, allowed for some sovereignty for republics and some autonomy for regions without breaking up the country. However, these ideas had brought nothing but chaos, and many Russians considered them broadly indefensible in 1999, in the wake of the collapse of the economy and renewed war in Chechnya. Restoration of central authority was a more attractive proposition. What remained to be decided as Yeltsin's presidency ended was not whether there should be some restoration of central state power but who was to bring this restoration about: regional leaders through Fatherland–All Russia or Yeltsin's designated successor? Divisions between provincial leaders, the fact that many of them were associated with the chaos of the Yeltsin years, and Putin's prosecution of the second Chechen war tilted the balance in Putin's favour in 2000. Thereafter provincial leaders had little option but to follow his lead and his ideas about how the recentralization of power would proceed (Sharafutdinova, 2013).

Once the initial steps had been taken towards shifting the balance of power in favour of the Kremlin, Putin was able to take more control over the regions as circumstances and his perception of his political needs dictated. The next major change came in 2004, as central control over provincial leaders was tightened after the Beslan tragedy, which brought changes to the electoral system (see chapter 9). Also important in provoking change in how provincial leaders were selected were the protests against the monetization of benefits in early 2005. The protests were over moves to replace the complex system of paying benefits to welfare recipients, in particular to pensioners, which had been made in kind. This system was complex in that the range of benefits and who was entitled to them was often opaque, leaving the state with open-ended commitments that were a burden on the budget. Benefits paid in kind included provision of housing and communal services, free transportation, utilities subsidies, health care, and things such as free or subsidised telephone services. Who was entitled to these and who gained from them was complex and uneven. Different categories of pensioners – for example, war veterans and people who had suffered political persecution – had different entitlements, and not all beneficiaries of in-kind subsidies and benefits were financially needy. The monetization reform was supposed to clarify whether benefits were in fact needed, to make their provision transparent, and to help reduce the burden to the budget of providing them. This would help to clarify the relationship between central and regional budgets too, since it would define more precisely what such payments would cost and who was to be responsible for their provision. In-kind benefits were to be replaced by cash payments for social care and for transportation, and there was to be a clarification of whether payments were to be made to different classes of recipients by provinces or the federal government (Sinitsina, 2009).

The wave of protests in early 2005 over the proposed changes raised fears of a 'colour revolution' in Russia, coming as they did just after the Ukrainian 'Orange Revolution' (see Robertson, 2011: 174–83). Beslan, the

'Orange Revolution' and the benefits protests created the belief that it was necessary to limit opportunities for popular mobilization against the regime and to strengthen ties with the provincial leaders. Elections for provincial leaders were therefore suspended. Appointments were to be made by presidential nomination and be ratified by local legislatures. If a legislature rejected a nomination twice, the president had the right to disband it and appoint a temporary provincial leader until such time as a new legislature was elected. This innovation, explained by Putin both as a necessary response to the failures of the local administration that had helped create the tragedy at Beslan and as the means of controlling separatism, was similar to the mechanism for appointing a prime minister: presidential nomination, legislative right of refusal to ratify the nomination a number of times, followed by dissolution of the legislature if it pushed its disobedience too far.

Reform results

In practice, Putin's new controls over provincial leaders did not lead to much turnover in appointments (there was more turnover under Medvedev, as we shall see below). Most of the provincial leaders whose terms finished after the abolition of elections and the adoption of presidential appointment were reappointed (Chebankova, 2007). What did change was that provincial leaders were now much more clearly subordinated to the president and a part of the 'power vertical'. This was highlighted symbolically by the regular meetings that took place between them and Putin (and later Medvedev). These meetings, which were televised, saw provincial leaders reporting their successes to Putin and being berated by him for their failings. Such meetings were supposed to show that the president was in control and that the provincial leaders were being made to toe the line. They exemplify the personalized system of politics that took shape around Putin and that remained when Medvedev took over from him between 2008 and 2012. The president, and the president alone, held others to account and was the guarantor of policy uniformity across Russia; it was his interventions, rather than their adherence to laws or bureaucratic procedures, that brought regional leaders into line.

The meetings with the president showed that provincial leaders were not going to challenge the regime and were now integrated into it. Regime consolidation, however, is not the same as greater state functionality, and the reassertion of central authority did not translate automatically into improved governance. But this was necessary if Russia was to modernize its economy, as both Putin and Medvedev wanted (see chapter 10). In 2007 a new system for evaluating provincial leaders' performance was put in place, initially, according to forty-three indicators. This was supplemented by the addition of more indicators in 2009, so that 295 areas came under review. Good performance on the annual report on these indicators was to be rewarded by special grants to successful regions. Poor performance was supposed to lead to censure. The enlarged list of indicators covered a wide range of social issues: education, housing provision, health care, mortality rates, crime rates, budgetary performance, forward planning, administrative organization and local satisfaction, among other things. As Petrov (2010: 285–6) has noted, this was a complex range of indicators and open to abuse. Statistics for some were missing, and others could be fudged or gamed to avoid censure and falsely claim success.

The number of indicators that were used to evaluate provincial leaders' performance were reduced in 2012 to eleven. This should have made it easier to check on them and focused efforts on a smaller number of policy areas. In practice, performance was often still assessed against a wide number of unwritten criteria (Slider, 2012: 160–1; 2014, 167–8).

Chief among the unwritten criteria was the mobilization of political support for Putin and United Russia at election time. There is good evidence that ensuring turnout and support was a more important measure of success than the written criteria. Reuter and Robertson (2012) make the case that regimes such as Putin's that manage elections to create a version of legitimacy have a tendency to promote politically loyal personnel over administratively competent ones. The fate of central political leaders is dependent more on the demonstration of regime control over political life at election time than on ensuring the broad satisfaction of people's needs in the regions. This is potentially a short-term strategy. Over the short term, central leaders can stay in power by having their provincial clients manipulate electoral politics to provide them with demonstrations of support. Over the longer term, however, this can lead to the accumulation of problems that politically loyal but administratively poor appointees cannot solve and have a negative effect on economic development. Obviously, repeated poor performance economically will over time be detrimental to support for the regime, as general living standards suffer and as the accumulation of resources to pay off elite supporters becomes more difficult. Putin and Medvedev both favoured short-termism, as 'gubernatorial reappointment decisions in Russia were based largely on the governor's ability to mobilize votes for United Russia', and 'a governor's ability to do better than we might otherwise expect in turning out United Russia voters is consistently the best predictor of whether he or she will keep his/her job, and when United Russia performs poorly, governors are much more likely to be replaced' (Reuter and Robertson, 2012: 1035; Reisinger and Moravski, 2013) Failure to secure a high vote for United Russia was one of the reasons behind the removal of Eduard Rossel, for example, in 2009. Rossel, who had been governor of Sverdlovsk oblast' since 1991, had been late joining and allying his political machine to United Russia, signing up only in 2007, and had not produced strong results for the party.

This short-term strategy was modified only slightly under Medvedev. From 2009, the party that won the most seats in provincial legislatures would be allowed to nominate a candidate for the post of provincial leader for presidential approval. In effect this meant that United Russia – now the dominant party in regional as well as national elections – was always the party that was charged with making nominations. Local United Russia deputies would nominate someone from the local political machine, someone who was part of the local power structure. Putin was also the head of United Russia during Medvedev's presidency, so that there was great continuity in the rationale behind appointments. United Russia's dominance in elections to provincial legislatures was based on the same kinds of electoral fraud and restriction of competition (not registering opposition candidates, for example) as take place in national elections (Golosov, 2011b; Ross, 2010, 2011; see also chapter 9).

There was an increase in the rate of replacement of provincial leaders under Medvedev, but this higher turnover was in part because many regional leaders were ageing. The only major difference between the two presidencies was that many of the appointees under Medvedev had done a period of service in Moscow rather than coming direct from a local political machine (Blakkisrud, 2011: 391). This, as has been pointed out, resembles the Soviet practice of trying someone out under observation in Moscow before appointing them to a regional post (Petrov, 2011: 93). Appointees who came from Moscow are called 'Varangians', after the Viking outsiders who were 'summoned' to rule and bring order to the Kievan Rus' in the ninth century. The label is not totally accurate: some of the latter-day Varangians struggled to control competition between factions in the regions that they were appointed to rule and were replaced after a brief period in office. The name is, however, accurate in that it reveals the intention behind the appointment of outsiders: they were supposed to deliver political control. Not all incumbents have been replaced by outsiders. Outsiders were less likely to be brought in to head republics, for instance, since ethnic sensibilities needed to be taken into consideration. Ilyumzhinov was replaced as head of Kalmykia by another ethnic Kalmyk, Aleksei Orlov, who had had a long career in the republic. In Tatarstan, Shamiyev was able to arrange to be replaced by his prime minister, Rustam Minnikhanov. Some of Moscow's appointees had mixed backgrounds. Vladimir Miklushevsky, for example, who had been a deputy minister for education in Moscow and then been sent to be the rector of the Far Eastern Federal University, based in Primorskii krai, was appointed in 2012 as governor of the region. He was also made a member of the presidential Council for Science, Technology and Education, which consolidated his links with Moscow.

Where a replacement was particularly politically important, central political experience and loyalty were at a premium. The two clearest cases of this are Chechnya and Moscow. The second war in Chechnya was prosecuted more successfully than the first, in part because of the successful co-option of part of what had been the Chechen opposition alienated by radical Islamist elements of the anti-Russian revolt. Ahmad Kadyrov, a former rebel, and former mufti of Chechnya, was installed as head of the Chechen administration by Putin.

Kadyrov used militia loyal to him, and led by his son Ramzan, to suppress pro-independence forces, and considerable powers were devolved from Moscow, along with financial transfers, to build up his strength. Kadyrov was assassinated in June 2004. His son was then too young to take over, so Putin appointed a caretaker president until 2007, when Ramzan reached the legal age to be appointed. Ramzan Kadyrov's loyalty to Putin, which has been reciprocated, has seen Chechnya produce high – and probably fraudulent – election results in favour of Putin and United Russia. He has been an ardent promoter in the republic of a Putin cult of personality, alongside a cult of his own. He has threatened Putin's 'enemies'; members of his militia have been implicated in the murder of the opposition leader Boris Nemtsov, and he has posted pictures of opposition leader Mikhail Kasyanov seen through sniper's sights. Chechnya's human rights record and corruption have been appalling under Kadyrov's rule, and it has regularly flouted the authority of federal representatives and ministries. There has been hardly any comeback against Kadyrov for his actions, however; indeed, he has generally been indulged by Putin because of his loyalty (Dannreuther and March, 2008; Sakwa, 2010b).

Lack of loyalty and the possibility that he might be an electoral liability led to the downfall in 2010 of Yurii Luzhkov, Moscow's longstanding mayor. Luzhkov had expressed doubts about Medvedev's leadership, an implicit criticism of the Medvedev–Putin 'tandem'. For many, Luzhkov personified the opposition critique that United Russia was the 'party of swindlers and thieves' (see chapter 9) because his wife had amassed a huge fortune through property deals in Moscow. Moscow was the centre of opposition to Putin, and putting the city under closer control in advance of the 2011–12 election cycle was a priority. The regime was well aware that protests over electoral irregularities in capitals such as Kiev had been the motor that had driven 'colour revolutions' in other post-communist polities. Luzhkov was replaced in September 2010 by a Putin loyalist, Sergei Sobyanin, who had experience of regional administration (he had been governor of Tyumen oblast' for four years), but who had spent most of his political career working for Putin as a deputy prime minister and as head of the presidential administration.

The reforms introduced by Putin and Medvedev have been less than effective as a means of building up the administrative capacity of the Russian state at local level than they were at making sure provinces gave their support to Putin. The quality of governance in the provinces has varied widely as a result. Overall, indicators of poor governance, such as corruption and lack of public trust in regional authorities, remain high (Panfilova, 2016). As central government pushed back into the provinces through the *polpredy* and tried to restore the authority of federal ministries and agencies, it also created confusion over where authority lies in the regions. Provincial and federal bodies have duplicated each other and got in each other's way, and provincial leaders do not have the means to coordinate the actions of any of the competing parts of the bureaucracy operating in their territory (Slider, 2012: 161).

The democratic discontents of regional politics

The failure to reform provincial governance, together with the use of provincial leaders to support the regime rather than to govern, provides an example of how state development, as the building up of governmental capacity through the growth of public administration and organizational integrity, can be sacrificed for regime consolidation.

There are dangers in this, however. One benefit of having provincial leaders accountable – however imperfectly – to their electorates under Yeltsin was that responsibility for development and local conditions was not laid solely at the feet of the central government. Moreover, popular reactions and mood could be gauged through local elections, and provincial leaders were able to provide feedback on popular discontent through their places in the Federation Council. This was far from perfect, of course, given the many failings of local democracy. However, the move to appoint provincial leaders after 2004 removed even this imperfect mechanism. This was compounded by increased control over elections to provincial legislatures (Ross, 2011). Provincial leaders had to control elections to secure victory for United Russia and to show that they would be able to ensure majorities for the party in Duma elections. The price paid for the erosion of feedback from the provinces has been significant. One of the reasons why there were demonstrations over the monetization of benefits in 2005 was because the provincial leaders' warnings about what the proposed reforms would do were ignored. The response to the protests – placing provincial leaders even more under the thumb of Moscow – weakened the mechanism even more and led to overcentralization, a loss of responsiveness to local concerns, and a loss of ability to see how particular local problems add up to general complaints about politics and economics. The result was that Putin increased his control over the 'steering wheel', as Petrov (2011: 109) has put it, by reining in provincial leaders, but 'the connection between the steering wheel and the road wheels has weakened in the process' (see also Moses, 2010).

Finding a solution to these problems has proven elusive. The regime wants different kinds of performance from provincial leaders, and changes designed to get one kind can work against others. It is sometimes not even clear what any changes are supposed to encourage. A concession over the appointment of provincial leaders was made after the demonstrations that accompanied the 2011–12 national electoral cycle: direct elections of provincial heads of administrations were restored from October 2012. What this was supposed to do was not totally clear, however. The change addressed complaints about Russia's democratic deficit and as such was a tactical move to dampen protest. Restoring elections re-creates some level of responsibility for development at the provincial level and a feedback mechanism linking the provinces and Moscow.

However, the restoration of elections was also a means of developing political control (Golosov, 2012a). One of the reasons for the poor performance of United Russia in 2011 was the weakness of regional political machines where provincial leaders who had developed organizations to control local politics had been replaced by administrators (Reuter, 2013). Restoring elections incentivised leaders to develop or strengthen their control so they could win elections both for themselves and for Putin and United Russia. Incentivising provincial leaders' development of political machines means, however, that provincial elections will be less effective both as feedback mechanisms and as a means to hold provincial leaders accountable. Moreover, stronger local political machines can act as shelters for corruption, since they involve patronage, favour swapping and resource transfers and, as a result, inhibit economic development. Most of the gubernatorial elections have not been that competitive. Like elections to regional legislatures, they have been characterized by the exclusion of opposition candidates and the use of administrative resources to make sure that the vote has gone the 'right' way (Golosov, 2014). The only exception to this was the election to the Moscow mayoralty in 2013 that Alexei Navalny was allowed to contest. Against expectations, Navalny was allowed to stand against Sergei Sobyanin and organized a grassroots campaign that was very effective and was supported by much of the Russian opposition (Orttung, 2013). Navalny

Alexei Navalny at a protest rally, Moscow, 2013

was probably allowed to compete to avoid protest in Moscow over the election, which may actually have been held early to cap protest. Sobyanin resigned as mayor to instigate it, and the expectation was that Navalny would do badly and that this would weaken the opposition movement. In the end Sobyanin won in the first round of the election (the election was held under the same rules as presidential elections), but only just, with 51 per cent of the vote. Navalny did better than expected, with 27 per cent, and the CPRF candidate came third, with 10 per cent. The ploy of using the election to show that the regime had majority support in the capital worked but was not as effective as the Kremlin's strategists had hoped.

Conclusion

The changes that have taken place in centre–periphery relations under Putin have been some of the most extensive of his rule and have involved modifications to the federal legislatures, fiscal policy, personnel and elections. The extent to which they have produced change, however, is very varied. The power of the president over provincial politicians is different. Provincial politicians have been brought to heel and have been compelled to provide the regime with support electorally. Their autonomy over policy has been reduced formally, if not in practice, by the introduction of performance measures, the most important of which is not policy delivery, however, but the provision of political support to Putin and United Russia. This support, at all electoral levels, has undermined both sub-national democracy and the improvements in governance that Putin and Medvedev want and that Russia needs for its long-term economic health. The decline of local democracy and the continued institutional variation that exists between Russia's federal units mean that we have to question whether Russia is a federation. In terms of political management it is a unitary state, and the conduct of centre–periphery relations has become even more subterranean than it was under Yeltsin during the mid-1990s when bilateral treaties were being signed. Competitive politics is essentially dead in regional politics and the relations between the centre and provincial leaders are defined not by law but by a mixture of threats and mutual dependency that are opaque in nature. This means that there are still great variations in how regional politics operates and in its relations with the Kremlin, so that Russia has become 'a quasi-unitary state in federal clothing' (Ross, 2012: 151). This shift away from federalism to a form of centralization has not made the Russian state function better, however, since it has been concerned more with control over politics than with policy implementation.

8

Political Parties and Opposition

Introduction

Modern democracy is based on the existence and health of political parties. Democracy has historically been legitimized through enlarged popular participation in political life and government accountability, and parties are essential both to participation and to holding government and politicians accountable for their actions. Parties do this directly when they censure their own leaders for their failings. Voters can transfer their support to another party to discipline politicians of whose actions they disapprove or who have failed to deliver political outcomes that people desire. Modern democracy is party democracy. Where parties fail, either because the party system is too fragmented or because parties cannot compete effectively, democracy also fails. Popular representation is weakened or debased, and government accountability declines so that politicians can use power for personal rather than public ends.

Russia's problems in developing democracy have been because of excessive fragmentation of its party system and because of barriers to effective party development and competition. Excessive fragmentation was a legacy of the weaknesses of parties in Russia as the USSR ended, and it continued through the Yeltsin presidencies of the 1990s. This weakness meant that parties could not act as a constraint on the president's rule. The restriction of competition that followed Putin's election in 2000 reduced the number of parties that could take part in elections. Putin's policies towards parties did not develop party competition, however. United Russia was created to be an electorally dominant party, supported by other so-called project parties – parties that were established from within the executive to structure voter choice and limit effective opposition. More restrictions on which parties could compete electorally and the resulting narrowing of electoral choice (see the next chapter) split the party system. On the one hand, and represented in the Duma, were the pro-government parties and the 'systemic' opposition – opposition that is casual and half-hearted in its criticism of Putin. On the other were the 'non-systemic' opposition parties, which had no parliamentary representation at the national level. This non-systemic opposition continued to suffer from high degrees of fragmentation. As a result, and overall, Russia continues to have a party system, shaped above all else by the demands of regime consolidation, that is dysfunctional for democratic development (Robinson, 2012).

The development of Russia's party system from *perestroika* to Putin

The development of Russia's party system has gone through several stages, defined largely by the political events and actions of the country's leaders. Politics rather than socio-economic or sociological factors (such as gender, age, education, class or ethnicity) has generally been the primary influence on party formation and consolidation.

The first stages: political parties and perestroika

The liberalization of Soviet politics allowed by Gorbachev's policies led to a surge of social organizations appearing from 1987 onwards. These social organizations were labelled 'informal groups', and many of them were non-political groups of individuals with shared interests and hobbies. The first politically orientated groups were generally formed to lobby on a particular issue – environmental groups protesting some local planning issue – or were discussion circles created to support *perestroika*, which often presented themselves as 'popular fronts for *perestroika*'. They played a minimal role in the 1989 elections to the Congress of People's Deputies but began to develop in response to the failings of those elections and the disappointments of pro-reform liberals at the first convocation of the congress (see chapter 3). In the Baltic republics, the popular fronts' growth as pro-independence organizations accelerated, while, in Russia, they linked with radical deputies from the congress's Inter-Regional Deputies Group in January 1990 to form Democratic Russia.

The creation of Democratic Russia gave Russian liberals a vehicle to compete in the March 1990 election to the republican Congress of People's Deputies. Their success in taking about 40 per cent of the seats paved the way for Russia's declaration of sovereignty and eventually for Yeltsin's election as president in June 1991 (see chapter 3). It also led to some party development from other parts of the political spectrum, as conservative nationalists and communists began to create their own political organizations. These developments did not create a strong social basis for political parties. Whether democratic or not, the groups and parties were mostly organizationally weak and their membership was small. They were weak because they were fractious, often divided over members' views on the Soviet system and the merits of its survival. Involvement in many of the overtly political informal groups was modest. Most people were still employed by the state and were dependent on their employer for such things as housing and welfare. Political activism tended to be limited to the larger cities, where there was a greater chance of anonymity and more opportunities if activism brought censure from the authorities (Fish, 1995). This meant that the groups such as Democratic Russia were unable to develop strong local roots. They remained relatively amorphous peak organizations, founded around a leader – in Democratic Russia's case, Yeltsin – and were more like movements than mass parties with large memberships.

Parties and the constitutional struggle, 1992–3

The collapse of the Soviet Union ended the *raison d'être* of movements such as Democratic Russia, which declined to a rump in December 1991 and splintered as a parliamentary force (Brudny, 1993). Yeltsin didn't put any effort into creating a new presidential pro-democracy and pro-economic reform party. Part of his argument for emergency powers as president was that parties were weak. In Yeltsin's view, it was the job of parties to unite behind him rather than his job to create a party that could support reform (Robinson, 2000: 18–19). But his unwillingness to create a pro-reform party left the door open for a large number of democratic parties to form. The same was the case for anti-reform groups. A successor party to the CPSU would have been the natural focus of any opposition, but the Communist Party of the Russian Federation (CPRF) took time to emerge because of the ban on the CPSU that Yeltsin had issued in the wake of the August coup (March 2002). A plethora of groups claimed to take up the mantle of the CPSU while this ban was fought through the Constitutional Court.

The end of the USSR did not, therefore, lead to a consolidation of political parties. Parties continued to be small and often fractious, with shallow social roots, and were often referred to as 'sofa' or 'taxi' parties because all of their members could supposedly fit on one couch or in the back of a cab. For these reasons, popular attitudes towards them were broadly negative (Wyman et al., 1995). Parties were also politically ineffective. The mass of people took part in politics through official channels, such as the referendum on reform and the future of the Congress of People's Deputies and the presidency in April 1993, and political organization took the form of movements to overcome the weakness of the parties. One of the most notable was the 'red–brown' coalition, the mobilization of communist (red) and nationalist groups (often on the far right with fascist overtones, hence 'brown') against the 'betrayal' of Russia through capitalist reform. It was supporters of parties linked to the 'red–brown' coalition who reacted violently to Yeltsin's efforts to disband the congress in September–October 1993 and who prompted the military action that finally dissolved it.

Parties under Yeltsin, 1993–9

The immediate post-Soviet period saw the creation of a few political parties but not the creation of a party system. A party system is the set of interactions between parties that influences how they act and the type of competition for power between them. During both the struggle against the USSR in the last years of *perestroika* and that between parliament and president over the constitution, there was relatively little interaction between political parties. Interaction between parties and the government was much more important. The establishment of a new parliament, the Duma, gave party building a new impetus and began to create the basis for a party system as interactions between the various groupings began to influence their behaviour. This inchoate party system was, however, still very fragmented (there were lots of parties) and highly polarized (the distance between the factions was great). Fragmentation and polarization meant that Russian voters had a great deal of choice but that the system was very fluid and unstable, thus limiting the extent to which parties could act in concert to restrain the executive and create political accountability.

The electoral rules for the new Duma reserved half of its 450 seats for deputies taken from a proportional party list. The idea of this was to encourage party development (see chapter 9). Theoretically, the PR element should have had a centripetal effect, mechanically forcing cooperation between politicians and parties over time to consolidate and forge a smaller number of effective parties – that is, parties that would have a chance of getting across the 5 per cent threshold needed to secure some of the seats distributed through the PR vote; not to cooperate and coalesce into party groups that had a chance of getting over this threshold should have been irrational.

The parties that fought the 1993 election were mostly established for the election, the exceptions being the CPRF and the LDPR. The CPRF had been founded in February 1993 following the partial lifting of the ban on the old CPSU and was its national successor. Rurally based elements of the latter had founded the Agrarian Party as a sectoral (agricultural) successor to the CPSU, and the Agrarian Party was to act in concert with the CPRF for most of the 1990s. The CPRF was the only mass party to compete in the elections in 1993 and afterwards. It had regional organizations throughout Russia and a large and relatively active membership of about 500,000. It also represented a fairly clearly demarcated social constituency of people who had lost from the demise of the USSR because they were more dependent on the Soviet economic system for their incomes and welfare: older people and pensioners and less educated and unskilled workers. The CPRF's organization and relatively consistent vote meant that it was always a strong contender in elections in the 1990s (see chapter 9). As the successor to the CPSU, the CPRF had the advantage of a clearer identity than other political parties, though this advantage was a double-edged sword. Its electoral success, especially in 1995, could be (and was) used to turn the more important presidential election into a referendum on communism, with the party portrayed as the bogeyman threatening a return to the past.

Zhirinovsky's LDPR had been founded in April 1991 but had been a marginal political party before the 1993 elections. It had allegedly been created at the instigation of the CPSU and the KGB as a means of confusing the electorate (Yakovlev, 2003: 573–5). This would make the LDPR the first of what were later known as 'project parties' – parties set up specifically to deny votes to real independent political forces. Project parties deliberately – and usually through their name – occupy the same policy space as an existing party. The LDPR, as its name suggests, was supposed to take votes from liberals and democrats, but, as wags pointed out, it is 'not liberal or democratic, or much of a party', since it is nationalist, dismissive of democratic values, and dependent on its leader, Zhirinovsky, and his propensity for gathering support through outrageous political rhetoric and stunts.

Since there were few well-established parties to contest the elections in December 1993, some had to be created. One source was the government itself, from which emerged two parties, Russia's Choice and the Party of Russian Unity and Accord. Their establishment was the first of several attempts across the 1990s to form parties and secure a stable source of support for Yeltsin, and later Putin, in the Duma. Our Home is Russia and Unity succeeded Russia's Choice and the Party of Russian Unity and Accord in the 1995 and 1999 Duma elections. Like other parties formed from within government elsewhere, most of these – the exception, as we shall see, was Unity – were unstable. Their existence and relative electoral success depended on their founders' and leaders' continued access to government resources. The parties faded from prominence when the composition of government changed, as it did after the 1993 and 1995 Duma elections, and leaders' access to official resources ended.

Other parties were often hurriedly put together as alliances of like-minded politicians or to appeal to specific sectors of the population. An example of the former would be Yabloko (meaning 'apple' in Russian, but the name was an acronym of its initial leaders' names, Grigory Yavlinsky, Yuri Boldyrev and Vladimir Lukin). Yabloko was able to get over the 5 per cent threshold in 1993, in 1995 and in 1999 because it was the non-government liberal party – i.e., it was not held responsible for the failures of economic reform and was a critic of the democratic failures of the administration in the 1990s. This gave it a niche position in the Russian political system, but not one it was able to expand upon. Part of the pro-liberal reform vote went to pro-government parties. Yabloko failed to link up with other democratic parties because of doctrinal differences and personality clashes between its main leader, Yavlinsky, and other democrats. These failures in part reflected a complacency over its place as the only successful democratic opposition party. Over time, Yabloko's appeal waned as the room for opposition parties narrowed under Putin (White, 2006).

A successful tactic in 1993, when the electoral field was full of relatively unknown political parties, was to try to catch the vote of a specific section of the Russian populace, as Women of Russia did – though its achievement that year in getting over the 5 per cent threshold was not to be repeated. This was probably in part because of the rise of the CPRF's electoral fortunes in 1995 and in part because the success of Women of Russia in 1993 encouraged many other groups to join in the electoral fray. The electoral field in 1995 had many more groups that appealed to sections of Russian society, such as the Russian Muslim Public Movement, and two electoral blocs that sought to appeal to women, pensioners, the disabled, war veterans and youth. Like Women of Russia, none of these blocs managed to reach the 5 per cent threshold.

The large number of parties formed for the 1993 election should have been reduced thereafter if the centripetal forces that PR is supposed to produce had worked. But this reduction did not occur, as a large number of centrifugal forces in the Russian political system nullified the theoretical centripetal pressure of the PR system.

CPRF leader Gennady Zyuganov and supporters in Red Square celebrate the 130th anniversary of Lenin's birth

The first of these forces was the electoral system itself, which was a mixed system rather than purely PR. Half the seats were distributed to parties through PR, but half were contested through single-mandate districts (SMD) that were fought on a first-past-the post or plurality basis – i.e., the candidate receiving the most votes in a constituency would win the seat even if they did not have a majority (over 50 per cent of votes). Politicians did not, therefore, have to be loyal to a party to have a chance of winning a seat in the new parliament; they were as incentivised to build up their personal following and compete for a seat as an individual as they were to support party development. The mixed electoral system sent out mixed signals, in other words, as to what was best for politicians and undermined 'the ability of candidates or parties to learn over time and begin to make decisions that yield[ed] issue-based partisan competition' (Smyth, 2006: 195). Independents did consistently well in the elections of the 1990s until they were squeezed out by United Russia in 2003 and removed from the system entirely when the SMD vote was abolished between 2005 and 2016.

Second, consolidation did not occur because of the sequencing of Duma and presidential elections. Elections to the Duma elections always preceded presidential elections. This gave politicians an incentive to run a party in the Duma elections or to join an electoral association formed from a bloc of parties to see if they stood a chance in the presidential elections. Thirteen parties competed in the 1993 Duma election. Those that did not secure 5 per cent of the vote and parliamentary seats should have disappeared as politicians learnt to cooperate. Instead there was an oversupply of forty-three parties and electoral associations in the 1995 Duma election. The number of parties in 1999 fell to twenty-eight, but this was still a far larger number than could hope to get over the 5 per cent threshold. This oversupply was one of the distorting effects of presidentialism on the Russian political system. Politicians' personal desire to capture the presidency, or to show that they had a constituency that would be useful to the president if incorporated in his coalition, created what Hale (2006b: 19–20) called 'party substitutes' rather than political parties.

Party substitutes were also common at local and regional levels, and their weakness at regional level was one of the causes of the third factor that undermined the consolidation of political parties. Aside from the CPRF, political parties generally failed to develop strong local organizations and hence lacked the means to develop stronger ties to voters through local campaigns and representation. One of the main reasons for this was the lack of turnover in regional political elites and the fragility of local democracy (see chapter 7), both of which meant that elites had small need for political parties to organize and control access to office in the regions (Hale, 2006b). Regional parties developed only rarely, as when leaders were unsure of their hold on power and promoted local democracy and parties as a hedge against losing office (Gel'man and Golosov, 1998). Local so-called parties of power – party substitutes that were generally just fronts for elite interests – squeezed out national parties in the regions at all levels. Most candidates in the 1990s fought elections for the post of regional governor without party affiliation. Even where parties did manage to get candidates for governorships to declare for them, they often did not retain their loyalty post-election, as successful candidates moved away from parties, particularly opposition parties. At the end of the 1990s one survey found that only 11.5 per cent of deputies in regional parliaments had an affiliation with a national party, and most of these (7.3 per cent) were affiliated to the CPRF (McFaul, 2001b: 1169).

The cumulative result of party weakness in the 1990s was that the party system in Russia was highly fragmented (Robinson, 1998). Fragmentation meant parties were unable to cooperate and act in concert to restrain the executive and create political accountability. This failure was one of the reasons why they were held in low public esteem. By the mid-1990s, a majority of Russians (54 per cent) distrusted parties; 75 per cent thought that there were too many of them, and only 17 per cent trusted them to some extent (Colton, 2000: 106–7). From the mid-1990s and through the first decade of the twenty-first century, one-third of Russians consistently thought that there needed to be only one party, and a plurality (anywhere between 40 and 59 per cent) thought that there should be between two and five parties (ibid.: 106; Levada Tsentr, 2010). Over time, distrust in parties hardened: by the early 2000s, the number of Russians stating that they trusted parties was down to 2 per cent in some surveys. This level of distrust contributed to the wider dissatisfaction with democracy in Russia, with people frequently exhibiting the highest levels of disapproval and distrust in democracy in international surveys (Shlapentokh, 2006: 156–7).

Putin and the consolidation of the party system

The failures of political parties and the low public esteem in which they were held simplified the political management that transformed the party system under Putin. The weakness of Russia's political parties was converted into a source of strength for the Putin regime and became one of the planks supporting the president's power. Controlling the party system was a way of controlling elections (see chapter 9), weakening the autonomy of regional leaders (see chapter 7) and ensuring Putin's domination of Russian political elites generally. The development of political authority through parties – part of what came to be called the system of 'managed democracy' – created a new dividing line between what are commonly called the 'systemic parties' (including the 'systemic opposition') and the 'non-systemic parties' (most of which oppose Putin). The former were the parties that were allowed to continue to win seats in the Duma, a list that includes some older organizations such as the CPRF and the LDPR. The latter include established parties that were excluded from representation at the apex of the Russian polity (although they occasionally win some seats at local and regional levels), new opposition parties that emerged under Putin, often as established parties split, and an array of civil society groups that campaign on political issues ranging from human rights to environmentalism.

Controlling the party system

Controlling the party system was the easiest way for Putin to consolidate his power after 1990. Despite its fragmentation, the party system and elections were the main arenas from which challenges to leadership might emerge. The dangers of this were highlighted by the 'colour revolutions' that overthrew established rulers or their designated successors in Serbia (2000), Georgia (2003), Ukraine (2004–5) and Kyrgyzstan (2005). The common denominator among the 'colour revolutions' was mobilization against the incumbent president around elections, driven by a loosening of political control at a time when incumbent presidents were unable to discipline elite factions and control political competition (Hale, 2005, 2015).

Avoiding overthrow through loss of authority over political competition requires *over*-securing control. Elections should achieve not just victory but acclamation of the regime and its 'right' to occupy office and hold power. This meant securing oversight over the media, something that Putin achieved relatively early on, and weakening the autonomy of such powerful groups as business and regional elites (see chapter 5). It meant electoral fraud to ensure large electoral majorities that 'showed' the legitimacy of the regime and the futility of launching a challenge to it (see chapter 10). Control of political parties was the link between control over the media, elites and electoral results. It meant that elite factions could not create parties and test whether they had enough support for a run at the presidency and that voters would be forced to choose at elections between officially licensed political parties. These parties would not protest electoral fraud and would be compliant in the Duma. Domination in the Duma meant that elite factions that might be tempted to break with Putin would be denied the allies that Yeltsin's rivals had enjoyed before 1993 in the old Supreme Soviet and Congress of People's Deputies and after the August 1998 economic crisis in the Duma. Defectors from the regime without allies in parliament would be easier to censure.

Management of the party system addressed these issues by regulating the number of effective political parties (that is, the number of parties that could compete for office), manipulating the electoral space by establishing project parties, and building a parliamentary party for Putin. Controls on the number of effective parties were created by changes to electoral law and by the 2001 law on parties (amended in 2004; Wilson, 2006, 2007). The latter introduced tighter rules on party financing and on the standards that parties had to meet to be registered, while the 2004 amendment demanded that parties have to have at least 50,000 members, who must be Russian citizens over the age of eighteen, and branches in at least half of the country's republics and regions. This last was supposed to prevent the creation of ethnic parties, which would struggle to organize outside of their home region. Further controls were put on the organization of minority parties, as having a religious or racial bias or being based on a single occupational category was prohibited. Parties are forbidden from taking part in 'extremist activity'.

The registration requirements set a high bar for parties to meet and provide grounds for preventing registration or for banning parties. Potential electoral competition is limited, since only parties can nominate candidates for elections. In 2007, for example, the Republican Party of Russia was dissolved by the Supreme Court after the Ministry of Justice deemed that it had improperly organized a party congress. It was allowed to re-register in 2012 only after the European Court of Human Rights ruled its dissolution was in breach of the European Convention of Human Rights (it later joined with the People's Freedom Party, PARNAS, to form RPR-PARNAS).

Rules on finance set limits on how much money parties can legally raise from private donors and made it illegal to accept money from abroad or from Russian firms that are more than 30 per cent foreign owned. Parties receive finance from the state according to the number of votes that they receive. Initially this amount was modest, but the sum per vote increased fortyfold between 2001 and 2009 (Hutcheson, 2012: 269). This created a huge difference between the financial fortunes of those parties that secured Duma seats and those that did not. Income from the state enabled those that were successful to spend more money on advertising and campaigning and gave them an incentive to moderate their opposition to Putin to ensure that they participate in elections and maintain their income stream from government coffers (Hutcheson, 2012).

Rules on party registration were combined with changes to electoral laws in 2005 (the raising of the threshold for securing seats through the PR vote from 5 to 7 per cent and the abolition of single-mandate district [SMD] seats) to limit the number of parties competing and securing seats in parliament (see chapter 9). This did not prevent the overall creation of parties, but it did limit the number that were effective. By the end of 2016 there were some seventy-six registered parties. This gives an impression of democratic openness, but most registered parties are politically invisible: the Russian Gardeners' Party, for example, has not pruned United Russia's electoral support. Many of the other parties registered by the Ministry of Justice (2016) are either project parties or, like the Cossack Party of the Russian Federation, a sop to a special interest group useful to the Kremlin.

Project parties – set up as 'independent' parties by the Kremlin to impact the vote of potential rivals to United Russia – have assisted control of Russia's political space. They were often formed with the involvement of the presidential administration, with Vladislav Surkov, the first deputy head of the presidential administration between 1999 and 2011, as their *éminence grise*. Rodina (Motherland), which was set up in August 2003 to take votes away from the CPRF, included a mix of ex-CPRF and nationalist politicians. The party was initially successful, and in the December 2003 Duma election took 9 per cent of the PR vote. Some of its vote might previously have gone to the LDPR or United Russia, but most of it came at the expense of the CPRF, whose share fell from 24.3 per cent in 1999 to 12.6 per cent in 2003. In 2006 Rodina was combined with some other small parties to create A Just Russia (Spravedlivaya Rossiya), which was described as a social democratic rather than a nationalist or left party (Sakwa, 2011: 221–2). A Just Russia did less well than Rodina in drawing votes away from the CPRF in 2008, when it took 7.7 per cent of the total, but the CPRF's share still fell to 11.7 per cent on account of the strength of United Russia. In 2011, its vote went up to 13.2 per cent, while the CPRF's went up too, to 19.7 per cent. Both were protest votes, since Russia was still feeling the effect of the 2008 financial crisis, which impacted United Russia and Putin's popularity. If A Just Russia had not been in the election as a project party, the CPRF's gains would probably have been greater; the 2011 'revolt' at the ballot box was therefore managed to an extent by its existence. In 2016, the shares of both the CPRF and A Just Russia fell back again, to 13.3 and 6.2 per cent respectively), as the political situation was calmer and Putin had reasserted his control. Zhirinovsky's LDPR has performed the same function, picking up votes that might have gone to regime opponents in both parliamentary and presidential elections: Zhirinovsky has been the perennial also-ran in every Russian presidential election except that of 2004.

United Russia: 'hegemonic', 'dominant' or Putin's personal party?

The creation of project parties helped to support the establishment of a parliamentary party for Putin, United Russia (Edinaya Rossiya). The benefit of setting up a party that could capture seats in the Duma had been recognized during the Yeltsin presidencies. In 1993, for example, Russia's Choice and the Party of Russian Unity and Accord were formed from within government to try to create a pro-government party in the Duma. Our Home is Russia was established for the 1995 Duma election. None of these parties had been successful, in large part because elite infighting meant they were unable to monopolize the 'administrative resources' (the aid that government and local authorities can give to a party) and use them to campaign and pressurize voters to support them at the ballot box.

United Russia's roots were also in Unity – a party created to support the government – which became associated with Putin after his appointment as prime minister in August 1999. It was competing with Fatherland–All Russia, which was the electoral wing of regional leaders trying to manoeuvre themselves into a position to control Yeltsin's succession. Putin's popularity and media support gave Unity a far greater share of the vote than had been expected. Fatherland–All Russia, with its strong support from regional administrations, also picked up seats in the SMD vote (see next chapter). Between them, Unity and Fatherland–All Russia had 31 per cent of the Duma seats – more than the CPRF, which had topped the poll. Unity's association with the new president, Putin, lead many independents and Fatherland–All Russia deputies to join it. At first Unity collaborated with the CPRF to divide up offices within the Duma administration between them. However, in July 2001, as Putin consolidated his power, Fatherland–All Russia merged with Unity to form the Union of Unity and Fatherland. In December of the same year it adopted a new name, the All-Russian Party of Unity and Fatherland, before finally settling in 2003 on the name United Russia (for more details on the party's formation, see Hale, 2004; Roberts, 2012a).

United Russia has a majority in the Duma and is the undisputed 'party of power'. Its dominance has been ensured by changes to electoral laws in its favour and because Putin's increasing control over regional politics has forced most regional leaders to support it (see chapter 8). United Russia expanded rapidly after 2003, opening branches in all of Russia's regions, developing youth and supporters' associations, and forging links with a wide variety of civic organizations (some of which were set up to liaise with it). Consequently, it became the largest party in the country, and by the end of 2016 it had over 2 million members, 2,595 local branches, and 82,631 grass-roots organizers.

The growth and dominance of the party raised questions about its nature. Clearly it was a mainstay of the Putin regime, since it controlled the Duma, prevented opposition from emerging, and was used as a vehicle for incorporating elites into the political system. However, does the party have any power in its own right? Political parties in democracies and non-democracies can act as constraints on politicians, censuring them, removing them from office, and trying to ensure that they make policies and laws that are in line with party ideology. There are differences in how they do this in democracies and non-democracies, of course, but if United Russia was to expand its political power this would have implications for the development of the whole Russian political system. Since the party evolved at a time when the quality of Russian democracy was declining, the most obvious question about its nature is to ask whether it was becoming what is known in other non-democratic states as a 'dominant' or 'hegemonic' political party. Dominant parties are able to secure electoral victories over time. They thus come to have control over government formation and policy and can use this to develop patron–client networks that give them an unfair electoral advantage. This advantage then ensures that the dominant party stays in office. Hegemonic parties are more prevalent where electoral competition is limited and subject to official manipulation – as it is in Russia – and are used as vehicles for the ruling elite to show that their electoral victories have legitimacy. In both cases a party has some power in its own right. It is an important part of the machinery of government, it organizes patronage, and it is the institution that arbitrates between different elite demands. This can give the party a role in deciding on leadership succession and access to office, alternating favour between different factions, making sure that any leader is supported by a majority of elite members, etc. By performing these functions, a dominant or hegemonic party can play a powerful stabilizing role. Elite division and competition can be contained within the party and is less likely to spill out into the wider political arena and undermine the regime. Some dominant parties, such as Mexico's Party of the Institutionalized Revolution, have gone so far as to rotate access to executive office (in Mexico's case, the presidency) so as to give all factions a turn in office and at the public finance trough. Clearly, where such arrangements occur, the party is a powerful force for the stabilization of regime politics and is one reason why non-democratic regimes based on a political party last longer than other forms of non-democratic regime. When parties are involved, there is a wider social interest in the perpetuation of non-democracy from party functionaries and all of a party's appointees and beneficiaries in the economy, bureaucracy and security services (Geddes et al., 2014).

A United Russia campaign poster for the 2007 Duma election: 'Moscow votes for Putin!'

Despite its wobble in 2011, United Russia is clearly dominant electorally. Its dominance, and the efforts that have been made to support it through voter fraud and rule changes, mean that it is a hegemonic party: no other party has been allowed to compete with it on a level playing field, and it is set up to be a 'winner' and legitimate the regime. This does not mean that it has any independent power, however. There was some expectation that United Russia was becoming a dominant party in the mid-2000s, based on the fact that membership was increasingly a route to access office, to remain in office, and to access economic rent. Few regional leaders, for example, remained outside of the party. Those that did generally had some independent source of power, and even then many still joined United Russia to signal that they supported the regime and understood the rules of the political game (Reuter and Remington, 2009; Reuter, 2010; White, 2011).

But this did not necessarily mean that United Russia was developing as an independent force in politics to the point where it was able to control access to office as a party, as an institution that had powers in its own right. It was highly centralized and under Putin's control rather than being an administrator of its own affairs. United Russia membership was a means of gaining access to office and patronage, but access to the benefits of being a party member flowed from loyalty to the regime rather than from the party. Overall, it was just one means for the Kremlin to manage elites (Slider, 2010). Taken 'at face value', United Russia looked to be a solution to the issue of how to organize access to power, but, like the parties that preceded it, it was actually quite weak, and it didn't function as a dominant party (Roberts, 2012a: 4–5, 2012b). Its roles were to do more with political communication, mobilizing support and testing ideas for Putin than actually deciding how Russia is ruled. This has led to its being labelled as a particular variant of the dominant party type: it is a 'personalized dominant party' that lacks autonomous agency (the ability to independently shape policy, for example) and is intimately bound up with the rule and leadership style of the leader, Putin (Isaacs and Whitmore, 2014).

The long-term survival of United Russia as a personalized party is doubtful. Putin's supporters often argue that 'no Putin = no Russia', but 'no Putin = no United Russia' is a much more plausible equation, especially since Putin's attitude towards the party has always been ambivalent. He chaired it while prime minister without being a member and has only once stood at the head of its party list for Duma elections, in 2007. Partly this ambivalence comes from the desire to represent Putin as 'above' party politics; he was most involved in United Russia when he was not president and not the 'leader' of the whole nation. However, we cannot discount the possibility that his ambivalence is also because he doesn't want to see any transfer to the party of his authority so that it becomes something more than a personal machine. United Russia's sometimes less than stellar performance as a mobilizer of political support probably reinforces this ambivalence. It has sometimes struggled to bring out the vote when it has been used in the regions to put loyal bureaucrats in power rather than strong local politicians (Reuter, 2013). This demonstrates Putin's dilemma: he needs good administrators in office to run Russia if he wishes to modernize it, but he also needs strong politicians who can develop networks that can be activated to support him at election time. A good administrator and a strong politician will rarely be found in the same individual, however, given that political strength in Russia is based on patronage and the subversion of administrative order and procedure.

No real answer has been found to this dilemma. One prospective solution has been to create a parallel organization to United Russia to give Putin another lever for rallying support. Before the 2011 election Putin announced the formation of such an organization – the All-Russian National Front – which was formed as a social movement to support United Russia, but its founding conference was not held until June 2013, when Putin was elected as its leader. Its role has changed during this time, from that of a political party to that of a watch-dog. It has become a quasi-state organization that checks on the implementation of government policy and the loyalty of government officials (Lassila, 2016). The need for such an organization shows that neither United Russia nor the institutions of the state that were supposed to monitor policy implementation and check corruption are up to the job. The creation of another organization answerable to Putin looks like an attempt to get strong politicians who are bad administrators to do a little better. It also gives Putin a possible replacement for United Russia, an organization that is not a party but an 'all-Russian' movement and which can stand for election.

The systemic opposition

It is open to question how far there is any opposition from parties in the Duma. Formally, Rodina, A Just Russia and the LDPR are all in opposition. So too is the CPRF. However, all are clearly also part of the political system, and their continued ability to compete for votes depends on their being allowed to compete. For this reason, they have all been labelled as part of the 'systemic opposition'. This term denotes that they are a part of the political system – i.e., while not being a part of government, they hold seats and positions (such as Duma committee chairs). It also denotes that they are *of* the system, either directly created by it, in the case of the project parties, or reliant upon it.

This applies to the CPRF as well as to the project parties. Its ability to exist and the level at which it can compete is determined by the regime. The CPRF has become less and less clearly an anti-systemic party over time. As a result, the differences between it and other Duma opposition parties are not as great as rhetoric might sometimes lead us to suppose. From its inception it has depended on its ability to win seats to give it access to state resources that it can use to support the party organization. This has not changed, but its ability to win seats has been challenged by the creation of United Russia and the project parties. The CPRF has therefore had to collaborate with the regime in order to survive. There is some evidence that it has done this by moderating its policy positions, providing support for the regime (over some foreign policy issues, for example) and by not contesting political reforms, especially not of party registration and electoral laws. The CPRF benefited from the latter changes, since many of the smaller political parties on the left that had nibbled at its vote in the 1990s were removed from the electoral arena.

The *de facto* demise of the CPRF as an anti-systemic party – at best it might be labelled a 'semi-opposition party' (Gel'man, 2005: 228–9) – and its reliance on the state point to Russia having a 'cartelized' party system (Hutcheson, 2013). In such a system there is a high degree of penetration of parties by the state, the membership does not play a great role in the life of the party, and there is controlled electoral competition as parties conspire with one another to try to raise the barriers of entry for new electoral forces. In Russia's case this conspiracy is driven from the regime rather than achieved by organic cooperation between parties, but the CPRF has colluded with it, and the outcomes have been the same: the number of effective parties – that is, parties able to compete and win seats in the national parliament – has declined, and an electoral status quo has been created in which only United Russia, the CPRF, the LDPR and one or more project parties can be successful.

The dilemmas and difficulties of the 'real' opposition: non-systemic forces and civil society

As the party system became cartelized, those parties that were not able to join the cartel, or even take part in national elections, were forced into what has been called the 'non-systemic opposition'. Unlike the project parties or semi-opposition parties, this opposition has no loyalty to, and does not collude with, the Kremlin (Gel'man, 2005). The consolidation of the party system as a type of cartel made for a larger opposition; more parties were pushed out as they lost the right to contest for parliamentary seats or failed to win seats. As more groups were forced out, they added to the range of ideological groupings; however, this didn't make the opposition any stronger by deepening its overall social support.

The widening of opposition rather than its deepening in the 2000s renders the term 'non-systemic opposition' somewhat problematic despite its common usage (Bol'shakov, 2012). The main problem with the term is that it implies a large degree of unity between oppositional groups. This, as we shall see, is far from the case; the opposition has generally been highly divided both within and across ideological lines. It might, as David White has suggested, be better to talk about a 'non-systemic party system', since this better captures its diversity.

Another advantage of the term 'non-systemic party system' is that it draws a distinction between civil society and parties as a part of *political* society. Civil society, as a broader public sphere of social organizations, is a source of political party development, and linkages with civil society interests and organizations can be a resource for political parties. The relationship between civil and political society is a fluid but vital one (White, 2015). One of the tasks of opposition parties if they wish to take power, or if they wish to force or participate in regime change, is to mobilize civil society actors in their support. This can be used to stall repression by creating fear that it will lead to a social backlash. Finally, mobilization can help parties become players in any move to alter regime politics, since it shows that they might be effective partners.

Given that the opposition could appeal to a wider range of ideological positions, its widening into a kind of parallel party system should have made mobilization of support easier. Working against this was their inability to rally electoral support as the rules changed and United Russia grew in popularity. Liberal parties, whether economically liberal such as Union of Right Forces or more socially liberal such as Yabloko, faded under new electoral rules and economic conditions. Their ideas on economic reform were tainted by the experience of the 1990s and were not needed as the economy grew. Yabloko also suffered from the fact that it had been around since 1993 and had never really made an impact. Casting a ballot for Yabloko began to look like a wasted vote as time progressed. The fact that some economic liberals were in government – such as the finance minister Aleksei Kudrin – meant that it was possible for some liberal voters to plump for United Russia rather than supporting Yabloko as the perennial liberal opposition.

Marshalling support for oppositional politics was not just hampered by economic growth and Putin's popularity. Access to the media was severely restricted for oppositional politicians, as the regime began to reassert control over television in 2000 as part of the move to restrict the political power of oligarchs. Laws against extremist propaganda have been used to silence criticism, since what is defined as extremism is open to broad interpretation. There has been self-censorship as businesses with media interests have softened criticism of the government to protect themselves from official action. Independent journalists have been silenced, have gone into exile or have been murdered, the most notable case being that of Anna Politkovskaya, who was assassinated in 2006 after a long career exposing human rights abuses in Chechnya. Many other journalists have been threatened or assaulted.

The main news media, in particular television, have become propaganda arms of the state. Opposition politicians have had to rely on web-based communication, notably social media, to try to reach an audience. Although internet usage has grown in Russia, with 43 per cent of the population having access to the web by 2010, it has not replaced television news as the country's main source of information (Oates, 2013: 55, 59–60). Of course, the information that people receive from the web is not solely from the opposition. Russia has not developed the same level of control over the internet as has China, but it has increased surveillance of the web (Oates, 2013; Soldatov and Borogan, 2015). For every anti-Putin blog or meme there is a pro-Putin blog or meme, some of which are posted from organized troll factories that are used to flood the internet with pro-Putin and anti-Western content. Despite this, the internet is a way of making connections for opposition politicians. Aleksei Navalny, who emerged as a leading opposition spokesman and figurehead during the 2011 and 2012 demonstrations, came to prominence through online activism. His *Rospil*, *FBK* (Fund for the Struggle against Corruption) and *Rosyama* websites allow Russians to report corruption and holes in roads (which by law have to be filled). These sites were linked to Navalny's social media sites and generated considerable traffic, popularizing Navalny's description of United Russia as the 'party of swindlers and thieves' in the run-up to the 2011 Duma election. Social media was important in helping to spread word about the demonstrations in protest at electoral malpractice in 2011 and 2012. However, as the decline in activity between 2012 and 2017 showed, it is hard to sustain mobilization in support of opposition through social media alone.

A second factor that limits the ability to rally in support of the opposition is that, since 2005, civil society has been subject to co-option by the regime via the Public Chamber (Obshchestvennaya palata). This was set up to provide a forum for NGOs to discuss policy initiatives. Its first forty-two members were selected by Putin. They then voted to select another forty-two members, and these eighty-four members chose another forty-two to fill the 126 places in the chamber. The members were from mixed backgrounds. While they were supposed to represent NGOs, the method of their selection meant that some of the most vocal NGO critics of Russian policy over issues such as human rights were not chosen The Public Chamber has done some good things – for example, working on the problem of recruits in the Russian armed forces being bullied. However, the consensus is that it is really effective only where it is in line with presidential aims, and it has not raised any issues that would substantially embarrass the regime (Evans, 2008; Richter, 2009). It gave privileged access to some NGOs and the possibility of such access to others if they behaved. There have also been some public chambers created at sub-national level to co-opt local social organizations (Gilbert, 2016: 1569–70).

Where NGOs have not toed the regime's line they run the risk of repression or suffering official harassment. Human rights workers in particular have been subject to violence, including murder. Many human rights organizations and groups involved in such activities as election or environmental monitoring have connections with international organizations, which has made them vulnerable to accusations of working against Russia's national interest. Restrictions on foreign NGOs working in Russia were introduced in 2005. Laws passed in 2012 and 2015 made it compulsory for Russian NGOs in receipt of foreign funds to register as 'foreign agents' and gave the authorities the right to close any organization that violated the order. These laws have been used, for example, to target Amnesty International's Russian branch and Memorial, bodies that are seen as politically liberal, which have defended Russian political prisoners and investigated rights abuses in areas where Russia has military involvement, such as Eastern Ukraine, Crimea and Chechnya.

Finally, civil society is an area of regime mobilization. Like the effort to institutionalize NGOs with the Public Chamber and the limits on electoral activity, this mobilization took off after the colour revolutions in Georgia and Ukraine. The main focus in the mid-2000s was on organizing youth using a group called Nashi ('Ours'), established as a Kremlin initiative with the involvement once again of Vladislav Surkov from the presidential administration. Surkov argued that the role of Nashi was to 'defend Russia's youth from the political manipulations of the West' (Ambrosio, 2009: 63). Thanks to official support and resources, Nashi soon developed as an extensive organization with a large membership. It propagandized for the regime, took part in counter-demonstrations to the opposition, and generally sought to socialize young Russian adults into supporting the regime (Atwal and Bacon, 2012; Lassila, 2014). After the overthrow of the Yanukovych regime in Ukraine following the Maidan demonstrations in December 2013, Nashi was supplemented by the Anti-Maidan movement, which held a series of demonstrations to support Putin's actions in Crimea and Ukraine and picketed opposition offices. The group's declared aims according to its manifesto are 'to prevent "colour revolutions", riots, chaos and anarchy' and to preclude Russian cities hosting 'forces that hate a strong and sovereign Russia and which have approval and support from abroad' (https://antimaidan.ru/page/9). The group is supposedly an umbrella organization supported by a mixture of NGOs, some clearly 'patriotic' and military (the Russian Union of Afghan Veterans, the Union of Russian Paratroopers), others charitable and cultural (Foundation for Children with Cerebral Palsy, the Russian Musical Association), and some bizarre (the Night Wolves Motor Cycle Club, Putin's favourite Orthodox Christian nationalist biker gang; see Zabyelina, 2017).

Strictly speaking, neither Nashi nor the Anti-Maidan movement are really civil society organizations. They are semi-state bodies founded with the participation of government officials. However, their presence, and the fact that some very normal-looking civil society organizations join them, shows the extent to which civil society has been co-opted. At other levels of the political system the regime has actively promoted NGO development and created organizations – project NGOs if you like, or GONGOs (government-organized non-governmental organizations) – so that they are aligned with the system from the onset. For example, business associations, which might usually be thought of as natural allies for economically liberal parties such as Union of Right Forces have been created by the state. As a result, part of economic society (business) is not allowed to develop organic civil society offshoots and use them to negotiate with political society in the form of parties. The two main business associations act as means of communication between officials and business and as channels for organizing business support for the regime (see Gilbert, 2016, for other examples of where the regime has 'crowded out' independent social organizations).

Civil society co-option, repression and mobilization, together with limited access to media, have meant that the public sphere has largely been closed to the non-systemic political parties. This has had a profound effect on their popularity. Opinion polls show that Russians believe that the country needs a political opposition, although the numbers in favour fell over the Putin years: in 2004, 61 per cent of those surveyed by the Levada Tsentr (2016) said that a political opposition was needed, but by 2016 this had fallen to 52 per cent. Belief in the need for an opposition doesn't translate into support for the non-systemic opposition politicians and parties, however. Indeed, the distinction between systemic and non-systemic opposition is not one that many Russians appreciate. Name recognition is lower for non-systemic than for systemic opposition politicians: Zhirinovsky and the CPRF's Zyuganov were recognized by a majority of poll respondents, but no non-systemic politician was. Zhirinovsky, Zyuganov and A Just Russia's Sergei Mironov were also more trusted (by 21, 20 and 10 per cent of poll respondents respectively) than non-systemic politicians, none of whom was trusted by more than 4 per cent of respondents. The regime's policies of party system management, of maintaining an official and semi-official opposition while demonizing the non-systemic parties and politicians, has been successful; Russians have taken on board Putin's (2014a) argument that there is a 'nationally oriented opposition' that is very different to 'the so-called non-systemic opposition'.

Some of the problems of non-systemic parties are a result of their failings. Chief among these are the inability of opposition forces to work together. There has been a failure among all opposition parties to form general alliances to create an actual 'non-systemic opposition' rather than a series of 'non-systemic oppositions'. The non-systemic parties have a common aim in wanting the removal of the Putin regime, even if they disagree about what should replace it. This should give them some common ground around which to organize, particularly over elections, and there have been several attempts to build a larger opposition movement. The Other Russia coalition, for example, combined groups from across the political spectrum between 2006 and 2008. Its members included liberal groups and politicians such as the United Civil Front, led by the former chess champion Garry Kasparov, the former prime minister Mikhail Kasyanov, representatives from the hard left such as Sergei Udaltsov from the Russian United Labour Front, and the 'psychedelic-fascist-pseudo-revolutionary' Nationalist Bolshevik Party led by Eduard Limonov (Judah, 2013: 203). The Other Russia organized a series of 'dissenters' marches' in Moscow and St Petersburg but was never a stable organization.

Fragmentation is a major problem for the opposition even when there is more ideological congruence between groupings than there was in the Other Russia. Plans to merge Union of Right Forces with Yabloko foundered over policy and leadership questions in 2006. Discussions for a merger between three other liberal parties – RPR-PARNAS, the Progress Party (Navalny's party) and the Party of 5th December – failed in 2015. There have also been splits within parties. The result has been that most parties are very small, with only a few thousand members and limited resources.

Fragmentation has made it hard to build on what limited success the opposition has had. The main success was the demonstrations that followed the December 2011 Duma election, which saw up to 100,000 protesters take to the streets in Moscow behind the slogans 'For honest elections' and 'For a Russia without Putin' (Greene, 2013, 2014; Robertson, 2013). The Moscow demonstrations were by far the largest, but there were protests across Russia in most major cities. The cooperation that was shown by opposition groups during the planning and execution of the main marches in Moscow seemed to signal the 'emergence of a significant, robust, and durable protest movement' for the first time (Greene, 2013: 40). Opposition politicians tried to institutionalize their cooperation by forming a Coordinating Council of the Russian Opposition, a committee of forty-five people elected in October 2012 by an online poll in which over 80,000 people voted. To ensure representation of all ideological factions, there were different lists for liberals, nationalists, the left, and civil society activists. The list of representatives elected was a who's who of the opposition (with no Yavlinsky or official Yabloko presence), but cooperation didn't materialize. The council was soon riven by disputes over procedure, over a common programme and over tactics, and it was dissolved a year after it was elected. Efforts to cooperate in the run-up to the 2016 Duma election foundered as opposition leaders could not agree on whether to participate in or boycott the poll. The only real success that the opposition had after 2011–12 was Navalny's campaign for the Moscow mayoralty, which saw him win 27 per cent of the vote, much more than was predicted. Even that came at a cost. Navalny was supported by RPR-PARNAS, but this was one of the reasons that led RPR-PARNAS's co-founder Vladimir Ryzhkov to quit the party. Navalny was also unable to get much of the non-systemic opposition to join his campaign for a boycott of the 2018 presidential election.

The small size of opposition political parties and their fractiousness have meant that they have not penetrated Russian society to any great extent or been able to forge links with civil society. They are very dependent on their leaders, many of whom have far higher public profiles than the parties they lead. A case in point is Navalny and the Progress Party, which has not been able to register officially. This makes the loss of a leader through arrest, assassination or exile especially damaging. Navalny has been tried and sentenced several times and undergone long periods of house arrest, as have other prominent opposition figures such as Udaltsov and Ilya Yashin. Boris Nemtsov was murdered in Moscow in February 2015. Garry Kasparov has been in exile since 2013. The opposition is in many ways a mirror of the system that it is protesting against, as personalized as the Putin regime.

The opposition has been unable to capitalize on splits in government support when they appear. Protests by long-distance lorry drivers against changes to road taxes in late 2015, or protests against housing demolition in Moscow in 2017, often involve aspects of social justice and the potential for political mobilization. The drivers' protest, for example, was motivated in part by the fact that the firm that was to implement the new payments scheme was linked to the son of one of Putin's billionaire friends, Arkady Rotenberg. It was a protest against cronyism as well as an economic protest, and it revealed a split in Putin's support: many of the protesters had been involved in the pro-Putin Anti-Maidan movement. But the weakness of the opposition means that it cannot exploit feelings of ill-will about issues such as cronyism and translate them into broader mobilization. This makes it very uncertain that protests such as the anti-corruption demonstrations of 2017 can be sustained. While Navalny's social media campaign over Prime Minister Medvedev's alleged corruption brought many people out onto the streets, including many younger people for the first time, it is not clear that protests can be developed into a wider movement for change that can force concessions from the regime. Navalny's success as an anti-corruption campaigner did not force the regime to put him on the ballot for the 2018 presidential election. He thus launched a campaign calling for a boycott of the election, but this had only limited success.

Conclusion

The failure of Russian political parties to act as a constraint on the country's rulers has been central to the failure of democracy and to the consolidation of power in the Kremlin. The lack of success in developing strong party politics has many dimensions to it. There are historical reasons, electoral and sociological factors, and the distorting effect of presidential power. Over time, however, it has been a matter of design: party politics has failed because the Putin regime has not seen the need to support party development and has actively restricted the ability of new parties to form and thrive. It is content to rest on the support of United Russia and the 'systemic' parties that cooperate with it, and party politics have not been allowed to put in place constraints on regime behaviour, propose alternative paths of political and economic development, or create structures that can regulate the transfer of executive power. The weakness of parties, the hollowness of systemic parties, and the small size of opposition parties help to make the Russian political system generally under-institutionalized and dependent on Putin. This helps create uncertainty. Without strong parties it is hard to see who – apart from Putin – can rule Russia. The weakness of parties thus has implications for what type of political system the country has and what type of political system it might have in the future, issues that we will return to in the final chapter. Without stronger parties it is less likely that Russia will develop impersonal political power, democratic or otherwise, that is easily transferred from one leader to another.

9
Elections and Voters

Introduction

A primary function of elections is to legitimate a political system by having the selection of rulers approved by voters. This may or may not involve their bringing about changes in who rules through free and fair competition. Where there is not free and fair competition between candidates, their chief function is acclamatory: the representation of voters' preferences about who is in charge and to what ends are secondary to the legitimation of power through a public display of approval for a country's rulers. Soviet elections were essentially acclamatory, held to display popular acquiescence to the power of the Communist Party of the Soviet Union. Reform under Gorbachev allowed voters to withdraw their approval, and elections became imperfect plebiscites on whether the CPSU should stay in power. By voting against the CPSU, voters did not necessarily choose a deputy or leader who shared their policy preferences but were able to express their discontent with their existing rulers. To a large extent, Russian elections, at least at national level, have remained plebiscites on whether those in authority should remain in power rather than a means of allowing voters to match their preferences and interests to potential rulers. The acclamatory nature of elections was slightly weakened in the 1990s but strengthened again under Vladimir Putin. This shift raised questions about the democratic nature of Russian politics and heightened the divide between the systemic and non-systemic parties and opposition that was discussed in the last chapter.

Elections under Yeltsin

The first free election in Russia was the 1991 presidential election, which Yeltsin won with 59.7 per cent of the valid votes. By winning more than 50 per cent in the first round Yeltsin did not have to compete in a second-round ballot between the two candidates topping the first round. Only once, in 1996, has a Russian presidential election gone to a second-round vote.

The system of electing the Russian president has remained largely the same since 1991, but the electoral system for parliament changed considerably as a result of the power struggle between Yeltsin and the Congress of

People's Deputies and Supreme Soviet. The defeat of the Congress and Soviet in October 1993 enabled Yeltsin to force a vote on a new constitution. This referendum was held on the same day – 12 December – as the election for the new parliament that the constitution was to establish. Legally, referendums in Russia were binding if half of the electorate voted for a proposition. Yeltsin decreed that the constitution would be ratified if half of the electorate took part in the poll rather than voting in favour of the new constitution, and that the constitution could be accepted by a majority of voters rather than by a majority of the electorate. Yeltsin's intervention proved necessary as turnout was much lower than in previous votes. Officially, 54.8 per cent of registered voters took part in the poll, so that the 50 per cent threshold required for the constitution was met. More than half of those who voted – nearly 33 million people, or 54.4 per cent – approved the new constitution, so it was accepted and came into force on 25 December 1993. However, this meant that the share of the total electorate (just over 106 million people) that voted for it was only 30.7 per cent, and seventeen regions and republics of the federation voted against acceptance (Sakwa, 1995: 211). There were strong and credible accusations that actual turnout was below the 50 per cent necessary even under the terms of Yeltsin's decree for ratification, and that ballots had been stuffed with 'yes' votes to pass the constitution.

The 1993 Duma election

One reason that the ratification of the constitution wasn't challenged was because the best platform for making the challenge, the Duma, was weak (see chapter 6). This weakness was both a product of constitutional design and because of the fragmentation of the deputy body created by the electoral system.

The new electoral system was a mixed system. Half of the Duma's 450 seats were to be elected by proportional representation (PR). Voters would choose from a list of parties. The 225 PR seats would be divided among those parties that received over 5 per cent of the national vote. The remaining 225 seats would be elected from single-mandate districts (SMD) on a first-past-the post or plurality basis – i.e., the candidate receiving the most votes in a constituency would win the seat even if they did not have a majority (over 50 per cent of votes). To be valid, there had to be a turnout of at least 25 per cent. The intention of having a mixed system was at least in part to encourage the development of political parties. PR demands the creation of parties and should lead to their consolidation. Parties that do not receive more than 5 per cent of the vote should be seen as unviable by both the politicians who lead them and their supporters. Voter allegiance should thus move to viable parties to get their interests represented in parliament; politicians should look to improve their electoral fortunes by merging parties that share ideological positions but that cannot individually cross the 5 per cent threshold. This consolidation should, in theory, be 'mechanical', produced by the PR electoral system automatically as it incentivises voters and politicians to act rationally to increase their representation.

The influence of PR on party formation and consolidation was mitigated by other factors, as we saw in chapter 8, and by the existence of the 225 plurality SMD seats. In 1993, candidates for these seats were not identified by party label on the ballot, making it difficult for voters to carry their party vote over to the SMD seat vote. There was little that parties could do to increase the name recognition of many of their candidates, given that the elections and the electoral system were created in haste and that most of the parties that fought it were either newly formed (such as the government parties, Russia's Choice and Russian Unity and Accord, or the liberal party Yabloko) or had

TABLE 9.1 Duma election, December 1993 (parties getting over the 5 per cent threshold are marked in bold)

	Votes %		Seats		
	List	SMD	List	SMD	%
Valid votes	50.6	50.6			
Invalid votes	3.7	4.0			
Total votes (% of electorate)	54.3	54.6			
Liberal Democratic Party of Russia (LDPR)	21.4	2.7	59	5	14.3
Russia's Choice	14.5	6.3	40	30	15.6
Communist Party of the Russian Federation (CPRF)	11.6	3.2	32	16	10.7
Women of Russia	7.6	0.5	21	2	5.1
Agrarian Party of Russia	7.4	5.0	21	12	7.3
Yabloko	7.3	3.2	20	3	5.1
Russian Unity and Concord	6.3	2.5	18	1	4.2
Democratic Party of Russia	5.1	1.9	14	1	3.3
Movement for Democratic Reforms	3.8	1.9	0	4	0.9
Civic Union	1.8	2.7	0	1	0.2
Future of Russia	1.2	0.7	0	1	0.2
Cedar	0.7	0.5	0	0	0
Dignity and Charity	0.7	0.8	0	2	0.4
Independents	—	45.2	—	146	32.5
Against all	3.9	14.8	—	—	—
Others	0.0	0.7	0	0	0
Invalid ballots	6.8	7.4			
Total	100	100	225	224[a]	100

Note: [a]One seat left vacant in Chechnya.

only recently been unbanned (such as the Communist Party of the Russian Federation, the CPRF). Unsurprisingly, independent candidates dominated the SMD vote (see table 9.1). Only Russia's Choice, the CPRF and the Agrarian Party managed to win any number of SMD seats – the first was helped by having some recognizable names on its list and the latter two by having politicians who were well known locally.

Voting for the PR list was fragmented in a different fashion. Many of the parties fighting the election were only recently formed and had therefore acquired little deep partisanship. The exceptions here were the CPRF and, to a lesser extent, the Agrarian Party, which was in many ways the rural branch of the CPRF and worked closely with it in the Duma. The CPRF had more loyal partisans because it was the successor party to the CPSU and was the natural party for those who had lost most through the demise of the USSR and its economic system. These voters were often, but not exclusively, older and less well educated, lived in smaller cities, and were blue-collar workers. However, the CPRF's vote was still smaller than it was to become later in the 1990s because it was still reorganizing after the ban placed on the old CPSU following the August 1991 coup. It also had to compete for votes against the surprise winner in the 1993 PR elections, Vladimir Zhirinovsky's Liberal Democratic Party of Russia (LDPR). The LDPR polled surprisingly well, outperforming all pre-election forecasts and also captured some of the protest vote against the changes that Russians had been living through since 1991: male blue-collar workers from small towns and cities were strong LDPR voters. In addition, it was the beneficiary of electoral fraud used to boost turnout so that the constitution could be passed. Many regional electoral commissions allegedly evened out the tally between the referendum vote and the PR list vote by casting ballots for the LDPR in the latter.

The LDPR was helped to top the poll by the fragmentation of the pro-government and centre vote between Russia's Choice (founded by Yegor Gaidar and representing the economic liberal wing of the government), Russian Unity and Accord (representing a more conservative and patriotic platform), Yabloko (the Yavlinsky–Boldyrev–Lukin bloc, a non-government liberal party) and several other smaller liberal and centrist groups and parties. The PR results of the 1993 election *should* have taught liberal and centrist politicians that they needed to cooperate. However, the mechanical effects of PR did not work. Parties formed from within government largely disintegrated after their modest electoral performance, as government changed and new pro-government parties were formed to fight the next round of elections, and because politicians had other means of entering parliament through the SMD elections.

The results of the election to the 178 seats of the Federation Council (each unit of the federation had two seats on the council) largely reflected the Duma SMD votes. Fewer candidates contested each of the Federation Council seats than the SMD seats so that voters' choices were more structured. Russia's Choice did better than it did in the SMD vote. Overall, the election was dominated by independents and proved a victory for regional economic and political elites.

The 1995–6 and 1999–2000 electoral cycles

The first Duma had a two-year term, so that the second Duma election took place in December 1995. Yeltsin had to stand for re-election as president in 1996. Thereafter, and until the presidential term was changed in 2012 from four to six years, Duma and presidential elections were in lock-step, the period between them being shortened from six to three months after Yeltsin's retirement in December 1999 brought presidential elections forward from June to March. This timing meant that Duma elections became trial runs for presidential elections. How well parties performed in the former became a predictor of how the vote might be distributed in the latter. This created an incentive for politicians to fly electoral kites in the Duma elections to see if they stood any chance in the presidential elections. Few did, but if a politician could win a large enough vote share they might gain some bargaining power with a front-runner in the presidential election for office or favour.

There were other factors that increased the number of parties running in Duma elections besides their timing. As mentioned above, government parties changed between elections as participation in government changed. In the December 1995 Duma election, the main government party was Our Home is Russia, which replaced Russia's Choice (now a rump liberal party) and Russian Unity and Accord as the pre-eminent government party. Many other parties that had competed in 1993 had weakened or disappeared and there was a rush to fill their places. The electoral outcome was something of a mess. On one hand, the PR vote was consolidated for three parties that had secured seats through PR in 1993: the CPRF, the LDPR and Yabloko. Our Home is Russia picked up 10.1 per cent of the PR vote and ten SMD seats, which was a weaker performance than the pro-government parties had achieved in 1993. This can be explained by the fact that Russia was still struggling with economic downturn and by the unpopularity of the first Chechen war. But poor performance was also because of the large number of parties and electoral associations taking part, resulting in a fragmentation of the vote. Only four of the forty-three – the CPRF, the LDPR, Our Home is Russia and Yabloko – made it over the 5 per cent threshold, and these four shared all the 225 PR seats between them despite gaining only just over 50 per cent of the valid votes cast. This meant that proportional representation was not really that proportional: nearly half the votes cast did not get translated into seats (see table 9.2).

The only party to be successful was the CPRF, which increased its vote share from 1993 as it was better established organizationally and the focus of opposition to Yeltsin in the Duma. It was also the only party to retain most of its voters – 60 per cent – from the previous election; none of the other

TABLE 9.2 Duma election, December 1995 (parties getting over the 5 per cent threshold are marked in bold)

Position in list vote at previous election		Votes %		Seats		
		List	SMD	List	SMD	%
	Valid votes	64.4	62.9			
	Invalid votes	1.3	1.4			
	Total votes (% of electorate)	65.7	64.3			
3	**CPRF**	22.3	12.6	99	58	34.9
1	**LDPR**	11.2	5.4	50	1	11.3
	Our Home is Russia	10.1	5.5	45	10	12.2
6	**Yabloko**	6.9	3.2	31	14	10.0
4	Women of Russia	4.6	1.0	0	3	0.7
	Communists of the USSR	4.5	1.8	0	1	0.2
	Congress of Russian Communities	4.3	2.9	0	5	1.1
	Workers' Self-Government	4.0	0.7	0	1	0.2
2	Russia's Democratic Choice[a]	3.9	2.6	0	9	2.0
5	Agrarian Party of Russia	3.8	5.9	0	20	4.4
	Great Power	2.6	0.6	0	0	0
	Forward Russia!	1.9	1.5	0	3	0.7
	Independents	—	31.2	—	77	17.1
	Against all	2.8	9.6	—	—	—
	Others	15.3	19.7	0	23[b]	5.1
	Invalid ballots	1.9	2.3			
	Total	100	100	225	225	100

Notes: [a]The renamed Russia's Choice.

[b]Twelve small parties won twenty-three seats.

parties that crossed the threshold managed to carry over more than half of their voters (White, Wyman and Oates, 1997: 789). This was because of its place at the head of the opposition to Yeltsin and because it retained its social base among older, less well-educated and working-class voters nostalgic for the certainties of Soviet rule. The relative solidity of the CPRF vote helped to make attitudes to the Soviet regime the main predictor of how people cast their ballots. Those with a positive attitude towards the USSR voted for the CPRF, while those with a negative view voted for other parties (Rose et al., 2006: 118–20). As in 1993, the failure of parties holding similar ideologies to forge alliances both prevented them from achieving a higher vote or getting across the 5 per cent threshold and acting as a break on voter volatility.

The results of the December 1995 election should have made the CPRF's Gennady Zyuganov the front-runner for the 1996 presidential election. However, the double-ballot majoritarian system used in presidential elections focused voter choice: the key questions were whether there would be a candidate who could win outright in the first round with more than 50 per cent of the vote and, if not, who would be the top two candidates to face off in the second round of voting. It was unlikely that Zyuganov would win the presidency in the first round, despite the CPRF's success in the Duma vote. It was also unlikely that he would win a second-round vote, since the total non-communist vote was larger than that of the left. The main issue at stake in the presidential election was who would share top position with Zyuganov and thereby stand a good chance of securing the presidency in the second ballot.

Yeltsin's chances of being this other candidate on the second ballot looked slim initially. However, big businesses – the oligarchs – rallied behind him, seeing him as the only plausible non-communist candidate. The election was turned from a vote on Yeltsin's competence as an administrator into one on whether the changes of the late 1980s and early 1990s should be repudiated. Many Russians were not prepared to do this even though they were dissatisfied with Yeltsin, who was therefore able to win the second-round vote with the support of transfers from other candidates – and because voters were 'forced' to choose between communist and anti-communist candidates (White, Rose and McAllister, 1997: 263). Yeltsin's margin of victory was quite wide at 14 per cent, but he secured only 54.4 per cent of the vote; nearly

TABLE 9.3 Presidential election, June–July 1996 (candidates going through to the second ballot are marked in bold)

| | First round | | Second round | |
	Number	%	Number	%
Electorate	108,495,023		108,600,730	
Valid votes	74,515,019	68.7	73,910,698	68.1
Invalid votes	1,072,120	1.4	780,592	1.1
Total votes (% of electorate)	75,587,139	69.7	74,691,290	
Yeltsin, Boris	26,665,495	35.8	40,203,948	54.4
Zyuganov, Gennady (CPRF)	24,211,686	32.5	30,102,288	40.7
Lebed, Aleksandr	10,974,736	14.7		
Yavlinsky, Grigory (Yabloko)	5,550,752	7.4		
Zhirinovsky, Vladimir (LDPR)	4,311,479	5.8		
Fedorov, Svyatoslav, Gorbachev, Mikhail, and six others	1,636,950	2.2		
Against all	1,163,921	1.6	3,604,462	4.9

5 per cent of voters declared that they wanted neither Yeltsin nor Zyuganov by voting 'against all' (see table 9.3).

The basic patterns established in the 1995–6 electoral cycle and between the 1993 and the 1995 Duma elections carried across to the 1999–2000 election cycle. Fewer parties and associations competed in December 1999 – twenty-eight as opposed to forty-three – but this was still far more than could secure election. Six parties made it over the threshold, with a vote share of 77.3 per cent, so that there was less disproportionality than in 1995 (see table 9.4). Thanks to its social base, established organization, and oppositional status, the CPRF topped the poll again. Yabloko and the LDPR also reached the threshold, and for the same reasons as in 1995, although the former was beginning its slide into electoral irrelevance. There was still a high degree of

TABLE 9.4 Duma election, December 1999 (parties getting over the 5 per cent threshold are marked in bold)

Position in list vote at previous election		Votes %		Seats		
		List	SMD	List	SMD	%
	Valid votes	60.5	60.3			
	Invalid votes	1.2	1.3			
	Total votes (% of electorate)	61.7	61.6			
1	**CPRF**	24.3	13.4	67	46	25.1
	Unity	23.3	2.1	64	9	16.2
	Fatherland–All Russia	13.3	8.6	37	31	15.1
	Union of Right Forces	8.5	3.0	24	5	6.4
2	**LDPR**	6.0	1.5	17	0	3.8
4	**Yabloko**	5.9	5.0	16	4	4.4
6	Communists of the USSR	2.2	0.7	0	0	0
5	Women of Russia	2.0	0.5	0	0	0
	Party of Pensioners	1.9	0.7	0	1	0.2
3	Our Home Is Russia	1.2	2.6	0	7	1.6
	Others	3.1	6.0	—	8	1.6
	Independents	—	41.7	—	114	25.3
	Against all	3.3	11.6	—	—	—
	Others	2.9	0.6	0	0	0
	Invalid ballots	1.9	2.2			
	Total	100	100	225	225	100

electoral volatility as old parties faded from view or saw their votes decline; that of the LDPR, for example, fell to 6 per cent.

The beneficiaries of this volatility were the new parties formed from within government (Unity and Union of Right Forces) and by a set of powerful regional leaders (Fatherland–All Russia). These parties – in particular Unity, which became associated with Putin after his appointment as prime minister in August 1999, and Fatherland–All Russia, as the electoral wing of regional leaders – could call on significant administrative resources to support their campaigns. The media support that was given to Unity, its piggy-backing on Putin's growing popularity, and the desire for stability after the chaos of the Yeltsin era structured the vote to a far greater extent than had previously been the case. Television is the main source of information for most Russians, and TV support has therefore had a very large influence on voting behaviour and support for the government party (Enikolopov et al., 2007). Fatherland–All Russia in particular, with its strong support from regional administrations, also picked up seats in the SMD vote. The CPRF, thanks to its stronger organization and support from some regional administrations, also won seats in the SMD votes, but as in previous years the largest bloc of deputies elected to the SMD seats were independents.

The CPRF topped the PR poll, but the real election winner was Unity, which secured 10 per cent more of the vote than Fatherland–All Russia. This result came from a swing away from Fatherland–All Russia over the last months of 1999 as Putin's popularity grew and he conducted the second Chechen war as prime minister. Putin's association with Unity attracted a wider spectrum of voters than any other government party had managed to capture and reduced the credibility of Fatherland–All Russia's claim to be the party of order that the country needed after the crises of the later Yeltsin years. Putin's personality, youthful and publicly untainted by the compromises of the Yeltsin era, and his prosecution of the war attracted voters – nationalists, those on the centre-left, people who had lost out economically in the 1990s – who had been reluctant to support government parties associated with Gaidar (Russia's Choice) or Chernomyrdin. The combined vote of Unity and Union of Right Forces encouraged Yeltsin to resign early and make Putin acting president in the run-up to the presidential election. The poor showing of Fatherland–All Russia effectively ended any challenge by regional leaders for the presidency. Putin, as the candidate associated with both Unity and Union of Right Forces, thus had a clear run against Zyuganov, as there were really no other heavyweight candidates in the race. In many ways, the first round was a contest between Putin and Zyuganov to see if the latter could garner enough votes to force a second ballot. To try to avoid this, the campaign was skewed in the media towards Putin, with television coverage focused disproportionately on his campaign (although he actually didn't formally campaign at all). Putin received nearly half the TV coverage overall, against Zyuganov's 11.4 per cent (Raskin, 2001: 10). Media bias and Putin's popularity and promise

TABLE 9.5 Presidential election, March 2000

	Votes	%
Electorate	109,372,046	
Valid votes	74,369,773	68.0
Invalid votes	701,003	0.6
Total votes (% of electorate)	75,070,776	68.6
Putin, Vladimir	39,740,434	52.9
Zyuganov, Gennady (CPRF)	21,982,471	29.2
Yavlinsky, Grigory (Yabloko)	5,722,508	7.9
Tuleev, Aman-Geldy	2,217,361	3.0
Zhirinovsky, Vladimir (LDPR)	2.026,513	2.7
Titov, Konstantin	1,107,269	1.5
Pamfilova, Ella (For Citizen's Worth) and four others	1,585,625	2.0

of stability worked: he won a majority in the first round of 52.9 per cent, thus avoiding a second round (see table 9.5).

Back to acclamation: the 2003–4 and 2007–8 electoral cycles

Putin's win in March 2000 marked the start of a shift in Russian electoral politics. Stability has always been one of Putin's main aims, and instability in elections could easily produce instability elsewhere. The cycle of holding Duma elections involving a large number of parties just before presidential elections threatened to throw up contenders for the post of president. Elections were moments when elite divisions and contestation of power could become public, as when regional leaders had mounted challenges to Yeltsin's control over his succession by launching Fatherland–All Russia. They also provided the best opportunity for both elites and people to act and ally to get rid of an otherwise immovable leader who has outlived their political functionality, as the 'colour revolutions' in other post-Soviet states showed (Hale, 2005, 2006). Managing elections therefore means lessening instability and is important for political survival. Controlling one election can reduce the chances of revolt at the next. The more a president can manipulate an election, for example, by securing a large majority to continue in power, the higher the costs of challenging him will appear to potential rivals.

The 2003–4 electoral cycle

Putin's efforts to control electoral competition and the instability that it could create pre-dated the 'colour revolutions' because he was also interested in securing a parliamentary majority that would help him control legislation. At first this majority was secured via compromise in the Duma rather than through the ballot box. Unity and Fatherland–All Russia deputies merged to form United Russia, and many of the independent deputies elected to SMD seats joined the party because it was now dominant in the Duma and had the power to distribute positions of influence and the privileges that came with them. United Russia was able to dominate elections to a far greater extent than previous government parties, partly because of its association with Putin (who was not a member). The results that the party achieved were a reflection of his popularity and approval ratings, which hovered around the 60 per cent mark for most of this period.

Putin's popularity, and United Russia's riding on its coat-tail to electoral success, was also based on economic growth, a desire for stability, and the fact that Putin was ideologically opaque. Economic growth was important because many Russians vote not according to how well off they are personally but according to how much better off they see the country becoming (McAllister and White, 2008b). This is called sociotropic voting. Naturally, if you think the country is becoming better off, you might consider that your own economic circumstances will improve as well, so it is not a totally altruistic position. However, it does mean that people in power can gain electoral advantage from economic success much more quickly and more broadly from a positive national economic outlook: economic growth does not have to trickle down to people before they start to vote for incumbents who can claim responsibility for national economic success.

Sociotropic voting was not the only factor that drew people to Putin and United Russia. They also picked up votes as Putin's ideological opacity squeezed the votes of other parties and leaders. Putin's anti-oligarch stance attracted those who were concerned with social justice, but he was still pro-capitalist, so he didn't alienate voters who were economic liberals. In that he talked of making Russia a great power again, he could attract votes from nationalists such as Zhirinovsky, but he had also been broadly supportive of better relations with the West during his first years in office and so could attract voters who were more internationalist in their outlook.

This combination of factors attracting votes to Putin and United Russia was helped by the start of what was at the time labelled 'managed democracy', or 'managed pluralism' (Balzer, 2003). This was the much more active engagement of the presidential administration in political management and in the affairs of other political parties to weaken them. The first moves were made to dominate the electoral system by creating and supporting parties that would take votes from opposition parties and complement the capture of votes by United Russia as Putin's party. The first 'project party' (see chapter 8) was Rodina (Motherland), which was formed in August 2003. Rodina was a left nationalist party designed to occupy some of the electoral space taken up by the CPRF and to complement United Russia, which was a centre-right nationalist party. The CPRF was also weakened by its loss of control in the Duma following the establishment of United Russia, and it lost committee chairs and posts, resources that had been used in the 1990s to support its organization. The loss of influence in the Duma also precipitated a split in the party's ranks (March, 2004). Finally, a law was passed in June 2001 that placed some limits on the registration of parties (see chapter 8). Although this did not immediately impact on the parties that had previously managed to cross the PR threshold, it did begin to restrict the formation of electoral associations that had been such a prominent feature of elections in the 1990s.

The combined weight of these factors brought elections for the Duma under far greater control than previously. In December 2003, United Russia dominated both the PR and the SMD votes (see table 9.6), taking the largest share ever of the PR vote. The main losers were the CPRF, Yabloko and the independents. The CPRF's vote fell from 24.3 to 12.6 per cent, and it won only twelve SMD seats against the forty-six it had secured in 1999. Some of that vote loss probably went to Rodina, which took 9 per cent of the PR vote and eight SMD seats. The CPRF's share was probably also squeezed by demographic changes, as its elderly voters began to die off or were no longer available to work for the party. Although it was to recover slightly in the 2011–12 electoral cycle, where it attracted some of the protest vote cast in those elections (see below), it could not rebuild its share to the high of 1995.

Yabloko's vote share in the PR vote declined less precipitously than the CPRF's, shrinking from 5.9 to 4.3 per cent, but this left it below the 5 per cent threshold for the first time, and it has never recovered. An alliance before the election with Union of Right Forces, with which it shared many liberal political and economic positions, would have benefited both parties, but personality differences between leaders and a refusal to compromise meant that both failed to cross the threshold. As a result they were both increasingly marginalized and began to drift towards what was later to become called the 'non-systemic opposition' (see chapter 8). Finally, independents, who had dominated the SMD vote, were squeezed out by United Russia, which took 102 seats; their share of seats fell from 114 to 68, a sign that regional elites had transferred their allegiance to United Russia and to Putin.

The victory for United Russia in December 2003 cleared the field for Putin in the 2004 presidential elections (Sakwa, 2005). He won in the first round with 71.3 per cent of the valid vote (see table 9.7). The election was barely a competition at all. Neither the LDPR's Zhirinovsky nor the CPRF's Zyuganov stood; both parties ran obscure candidates instead. No other party formally fielded a contender, although Sergei Glazyev was associated with Rodina and Irina Khakamada with Union of Right Forces. The poverty of the opposition to

TABLE 9.6 Duma election, December 2003 (parties getting over the 5 per cent threshold are marked in bold)

Position in list vote at previous election		Votes %		Seats		
		List	SMD	List	SMD	Total, %
	Valid votes	54.8	54.3			
	Invalid votes	0.9	1.1			
	Total votes (% of electorate)	55.7	55.4			
	United Russia	37.6	23.2	120	102	49.3
1	**CPRF**	12.6	10.8	40	12	11.6
5	**LDPR**	11.5	3.1	36	0	8.0
	Rodina	9.0	2.9	29	8	8.2
6	Yabloko	4.3	2.6	0	4	0.9
4	Union of Right Forces	4.0	2.9	0	3	0.7
	Agrarian Party of Russia	3.6	1.7	0	2	0.4
	Pensioners–Fairness	3.1	0.5	0	0	0
	Rebirth–Party of Life	1.9	2.6	0	3	0.7
	People's Party	1.2	4.4	0	17	3.8
	Others	1.7	3.9	0	3[a]	0.7
	Independents	—	26.8	—	68	15.1
	Against all	4.7	12.9	—	3	0.7
	Invalid ballots	1.6	2.1			
	Total	100	100	225	225	100.0

Note: [a]Three small parties won one single-member seat each.

Putin was made clear during the campaign when one of the contenders, Sergei Mironov, the chairman of the Federation Council, remarked that 'We all want the next president to be Vladimir Putin.' Mironov's reward was to go on to be one of the leaders of another 'project party', A Just Russia, which was founded in October 2006 when Rodina was merged with several smaller parties.

The 2007–8 electoral cycle

The results of the Duma and presidential elections in 2003–4 were votes in favour of Putin and the stability and growth that he was thought to have brought to Russia. Both were essentially plebiscites on whether Russians supported Putin, and this aspect of elections became more marked in the next electoral cycle (Hanson, 2011).

TABLE 9.7   Presidential election, March 2004

	Votes	%
Electorate	108,064,281	
Valid votes	69,504,609	64.3
Invalid votes	695,976	0.1
Total votes (% of electorate)	69,581,761	64.4
Putin, Vladimir	49,565,238	71.3
Kharitonov Nikolai (CPRF)	9,513,313	13.7
Glazyev, Sergei	2,850,063	4.1
Khakamada, Irina	2,671,313	3.8
Malyshkin, Oleg (LDPR)	1,405,315	2.0
Titov, Konstantin	1,107,269	1.5
Mironov, Sergei	524,324	0.8
Against all	2,396,219	3.6

The first reason for this was the changes made to the electoral system and party registration (see chapter 8) after the siege at Beslan in September 2004. All 450 seats in the Duma were now to be elected by PR. The threshold for securing seats in the Duma, raised from 5 to 7 per cent, had already risen in 2002 (a minor change was made to the law in 2009: parties gaining more than 5 but less than 6 per cent would get one seat, while those receiving more than 6 but less than 7 per cent would get two seats; no parties met these conditions in 2011). Another amendment to this law in 2006 removed the possibility of voting 'against all'. This had been a significant category – 4.7 per cent (i.e., just under the 5 per cent threshold) in the 2003 Duma election and 3.6 per cent (more than the bottom three candidates had polled collectively) in the 2004 presidential election (McAllister and White, 2008a). These changes narrowed the choices that Russians would be offered at the ballot box and gave the Kremlin greater control over manipulating elections (see below) by keeping parties critical of the government and Putin below the threshold – contrary, of course, to the idea that PR produces broad representation of popular political views (Golosov, 2012a). Parties could be turned down for not meeting registration criteria, and regional elites lost their ability to manage electoral outcomes in SMD seats and to sponsor alternatives to the central government's party in the way that they had with Fatherland–All Russia in 1999. The removal of SMD seats also ended the representation of smaller parties, some of which had always managed to secure a few seats.

The second reason elections became more plebiscitary was because the Kremlin transformed them into vehicles for supporting Putin. Putin's decision to abide by the constitution, and so not to stand for a third term in 2008, made it imperative that United Russia gain a majority. The party, as Putin (2007a) noted not long before the 2007 Duma elections, was far from a coherent body in terms of ideology or organization. However, Putin argued, if people voted for United Russia, he would gain 'moral authority' to demand that the Duma and the government work to the agenda he had set out. A vote for United Russia was thus a vote for Putin and his ability to continue to work as prime minister, the post he was due to take when Medvedev succeeded him as president in 2008. A strong vote for United Russia was thus essential to show that Putin was in charge, to clear the ground for his chosen successor, and to constrain his successor both morally (Medvedev would be working to Putin's agenda since that was what people had voted for at the Duma elections) and practically (a United Russia majority would prevent the new president from acting against Putin as prime minister).

Putin won his plebiscitary elections in 2007 and 2008 (see tables 9.8 and 9.9). United Russia received 64.3 per cent of the vote. The CPRF vote remained

TABLE 9.8 Duma election, December 2007 (parties getting over the 7 per cent threshold are marked in bold)

Position in list vote at previous election		Votes	%	Seats	%
	Electorate	109,145,517			
	Valid votes	68,777,136	63.01		
	Invalid votes	759,929	0.70		
	Total votes (% of electorate)	69,537,065	63.71		
1	**United Russia**	44,714,241	64.3	315	70.0
2	**CPRF**	8,046,886	11.6	57	12.7
3	**LDPR**	5,660,823	8.1	40	8.9
	A Just Russia	5,383,639	7.7	38	8.4
7	Agrarian Party	1,600,234	2.3	0	–
5	Yabloko	1,108,985	1.6	0	–
	Civic Strength	733,604	1.0	0	–
6	Union of Right Forces	669,444	0.9	0	–
	Patriots of Russia	615,417	0.9	0	–
	Party of Social Fairness	154,083	0.2	0	–
	Democratic Party of Russia	89,780	0.1	0	–

TABLE 9.9 Presidential election, March 2008

	Votes	%
Electorate	107,222,016	
Valid votes	73,731,116	68.8
Invalid votes	1,015,533	0.9
Total votes (% of electorate)		69.7
Medvedev, Dmitri	52,530,712	70.3
Zyuganov, Gennady (CPRF)	13,243,550	17.7
Zhirinovsky, Vladimir (LDPR)	6,988,510	9.3
Bogdanov, Andrei	968,344	1.3

low and its seat share fell because of the removal of the SMD vote. Besides United Russia and the CPRF, only the LDPR and the new 'project party', A Just Russia, got over the 7 per cent threshold, but the combined vote of all the other parties – including Union of Right Forces and Yabloko – did not collectively add up to the threshold. Medvedev was equally successful in the presidential election in March 2008, when he secured just over 70 per cent of the vote, down only very slightly on Putin's poll in 2004. The political aims of the changes made to the electoral system and party registration between 2002 and 2005 had paid off, helped considerably by economic growth throughout this period, which peaked just after Medvedev's election in 2008. A large proportion of the popularity of Putin, and hence of United Russia and Medvedev, was tied to this success, as people were very positive about the national economic outlook (McAllister and White, 2008b). However, the changes to the electoral system brought one other factor into play in securing the results that Putin wanted: electoral fraud.

The spread of electoral fraud

There had always been an element of Russian elections that was unfair: the presentation by the media of a skewed picture of the competing parties and candidates. Local authorities had also influenced voter behaviour and electoral outcomes before the mid-2000s through the use of what were euphemistically called 'administrative resources' (Fish, 2005: 33–67). These practices were extended and amplified from the mid-2000s. Putin's increasing control of the political system and United Russia's growth as the sole government party created more incentives to engage in electoral fraud, a clearer target (United Russia) and, because the media were cowed, fewer risks attached.

Assessing the scope of electoral fraud is not easy, since it is largely hidden from view. Myagkov, Ordeshook and Shakin (2009) have argued that some indication can be gained by looking at turnout and the vote for the main

'I didn't vote for these bastards' (the United Russia logo adapted by Alexei Navalny to show the United Russia bear with a bag of swag), 'I voted for some other bastards' (logos of Yabloko, A Just Russia and the CPRF). 'I demand a recount!'

government party. Where turnout is higher than the national norm and there is also a disproportionately high vote for the government party or candidate, there is a good chance that something has happened fraudulently to inflate the numbers in favour of the government. Myagkov and his colleagues report such outcomes across elections from the Yeltsin period through to the 2007 Duma election. There were disproportionately high swings to Yeltsin in 1995 in the second round of the presidential election; turnout increased in some regions, a higher than normal amount of which went to Yeltsin (ibid.: 75). These effects were most marked in the ethnic republics of Russia rather than its regions (see chapter 7 for the differences), since levels of democracy in the republics were frequently lower and political control by elites therefore higher.

There was some prevarication over using fraud to support Putin in 2000 since his power was not yet established. However, in both the Duma election of 2003 and the presidential election of 2004, extra turnout led to a disproportionately high advantage to Putin and United Russia. In short, as United Russia and Putin became established, votes were 'created' for them by local administrations. Myagkov et al. (2009: 110) estimate that as much as 25 per cent of Putin's vote in the 2004 election was the result of fraud. Again, and as in the 1996 presidential election, this problem was worse in republics than in oblasts. However, in a follow-up study of the 2008 presidential election,

Lukinova, Myagkov and Ordeshook (2011) argue that electoral fraud had, like cancer, 'metastasised' from republics to other areas of Russia. Oblast' leaders began to believe it was 'personally costly to have one's area of control show less enthusiasm for the Kremlin-sanctioned candidate than elsewhere' (ibid.: 620) and so helped ensure that Medvedev's vote was roughly equivalent to Putin's in 2004 (see also White, 2016).

The system wobbles: the 2011–12 electoral cycle

The growth of fraud alongside the controls placed on elections under Putin meant that both their 'fairness' and their 'freeness' were compromised. It increasingly came to look as if Russia had an 'electoral authoritarian' regime, where elections were used to legitimate the power of an incumbent ruler rather than to pose effective checks on that power or to remove them from office (see chapter 12). This was not necessarily a political problem for Putin. Despite the changes to the system and people's awareness of manipulation, a majority of Russian voters saw elections as broadly legitimate, and many were happy to tolerate manipulation in return for economic growth (White and Feklyunina, 2011).

Electoral fraud and manipulation were to become issues, however, when economic growth slowed after the international economic crisis hit Russia in late 2008. The crisis saw a growing disenchantment with Putin and Medvedev, both of whose approval ratings fell (see figure 5.3, p. 103). Although economic recovery was comparatively quite quick after the major contraction of the Russian economy caused by the crisis, a sizeable section of the Russian electorate was alienated from the regime by the economic losses that they had suffered (Chaisty and Whitefield, 2012, 2103). There was also some negative popular reaction to the way in which Putin decided that he would return to the presidency, pushing Medvedev aside. This reinforced dissatisfaction with United Russia as a party of power, dissatisfaction that was summed up by anti-corruption campaigner and blogger Aleksei Navalny's labelling of it as the 'party of crooks and thieves'.

Cumulatively, crisis, arrogance and dissatisfaction with United Russia created a groundswell of opposition in late 2011 (White, 2013). Opposition was particularly strong in urban areas and among what many analysts in Russia saw as the 'new middle class', sometimes also called the 'creative class', that had been created by economic growth under Putin. There were strong warnings from before the election that this socio-economic group was alienated from what was for them an 'aging' political brand (Belanovsky et al., 2011). Expression of this discontent was articulated and mobilised through social media.

Dissatisfaction with the political system had nowhere to go electorally because of the control that had been built up during the 2000s. United Russia won with just under 50 per cent of the vote, but this was damaging to its image, and also to Putin, since this was a fall of 15 per cent on its vote in 2007 (see table 9.10). Some of this fall was the result of a slightly lower turnout, while some of it was because the share gained by other parties grew. The CPRF's vote went up by 8 per cent, the LDPR's by 3 per cent, A Just Russia's by nearly 6 per cent, and Yabloko's doubled, although it still fell well short of the 7 per cent threshold. This increase in votes for all the other main parties was probably the result of a popular response by some voters to the call by Navalny for them to cast their ballots for any party other than United Russia.

TABLE 9.10 Duma election, December 2011 (parties getting over the 7 per cent threshold are marked in bold)

Position in list vote at previous election		Votes	%	Seats	%
	Electorate	109,237,780			
	Valid votes	64,623,062	59.2		
	Invalid votes	1,033,464	0.9		
	Total votes (% of electorate)	65,656,526	60.1		
1	**United Russia**	32,371,737	49.3	238	52.9
2	**CPRF**	12,599,420	19.2	92	20.5
4	**A Just Russia**	8,695,458	13.3	64	14.2
3	**LDPR**	7,664,516	11.7	56	12.4
6	Yabloko	2,252,327	3.4	0	
9	Patriots of Russia	639,067	0.9	0	
	Right Cause	392,727	0.6	0	

The 7 per cent threshold meant that United Russia's share of 49.3 per cent translated into 52.9 per cent of the seats, but this was not viewed as legitimate and was a humiliating slump in the proportion from 2007, when it had captured 70 per cent of seats. United Russia almost certainly did win a plurality of votes, as official results showed, but there was a comprehensive feeling that it had not won as large a share as reported and that the outcome was brought about by widespread electoral fraud. Online reporting bolstered this feeling. More than 1,500 violations were reported on election day to one of the main NGOs tracking electoral fraud, GOLOS ('Voice') – violations that included such things as voters being bussed from polling station to polling station to vote several times for United Russia. GOLOS also reported several regions where there was abnormally high turnout as well as an abnormally high vote for United Russia, the same predictor of electoral fraud that Myagkov, Ordeshook and Shakin (2009) identified in earlier elections. The most grievous and blatant of these abuses was in the Chechen republic,

The late Boris Nemtsov at the December 2011 For Fair Elections rally

where a turnout of 99.5 per cent was matched by a vote of 99.5 per cent for United Russia (GOLOS, 2011: 10). Large-scale fraud was also suspected in Moscow, where the party polled more strongly than opinion polls would have indicated. A conservative estimate put the scale of this at 635,000 votes, but it is possible that United Russia gained up to 1 million more votes than it should have done and that United Russia's vote share in the city was inflated by about 11 per cent (Enikolopov et al., 2013).

The perceived injustices gave the non-systemic opposition a powerful fillip and led to large-scale demonstrations against Putin and for free elections in Moscow and across Russia (see chapter 8). These demonstrations forced some concessions from the authorities, which promised to police the March 2012 presidential election more carefully and to ensure fairness by putting webcams in polling stations.

The relatively poor showing of United Russia at the Duma election increased the need for Putin to do well at the presidential election to shore up his authority and to ensure that he could control intra-elite competition. The campaign for the presidency was therefore more heated than in either 2004 or 2008. The Kremlin firmed up Putin's vote by concentrating on mobilizing his core supporters and turning the election into a 'loyalty to Russia' test. The election, Putin argued in his main campaign address, was about 'people like us. ... We are prepared to work for the good of the Motherland ... [we will not allow others to] dictate their will to us, since we have a will of our own.' This campaign theme was not only aimed at rallying Putin voters to the flag; it was also a pre-emptive move against further protest. It contrasted

Putin – as defender of a form of Russianness – with the opposition, portrayed as metropolitan and 'cosmopolitan', in order to disarm potential protesters and provide grounds for the repression of opposition if it became necessary.

There was never any doubt that Putin was going to be re-elected in 2012; the issue was not winning but the size of his victory (see table 9.11). Officially, this was handsome: 63.6 per cent of the vote – less than his share in 2004 and Medvedev's in 2008, but still substantial. There were, however, charges of electoral fraud. Again, there were statistical anomalies in the vote caused by variance in turnout across regions and the disproportionate share of the excess that went to Putin. One estimate puts the number he gained from these anomalies at about 7 million votes (Kobak et al., 2012: 4). Removing these from Putin's official tally would reduce his share of the vote to just over 50 per cent. He would therefore have won on the first round even without fraud (assuming that the number of votes for his opponents stayed the same), but not with the ringing endorsement that he sought and that many believed was necessary for him to control the Russian political system. Fraud ensured that this endorsement was forthcoming and demonstrated to any potentially recalcitrant members of the elite that Putin could produce the results that he required. It also served to bind to him, and to the political machine that he had built, those who engaged in electoral fraud. Still, the result showed worrying political divisions in Russian society for the Kremlin. Putin's vote was less than 50 per cent in such major metropolitan areas as Moscow and St Petersburg. This reflected economic and social differences between Russia's regions that were potentially politically dangerous. Protest over electoral fraud and manipulation that brought down many post-Soviet regimes was focused in capital cities. A great electoral divide between Moscow and other parts of Russia creates an environment in which dissatisfaction can

TABLE 9.11 Presidential election, March 2012

	Votes	%
Electorate	109,860,331	
Valid votes	70,864,974	64.5
Invalid votes	836,691	0.7
Total votes (% of electorate)	71,701,665	65.2
Putin, Vladimir	45,602,075	63.6
Zyuganov, Gennady (CPRF)	12,318,353	17.2
Prokhorov, Mikhail	5,722,508	7.9
Zhirinovsky, Vladimir (LDPR)	4,458,103	6.2
Mironov, Sergei (A Just Russia)	2,763,935	3.8

be mobilized. Such mobilization was limited in 2011–12 and was potentially reversed by the post-electoral fragmentation of the opposition and the wave of nationalist sentiment that restored Putin's approval ratings following the annexation of Crimea in 2014.

The 2016 Duma election and 2018 presidential election: manipulating the electoral system and turnout

The restoration of Putin's popularity through the annexation of Crimea and clamping down on protest did not totally remove the fear that elections would be marred by protest. Changes to the length of the presidential term meant that the Duma election of 2016 would be the first not to precede a presidential vote since 1993. The presidential election would follow the Duma election only in 2018. This was always going to make the Duma election less febrile, as it would not be predicting a presidential election and the strength of competition over the presidency, nor would dissatisfaction with its spillover into a presidential election. Putin's regime decided to adopt a 'belts and braces approach', however, and changed the election law and timing to ensure that the Duma election would be protest-free. Its traditional date in December was brought forward to mid-September. This would mean that many people would not be able to vote as they would be on holiday, and students would be on vacation and dispersed. As many feared, turnout was very low, at 47 per cent of the electorate, the lowest that there had ever been for a Russian national election. The old mixed system that had been used between 1993 and 2003 was restored, with half of the 450 seats elected through PR, with a 5 per cent threshold, and half through SMD on a plurality basis. This was supposed to guarantee that United Russia would be able to win a majority of seats. Even if it didn't perform spectacularly in the PR vote, the co-option of regional elites into United Russia meant that this would be compensated for in the SMD vote, especially as the district boundaries of these seats were often gerrymandered to combine rural and urban areas. This would split up the urban vote, weakening the chances of parties other than United Russia, which polled better in rural than in urban areas.

The strategy paid off (see table 9.12). In contrast to previous elections, the SMD constituencies were not contested by strong independents, since local elites had been absorbed into United Russia, which won 203 out of the 225 seats. United Russia's PR vote went up moderately from its poor performance in 2011, climbing by just under 5 per cent to secure more than 50 per cent of the vote. After that, the results were pretty much par for the course. Only the CPRF, the LDPR and A Just Russia managed to get over the 5 per cent threshold, and all of them saw their vote share decrease apart from the LDPR, which gained a modest 1.5 per cent. Yabloko once more failed to cross the PR threshold and did not win any SMD seats. The other main liberal party, RPR-PARNAS, did not even manage to obtain 1 per cent of the vote.

TABLE 9.12 Duma election, September 2016 (parties getting over the 5% threshold are marked in bold)

	Electorate	110,061,200					
	Valid votes	51,339,235					
	Invalid votes	982,596					
	Total votes (% of electorate)	47.8					
Position in list vote at previous election		Votes %		Seats			
		List	SMD		List	SMD	Total (%)
1	**United Russia**	54.20	50.12		140	203	76.3
2	**CPRF**	13.34	12.23		35	7	9.3
4	**LDPR**	13.14	10.09		34	5	8.7
3	**A Just Russia**	6.2	10.0		16	7	5.1
	Communists of Russia	2.27	3.68		0	0	0.0
5	Yabloko	1.99	2.64		0	0	0.0
	Other parties	6.38	8.28		0	2[a]	0.4
	Independents	—	0.85		—	1	0.2
	Total	100	100		225	225	100

Note: [a]Rodina and Civic Platform won one single-member seat each.

The move back to the old electoral system gave United Russia over 100 more seats in the Duma than it won in 2011 on just a 5 per cent increase in the vote. There is evidence that there was considerable fraud to secure this victory (Baryshnikov and Coalson, 2016). As in previous elections, districts that reported above average turnout also reported that the bulk of the extra votes were for United Russia. The extent of this fraud may have been a little more concentrated than it was in 2007 and 2011, less 'metastasised' and more focused on republics. The worst, as usual, was Chechnya, which had turnout of 94 per cent, nearly double the national average of 47 per cent, and 96 per cent of the PR vote went to United Russia. Irregularities in other republics such as Dagestan and Kabardino-Balkaria were not quite so blatant, but higher than average turnout and votes for United Russia were still posted. Most Russian regions, with a few exceptions such as Kemerovo, saw voting figures for United Russia around or below the national average. Suppression of turnout rather than artificially high and inflated turnout seems to have been as effective as fraud in some of these regions. Turnout in Moscow, for example, was only 35 per cent, and United Russia polled only 37 per cent of the vote. Some of the low turnout was probably a result of moving the polling date from December to September, but it also may have been the case that non-United Russia voters simply didn't bother to vote, seeing it as a waste of time.

Putin seems to have traded off high turnout for headlines about United Russia's seat majority in the 2016 Duma election. Pressure was applied to raise turnout in the 2018 presidential election, however, since Putin wanted to demonstrate his personal dominance of the political system. Alexei Navalny, the opposition leader banned from competing in the election, tried to deny Putin a boost in legitimation by running an electoral boycott. But not all opposition forces agreed with this strategy, and two candidates associated with the opposition, Yabloko's Yavlinsky and the TV presenter Ksenia Sobchak, did run. In total there were eight candidates, including Zhirinovsky and a CPRF candidate, Pavel Grundin. Public authorities and organizations, and many private firms, were pressurized to get the vote out to counter Navalny's campaign. The aim of the official campaign was, allegedly, to achieve a turnout of 70 per cent and for Putin to get 70 per cent of the vote. In the end turnout was close to the target, at 67.5 per cent. People were induced to vote by online operations, competitions at polling stations and, at some stations, the offer of cheap goods. There was also fraud to boost both turnout and Putin's vote. Several election officials were caught on camera stuffing extra votes in ballot boxes, while some voters were seen to be voting more than once. The electoral register was purged of at least 1 million names so that turnout would look better. There was fraud again with very high turnouts in some regions and excess votes going to Putin. Turnout in Yamal-Nenets, for example, was 91.9 per cent and Putin got 85 per cent of the vote; in Chechnya it was 91.5 per cent, with Putin's share at 91.4 per cent.

The differences between the 2016 Duma election and the 2018 presidential election are telling. Low turnout and more focused electoral fraud in 2016 alongside changes to the electoral system enabled a United Russia victory without provoking protest. The 2016 election seems to have been designed to avoid confrontation, while the longer gap between Duma and presidential election would allow any tumult arising from the former to die down before the latter. At the same time, however, lower turnout meant that the Duma's legitimacy was lessened (even further) in comparison to that of Putin. Both elections were acclamatory, but the presidential election was managed to produce a roaring acclamation rather than the quiet approval of United Russia produced by the Duma election. Both elections thus reaffirmed the extent to which the Russian political system revolves around Putin, his persona and popularity, and the weakness of United Russia as an autonomous political force. This, however, begs the question of what will happen in 2024, when Putin's fourth presidential term ends and (at least as the current constitution stands) he is not eligible for re-election.

Conclusion

The development of Russian elections has been shaped by the needs and actions of the country's rulers. Gorbachev made changes to try to accelerate the pace of reform. Yeltsin created a system that helped to fragment parties. Both Gorbachev and Yeltsin's politics had unintended consequences: Gorbachev's reforms accelerated the demise of the Soviet system, while Yeltsin's reforms led to electoral instability as Duma elections became trial runs for presidential elections and party fragmentation weakened democracy. Putin's reforms decreased competition and fragmentation, but at a cost to democratic choice and electoral fairness. The electoral system had been far from perfect or effective in holding politicians to account in the 1990s, but it had at least been pluralist. Any pluralism in the electoral system after 2000 was 'managed' and lessened over time as reforms and party registration enabled both central and regional political elites to produce results that bolstered Putin's control. Electoral fraud and the degree of control over parties that could effectively fight elections (i.e., have a plausible chance of winning seats) have led one leading Russian specialist to argue that 'the country could avoid spending any money on elections and simply appoint members of parliament', except for the fact that 'Russian authorities ... have no other source of legitimacy' (Golosov, 2012b: 18). Elections under Putin have reduced the pursuit of legitimacy to securing large numbers of votes for United Russia and himself, rather than the pursuit of legitimacy through accountability and the provision of representation. This is not too dissimilar to the function that elections played under the Soviet system: acclamation. Such a legitimation strategy cannot work for ever; all political stratagems cease to work eventually, as the CPSU discovered. But it will be a long struggle to compel elections in Russia to do more than produce acclamation.

10
The New Russian Political Economy

Introduction

Problems of transition and managing the movement from a centrally planned economy to a market economy have been among the most important issues for the Russian state. Economic reform was the means by which Yeltsin tried to rebuild the post-Soviet state and defeat his political enemies. Compromise over reform shaped how he came to rule. Economic stability and growth were fundamental to the popularity of Putin and United Russia, and hence to Putin's ability to build up his control over the political system. Economic issues have thus shaped politics, but political forces and considerations have in turn shaped the economy. Russia's version of capitalism is a form of 'political capitalism'. All forms of capitalism are subject to political regulation; indeed, the way that this regulation takes place is one of the key factors that determines the type of a country's capitalism. In most varieties of capitalism, the profit motive is not routinely subordinated to political logics except in times of national emergency (Ganev, 2009). This is not the case, or not routinely and automatically so, in political capitalist systems.

The key question is whether or not political capitalism is designed to develop a state that can grow and secure a market economy. Economically backward states, as Alexander Gerschenkron (1962) argued, do not have time to build the social and economic institutions that create development. These institutions take time to evolve organically, time that the economically backward do not feel that they have because they fear being left even further in the wake of early modernizers. Thus, for example, instead of waiting for a financial sector to develop over time, and for that financial sector to direct investment into economic activity that creates development, the state uses its political authority to take resources from what Gerschenkron called 'old wealth' and to redistribute these from consumption to investment. Politics supplants the market logic of profit, seeking to create economic development. A developmental state represents and acts for a general social interest, the interest that all of its citizens have in securing economic growth. The ultimate hope is that such economic growth prompts social and institutional modernization; it should produce social classes that want, and are able, to make capitalism work with less direct intervention by the state.

197

The developmental state is, ideally, one that undermines the conditions that called it into existence in the first place.

Building a developmental state is, however, a difficult trick to pull off. Only a few states are lucky enough to be able to put in place institutions that create economic growth and modernization. Political capitalism often sees state officials satisfying their private desires instead of serving the general interest. When this occurs, the state doesn't mobilize resources to create the conditions for growth but, rather, is seen as a vehicle for enrichment and as an economic resource to be consumed. In this situation, the state becomes fragmented and unable to work to produce growth or modernization. Such states cannot represent a common interest. Instead what emerges is 'a privilege-centered polity where *de facto* control over assets is asserted by means of fragmented and personalized enforcement mechanisms. The boundaries of the state are porous and liable to be transgressed by social predators, and the de-bureaucratization of the public domain resulted in diminished levels of stateness' (Ganev, 2009: 672). Bureaucratic hierarchy and control are weakened and decline, as does the idea that the state is the servant of society. When this occurs the state is an obstacle to growth rather than its facilitator. Corruption, theft of state resources, and abuse of one's office in order to sequester wealth that is created by others is a common occupation of state officials. Economic growth, and consequently modernization, is imperilled. The state cannot use what resources it has to encourage economic development (for example, investment in infrastructure that creates employment and demand for goods and services) because, through the weakness of bureaucratic systems and accountability, these resources are stolen by its officials and/or used inefficiently. Society likewise lacks the motivation to grow the economy. Bureaucratic predation through corruption and the seizure of private assets means that there are few incentives to accumulate economic wealth. Alternatively, where wealth and resources are acquired, there is reason to ship them out of the country as quickly as possible so that corrupt officials cannot steal them. As a result, domestic savings, the basis of economic investment, are lower than they should be, and this negatively impacts economic growth.

Russia has struggled to build a developmental state. It experienced rapid economic growth during the Soviet period but with very different institutions to those of its capitalist rivals. The Soviet state was a developmental one, but its form was not capitalist. Over time, its ability to engender growth declined and it began to fall behind other industrial nations economically. This was one of the reasons for the Gorbachev reforms and the collapse of the USSR. The disintegration of the Soviet system and the attempt to introduce the institutions of a market economy – private property, market exchange – created economic chaos and a depression that was the largest that any economy has suffered in modern times. The task of post-Soviet Russian rulers has been to restore growth, catch up with other industrial economies, and establish new institutions to make this growth sustainable, and the country's economic history has been shaped by efforts to try to create a positive, developmental form of political capitalism and avoid a negative, predatory form. Roughly, the early 1990s saw an attempt to develop the institutions of capitalism rapidly through radical reform. The aim was to achieve strong control over a few instruments of economic policy and to use these to force through marketization, but this effort failed and a predatory form of capitalism was created. The 2000s saw the chaotic nature of Russian capitalism tamed and growth was restored, though this was primarily the result of external factors (the rising price of oil), so that the building of institutions that could support economic development and a less rapacious form of political capitalism remain an issue (Myant and Drahokoupil, 2011; Robinson, 2013a).

The Yeltsin legacy

The Russian government that came to power in the last few months of 1991 had to take responsibility for the economy, which had begun to fall into recession. As was pointed out in chapter 2, there was a significant gap between the pace of political change and the pace of economic change. Political change had been pushed forward by Gorbachev and had undermined the CPSU's control over national government. Economic change had been much slower. As the CPSU's political power imploded, economic elites, from ministers down to factory directors, had begun to take over the properties and assets that they managed in a wave of 'spontaneous privatization' (Johnson and Kroll, 1991). This meant that *de facto* control over the economy was more deeply embedded than ever in the networks of support that administrators had put in place to protect themselves from the vagaries of the planned economy. The chief resource that these networks gave their members was not capital as it exists in market economies (money, formal property rights) but *relational* capital, the store of personal ties, connections and mutual aid that came through interactions with other economic actors established over time (Gaddy and Ickes, 2002: 55–8). Economic administrators derived status and power from this control over property. Ordinary people were dependent on them for work and frequently for access to things such as housing, health care and the means to life, which were distributed through workplaces. This dependence increased as the economy contracted, and supplies of goods and services became erratic as the Soviet system collapsed. There was thus a great deal of continuity within the economy and the system of power relations that it contained even as the USSR ceased to exist: the economic *nomenklatura* changed less than the political *nomenklatura*.

Radical economic reform was supposed to change this and to do so with minimal administrative support from the central government. It was aimed at altering the system of economic exchange and the balance of power between anti-reform interests and the state. The new Russian government sought to alter the system of economic exchange, and hence realign social structure and the relative powers of the state and economic managers (see the discussion in chapter 4), but it didn't have the administrative capacity to make such changes through direct interaction with every part of the Russian economy. Power in the regions rested in the hands of the bureaucrats and economic managers who knew only the Soviet system and who were used to operating that system to their own advantage. These officials were not sympathetic to Yeltsin or understanding of reform, so the administrative system Yeltsin inherited was not one that could be used to support reform. Economic reformers argued that the inherited Soviet system didn't need to be used to implement change: radical economic reform, 'shock therapy', promised that the legacies of the Soviet era could be tackled through economic policy alone. Compliance with government policy depended on persuading people that there was a 'credible commitment' to reform, that the government was dedicated to reform and would pursue it no matter what, and that evading its implementation would only lead to the pursuit of more policies to keep reform on track. Soviet legacies would therefore be diluted as reform provided incentives to act differently and empowered the state and new economic groups relative to the old *nomenklatura*.

However, the political struggles that occurred under Yeltsin meant that it was impossible to make a credible commitment to reform (see chapter 4). Reform could not be pushed through, and what Joel Hellman (1998) has called a 'partial reform equilibrium' emerged. This enabled those economic actors who were able to take advantage of reform – reform's 'winners' – to make enormous profits, rents, at the expense of the state, workers and households. The 'partial reform equilibrium' helped Yeltsin politically, but it was unstable and an economic disaster, as can be seen in table 10.1.

TABLE 10.1 Selected economic indicators, 1992–8

	1992	1993	1994	1995	1996	1997	1998
GDP (%)	−14.5	−8.7	−12.6	−4.2	−3.5	0.8	−4.6
General government balance (% GDP)	−18.8	−7.3	−10.4	−6.0	−8.9	−7.9	−8.0
Industrial production (%)	−18.2	−14.2	−20.9	−3.0	−4.0	1.9	−5.2
Fixed investments (%)	−40.0	−12.0	−27.0	−13.0	−18.0	−5.0	−6.7
Trade surplus (US$ billion)	10.6	15.4	17.9	20.4	26.9	19.8	14.4
Metals, metal products, fuels and precious stones as a % of total exports	68.5	69.9	71.6	68.0	71.1	71.8	69.7
Wage arrears (US$ million, end of year)	69	614	1,183	2,884	6,221	6,657	8,240
Income inequality (Gini coefficient)	37.1	46.1	44.6	47.1	48.3	–	–

Source: Robinson, 2013b: 32.

This instability was the result of the problems caused by the different forms taken by 'winning' in Russia's partially reformed economy and the ensuing fiscal problems for the state. The different forms of 'winning' are summarized by the two terms most often used to describe the Russian economy in the 1990s: 'virtual economy' and 'oligarchic economy'. 'Virtual economy' is a term created by two American economists, Clifford Gaddy and Barry Ickes (2002), to describe how most of Russia's economy dealt with reform. Pressure from Gaidar's reformist government to commercialize economic activity in 1992 was met with resistance from large segments of industry. This was because many factory managers were uncertain what would result if they attempted to commercialize, to reshape their economic activity, to abandon subsidies and 'soft budget constraints' (see chapter 2) and to produce for profit. Firms therefore carried on as usual, re-creating the 'soft budget constraints' of the past using the networks of relational capital inherited from the planned economy. Relational capital – the trust that factory managers had in each other and the ties that they had to local authorities – enabled them to ignore reform. Instead of commercializing their relations, firms traded with one another on credit and operated a barter system. The need to earn money through commercial activity to pay one's bills was further sidestepped, as firms skimped on wages or made payments in kind (in the form of some of the factory's product) and avoided paying their energy and tax bills, often with official connivance – or, again, paid them in kind.

These actions covered up ongoing inefficiencies in Russian industry, protected old power relations in the economy, and transferred resources from households (in the form of workers' wages) and society (in the form of unpaid tax bills and energy bills) to factory managers on the basis of fictitious prices. Factories hid their inefficiency and made a 'profit' by coming up with prices that covered their costs and their tax bills. Firms and local authorities colluded with each other. The main outcome of this was the re-creation of subsidies. Some were local in origin, as, for example, when a regional tax office accepted payment in kind made at an inflated value in lieu of taxes. Others came from the centre. Parliament, for instance, took over the Central Bank of Russia during its struggles with Yeltsin in 1992 and issued money to firms so that they could pay off their accumulated debts to each other (the debts soon built up again). Corruption frequently oiled the wheels. Regional tax officials who took payment in kind might be bribed to do so, for example. Barter arrangements between companies could also be facilitated by corrupt side payments.

The growth of the virtual economy refashioned the subsidies and the transfers of resources from sectors that could have earned a profit on global markets to unprofitable and/or unreformed sectors of the Russian economy. In effect, this re-created a kind of political interference in the economy that had existed under the CPSU, although this was now much more chaotic. The scale of the subsidies was large. By the end of 1993, overdue payments of wages, taxes and inter-firm debt was equivalent to over 15 per cent of GDP (Tikhomirov, 2000: 22–3). Wage arrears grew throughout the Yeltsin era (as can be seen in table 10.1). Tax arrears meant that there was no chance of the government balancing the budget; as table 10.1 shows, the government balance was in the red across the Yeltsin era. The collapse of the Soviet economy and system plunged Russia into depression, with contracting GDP and slumps in industrial production year on year (with the slight exception of 1997) and in investment. Instead of attracting investment Russia witnessed vast amounts of capital flight, as individuals sought to protect earnings against political and economic instability (Tikhomirov, 1997; Robinson, 1999b). This flight also weakened government revenue collection as the money was hidden from tax collectors.

The spread of virtual economy practices meant that there were no counter-vailing positive economic trends. Economic policy-making, after the first rush of radical economic reform, was more about firefighting, dealing with the crises that afflicted the economy and the state budget, than about planning an exit from the country's woes. Overall, this meant that the structure of the Russian economy and its relationship to the wider world economy remained largely unchanged. Russia maintained Soviet patterns of trade, exporting energy and raw materials (see table 10.1). While this generated a trade surplus, it didn't work through the economy to help its modernization: a large part of the surplus was converted into subsidies for the virtual economy, as resources were 'injected into illiquid parts of the economy not in the form of money but in the form of fuel' (Shleifer and Treisman, 2000: 76). There was also continuity in economic management. The failure to alter economic exchange meant that, as initial rounds of privatization happened, the people best placed to exploit them were existing managers. The degree of insider takeovers during privatization was thus very high and management turnover very low. Insider control rebuffed foreign capital that would have balanced out the power of managers holding relational capital. This cut off large swathes of Russian industry from investment and technological inflows that might have relieved its relative backwardness. Foreign involvement was limited to the energy industry and a few service sectors – such as catering and accountancy – which had been chronically underdeveloped in the Soviet economy.

The development of the virtual economy, and in particular its effect on the government's revenue and budget, was one of the reasons for the estab-lishment of the oligarchic economy – a side effect of efforts to raise revenue for the government. The first of these was the 'loans for shares' scheme, described above, announced in 1995, which accessed a modest amount of money that had been accumulated after 1991 by new commercial banks through financing trade deals and currency speculation. But the loans for shares deals massively inflated the worth of these banks and their owners and turned them into financial-industrial groups that controlled a substantial share of Russian industry and its export sectors (Johnson, 1997; Guriev and

Rachinsky, 2005). In all probability the expansion of the banks and the trans-formation of their financial assets into control over real assets would have happened anyway, but the loans for shares scheme raised the public profile of the banks and created the idea of Russian oligarchs and of their closeness to power (Barnes, 2006: 114). This image was cemented in the popular mind by their support for Yeltsin in the 1996 presidential election, but economically the oligarchs were more enriched as the government shored up its finances by borrowing from them direct. This borrowing took the form of the banks buying short-term government bonds. The sale of bonds began in late 1994 and by spring 1997 equalled 12 per cent of GDP. This was very profitable for the banks, since interest rates were very high to encourage lenders to roll debt over into fresh bond issues. The speed and extent of the growth of the short-term bond markets eventually exceeded the capacity of domestic Russian banks to fund loans to government in this way. At the end of 1996 the market for government short-term debt was opened to foreign lenders, who would work through Russian banks to buy government bonds.

The development of the oligarchic economy alongside the virtual economy created two sets of winners from economic change, the old industrial elites and the new oligarchs. The emergence of these winners, alongside the contraction of state spending caused by radical economic reform and the collapse of the government's finances, created a deep gulf between rich and poor. This can be seen in the bottom line of table 10.1, which records the growth of income inequality in the 1990s through a standardized measure (the Gini coefficient). The higher this coefficient is on a scale of 1 to 100, the greater is the gap between the top and bottom income groups. Some change was to be expected, as Soviet income policies ended with reform, but the growth of inequality – in 1988 the USSR had a low Gini coefficient of 23.8 – was more rapid and higher in Russia than in other post-socialist states in Eastern Europe undergoing reform (Robinson, 2001: 429). Another sign of the stress on the general population was the declining birth rate and excess morbidity that carried over from the Soviet era, when the average age of death had begun to fall, particularly for men. This created a potential demographic crisis as the Russian population was declining, so that there was a threat of a declining workforce.

More pressing politically than these issues, however, were the budgetary problems created by the combination of 'virtual' and 'oligarchic' economies. Hellman's (1998) idea of partial reform argues that the power of winner groups to block further reform creates an 'equilibrium' – i.e., the power and dominance of winner interests is so great that partial reform is locked in and cannot be overturned. However, winner interests were not uniform in Russia. In the oligarchic economy, rent was taken from government bonds and by the transfer of property to banks through schemes such as loans for shares. In the virtual economy, it was taken by tax avoidance, wage arrears and non-payment of other debt. (It should be noted that financial-industrial groups in the oligarchic economy also made money through these practices.) These different forms of rent-seeking were irreconcilable and left no room for the state to fund itself and fulfil its functions. There was little money for the basic tasks of government, such as providing for defence, paying welfare to the needy, maintaining health-care systems, and paying the wages of government employees (policemen, teachers and doctors as well as bureaucrats), let alone for desirable projects such as infrastructure and economic development programmes. Virtual economy practices such as the non-payment of taxes, payment in kind at low rates, and untaxable inter-enterprise barter trade seriously weakened the government's revenue-raising power (Easter, 2012: 130–4). Borrowing covered some of the shortfall and provided banks with revenue, but it was not a good solution to Russia's fiscal problems. Sums raised through borrowing had to be paid back or rolled over and were very expensive because of the high rate of interest on Russian government bonds. Paying back money or rolling over debt into fresh bond issues required, respectively, tax collection or faith that there would be tax collection in the future.

Something had to give if the Russian state was to survive financially; the partial reform equilibrium could not hold. The first efforts at breaking the equilibrium came early in 1997, after Yeltsin's re-election to the presidency, when he promoted economic liberals in government and introduced a whole raft of measures to improve tax collection. The main targets of these measures were firms in the oligarchic economy, which were to be forced to pay their taxes and to pay them in cash. This, it was hoped, would lead them to demand payment from their customers in cash, so that barter and payment in kind would be squeezed out across the economy and the virtual economy would shrink. While this happened, more money would be borrowed through the Russian banks from abroad to cover immediate spending needs (Robinson, 2001).

This plan to restore state finances foundered, not because of concerted action by winner groups, but because of the weakness of government and external factors. The most politically visible winner group, the oligarchs, did not act collectively as an oligarchy. Instead they reacted to the tax squeeze on their firms by fighting viciously over loans for shares deals. This conflict dragged in government members, who were accused by losers in such deals of corruptly favouring winners, and exposed the fragility of the government. Reform measures were also held up in the Duma, which at this time had a Communist Party plurality that objected to reform measures. The domestic political problems of improving the government's revenues were then compounded by international economic factors. A dip in oil prices in the spring of 1998 meant that essential revenue dried up. At the same time, international lenders, who now underwrote government borrowing on the short-term bond market, began to withdraw their money, as the 1997 Asian crisis undermined confidence in emerging economies. Together, these factors proved too much for either government or economy to bear (Robinson, 2009). In August 1998, efforts to prop up the rouble and honour debt payments failed. The government debt market collapsed, the rouble had to be allowed to float, leading to its rapid devaluation, and a moratorium on debt repayments was announced.

Putin or oil? Change in the Russian economy, 2000–8

The August 1998 crisis showed that the oligarchic and virtual economies were not compatible because of the damage that they did to the state's finances. Fortunately for Russia, and for Putin once he came to power in late 1999, the 1998 crisis began to wear away the basis of the virtual economy and helped to create political conditions for controlling the oligarchic economy. Virtual economy practices began to decline because of the stimulus provided to the Russian economy by the crisis. As the rouble depreciated, foreign goods became more expensive. This provided some stimulus for Russian manufacturing and began to bring online some of the productive capacity that had fallen into disuse during the recession of the 1990s. It also became more expensive to move money abroad, so that more cash remained in the Russian economy. The monetization of the Russian economy, the aim of reformers in the early 1990s and again after 1996, was therefore gradually achieved after 1998, helped along by reforms initiated by Putin once he became president in 2000. The reform of both income taxes and taxes paid by major firms increased payment of revenue across the Russian economy, since it became easier to pay in cash rather than in kind. Regional control over tax collection was weakened, so that there were fewer opportunities for businesses to strike local deals to avoid tax or to pay in kind. As people paid their taxes, the government's revenues and ability to pay its bills and welfare commitments increased.

Government revenues also increased through energy exports, particularly of oil. Russia's economy had always been heavily dependent on energy exports, as well as the sales of some other basic commodities such as metals (see tables 10.1 and 10.2). After the 1998 crisis, the export of oil rose, first in volume and then in value. The increase in volume was because the owners of oil firms sought to add to the revenues they earned from their assets because they were fearful of a backlash against the privatization programmes of the 1990s, particularly the loans for shares programme. This fear was created first by the unsettled political environment created by the August 1998 crisis and then, as that environment settled, by Putin's promise during the 2000 presidential campaign to 'destroy the oligarchs as a class'.

Putin attacked, though did not destroy, the oligarchs after his election as president in March 2000 by moving against Boris Berezovsky, who had a wide range of financial and industrial interests as well as control over ORT, the main state television broadcaster, and Vladimir Gusinsky, who had banking interests and controlled NTV, the main independent TV station. Berezovsky and Gusinsky were stripped of their media interests and some of their other assets and fled Russia in early 2000 to avoid further prosecution. Putin met the remaining oligarchs in July 2000 and promised that there would be no further actions against them so long as they stayed out of politics (Rutland, 2003; Hanson and Teague, 2005; Tompson, 2005; Sakwa, 2008). The government, Putin argued, was going to be 'equidistant' from oligarchs from now on and not play favourites.

The response of the oligarchs was politically muted, but they continued to pump oil at increased rates. This also generated revenue for the state, since the oligarchs were now more diligent in paying taxes. The export value of oil, gas and metals nearly doubled in dollar terms between 1998 and 2002. Six major private oil firms accounted for nearly all of these additional exports, which accounted for about a quarter of Russia's growth between 2001 and 2004. As table 10.2 shows, the government's fiscal balance began to rise and became positive in 2000 (measured as a percentage of GDP). However, the budget surpluses enjoyed by the government until late 2008 were based on oil income, which rose dramatically after 2003 as global energy prices rocketed upwards as a result of shortages (caused by growing demand from China and the rest of the expanding world economy) and political instability in the Middle East (in particular Iraq, where oil production slowed because of the war).

The net effect of these changes was that the Russian economy recovered and flourished across the 2000s. As table 10.2 shows, GDP and industrial output grew between 1999 and late 2008 by about 7 per cent a year. As GDP and industrial output picked up, incomes and living standards rose too, providing strong performance legitimacy for Putin and for United Russia (see chapter 9). The boost to the country's economic fortunes was not the result of changes in how well the economy was run, however. Overall, governance didn't improve, and economic reform was often compromised by the poverty of public administration (see the lack of change in governance indictors in figure 1.1, p. 16) and political risk; when reform looked likely to provoke a public backlash, the oil-rich administration backed away from it. The monetization of welfare benefits in 2005 is a case in point. Many welfare payments were paid in kind as a legacy of Soviet social policy to groups such as veterans, who received free transport, medicine and health care. Plans to replace the benefits in kind with cash payments largely failed, since poor public administration meant that much of the reform could not be implemented, and certain key provisions of the policy were delayed following protests (see chapter 8).

There were other continuities too. Corruption continued more or less unchecked despite Putin's frequent promises to rein it in. Russia remained one of the most corrupt states in the world, and bureaucratic predation on the economy remained high (Holmes, 2008). Political connections continued to

TABLE 10.2 Selected economic indicators, 1999–2017

	1999	2000	2001	2002	2003	2004	2005	2006	2007	2008	2009	2010	2011	2012	2013	2014	2015	2016	2017
Government balance (% GDP)	-0.9	1.9	3.0	0.9	1.3	4.5	8.1	8.4	6.0	4.9	-6.2	-3.4	1.5	0.4	-0.7	-1.0	-2.4	-3.4	-3.2[a]
GDP (% change, real terms)	6.4	10.0	5.1	4.7	7.4	7.2	6.4	8.2	8.5	5.2	-7.9	4.4	4.3	3.4	1.3	0.5	-2.8	-0.2	1.4[a]
Industrial output (% change)	11.0	8.7	4.9	3.1	8.9	8.0	5.1	6.3	6.3	2.1	-10.8	8.2	4.7	2.6	0.3	-0.3	-0.8	1.3	0.7[b]
Metals, metal products, fuels and precious stones as a % of total exports	72.7	75.5	81.4	76.9	75.3	78.0	81.6	82.2	80.8	91.0	90.3	81.2	82.5	82.5	–	–	–	–	–
Income inequality (Gini coefficient)	–	–	39.6	35.7	–	–	37.5	–	43.6	42.2	40.0	40.9	41.0	41.59	–	–	–	–	–

Notes: [a] Forecasts.

[b] January–April 2017.

Sources: Robinson, 2013b: 37; World Bank, 2017b; Federal'naya sluzhba gosudarstvennoi statistiki, 2013: 36, 544; 2017; OECD, 2014; Ekonomicheskaya ekspertnaya gruppa, 2017.

allow businesses to accumulate wealth. Although privatization slowed in the 2000s, political connections were often used to secure control of successful companies through 'raiding', a kind of corrupt corporate takeover that often involved using law-enforcement officials to force company owners to hand over their firms to rivals with the right political connections (Sakwa, 2013b). Although incomes rose across Russia, large-scale social inequality persisted. As table 10.2 shows, the Gini coefficient dipped slightly in the mid-2000s but remained largely the same as in the 1990s. Apart from some individual cases, the super-rich were largely unaffected by Putin's rise to power. Russia continued to have a far larger number of billionaires than its economic size and structure would predict. One study estimated that the country should have ten billionaires. At the time it actually had fifty-three, an 'excess' of forty-three billionaires, one of the largest such excesses of the super-rich in any country of the world (Popov, 2014: 51). Although there were high-profile cases against some billionaires under Putin (see below), a study of the world's super-rich by the Credit Suisse Research Institute (2013: 28) noted that Russian billionaires had a higher 'survival rate than any other BRIC [Brazil, Russia, India and China, a label for the world's largest emerging economies] or G7 country', and that this probably showed a high level of 'state protection of billionaire interests' even in times of international economic crisis (see Novokmet et al., 2017, for the most extensive survey of economic inequality in Russia).

Much of the oligarchic economy and much of the oligarch's control over high-value assets therefore survived into the Putin era. The major exception to this involved the head of the oil giant Yukos, Mikhail Khodorkovsky, and the return of the company's assets to the state oil firm Rosneft (for a full discussion of the case, see Sakwa, 2009, 2014). Khodorkovsky was singled out for arrest, trial, imprisonment and appropriation of assets because he broke the July 2000 'deal' and did not keep out of politics. He tried to do deals that would have compromised state control over oil transportation and was disliked personally by Putin and key members of his team. The Yukos affair saw the return of significant assets to state control and was followed up by the seizure of other assets by the state (Shell and BP had to concede control over the Sakhalin-2 and Kovykta gas projects to Gazprom, for example), the blocking of sales of large firms to foreign companies, the placement of state representatives on the boards of major companies, the consolidation of energy holdings by state companies (Sibneft, Roman Abramovich's oil firm, was sold to Gazprom, for instance), and the rolling back of privatization of some major industrial firms, such as Kamaz (trucks). Overall, state ownership of Russia's equity market capitalization rose from 20 to 30 per cent between 2003 and mid-2006, and this was before the final redistribution of all of Yukos's assets or the transfers to Gazprom of major holdings in the Sakhalin-2 and Kovykta gas fields in late 2006 and 2007, as well as other smaller actions against business in the interest of state corporations (OECD, 2006: 32; Hanson, 2007).

The chief effect of these actions was not to make the state the engine of economic growth, however, but to consolidate the government's control of revenue sources so that its fiscal position was robust. In effect, Putin was running what Gaddy and Ickes (2010) have called a 'protection racket': most oligarchs got to keep their property and were supported by the state in return for paying taxes that could be used to prop up the rest of the economy. Increased state involvement in the economy backed up the protection racket that Putin used to control the oligarchs.

Economic growth did not mean that Russia became more competitive even as the market expanded within the country. Economic growth, particularly growth in industrial output, was protected and was not export-led, as innovation and change were weak. Industrial production could expand because there was a lot of under-used industrial capacity that had been put in place under the USSR and that was protected from competition. As seen in figure 10.1, the barriers to trade and investment in Russia were much higher than in many other advanced industrial economies. Figure 10.1a shows how regulated product entry is: on a scale of 0 to 6, Russia scores 3.16, far higher than an open market such as the UK (0.04), and far higher than other emerging economies such as South Africa (1.86) and Brazil (1.3). Innovation in the manufacturing sector, on the other hand, is much lower, as is shown in figure 10.1b. Only about 13 per cent of Russian manufacturing firms were engaged in innovation, far fewer than in other emerging economies or established capitalist economies.

Russia's manufacturing sector also benefited from the continuation of subsidies. As in the 1990s, the source of these subsidies was energy. Domestic energy prices remained below international market prices, thus continuing a key plank of what had been the virtual economy under Yeltsin, transferring value from the energy sectors to the rest of the economy, and in particular to the highly energy-inefficient industrial economy. There were also indirect subsidies, as the Central Bank of Russia intervened in currency markets to try to protect Russian industry from imports and maintain competitiveness. While this intervention slowed the appreciation of the rouble, appreciation remained significant and fast because of the large trade surplus created by the increased volume and value of energy exports. However, the bank could deal with this thanks to the massive revenues earned from oil and gas sales, and their intervention helped maintain some industrial competitiveness by leaving the rouble undervalued by about 10 to 20 per cent.

Finally, the revenues generated by record global energy prices and the availability of low-cost credit in the USA and Europe meant that it was cheap for Russia's major businesses to borrow in foreign currency: on average, the rouble cost of dollar loans between 2003 and mid-2007 was 1 per cent. There was therefore a flurry of borrowing by Russia's major firms, such as the aluminium concern Rusal, and by many state-owned firms, including the oil company Rosneft and the gas giant Gazprom. This borrowing was partly to

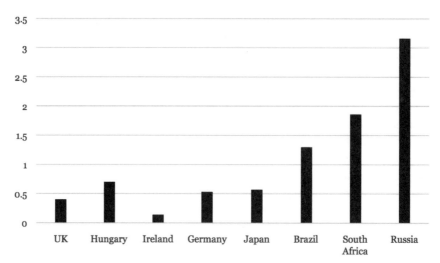

Figure 10.1a *Barriers to trade and investment (product market regulation indicator, 0–6) (data for various years 2008–10; Russia data for 2008)*

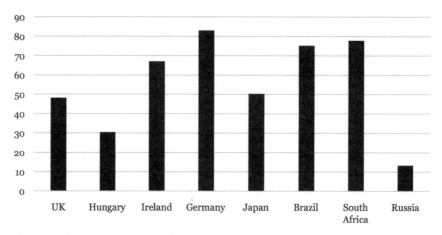

Figure 10.1b *Innovation in manufacturing sector (percentage of all manufacturing firms) (data for various years 2008–10; Russia data for 2008)*
Source: Adapted from OECD, 2014: 67, 119.

generate revenue for development in the absence of a developed domestic banking sector, partly to fund purchases outside Russia as firms bought both upstream and downstream and developed as global players in metals and energy. The borrowing on global markets suited the Russian government, since it created investment, and suited the firms involved, since it spread their assets and sometimes their ownership beyond Russia, thus freeing them from some of the risk to economic actors' property rights at home. The very low rates at which borrowing took place represented another subsidy from energy production to the borrowers (Robinson, 2011). External borrowing by industry, including state-owned firms and corporations, reached $307 billion in June 2008; the financial sector had borrowed another $200 billion by June 2008 – all told some 40 per cent of GDP (Connolly, 2009).

The growth that Russia experienced under Putin did not, therefore, exhibit as radical a break with the past as the headline figures of GDP growth might seem to indicate. Growth took place on the industrial platform inherited from the USSR and kept in place some of the transfers to industry inherited from the virtual economy and the structure of wealth created by the division of economic change into winners and losers. Overall, Russian industry remained relatively uncompetitive and didn't innovate to overcome this. Difficulties of attracting foreign investment meant that importing innovation from abroad was slow. While there was growth in other sectors of the Russian economy in the 2000s as trade, services and construction grew, these too were fuelled by income from energy sales. There were therefore strong doubts both about Russia's ability to compete with other emerging economies at the end of Putin's first two terms as president (Cooper, 2006) and about whether the economic 'success' that Putin had brought was sustainable (Hanson, 2007; Rutland, 2008; Robinson, 2009).

Crisis, 'modernization' and the return of Putin

By the end of Putin's first two terms as president, the Russian economy presented a strange picture. On the one hand there had been clear successes

Putin's tears in oil: graffiti in Perm satirizing Russia's dependency on oil

'If Russia has oil, I'm shopping in Milan.'

since 1999. Growth had averaged 7 per cent a year. Increased government revenue had produced large fiscal surpluses so that external debts were paid down and overall public debt was very low. External debt declined from 90 per cent of GDP in 1999 to about 12 per cent of GDP at the end of 2005. In June 2006 Russia announced that it would clear its remaining debt to the Paris Club of US$22 billion and settle an early repayment fee of US$1 billion (Robinson, 2009: 444). Foreign reserves grew to nearly US$600 billion, most of which was placed in two stabilization funds, the Reserve Fund and the National Wealth Fund. These were built up to be available to ameliorate the effects of fluctuating oil prices on the state budget and the economy more generally. But this positive picture was tempered by realization that the economy was highly dependent on energy exports. By 2008, 80 to 90 per cent of all oil revenues went to the federal budget and accounted for about half of that revenue. Any downturn in oil prices was thus going to be a major shock to the economy, but Russia had a stock of money to cope with such an upheaval.

Putin didn't want to draw on this money, however. As his first presidential term drew to a close, he began to talk about economic 'modernization' to protect Russia from the boom and bust cycles that can plague oil-rich economies. The agenda for modernization was essentially one of economic diversification: modernization was supposed to encourage non-energy sectors of the economy to grow and become sources of external revenue generation. The idea was to change the Russian economy but in a way that was gradual and cost-free politically. Putin proposed large-scale infrastructural developments and the promotion of some new national champions in new technology areas such as nanotechnology. There were also plans to attract more foreign investment. What these plans meant was that the basic structure of the economy – revenue earned from oil cushioning domestic

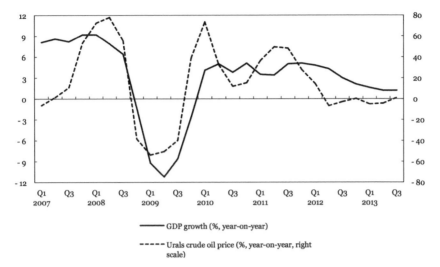

Figure 10.2 *Economic dependency on oil*
Source: Adapted from OECD, 2014: 15.

Russian manufacturing and consumption – would be supplemented rather than replaced by new sources of growth and high-value production. Over time the 'supplement' would hopefully grow and transform the basic structure of the economy so that the dependency on oil would decrease, but the basic pattern of the government presiding over the redistribution of energy rents would not be attacked directly or at potential political cost.

This scheme for gradual change was thrown into chaos almost immediately after Putin handed the presidency to Medvedev. The international financial crisis that had begun in the USA and Europe hit Russia in the autumn of 2008 as oil prices slumped. This had an immediate effect on Russian economic fortunes. As can be seen in figure 10.2, growth plummeted as energy prices fell (the price of oil dropped by $90 per barrel between July 2008 and the start of 2009 due to the slump in global demand). Industrial production also declined rapidly, and the government balance went back into the red as tax and excise duties dwindled (see table 10.2). The value of the rouble slid on foreign exchanges and the value of stocks on the Russian stock exchange fell. The drop in the value of both the rouble and stocks was inevitable given the predominance of energy stocks in the Russian market and the large foreign borrowings of many of the major Russian firms. The exchange rate of the rouble now pushed the costs of these foreign borrowings up dramatically. The collapse of the stock market and the exposure of major firms to their foreign debts were matched by a sharp contraction in lending by Russian banks. Interest rates rose as banks shifted their assets into dollars to avoid being caught by further falls in the value of the rouble and to service their foreign debts; the average rate charged to firms rose from 11 per cent in July 2008 to 17 per cent in January 2009.

The broadening financial crisis led to sharp contractions in construction, industrial production and wages and to an increase in unemployment. The headline figures were that, in 'the fourth quarter of 2008, industrial production decreased by 6.1% compared to the same period of 2007. Manufacturing activities fell by 7.7%, the real after-tax incomes decreased by 5.8%, and investment into fixed assets, by 2.3%' (Russian Government, 2009). This contraction continued in 2009. Unemployment rose from 6.1 to 8.4 per cent of the working-age population between 2007 and the end of 2009 (Robinson, 2013c: 457).

The initial response to the crisis was led by the Central Bank of Russia, which used its reserves to slow the depreciation of the rouble, to take pressure off firms that had to repay loans denominated in foreign currency, and to prop up the stock market. Tackling the crisis by defending the rouble was an expensive policy measure, but the currency began to stabilize in January 2009, which enabled firms and banks to cover a significant proportion of their foreign borrowings and more immediate debt obligations. At more or less the same time the policy response to the crisis began to widen as there was a shift from using financial resources for currency protection to direct economic stimulus by the state. The amount deployed in the stimulus package was substantial – equivalent to roughly 12 to 13 per cent of GDP in both 2009 and 2010 – and estimated as being the third largest worldwide at that time. Spending on social policy rose from 8.6 to 13 per cent of GDP between 2007 and 2010. Most of this increase was in pensions, where spending went up from 5.9 to 9.9 per cent of GDP (OECD, 2011: 97). Much of the rest of the stimulus went on subsidies to industry, particularly to the automobile industry and construction. State purchases were increased and preferential prices paid to Russian suppliers; there was direct support for industries affected by the downturn of the oil economy (such as transport firms) and support for regional budgets (Robinson, 2013c: 459–60).

Recovery was assisted from mid-2009 by the steady revival of oil prices, which dragged the Russian economy back up into growth (see figure 10.2). This was a considerable success for the Russian government; few other states that were as badly affected by the international economic collapse recovered as quickly, and most of the worst-affected eurozone states languished in the economic doldrums for several years. Russia's economic success was not complete, however. The main reason for this is that the 2008 crisis weakened confidence in the development 'model' of the 2000s. Growth was dependent on the price of energy, and the state had managed to capture most of the revenue from energy sales to avoid the types of crisis that had plagued it in the 1990s. The crisis of faith in the economic system was compounded by how discussions of 'modernization' developed during the recession. Medvedev argued that the true sign that the economic crisis was being dealt with was not a return to growth – that was a result of changing energy prices

– but economic diversification. This, he said, required institutional change to ensure that the crisis was not repeated in the future:

> I can tell you quite honestly that I am not happy with our economic structure. We were aware of this even before the crisis … What we really should have done is diversified the structure of our economy to a greater extent. … We entered the crisis with the same raw materials structure that we had in the past … Our economy's one-sided structure is reflected in the figures we are seeing today. … We will pull ourselves out of this crisis; however, the same situation could repeat itself several years down the road. The patterns governing this crisis are not fully clear, and nobody knows when we might have another one like it. Thus, we must begin creating a new economic structure now. (Medvedev, 2009a)

By arguing in this fashion, Medvedev created a rhetorical position from which the efforts of the government as a whole could only be found wanting. Economic recovery, which would have been the envy of most other governments, could be regarded as a form of failure since it was associated with rises in energy prices rather than with modernization; such a way out of the crisis, Medvedev argued in December 2009 – as the crisis was ending and growth returning to the economy – 'leads nowhere. We need to get out of the crisis by reforming our own economy.'

The type of 'modernization' that Medvedev was proposing involved political change that would increase the state's capacity to regulate the market without privileging elite interests (Medvedev, 2010). These reforms were obviously much more than economic policy matters and required a political consensus to deliver them that Medvedev could not secure. Faith in the country's economic future remained lower than should have been the case given the recovery effected by rising oil prices because sweeping reform, including political reform, was not possible. Capital flight continued and investment was low. One estimate is that 'offshore wealth is about three times larger than official net foreign reserves … and is comparable in magnitude to total onshore household financial assets. That is, there is as much financial wealth held by rich Russians abroad … than held by the entire Russian population in Russia itself' (Novokmet et al., 2017: 5). Continued capital flight, resulting in a serious shortfall in investment funds, is one reason that, as table 10.2 and figure 10.2 show, Russian economic growth slowed after 2012. The slowdown was not just the result of low confidence after the 2008 crash, but also because, in particular, underutilized industrial capacity left over from the Soviet period was either used up or had begun to reach the end of its useful working life. New sources of growth needed to be found and new means of financing, of investment, needed to be created. None of these things were possible in the absence of wider reform.

Putin's return to the presidency in March 2012 ended discussion of modernization via political reform. Spending on welfare that had been a part of the anti-crisis package was kept up for electoral reasons, and the drive for modernization became focused increasingly on the defence sector as much as the rest of the economy. 'The defence industry', Putin (2012c) argued, 'has always been an engine pulling the other manufacturing sectors along behind it', and 'we will have to modernize the entire defence industry and the way it works, and carry out the same kind of comprehensive and powerful modernization drive that was achieved in the 1930s.' This shift in focus was partly a response to foreign policy changes, as Putin began to lay more emphasis on the Eurasian Economic Union, and as relations with the West soured (Putin, 2014c; see also chapter 11). Welfare and increased defence spending helped to make the government balance negative after 2013, adding to the pressure on finance caused by the erratic recovery of energy prices, which did not reach the heights of the mid-2000s. Another consequence of lower energy prices was sluggish performance in growth. As table 10.2 shows, GDP growth was slow in 2013 and 2014, and the economy then went into recession in 2014, 2015 and 2016. Growth in industrial output remained low too.

International factors such as the sanctions put in place after Russia's annexation of Crimea did not help improve economic performance but have not affected the slowdown as much as changing energy prices. However, they have helped suppress the economy through isolation and by increasing the tendencies – already apparent as Putin began his term – to look to the regional economy and to defence-led growth. The slight rise in energy prices at the end of 2016 helped create some growth in 2017 but highlighted the fact that the overall structure of the economy, and the nature of the problems that it faced, had remained largely unchanged since 2008. Forecasts for economic change were therefore cautious (see, for example, World Bank, 2017c). As Medvedev had realized in 2008, the solution to Russia's problems required political action. This, however, does not seem likely to be forthcoming.

Conclusion

Putin's rule provided Russia with economic stability and growth until 2008, but there was a great deal of underlying continuity with the economy of the 1990s. Rising oil prices and increased output resulted in growth, but much remained the same: economically Russia is highly unequal, frequently corrupt and competitively weak. The increase in government intervention under Putin had some positive outcomes, such as the stabilization of the state's budget and the accumulation of reserves that could be used to deal with boom–bust cycles in oil prices. However, Russia is far from having a form of political capitalism that is positive. Corruption remains rife, and the development of a more robust system of political control under Putin did not improve governance in the country as a whole, as we saw in chapter 1 (see in particular figure 1.1). At best, the Russian state is partially developmental, able to control consumption to create a modicum of economic stability but not to develop administration and policy in a way that will transform the economy as a whole. At worst, the form of political capitalism is parasitical because of corruption and because the Russian people are denied opportunities for development while a super-rich social stratum of businesspeople and high state officials is protected. The economic winners of the 1990s remain largely in place and are as rich as ever. The economic losers of the 1990s saw their lot improve after 1998, so that living standards in the country overall reached about 70 to 75 per cent of the Western European average by the mid-2010s (Novokmet et al., 2017: 3), but credit for this was as much with changing global demand for energy as it was with the Russian government.

Russia might evolve out of this situation. Economic stability and experience of the market might over time produce social groups who become concerned to protect what they have politically against predation by state officials and their business cronies. The negative reaction to the economic crisis of 2008 from those who felt the Putin system of economic governance was not going to meet their longer-term economic interests might be a first sign of such social groups emerging. Opposition from such social groups is still weak, however, and it will be a long time before they can reshape Russia's political economy. While this is the case, reform of the economy will remain an issue, as the government is the only agency that is able to change the political conditions that shape Russia's political economy.

11
Russia and the World

Introduction

Russia inherited the bulk of the USSR's territory but not its great power status. The new Russia comprised 76 per cent of the area and 60 per cent of the population of the old USSR, but about 25 million Russians, or 17 per cent of the ethnic Russian population of the former USSR, now lived outside the country, and territory (such as Ukraine) was lost that had been viewed as a part of 'Russia' for centuries. Economically and militarily, Russia was weakened by a loss of productive capacity, the fragmentation of what had been a unified Soviet military economy, and a massive depletion of military materiel, weapons systems, personnel, equipment and bases. It also faced a series of new foreign policy problems: How would it deal with other post-Soviet and post-communist states, many of which were fearful because of their historic experiences with the tsarist empire and the USSR? What responsibilities did it have – if any – for ethnic Russians living in what were now sovereign states? How could it deal with the security problems that were created by the loss of some of its military and economic capacity and by the creation of new, and often weak states around its new borders? How would it build new relationships with the USA, China, what had been Soviet client states (such as Syria) and Europe, including the states that had been subject to Soviet domination in Eastern Europe? All of these questions begged other questions: What were Russia's national interests? What were its immediate and longer term interests, and how could they be aligned?

It is debatable whether these questions have ever been answered by Russia's leaders, who have struggled to find a role for the country after the Cold War. As Russia has struggled to define its role in the world, and as no other country has been able to assign it a role that it can tolerate, its relations with the West have worsened. Hope for good relations soured under Yeltsin, but did not die completely. Relations improved a little in the first years of the 2000s under Vladimir Putin but then deteriorated after the invasion of Iraq in 2003. Rather than provide a comprehensive blow-by-blow account of Russian foreign policy, this chapter will look at these issues to describe the main currents of the country's international relations under Yeltsin and Putin. First, however, we will look at the question of whether Russia's foreign policy is driven by global or domestic politics.

Drivers of Russian foreign policy

Arguments about the factors that have been the main driver of Russian foreign policy overlap with arguments about whether the West bears responsibility for the deterioration of relations. If Russian foreign policy is a reaction to global developments, then there is a possibility that it was 'lost' by the West, since the West bore most responsibility for shaping global politics after the Cold War. If it has been shaped by domestic politics, Russian politicians bear equal, and perhaps more, responsibility for the deterioration of relations.

Was Russia lost?

Russia suffered great humiliation and loss of power in 1991 when the USSR collapsed. The Warsaw Pact and alliances that had made the USSR a global power also collapsed, but those of the West endured. Russia became a supplicant to such Western international economic organizations as the IMF, the World Bank and the World Trade Organization. This uneven end to the Cold War meant that the West, and the United States in particular, was the dominant international power in the 1990s and had responsibility for shaping what US President George H. W. Bush defined in September 1990 as the emergent 'new world order'. This represented a unipolar moment: there was only one global power, the USA, which had the strength to make the international system. Since this system was, even if only briefly, unipolar, there was an overlap between international systemic factors that shaped Russian foreign policy and Western (but mainly American) actions.

Russian losses did not stop after the Cold War, because Western policy continued to push North Atlantic Treaty Organization (NATO) and EU expansion to the point where they became a threat to the country's security. Inevitably, Russia pushed back when it could – i.e., when it had some economic and military strength, and when its interests were too greatly infringed upon (Mearsheimer, 2014; Tsygankov, 2015). This argument echoes that made by Putin (2014b) after the annexation of Crimea in 2014, when he explained that, following the EuroMaidan revolt in Ukraine, Russia had 'found itself at a threshold from which it could not retreat. A spring that has been compressed will at some point snap back with force. We must always remember this.'

This argument privileges international factors to explain Russian foreign policy. Worsening relations with the West and increased Russian belligerence in dealings with its post-Soviet neighbours are reactions to external developments in the international system – the end of the Cold War, the loss of Russian influence and prestige, the corresponding growth of US and, to a lesser extent, European power, the shrinking of the zone of security that used to surround the country when it controlled Eastern Europe, the Caucasus and Central Asia, and its loss of international leverage as it forfeited its client states in Africa, Asia and the Middle East. How it has reacted to external events and loss is a function of both what happens around it – how its misfortunes grew over the Yeltsin years and how threatened it has felt – and the capacity it has to react. Hence, when it lacked economic and military capacity in the 1990s, Russia complained about the West's policies but was powerless to do anything about them. In the 2000s, when it had more capacity, it took action, launching diplomatic offensives against Western policy as well as military offensives in Georgia and Ukraine.

There is some truth, but only some, in the argument that Russia was lost. The truth of the 'West is to blame' argument lies in the fact that there has often been a failure in the West to realize how much some of its actions might be a problem for Russia. However, many of these actions have come *after* relations had deteriorated. George W. Bush's administration raised the prospect of Georgian and Ukrainian NATO membership in 2007 and 2008, and this helped provoke the war with Georgia in 2008, for example. But the actions of the Bush administration came after Russia had hardened its policy to the West over a whole range of issues, including the Iraq war (which was the fault of Bush) and 'colour revolutions' (which the West did not cause). The Bush administration's actions pushed a bad relationship into becoming a worse one, but they didn't create the bad relationship, which was caused by multiple factors, only some of which can be laid at the feet of the West.

Some of the points just made are contested. For example, some would argue that, while it may not have caused the 'colour revolutions', the West's support for them as potential democratization processes ignored Russia's concerns in the area and Russian perceptions that such events were counter to its interests. However, this begs the question as to whether Russia's interests were always legitimate and, if they were, whether it dealt with threats to its interests in the right way. The answer to these questions is generally going to be no: Russia's interests were not necessarily legitimate and it defended its illegitimate interests badly. The Orange Revolution in Ukraine in 2003–4 led to the formation of a government that was less sympathetic to Moscow and more pro-Western. This was seen as a defeat for Putin and a reduction in Russian influence. The Russian argument, and the argument of analysts who think that the West should not have become involved, is that the West should not have supported the new Ukranian government, since this was going to decrease Russia's sphere of influence. Accepting this line of argument means accepting that a state – any state – has a right to a sphere of influence just because it is bigger and better armed than the states around it. It means accepting that Russia therefore has a privileged sphere of influence in Ukraine and the former republics of the USSR, and this gives it a say in the domestic political organization of countries in its sphere. This is problematic. Russia obviously does not want Ukraine to be a security threat any more than, for example, France wants Luxembourg to be a source of insecurity for France. But this does not give Russia any rights over how the people of Ukraine dispose of their governments as long as this disposal does not cause physical harm to Russians or Russian territory (the same goes for France and Luxembourg). Russia had, and has, a right to be concerned about how changes in the government of Ukraine would influence Russian–Ukrainian relations and agreements between the two states, as well as about the possibilities of Ukraine cooperating militarily with NATO. Russia might also be concerned about the economic loss that comes with government change. But Russian reactions to these types of issues needed, and need, to be proportionate and lawful. Arguably, cutting off oil and gas supplies to Ukraine, as occurred after the Orange Revolution, or annexing Crimea and facilitating rebellion in Eastern Ukraine after the EuroMaidan were neither proportionate nor lawful, since they led Russia to break international agreements and laws.* Such actions convey the idea that Russia is a threat, so that, just as we can say that the West has 'lost' Russia, we can also say that Russia 'lost' the West. Misunderstanding has been mutual so it is hard 'to pinpoint the precise moment at which relations between Russia and the West went wrong. It may be that there was never a moment at which they were going right' (Conradi, 2017: 321).

A more serious charge against the West is that it did not rethink and reorganize the security architecture of Europe or of the world more generally in ways that would have allowed Russia to see itself in partnership with the West. Instead, it maintained and subsequently expanded NATO, so that Russia was inevitably going to be poorly served in post-Cold War global politics by international security institutions.

Again, there is some truth in this. The integration of Russia into structures of global governance after the collapse of the USSR was uneven. Quite quickly it joined some international organizations that it had previously scorned, such as the World Bank and the International Monetary Fund; both Russia and the West saw its membership of these bodies as necessary if the country was to complete economic reform. But in general there was little thought as to how organizations that managed global and European security would be reformed. The fundamental structures of the United Nations, for example, were not changed even though they had been designed to manage the conflicts of the post-Second World War world and reflected the balance of power from the 1940s. NATO, whose *raison d'être* was to protect Europe from the USSR, was extended as former Soviet allied states in Eastern Europe became members. There were some efforts to develop structures around NATO that could help manage relations with Russia (among other countries) (Smith and Timmins, 2001), but they were not able to ensure cooperation. As cooperation failed

---

* What about the actions of the USA in [insert the name of pretty much any country]? What about US spheres of influence ...? Two wrongs don't make a right, as your mother should have explained to you.

and relations worsened, it was easy for Russia to portray NATO as a hostile alliance, perpetuating itself by working to contain and isolate Russia. NATO expansion was described by Russia as a betrayal of Russian goodwill and of promises that expansion would not happen (Tsygankov, 2013; whether such promises were made is debatable; see Kramer, 2009). Since NATO expansion and EU expansion overlapped, they became seen in Russia as linked processes and as examples of victor's justice, or at least were presented as such, and condemned as unfair. This was one of the reasons why the crisis in Ukraine became so heated: discussions about Ukraine's relationship with the EU were seen as having broader security dimensions in Russia.

Bringing Russia back in

We should accept that the West is not blameless in the souring of relations with Russia. However, we need to go a bit beyond the 'West is to blame' argument because it controlled the international system in the 1990s to understand Russian foreign policy development. Explaining Russian foreign relations and foreign policy decisions means giving more weight to the impact of Russian domestic political development.

Dealing with Russia's new foreign policy problems following the Cold War meant securing a functioning state, one that was able to make agreements and honour them and provide security for its citizens. The choice was made at the end of 1991 to try to achieve state and regime building primarily through economic reform. Foreign policy was 'Atlanticist', orientated to the West, to support economic reform (this will be discussed below). However, there was no consensus on this, just as there was no consensus over economic policy. Many Russian politicians thought that radical economic reform policies ignored the country's actual economic interests, the fact that it had to develop and manage its relations with other post-Soviet states, and that it was not in Russia's interest to facilitate US global hegemony.

The lack of a consensus on foreign policy, together with the pro-Western nature of Atlanticism, linked foreign policy to struggles over domestic economic policy and constitutional order. Failures in one policy area – and there were to be plenty in economic policy, as we have seen – impacted other areas, weakening the ability of the government to hold a consistent course. As a result, foreign policy became one more area in which compromises could be made to lessen threats to Yeltsin's rule. As it was adapted to try to please different audiences, Russian foreign policy became a strange blend of pro- and anti-Western. The failure to reorganize security management organizations after the Cold War is not completely a tale of Western duplicity. Compromises over foreign policy were made by Yeltsin in the same way that he made compromises over domestic politics and economics, making it difficult to see how Russia could have been accommodated as a partner in reformed security organizations. In many ways the West overcompensated for the difficulties of working out how to institutionalize new arrangements by supporting Yeltsin with few conditions. Conditionality for the receipt of economic aid was far weaker for Russia than it was for other parts of the world and other post-communist countries (Stone, 2002). Yeltsin's war in Chechnya was not censured internationally. The expectation was that his survival would ensure Russian democratization and economic reform, and that democratization and the development of capitalism would in time make Russia part of the wider community of liberal democratic states.

Compromise over foreign policy helped to stabilize Yeltsin's rule and to ensure his political survival. It also made foreign policy pragmatic – anti-Western at times, pro-Western at others – according to the domestic political needs of the day. Over time this pragmatism led to Russia seeking advantage where it could by building relations with a broad range of states and leveraging influence where it could in these relationships to compensate for its position of relative weakness in international politics. There have been two problems with this. First, pragmatism can veer easily into opportunism and short-termism in the pursuit of advantage. Second, where democracy is weak, determining what is advantageous, and when advantage has been achieved, is very much under the control of political leadership. As a result, foreign policy becomes personalized in its formation and in whom it benefits.

The pragmatic consensus was a product of Yeltsin's efforts to survive politically and was maintained while he dealt with the various economic and political crises that beset him. This was to change under Putin as opportunities first presented themselves to build better relations with the West – opportunities that aligned with Putin's domestic agenda of consolidating political and economic control. However, when these opportunities faltered, when their alignment with Putin's domestic priorities changed, and as new opportunities for gaining foreign policy advantage presented themselves, it was easy for the president to change foreign policy and force it into a more anti-Western orientation. Again, this meant that foreign policy was at the service of the regime – was a prop for Putin's rule that was easily used, since he decided what was in Russia's interest and was able to decree that this interest had been achieved without being held to account by parliament, the media or the enfeebled opposition. Arguing this does not excuse the West from failure; not all Western policy towards Russia has worked, and much of it has failed or even been counterproductive. However, it does point to the better correlation of Russian foreign policy to domestic political developments and needs than to international balances and changes in relative power within the global system.

Russian foreign policy under Yeltsin

Russian foreign policy was initially and unambiguously pro-Western. This position was labelled 'Atlanticism', since it looked for support towards the countries of the North Atlantic alliance (NATO), in contrast to 'Eurasianism', which argued that Russia needed to build up its strength and alliances with other Soviet successor states and pursue its interests independently of the USA and its allies (Malcolm et al., 1996; Tsygankov, 1997). Yeltsin, foreign minister Andrei Kozyrev and politicians such as Yegor Gaidar all expressed Atlanticist views in 1992, making it the dominant view of foreign policy in the Russian government.

Initially, the prospects for an Atlanticist foreign policy looked promising. Western politicians realized that Russia had to be dealt with as an independent power after the August 1991 coup and were relieved to find that the government was willing to honour international agreements that Gorbachev had made. Moreover, they found that Russian politicians shared their concerns over such matters as nuclear proliferation, and were willing to work with Western powers to resolve them, and that the new Russian government was not interested in revising Russian borders to re-create an empire. Some progress was thus made in coping with the legacies of the Soviet collapse through multilateral agreements such as the Lisbon Protocol of May 1992, in which Russia and the USA worked with Belarus, Kazakhstan and Ukraine to amend the START I treaty to cover the nuclear weapons held by those countries and arrange their transfer to Russia. Russia agreed to honour Soviet-era borders with the other newly independent states and was prepared to guarantee the borders of Ukraine and Kazakhstan in return for their acceding to the Nuclear Non-Proliferation Treaty (this was done through the signing of the Budapest Memorandum in 1994, the memorandum that Russia broke in 2014 when it annexed Crimea).

Bill Clinton and Boris Yeltsin

However, cooperation was not to last. Foreign policy got dragged into the struggle over domestic economic policy and constitutional order that developed in 1992. The Congress of People's Deputies, the Supreme Soviet, and the Duma that was elected after 1993 had sizeable communist and nationalist factions which criticized Yeltsin's foreign policy as a betrayal of Russia, and this influenced the environment in which foreign policy decisions were made (Malcolm et al., 1996: 218). To many of Yeltsin's Russian opponents, Atlanticism was disdainful of Russian traditions. When Russia was side-tracked by the preferences of other states, the Atlanticists were open to the criticism that they were serving foreign interests. Russia did not have the strength to make its Atlanticist foreign policy look successful in practice. Its decline in military power, enfeebled economy and lack of allies after the collapse of the Warsaw Pact meant that Russia was unable to make positive contributions to international affairs when it did not have the support of more powerful states such as the USA.

Atlanticism was also vulnerable to the charge that it did not recognize Russia's interests in the former USSR. The initial hope of the Atlanticists was that they could settle relations with the newly independent states quite quickly. This was to be done by the replacement of the USSR with a new Commonwealth of Independent States (CIS), which was founded on 8 December 1991 by Russia, Belarus and Ukraine and joined a week later by the Central Asian successor states Moldova, Armenia and Azerbaijan. The agreement on the CIS was very vague. The only practical issue solved by the signatories was the recognition of existing republican borders as the borders of the newly independent states.

The formation of the CIS showed that Russia could not avoid being involved in the affairs of the other newly independent states. Unfortunately, the CIS was not much good as a vehicle for dealing with many of the issues facing the new states and neutralizing them. Its members' very different concerns meant there was no common interest underpinning the organization. Not surprisingly, the CIS never really functioned as a collective decision-making body (Robinson, 1999c; Sakwa and Webber, 1999). There were various attempts to develop it as both a collective security organization and an economic union, but securing cooperation that was meaningful proved difficult (Robinson, 2004; Kubicek, 2009). Throughout the 1990s and into the 2000s, Russia had to manage its relations with the rest of the former Soviet Union through bilateral treaties and agreements. This meant that it couldn't pull itself away from the post-Soviet space and orientate its foreign policy westwards.

The failings of the CIS showed up only over time, but they were foreshadowed by events in 1991 and 1992, which showed that Russia had to remain a major actor in the post-Soviet space. Russia was forced to intervene in the civil war in Tajikistan in 1992, when the collapse of the Tajik state threatened wider destabilization in post-Soviet Central Asia. Ethnic conflict in Transnistria (Moldova) and in Abkhazia and South Ossetia (Georgia) pulled its troops into peacekeeping duties, and it had to manage the division of former military assets such as the Black Sea fleet in Crimea and nuclear weapons. These developments, and worries over the citizenship rights of ethnic Russians who lived in other post-Soviet states, provided ample grounds for Yeltsin's critics to attack Atlanticism as a doctrine.

Criticism, and the fact that foreign policy became entrapped in the political struggles that were taking place in Moscow over the economy and between parliament and president, meant compromise and involved a greater focus on the former Soviet Union. This was a sop to nationalist and opposition forces, since it addressed their main immediate concerns about the fate of Russians in what were now foreign countries and the issue of Russian power within the former tsarist and Soviet 'empires'. As Lo (2002: 70) has argued, emphasis put on 'the primacy of CIS-related affairs ... [was] not because the Yeltsin administration was necessarily pursuing a more active policy towards the former Soviet Union, but because it felt the need to advertise that it was doing so.' To some extent this worked. Yeltsin managed to keep Kozyrev as foreign minister longer than he kept economic reformers in office. Kozyrev was replaced only in 1996, after the relative failure of pro-government and liberal parties in the 1995 Duma election and before the presidential election. His successor was Yevgenii Primakov, who had been on Gorbachev's Presidential Council and served as head of the Foreign Intelligence Service (SVR) between 1991 and 1996. However, the cost was that Russian foreign policy became very ad hoc. Policy seemed to be made on the hoof and frequently to consist of little more than playing to the public gallery in an effort to contain criticism and manage competing domestic political constituencies. Basic questions about Russia's interests and its long-term goals for its foreign policy went unanswered.

In policy terms, there was as much continuity as change after Primakov replaced Kozyrev (Lynch, 2001: 11). However, the idea was created that a consensus was developing over foreign policy (Lo, 2002: 5–6), which Primakov described as 'multipolar'. Unlike Atlanticism, multipolarism proposed promoting Russia as a global power by developing links with other states according to mutual advantage. Russia would cooperate with the West, but at the same time it would resist its use of military power and promote its own interests (Shearman and Sussex, 2000: 160).

This meant more rhetorical opposition to Western policies and a greater insistence that the West recognize that Russia had interests that had to be accommodated in some way.

The means by which Russia was supposed to achieve accommodation of its interests were multilateralism, an insistence on respect for sovereignty and non-interference in other states' affairs, and respect for the institutions of the global order, such as the United Nations, and international law. These themes were to carry over into the Putin era. The West's military, diplomatic and economic advantages, according to multipolarism, could be neutralized by working with other states and by insisting on the maintenance of international law and the use of multilateral institutions to respond to international security problems. This approach to foreign policy was driven by necessity as much as anything else. Yeltsin could not respond to demands made by opposition forces for a tougher line towards the West other than by using such mechanisms as Russia's permanent membership of the United Nations Security Council, with the threat of veto power that came with it, to try to gain some leverage in international politics.

However, recognizing Russia's weaknesses and using what tools were available to act on them were different matters. Russia's attention remained fixed on the West, particularly the USA. The country needed Western assistance financially – although the amounts that it received were frequently too little and could not overcome government weakness and inability to reform – and so Russia couldn't use even the limited powers that it had to their full extent. At most it could complain and alter Western foreign policy at the margins. Success was limited. NATO expansion went ahead, although Russia did get some representation and consultation rights,. Moscow's objections and prevarications delayed and hindered some of the West's efforts to intervene in Yugoslav conflicts. However, in the end Moscow was not able to prevent NATO's bombing of Serbia and forced resolution of conflicts in Bosnia and Kosovo. The most Yeltsin was able to achieve was some participation in the NATO intervention in Kosovo as a 'partner' (Levitin, 2000).

From pragmatism to confrontation: foreign policy under Putin

Improvements in relations on the surface, but tensions underneath, 2000–2

The development of Russian foreign policy under Putin was roughly similar to that under Yeltsin. Initially, there were hopes for improved relations. There were positive meetings between Putin and Western leaders, most notably the summit meeting in Slovenia in June 2001 after which President George W. Bush stated that he had looked Putin 'in the eye. I found him very straightforward and trustworthy – I was able to get a sense of his soul.' Cooperation did improve in 2000 and 2001, especially after 9/11. Putin was the first foreign leader to speak with Bush and offer condolences. He offered support to the Americans and linked 9/11 to Russia's struggles with terrorism in Chechnya, arguing that both were a part of a global 'war on terror'. Russia gave aid to the US-led coalition that removed the Taliban in Afghanistan and accepted the USA's move into airbases in Central Asia. At the time, these changes were seen as a major reversal of Russian foreign policy, as Putin put the country firmly in the 'Western' camp of 'civilized' nations that were united by common values and security concerns (O'Loughlin et al., 2004).

Support for US intervention in Afghanistan was a major change in Russian policy, coming as it did so soon after Russian objections to NATO's actions in Kosovo. However, post-9/11 support for American actions in Afghanistan was not a *carte blanche* from the Russians to the West or a licence for the USA to act unilaterally. Russia was angered by the withdrawal from the 1972 Anti-Ballistic Missile (ABM) Treaty announced by Bush in December 2001. This was a prelude to the USA announcing in 2002 that it would develop a new system of ABM defence in Europe with bases in Poland and the Czech Republic. Ostensibly the purpose of this new system was defence against nuclear attacks from Iran, which was trying to develop as a nuclear power. However, the ABM system looked to be directed against Russia's stock of nuclear missiles, since Iran was still some way from developing a nuclear arsenal.

Developments such as the US withdrawal from the ABM Treaty went against what Russia thought it was offering in the joint 'war on terror' – partnership. This should have been clear to the West, since Putin's accession to the presidency was marked by continuity in foreign policy overall rather than by change. Igor Ivanov, the foreign minister who had replaced Primakov in September 1998 when the latter became prime minister after the August 1998 economic crisis, was kept in place until 2004, when he was replaced by Sergei Lavrov. The June 2000 'Foreign Policy Concept' of the Russian Federation insisted that the basis of Russia's foreign policy was 'mutually advantageous pragmatism'. The concept also contained a warning for the West, as it argued that '[i]ntegration processes, in particular, in the Euro-Atlantic region are quite often pursued on a selective and limited basis. Attempts to belittle the role of a sovereign state as the fundamental element of international relations generate a threat of arbitrary interference in internal affairs' (Ministry of Foreign Affairs, 2000).

Breaking with the West: Iraq, neo-conservatism and 'colour revolutions', 2003–8

The issues of 'Euro-Atlantic integration', intervention and 'sovereignty' were to bring the improvement in relations following 9/11 rapidly to an end. The first line of fracture, after the ABM Treaty withdrawal, was the US push to extend the 'war on terror' from Afghanistan to tackle what Bush labelled the 'axis of evil': Iraq, Iran and North Korea. Russia saw this as an infringement on the sovereignty of these states and a sign that the USA was becoming an increasingly unilateral actor under the sway of neo-conservatives such as Vice President Dick Cheney and Defence Secretary Donald Rumsfeld. Cheney and Rumsfeld were associated with the neo-conservative 'Project for a New American Century', which had been pushing for a more assertive American foreign policy since the mid-1990s. Neo-conservatives argued that US foreign policy had lacked a sense of purpose since the end of the Cold War and should seek to repeat its 'success' under Ronald Reagan by bringing about 'regime change' in states that were opposed to American global leadership. As formulated by Kristol and Kagan (1996: 20), two of the movement's ideologists, complaints about US hegemony from countries such as Russia and China were not to be taken seriously but 'should be taken as a compliment and a guide to action'.

This was not an intellectual agenda that could serve as the basis for partnership between the USA and Russia. It not only ignored Russian interests but also devalued institutions such as the United Nations that Russia could use to influence international politics. The American push for war against Iraq over chemical weapons ran into Russian and Chinese resistance at the UN Security Council, and the Bush administration's decision to take what was in effect unilateral action in Iraq – the 'coalition of the willing' was created by the USA and was nothing without it – meant that, in Russia's eyes, the USA was moving from being a status quo power, one that was seeking to preserve the international system, to being a revisionist power, one that was seeking to change the way in which international politics occurred.

The Iraq war of 2003 would probably have been enough on its own to end the consensus over 'the war on terror'. The diplomatic arguments over whether Iraq was complying with international instructions to end its chemical weapons programme and destroy its stockpile gave Russia more options for partnership than it had had in the 1990s. The pragmatic pursuit of advantage became much more real as a possibility for Russia, as China, France and other states looked askance at US actions in the Middle East. The gains made by Moscow from pursuing relations with these states were not always great, since some of them were part of larger international organizations (for example, France, as a member of the EU) with which Russia was to come into conflict. Others, such as China, had their own interests and the power to pursue them independently of Russia. Still, links with China, and common concerns over sovereignty and the threat to it from neo-conservative ideas about 'regime change', meant that Russia had an ally in bodies such as the UN Security Council that could help it block American efforts to legitimize their policies through that body. As the war against the Taliban in Afghanistan dragged on, China was also to come to share Russia's concerns about the expansion of US influence in Central Asia.

One reason Russia became more worried about American influence in Central Asia was US support for 'colour revolutions', which saw the overthrow of incumbent presidents, or their nominated successor, in Georgia (the 'Rose Revolution' of November 2003), Ukraine (the 'Orange Revolution' of November 2004 to January 2005) and Kyrgyzstan (the 'Tulip Revolution' of February–March 2005 and a second, unlabelled, revolution in April 2010) (Bunce and Wolchik, 2011; Ó Beacháin and Polese, 2010). The role of the West in these upheavals was generally very small. There was some Western support for leaders who took power after the revolutions and hope that, thereafter, the countries concerned would pursue economic and political liberalization that would bring them closer to the West. Overall, however, the causes of colour revolutions in former Soviet states were internal, and the role of foreign actors was insignificant and came after the events.

The fact that colour revolutions were caused by internal factors did not assuage Russia's concern that they might spread to Russia itself. Both the Rose and the Orange Revolution saw the victory of candidates – Mikheil Saakashvili in Georgia and Viktor Yushchenko in Ukraine – who objected to Russian interference in their country's politics. Saakashvili and Yushchenko were keen both to reform their countries and to draw closer to the West. Successful reform had the potential to weaken Russian influence over both states. If economic reform led to greater wealth, the countries would be more integrated into the global economy and less reliant on Russia. Political reform, particularly democratization and the reduction of corruption, would weaken Russia's ability to interfere in their domestic politics, co-opting politicians and businesspeople. Successful reform might also open up the possibility of EU or NATO membership, or at least improved relations with those bodies, either of which would take Georgia and Ukraine further out of Russia's sphere of influence. Fear of losing influence in Kyrgyzstan was not as great a threat, since Kyrgyzstan's Tulip Revolution did not see the election of a leader who was as pro-Western. Still, the overthrow, first, of Askar Akayev and then of the successor regime of Kurmanbek Bakiyev made Russia nervous of other regimes falling in the post-Soviet space and the loss of influence this might bring.

Russian concern over American unilateralism and the non-status quo nature of the USA under George W. Bush meant that the country's foreign policy became focused increasingly on developing alliances to ensure that it could resist any unilateral actions. This meant greater cooperation with states that were equally as reluctant to accept Western leadership and putting more effort into countering Western influence in former Soviet states. Signs of this began early after the Orange Revolution, as gas deliveries from Russia to Ukraine were cut off or reduced several times in 2006 and 2008. Ostensibly, the disputes over gas were commercial in nature, but there was widespread suspicion that energy was being used as a political weapon to discipline Ukraine and other post-Soviet states (Nygren, 2008; Newnham, 2011). Russia began to position itself as an anti-colour revolution force, partly to counter and take advantage of other post-Soviet leaders' fears. Following a massacre of demonstrators in Andijan in Uzbekistan in 2005, for example, Western powers criticized the Uzbek government and banned arms sales to the country. Uzbekistan, which has had a hideous human rights record throughout its post-Soviet history, retaliated by throwing US forces out of the airbase they had been using to support operations in Afghanistan. Russia and Uzbekistan then signed a Treaty of Alliance Relations, which promised that each of the signatories could call on the other for support against both internal and external threats. Russia also began to assist friendly autocrats and governments in the post-Soviet space in managing elections to try to ensure sympathetic governments (Tolstrup, 2015). These actions increased the distance between Russia and the West as the divide between them began to be seen as an ideological one, a point to which we will return below.

In addition to providing support for friendly governments in the post-Soviet space, Russia began to pay more attention to developing regional security bodies that could be used to counter US influence. A Collective Security Treaty had been signed in 1992 between some of the CIS states. In 2002 this was changed to create a Collective Security Treaty Organization (CSTO), and in 2007 and 2009 the CSTO was expanded to include, first, a peacekeeping force and, second, a Collective Rapid Reaction Force. The intention of these developments was to make Russia the primary security partner of CSTO states (Armenia, Belarus, Kazakhstan, Tajikistan and, between 2006 and 2012, Uzbekistan) (Kropatcheva, 2016). The CSTO overlaps with the other regional organization that Russia used to counter Western influence in the post-Soviet space, the Shanghai Cooperation Organization, which developed in the early 2000s to bring together, initially, Russia, China and four Central Asian states (Kyrgyzstan, Kazakhstan, Tajikistan and Uzbekistan). India and Pakistan joined in 2017, and there are several other observer states, including Iran. One reason for these states to cooperate is a shared concern to combat terrorism in the region, and the organization has established several anti-terrorist structures to foster cooperation. However, the Shanghai Cooperation Organization is also seen as a means by which Russia and China can collaborate over security in Central Asia to weaken US power and work against regime change in the region (Ambrosio, 2008; Aris, 2009; Lo, 2008: 104–10).

While Russia worried about balancing Western influence, Western countries were concerned about Russian aggression. Events such as the assassination of Alexander Litvinenko in London in 2006 using polonium – a nuclear substance that is hard to find except from state sources – created tensions with individual Western states, not least the UK. Whether or not such events were officially sanctioned from the very top of the Russian political system is a matter of speculation (see Harding, 2016, for an argument that it was). However, the killings of Litvinenko and the journalist Anna Politkovskaya (also 2006), the assassination of Chechen exiles in Vienna, Istanbul and Dubai, the murders of human rights workers and politicians, such as Sergei Yushenkov and Yuri Shchekochikhin (2003), Natalya Estemirova, Stanislav Markelov and Anastasia Baburova (all 2009) and Boris Nemtsov (2015), and cases such as that of Sergei Magnitsky (who died in prison in 2009 following his investigation of official fraud) all created the idea that Russia was untrustworthy and aggressive. For some countries, such as the Baltic states and Poland, these actions fed into historical fears of Russian aggression; thus Russia's relationship with institutions of which they were a member, notably the EU, were complicated after the wave of accession of Eastern European states after 2004.

Neo-conservative foreign policy in the USA and events such as the Litvinenko assassination caused a deep estrangement between Russia and the West. Russia's view of the break was most fully articulated by Putin (2007b) in a speech to the Munich Conference on Security Policy. The problem with international politics, Putin argued, was the attempt to force unipolarity – US hegemony – on the world. This was 'not only unacceptable but also impossible in today's world … the model itself is flawed because at its basis there is and can be no moral foundations for modern civilization.' Efforts to force unipolarity on the world meant '[u]nilateral and frequently illegitimate actions' that 'have not resolved any problems … [but] have caused new human tragedies and created new centres of tension.' This was inevitable, as unilateralism and unipolarity, being impossible, lead to the '[u]ncontained hyper-use of force – military force – in international relations, force that is plunging the world into an abyss of permanent conflicts.' Moreover, the arrogance of unilateralism and unipolarity means that international law is ignored and potentially totally debased, since:

> independent legal norms are, as a matter of fact, coming increasingly closer to one state's legal system. One state and, of course, first and foremost the United States, has overstepped its national borders in every way. This is visible in the economic, political, cultural and educational policies it imposes on other nations. Well, who likes this? Who is happy about this?

Complaints about the United States 'overstepping' national boundaries and trying to impose its standards on other countries highlighted for Putin the need to defend national sovereignty against illegitimate foreign interference. This echoed the idea that Russia was a 'sovereign democracy' which had its own national traditions that were unique and that could not be judged by other states. This began a closer alignment between Russian foreign and domestic policies, as Putin's Munich speech laid the foundations of what was to become the 'cultural turn' in Russian politics towards conservative traditional values after his re-election in 2012. The cultural turn, as we saw in chapter 5, was premised on the idea that Russia's political health depended on the protection of Russia's 'state-civilization' against encroachment from foreign values and developmental models, something that could be achieved only by the protection of state sovereignty.

War with Georgia and the Obama reset, 2008–12

There was a brief hiatus between Putin's Munich speech in 2007 and the breakdown of relations that followed his re-election in 2012. This was partly because of the election of President Barack Obama in the USA in 2008 and partly because of Putin's replacement by Dmitri Medvedev as Russian president in the same year. The election of Obama ended the neo-conservative policies that had helped cause the growing rift with Moscow. Obama's administration was more committed to the development of a rule-based international order than the Bush administration had been. It was also more prepared to accept that there were limits to US power and influence and less inclined to think that it could will a new world order into existence.

These limits had been shown by one of the last gasps of neo-conservatism under Bush – the initiation of moves to make Ukraine and Georgia NATO members. Both countries were interested in NATO membership after their colour revolutions and were encouraged by the Bush administration despite Russian warnings that this would be seen as a hostile act. At the April 2008 NATO summit in Bucharest, the USA and Poland pressed for the adoption of membership action plans for the two countries, the formal stage for beginning NATO membership. In the end pressure from France and Germany meant that the plans were shelved. Instead, a vague promise was given that the two states would become members when they had fulfilled the entrance criteria, among which is a commitment to the peaceable resolution of disputes, including ethnic disputes. The promise, despite its vagueness, was met with hostility by a Moscow already angered by many Western states' recognition of Kosovo's independence from Serbia, Russia's historical ally in the Balkans.

The Bucharest summit and Kosovan independence formed the backdrop to the Russian–Georgian war in August 2008. The war has been explained both as the fault of the West (pushing Russia over Kosovo and NATO membership for former Soviet states – in other words, as another instance of the West 'losing' Russia) and as Russian aggression. Believing absolutely in the fault of either is too simplistic, however. Russia did feel aggrieved over Kosovo and ignored by the West. It was to get its 'revenge' by recognizing the independence of South Ossetia (the place where the war started) and Abkhazia, another region that had broken away from Georgia and that was a Russian protectorate. At the same time, the war was initiated by the decision of Georgia's President Saakashvili to attack South Ossetia (Allison, 2008; Cheterian, 2009; Asmus, 2010).

Whatever the cause of the conflict, the lessons learnt were, first, that the West was prepared to take only limited action to counter Russian aggression in the former Soviet Union and, second, that Russia was confident enough of its strength to take military action. The Obama administration, which took office in early 2009, tried to launch a 'reset' in Russian–US relations, but the improvement was briefer than either Obama or Medvedev would have liked. One reason for this was that there was continuity in Russian foreign policy. Lavrov remained foreign minister across the Putin and Medvedev presidencies, and Putin did not fully cede power over foreign policy to Medvedev. The type of thinking about state sovereignty and the need to protect it that Putin had articulated in Munich was repeated in documents such as the 2008 Russian 'Foreign Policy Concept' and the 2009 'National Security Strategy to 2020', with the latter mentioning the importance of culture, tradition and family values in a way that foreshadowed the cultural turn that was soon to take place (Ministry of Foreign Affairs, 2008; Security Council, 2009).

There were some gains made by both sides from the 'reset' (Deyermond, 2012). Obama dropped the Bush administration's plans for anti-missile defence systems in Eastern Europe, there was an agreement on nuclear arms reduction and the signing of a new Strategic Arms Reduction Treaty (START), and unanimity on sanctioning Iran over its development of nuclear weapons. Russia allowed the Americans to cross Russian airspace to supply coalition forces in Afghanistan. However, it was not possible to build on these successes to transform relations substantially and sustainably. Many Western policy-makers remained sceptical of Russian intentions to the point where they were accused of being 'Russophobic' (Tsygankov, 2009), although similar charges of anti-Americanism were laid against Russian policy-makers (Shiraev and Zubok, 2000). Mutual suspicion meant that relations were going to be easily upset, especially as some US and European politicians pushed for sanctions against Russian officials involved in corruption and the illegal detention and death of Sergei Magnitsky. An Act sanctioning officials involved in Magnitsky's death was passed in the USA in 2012 (other states and the EU have discussed passing similar acts). Russia responded by banning some American officials and the US adoption of Russian children.

Another blow to the reset came with the 'Arab Spring', the wave of regime change that began in December 2010 in the Middle East and North Africa. For Russia, Western action against the regime of Colonel Muammar Gaddafi in Libya together with support for some of the opponents of President Bashar al-Assad in Syria were more instances of interference in the affairs of sovereign states. Russia, along with China, protested when the West acted against authoritarian Arab states, seeing moves against Syria and Libya as hypocritical, since Western countries didn't dispute the suppression of protest in states such as Bahrain that were friendly towards them. Russian and Chinese objections forced the West to take unilateral action – the type of action that Putin had complained of in his Munich speech. Russia vetoed Western attempts to censure and take measures against the Assad regime and demanded that Assad be given a role in the resolution of the conflict as the legitimate ruler of Syria.

Putin's return to the presidency: Ukraine, Syria and confrontation

The Russian line on Syria and relations with the West hardened with Putin's return to the presidency in 2012 and the cultural turn that came with his campaign. This cultural turn, as we saw in chapter 5, drew a sharp distinction between Russian and Western values, and the argument was made that the loss of Russian values in the face of globalization and Western cultural hegemony would lead to the destruction of the Russian state. In short, Russia was openly, and officially, defining itself as ideologically opposed to Western liberalism. Action against Russian NGOs with foreign links, Russian policy on education about LGBT+ issues, links between Russia and conservative groups in Western countries (such as the French National Front) and the support of these groups for Russia (Chryssogelos, 2014) gave substance to this rift. In many ways the new split looked like a 'new Cold War', with Russia proposing an alternative value set and supporting forces in the West that shared its views, and there were commentators on both sides who were happy to push the comparison. However, this comparison can be stretched too far. Russia's geopolitical reach is a lot smaller than that of the USSR, and the anti-liberal message that it has been pushing resonates with local complaints about liberal democracy but offers no solution to these complaints in the form of a different socio-economic model. Even if Putin's message resonated with some Western anti-democrats and other illiberal politicians, it did not lead to Russia's restoration to super-power status.

The cultural turn that Putin made after 2011 did, however, help establish the ground on which the next, and most significant, crisis in Russia's external relations would take place – that in Ukraine, which took shape from November 2013 to February 2014. Ukraine's moves towards the West had abated after 2010, when Viktor Yushchenko, the 'winner' of the Orange Revolution, was replaced as president by Viktor Yanukovych, who had lost in that revolution. Yanukovych was more sympathetic to Russia, which had supported his bids for the presidency in 2004 and 2010. Yanukovych's power base was in Eastern Ukraine, where there are more Russian speakers and people who identify as ethnic Russians, and where the economy is closely linked to Russia's. Yanukovych pulled back from pursuing NATO membership, which had been one of Yushchenko's goals and one of Russia's principal bugbears.

Yanukovych's election was a gain for Russia, but Putin wanted to consolidate Russian influence in the post-Soviet region with states that he now described as part of the same 'civilizational' group as Russia. The Collective Security Treaty Organization had been developed as one way of achieving this. Putin now planned to extend the alliance of post-Soviet states by building up economic linkages between them. The Commonwealth of Independent States had given birth to multiple economic treaties and plans for economic integration, most of which had failed (Robinson, 2004). A Eurasian Customs Union between Belarus, Kazakhstan and Russia had been created in 2010, supposedly to eliminate tariff barriers to facilitate trade. This led to the proposal for a Treaty on Eurasian Economic Union, which was signed in May 2014 by the three countries to form a new Eurasian Economic Union (EEU) from January 2015. The EEU was supposed to establish a common market, much like that of the EU, based on free movement of goods, labour, services and capital. Like the EU, the EEU has policies on competition fairness and institutions such as a council, a presidency, a court and an economic commission, and there have been discussions on a common currency and a parliament. Armenia and Kyrgyzstan bowed to pressure and joined, bringing the number of member states to five by August 2015. Moldova has observer status, Tajikistan has begun negotiating membership, and Uzbekistan joined the CIS Free Trade Area, partly to ease pressures on it to join the full EEU.

The creation of the EEU, alongside the CSTO, began to put some flesh onto Putin's desire to push back against the process of European economic and security integration in the Euro-Atlantic area that Russia had been complaining about since the 1990s. The real prize, however, was to get Ukraine to join. Ukraine was the most important security and economic actor for Russia in the post-Soviet space, the one that it most feared withdrawing from its sphere of influence for economic and security reasons, and the most symbolically important. Along with Belarus, Ukraine was the state most culturally linked to Russia, sharing common history and, for Putin, values, since it was the birthplace of the first Russian state and the site of Russia's conversion to Orthodox Christianity (the Kievan Rus', founded in 882, which converted to Orthodoxy under Vladimir the Great in 988).

The election of Yanukovych as president in 2010 meant that Ukraine had a leader sympathetic to developing links with Russia. However, Ukraine was also in negotiations with the EU, and agreement had been reached on a free trade area before Yanukovych's election. There were also ongoing negotiations over an EU–Ukrainian association agreement that would have created mechanisms for greater cooperation and committed Ukraine to political and economic reform. In retrospect, there was little chance of Ukraine reaching a deal with the EU. Its human rights record worsened under Yanukovych, who had his rivals imprisoned on politically motivated charges. Reform would have threatened the oligarchic crony capitalist regime and corruption on which Yanukovych's power rested (Wilson, 2014: 51–60). But the fact that negotiations with the EU were kept up raised hopes that a deal would be reached among those sections of the population – liberals and nationalist – who were opposed to closer ties with Russia if this meant that Yanukovych's corrupt regime was strengthened. As the date for signing the document came closer in November 2013, there was a flurry of activity that went some way to meet the EU's demands for reaching an agreement. In the end, however, none was reached. Further discussions were pre-empted by Russia buying $15 billion-worth of Ukrainian bonds and reducing the cost of gas supplied to Ukraine. In return, Yanukovych agreed that Ukraine would join the EEU.

This was a temporary victory for Putin. Street protests against the abandonment of the EU association agreement escalated as the Ukrainian government dealt with demonstrators incompetently. Soon a full-scale stand-off on the Maidan Nezalezhnosti (Independence Square) in Kiev became a clash between the regime and the protesters. Attempts at mediation by both Russia and the EU were overtaken by events. The EuroMaidan protest, as the demonstration became known, transformed into a revolt against the government, which lost control of Kiev, large parts of Western Ukraine, and many of the most important cities in the east. Yanukovych fled to exile in Russia in February 2014.

The EuroMaidan protest, Kiev, 2014

Putin blamed the West for Yanukovych's fall and charged the EU with reneging on its promises to keep him in power (as if a few diplomats could affect what happened on the streets). The presence among protesters in the final days of conflict with the government of large numbers of far-right nationalist groups, some of which claimed descent from the pro-Nazi Ukrainian nationalist groups of the 1930s and 1940s, enabled Russia to argue that what had occurred was an illegal fascist coup that was anti-Russian. It defended its opposition to the EuroMaidan revolt as a defence of sovereignty, both its own and that of the legitimate Ukrainian government of Yanukovych. These claims became the pretext for Russia to seize the province of Crimea to protect the latter's Russian population and Russian military bases there. The seizure was disguised as a popular revolt by Crimeans, and a referendum was held to legitimate the province's becoming a part of Russia (the legality of the vote, the turnout, and the percentage of voters opting for union with Russia are all highly contested). The annexation of Crimea meant that Russia was violating the 1994 Budapest Memorandum, in which it had guaranteed Ukrainian territorial integrity as part of the deal to get Ukraine to hand over nuclear weapons on its territory. Further pressure was put on Ukraine in the east of the country, where Russia supported 'separatist' forces in what came to be known as the Donetsk and Luhansk People's Republics. These republics were supposedly set up by local pro-Russian militia but were in fact supported and armed by Russia. It was with a weapon supplied by Russia, and possibly manned by Russian troops, that separatists shot down Malaysian Airlines flight MH17 in July 2014, killing 298 passengers and crew.

The annexation of Crimea, the war in Eastern Ukraine and the downing of MH17 all caused a breakdown in Russian relations with the West. Sanctions were introduced against the country and against individuals and companies associated with Putin, by the USA, the EU, Japan, Switzerland and Canada. Russia retaliated with sanctions of its own, against some Western politicians who had led calls for sanctions and against agricultural imports from Europe. But the annexation worked for Putin domestically even as international relations worsened. The slogan *Krimnash* ('Crimea is ours') became a rallying cry, and Putin's popularity rose to new heights. There was a great deal of fear that Russia would continue to expand in Eastern Ukraine, perhaps taking much of the territory of Southern Ukraine to link up to Crimea and the disputed territory of Transnistria and reclaiming the historic territory of Novorossiya (New Russia, as the area north of the Black Sea had been known when it was incorporated into the tsarist empire at the end of the eighteenth century). Such fears have thus far proved unfounded. Russia has been content to alternate between being one of the brokers of ceasefires in Eastern Ukraine (the Minsk Process) and enabling its client militias in the region to violate them. The result is another 'frozen conflict', the first since the collapse of the USSR. This is a drain on Ukraine as it struggles to reform itself and a block on any future NATO membership, since states involved in conflict cannot join the organization, as well as a possible tool that can be used to leverage advantage for Russia in the future, because it retains the self-declared right to protect Russians in the breakaway republics.

The annexation of Crimea seemed to mark the nadir of post-Soviet Russian relations with the West. However, relations were to worsen further in 2015 as Russia took advantage of Western indecision over Syria and the use of chemical weapons by the Assad government to intervene in the conflict to support Assad. This was widely seen as an opportunistic move by Russia to support its client in the Middle East and to gain another point of leverage in international affairs. Again, Russia argued that what it was doing was defending a sovereign government from outside interference (by ISIS, among others). Russian action stabilized the Assad government and was presented as a heroic feat of arms by Russian forces. As with Ukraine, Russia's use of military power, this time directly, made it a central actor in talks around the conflict. However, it also brought its forces face to face with NATO member forces – US, French and British – both in Syria and along the latter's border with Turkey.

Intervention in Syria and Ukraine showed that Russia has regained strength and is willing to act aggressively in international relations. It is less clear what the country has gained by these actions beyond greater domestic popularity for Putin. Gains might have been made internationally if Russia's interests had been accommodated by Western governments, and some accommo- dation was threatened by the election of Donald Trump to succeed Obama as US president in 2016. Some of Trump's election statements were sympathetic to the conservative traditional worldview that Putin had been expressing, and he promised to review sanctions against Russia. However, scandal over Russian involvement in hacking during the US presidential election campaign, personnel changes, and an ongoing investigation of ties between Russia and members of the Trump administration seem to have blocked Trump from easing the post-Crimea sanctions regime and working for rapprochement. All that has been gained by Russia from Trump's election is some unease about the USA's commitment to NATO and the loss of American prestige as a global leader. The failure of the National Front's Marine Le Pen, an avowedly pro-Putin politician, in the French presidential elections in 2017 meant that European leaders were able to keep up a relatively united front on sanctions and relations with Russia. It can be argued that the fact that Russia was trying to make links with far-right European politicians, who are often far from the mainstream, shows how little success it has had getting its interests accepted by Western elites (Shekhovtsov, 2017). Moreover, because of its actions, Russia has proven itself unworthy as a partner in foreign relations as far as much of the Western foreign policy elite and large parts of Western public opinion is concerned. The complaint that Putin made about the USA in Munich in 2007, that it was a revisionist power destabilizing the world through unilateral action, is, for many, as good a description of Russia under Putin as it was of the United States under George W. Bush. While this is the case, the respect that Russia wants in international politics – something that Tsygankov (2012) has argued is a perennial aspiration of Russian leaders – seems as far away as ever.

Conclusion

Russia's international relations have brought it small benefits in the post-Cold War era in terms of fostering the development of a state that can both deal with security issues and provide welfare for its citizens. The chief beneficiaries of Russia's international relations have been its leaders. Foreign policy was an area where critics could be accommodated and at least partly neutralized under Yeltsin. This helped to keep Yeltsin in office, but Russia didn't look like a country able to become a full partner with the West in the development of post-Cold War global security. It was not strong enough to make itself a partner. It was prepared to work towards partnership with the USA in the 'war on terror' post-9/11, but the unilateral neo-conservative foreign policy of the Bush administration left little room for partnership to grow. A breakdown in relations was inevitable.

Preservation of the Russian political system has always been a goal of Russian foreign policy, just as it is for other states. In Russia's case, and as the 2000s progressed, this came increasingly to mean the preservation not just of the constitutional order but of the particular distribution of power under Putin – of the Putin regime. This was couched in language that linked the preservation of sovereignty and political order to themes of cultural identity. Differences in interests between Russia and the West hardened into rhetoric about differences that were essential in nature. It is hard to negotiate such differences away. Many Russian commentators hoped that the West would change to come closer to Russian official opinion through Trump and Le Pen, but this has not happened. Consequently, the future of Russian international relations looks to be little different to the recent past. The country will seek improved relations with states such as China that are sceptical about Western international leadership, but, as in the past, what Russia gains from these relations will often be small and dependent on its partners' willingness to accede to its wishes. In the case of powerful states such as China, this is far from guaranteed. In other cases, such as Venezuela or Syria, the states with which it can hope to have good relations are themselves too weak to add greatly to Russia's international prestige. Breaking this pattern will require more than change in foreign policy thinking. Since the Putin regime has invested so much in its rhetoric of civilizational difference over the last few years, it will probably require broader political change in Russian domestic politics.

12
What Kind of Polity is Russia?

Introduction

It has been argued throughout this book that Russian politics has been characterized by compromises that have sacrificed the development of the Russian state for the consolidation of political regimes. This compromise is detrimental to democracy, since the weakness of the state harms things such as the rule of law that are essential for democracy and encourages things such as corruption and personalized politics that are injurious to democratic political development. This still leaves open the question as to what kind of political system Russia actually has. Many answers to this question have been proffered by political scientists, and one of the purposes of this chapter is to go through some of their offerings. But before we do this we a need to ask ourselves two questions: What is being assessed when the Russian political system is being classified through conceptual descriptions? And how do we judge between different conceptual descriptions of the Russian polity?

The answer to the first of these questions is that, overwhelmingly, what is being assessed is the nature of the regime – what we defined in chapter 1 as the rules that govern how power in and over the institutions of the state is organized, the rules that determine who can access that power and what they can use it for. This is a standard practice, but it can lead to a tendency to overestimate political stability and assume that political development is a completed process. However, as has been stressed throughout this book, regimes and states are different in many ways, even if we often experience them as if they are the one and the same. Ideally we should keep in mind their differences when we classify the Russian political system, and this is something to which we will return in the course of the chapter.

The answer to the second question is that, usually, we judge between different conceptual descriptions of a political system in two stages. First, we list what analysts see as the essential features of the system. Second, we look to see if these essential features exist in the case being studied and if there are any we consider vital that have been left out. Thus we can assess whether there is a good fit between the conceptual description and classification of the system and the system as we see it, as well as whether the approach to classification we have taken is focused on the things that are most important about it. There is much merit to this approach, but it can leave implicit and unexplored how the political system might develop. Our expectations about what kinds of behaviour and development to expect from different types of political system are often unstated. How we see Russia's political system informs what we think the country might do next and how it will develop, and these impressions inform what we think policy towards it should be. Recognizing this gives us another criterion against which we can assess conceptual descriptions of political systems: How far do they help us conceive of possible futures for the polity that we are studying? Arguably, many conceptual descriptions of Russia provide partial answers to this question. This does not mean that they are wrong. Rather, it means that they focus on very specific features that do not necessarily give us as complete a picture as we might like of how Russia might develop in the future.

Although there are many different ways of describing the Russian political system, we will concentrate on the issue of hybridity. However, there are different approaches to hybridity. We will review these and argue that they are the best means of classifying the Russian system but that, to develop a conceptual description that can give us a full a range of developmental possibilities, we might need to go beyond ideas such as electoral authoritarianism, derived from comparative politics literature, and think of it as an example of a neo-patrimonial system.

Between extremes: regime hybridity and authoritarianism

Russia's political system has both democratic elements (elections, for example) and elements that can be associated with authoritarianism (controls over parties, for example). It is not surprising, therefore, that it is most commonly classified as a hybrid system that does not conform to straightforward definitions of either democracy or authoritarianism. We can divide definitions of hybridity into roughly two sets: those that come from comparative politics literature and are applied to Russia and those that have emerged from empirical studies of the Russian political system.

Hybridity and comparative politics

The two most common labels associated with regime hybridity in the comparative politics literature are 'electoral authoritarianism' and 'competitive authoritarianism', which are derived from the classic definition of authoritarianism: '[p]olitical systems with limited, not responsible, political pluralism, without elaborate and guiding ideology, but with distinctive mentalities, without extensive nor intensive political mobilization, except at some points in their development, and in which a leader or occasionally a small group exercises power within formally ill-defined limits but actually quite predictable ones' (Linz, 1970: 255). Authoritarianism allows for some political contestation – 'limited, not responsible political pluralism' – but the idea is that this neither influences policy-making nor determines who will access power.

Hybridity changes this idea about political pluralism subtly. In hybrid regimes, political pluralism is given an institutional space – elections and institutions such as parliaments and presidencies – through which to challenge incumbents and in which power is vested. However, elections are not free and fair and officeholders are not accountable. Rather, 'formal democratic institutions exist and are widely viewed as the primary means of gaining power, but in which incumbents' abuse of the state places them at a significant advantage vis-à-vis their opponents' (Levitsky and Way, 2010: 5). Regimes of this nature can emerge because of the gradual distortion of a democracy as officeholders twist the political system to give themselves an advantage. Alternatively, authoritarian rulers may introduce limited electoral competition when they find that they cannot rule by coercion, ideological control or the co-option of potential challengers through such mechanisms as granting access to economic resources. When this happens, elections move from being 'institutions of representation' to being 'institutions of domination' that are used as a 'last line of authoritarian defence' (Schedler, 2013: 59). In both cases the intent of rulers is to manage the uncertainty that elections create. Uncertainty is a necessary property of democracy, institutionalized in elections and the turnover of rulers. Authoritarian leaders are able to ensure that political outcomes are in their interest; they are therefore not subject to uncertainty; they know that they will be able to manipulate policy and the political system until they are able to obtain the outcomes with which they are happy. Democratic leaders cannot do this: elections force them to 'subject their interests to uncertainty' regularly and with no guarantees (Przeworski, 1986: 58).

The introduction of elections into an authoritarian system, or the continuation of elections where officeholders have begun to twist the political system to guarantee their advantage, does create a measure of uncertainty and so a hybrid political system. The key question then is whether the fix put in place by politicians to produce certain outcomes means that they can eliminate uncertainty. If this is the case, then hybridity decays and fully fledged authoritarianism exists, albeit under a façade of elections. Levitsky and Way's (2010: 5) definition of competitive authoritarianism insists that, for hybridity to exist, opposition parties have to be able to use democratic institutions 'to contest seriously for power', even if 'the playing field is heavily skewed in favor of incumbents. Competition is thus real but unfair.'

The extent to which competition is 'real but unfair' is influenced by both domestic and international factors. Domestically the 'realness' of competition depends on how much incumbent rulers can get away with. How far can they manipulate the rules that manage elections and party competition to get an advantage? To what extent can they marry the use of coercion with democratic practices to nullify the risks of such practices? Levitsky and Way (2010: 23) argue that the ability of incumbents to bend the political system their way depends on their 'organizational power' and the extent of a country's international linkages, on how cohesive the political system is under their rule so that their orders to subvert democratic norms are carried out and not contested. For Schedler, ability to sustain regime hybridity is a matter of institutional design and the tactics that are used by incumbents, both of which can affect the extent of their organizational power. Schedler (2013: 61–9) argues that there are 'menus' of 'institutional choice' and 'institutional manipulation'. These menus, and the choices that they offer, influence how far there is a division of power and how pluralism can exist and develop. The 'menu of institutional choice', which sets up the basic institutions of the system, includes things such as how far courts are independent, the nature of legislatures, rules governing elections, and the organization of parties and civil society. The more control that officeholders have over institutional design, the more they can build advantage into the system by giving themselves authority over appointments to courts, for example, or by choosing electoral systems that work best for them. The 'menu of manipulation' consists of the options that incumbents have to disempower institutions and suborn officials or break up the capacity of institutions that they do not control, as well as limiting pluralism by regulating the media or rigging voting.

Influence on the 'realness' of electoral competition internationally comes from a number of sources. Limits to electoral manipulation and abuses of the right to compete can be put in place by international election monitors, human rights campaigns, foreign governments who are queasy about doing business with hybrid regimes that play too fast and loose with democratic norms, and aid donors who insist on good governance and accountability. All of these are influenced by what Levitsky and Way (2010: 10) call 'linkage to the West'. The greater the number of ties to the West, whether concerned with trade, aid or diplomatic arrangements, the less able incumbents will be to fix political outcomes to their own benefit.

The extent to which politics can be controlled through organizational power or menus of manipulation, and the extent to which control can be exercised without constraint from overseas, determines the sustainability of hybridity – whether it reproduces itself, whether it collapses into fully fledged authoritarianism or whether competition leads to democratization. Analysts such as Levitsky and Way and Schedler are concerned primarily with these questions in comparative perspective – i.e., with uncovering the general factors that influence the political development of hybrid regimes.

Levitsky and Way (2010: 186–200) do, however, look at the wider set of post-Soviet states and argue that there is a tendency in the region towards the restoration of authoritarianism. Russia is used as a case study of how this happened. Unlike Eastern Europe, the post-Soviet space was a low linkage area. The USSR was more cut off from the West socially, historically and economically than its satellite states and was not integrated into European or international institutions as quickly as the Eastern European countries (see chapter 11). Russia resisted the development of links in the West for the region as a whole (as a 'black knight' protecting its influence in the region by opposing democratization) and was itself too big and too militarily strong and economically complex to be subject to great leverage from abroad. However, low organizational power in Russia meant that it was 'a stable competitive authoritarian regime through 2008' (ibid.: 186). This changed over the 2000s, and at a time when international leverage was most weakened by Russia's energy income windfalls. Organizational power was developed through the founding of United Russia, coercive capacity grew as Putin appointed loyalists from security services, and Putin gained greater control over the economy and legal systems so that opponents (such as Khodorkovsky) could be punished. This meant that there was gradual authoritarian consolidation over the course of Putin's first two terms as president. Real electoral competition died back to the point where it became impossible. Putin's ability to engineer Medvedev's succession for one term in 2008, while personally retaining much of the power that had been built up over the 2000s, meant that Russia now had 'a more stable – and closed – authoritarian regime' (ibid.: 200).

Schedler spends much less time on Russia as a case, but argues that there has not been a move from what he calls a competitive electoral authoritarian regime to a hegemonic electoral authoritarian regime. The difference between the two is, first, that the level of uncertainty faced by incumbents is higher, and there is a greater chance of losing power at an election, in a competitive regime than in a hegemonic system. Second, institutional strength is greater in a hegemonic system; regime institutions, in particular the ruling party, create a more predictable set of expectations so that politics is easier to manage (Schedler, 2013: 23–4). We can see that a hegemonic electoral authoritarian regime has emerged, Schedler (ibid.: 191–3) argues, when a ruling coalition has been in power for ten years or more and the coalition has a supermajority in the legislature: 'hegemonic regimes strive to assemble heterogeneous "oversize coalitions".' Being in power for at least ten years means that there is institutional strength, since there will be the expectation that the ruling coalition will inevitably retain power. A supermajority means power over the rules of politics, perhaps even over the constitution.

Part of the difference between Schedler's argument and that of Levitsky and Way is definitional. Schedler's hegemonic and competitive electoral authoritarian regimes occupy respectively the same space politically as a fully fledged authoritarian and competitive authoritarian regime in Levitsky and Way's schema. Hegemonic electoral authoritarian regimes and fully fledged authoritarian regimes with elections are both characterized by the ability of incumbents to fix politics, guarantee election results, and change rules to suit themselves; competitive electoral authoritarian and competitive authoritarian regimes try to emulate hegemonic/fully fledged authoritarian regimes by becoming stable and sustainable, but they don't always get it right and fail more often. The rest of the difference is down to the nature of the research methods used. Levitsky and Way's approach is qualitative and historical and based on two main variables, organizational strength and Western linkages. They therefore see the development of United Russia as a build-up of organizational strength which, added to Putin's succession in 2008, meant that elections became meaningless. The Russian system was therefore fully fledged authoritarian. Schedler's approach is quantitative, as he looked at eighty-five different cases. This complexity means that he is limited to talking about Russia in the 1990s and early 2000s rather than after 2003. If we apply the two tests that Schedler uses to distinguish between competitive and hegemonic electoral regimes – that a ruling coalition has been in power for ten years or more, and that the coalition has a supermajority in the legislature – then it looks more as if Russia has a hegemonic electoral authoritarian regime. Putin came to power in 2000; United Russia was founded in 2001, won its first elections in 2003, and has had a supermajority constantly in the Duma since then, with the exception of the years 2011–16, when it had a simple majority (over 50 per cent of the seats). Even then, however, it could rely on project parties to back it up and agree with it over changing the electoral system to give it a supermajority of parliamentary seats no matter the size of its vote share (Golosov, 2017). This supermajority was duly produced both at the 2016 Duma election, in terms of the number of seats that United Russia secured, and at the 2018 presidential election, in which Putin received a supermajority of votes from a larger voter turnout (see chapter 9). These supermajorities were secured using a full range of tools from the 'menu of manipulation': restriction of competition (the banning of Navalny from taking part in 2018), control over the media, use of the law and law enforcement against opponents, vote rigging, etc. Thus, despite United Russia's wobble in 2011, Russia looks like a hegemonic electoral authoritarian state.

This highlights some of the difficulties of using labels from comparative politics where hybridity is concerned. Russia can change more quickly than the labels used about it in the literature. It is not easy to run through the distinctions between different definitions of hybrid regimes and work out which should be applied at any point in time. For that reason, much of the literature on Russian politics has had a tendency to use the labels 'competitive authoritarianism', 'electoral authoritarianism' and 'authoritarian' loosely and sometimes interchangeably (e.g., Gel'man, 2014: 504); to use the labels or the idea of regime hybridity as simple empirical descriptors (there is authoritarianism and there are elections, therefore there is electoral authoritarianism) (Ross, 2005; Robinson and Milne, 2017); or to withhold any final judgement and leave the question of final classification to await developments (e.g., Zimmerman, 2015: 308–9). Others, meanwhile, have questioned the utility of mainstream ideas about hybridity and gone off in different directions altogether (Hale, 2015: 453–4).

Problems applying the definitions from comparative politics literature do not mean that we should abandon them entirely. It does, however, mean that we should be very specific about how and when we use them, and about what we are referring to when we do use them. Essentially, hybridity definitions in the comparative literature are about the place of elections in political systems that do not meet basic standards for classification as democracies. This is a very important question, but it doesn't tell us everything about how a political system works. Politicians may always have one eye on the next election, and this may shape their actions and policy choices. There is, however, more going on in a political system than elections, and we might want to account for this in how we classify a political system. Definitions of hybrid regimes tend to sweep all of this other stuff under the carpet of authoritarianism without really saying what it signifies except insofar as it might eventually come back to haunt a regime electorally. In other words, they don't really give us much sense of governance or decision-making, except that these are undertaken by incumbents lacking any accountability on a day-to-day basis. This thinness is a natural result of comparison: when you are looking at lots of cases there has to be a trade-off between scope and depth. This trade-off can be useful and tell us some interesting things, but it doesn't necessarily mean that the definitions allow us to gauge the wide number of ways in which a political system might develop.

Hybridity à la Russe

One alternative to the problems of using definitions from comparative politics is to develop definitions of hybridity that apply solely to Russia – something that has been done by Russian area specialists. One of the reasons for this offshoot was that area specialists were far more concerned than comparativists with the issue of informal institutions. While the latter recognized the importance of things such as corruption in hybrid regimes as a means of co-opting and controlling elites, they were more interested, for example, in formal institutions, which are easier to compare across cases, than informal institutions, which can vary widely. For area specialists, however, informality was a key aspect of governance and a point of continuity with Soviet politics.

Informal politics in post-Soviet Russia is based on unwritten rules that are not transparent or regularized. Informal ties, group loyalty and political and material rewards coexist with the formal rules of politics – with constitutional and legal norms. This creates what Ledeneva (2013: 20) calls the *sistema*, a paradoxical system of governance based on 'adhering to official rules and formal procedures but also following unwritten codes and practical norms'. This creates power that is 'obscure' in nature and frequently based around networks of influence that supplant formal institutional hierarchies (see also chapter 6). When Khodorkovsky broke these rules by ignoring Putin's July 2000 instruction to the oligarchs to stay out of politics and threatened to merge Yukos with an American oil firm, thus removing control of the company beyond the reach of the *sistema*, he was punished using the formal apparatus of the state, the legal system. Khodorkovsky was arrested, tried for tax evasion and theft, and sentenced to prison. Yukos and Khodorkovsky were not the only economic actors who could have been found guilty of tax evasion or other economic crimes. Others should have been punished too if the law, formal rules and procedures were adhered to. However, the use of formal, legal rules to punish is selective, applied only in particular cases where informal, unwritten rules have been transgressed rather than used universally and impersonally to regulate social, economic and political behaviour. This creates a means of control: anybody

> can be framed and found in violation of rules. While everybody is under the threat of punishment, the actual punishment is 'suspended' as it is not feasible to prosecute everyone. Accordingly, law enforcement is not impartial and is often mediated by informal leverage or informal command. To establish the rule of law would require reducing the use of informal governance and therefore incur a certain loss of manageability of the formal institutions required to control powerful clans. (Ibid.: 14–15)

Ledeneva's idea of *sistema* recognizes the way that formal and informal politics have been used to support Putin's power. The *sistema* clearly describes a form of hybridity, with what is hybrid now being defined by modes and codes of governance: on one hand, the formal, legalistic and bureaucratic-impersonal modes and, on the other, the informal, unwritten and personalized modes. The tension between these is not, however, a source of change. Ledeneva (2013: 250–2) sees internal tension between different modes of governance as secondary to the tension that exists between the Russian *sistema* as practices of governance and those that exist in the outside world. Change is more likely to come from outside than from within, where the challenges of change are too great.

Not all analysts of Russian politics see the coexistence of formality and informality as stable, however. Sakwa (2010b, 2011) describes a tension between what he labels the 'normative state', the formal-legal polity based on constitutional and legal forms, and the informal-personalized polity, which he calls the 'administrative regime'. Together the normative state and the administrative regime make up what Sakwa refers to as a 'dual state'. The idea of an administrative regime recognizes that there was a limit to the build-up of state functionality under Yeltsin, with the securing of a regime being more important than the creation of state capacity (Sakwa, 1997; see also chapter 4).

Securing a balance between the normative state and an administrative regime is difficult and not produced automatically. There is a competition between the two that is constant and unsettling (Sakwa, 2010b). The factions that vie for power in an administrative regime are at odds with the principles of the normative state. The struggle to bridge this gap and create stability is what drives Russian politics forward, creating new institutions and practices that attempt to align regime and normative state. We have talked about many of these institutions in the course of this book. One example is provided by project parties, which helped to stabilize the administrative regime by facilitating the management of elections. Such parties had to be created in line with the rules of democratic competition that are part of the normative state's constitutional democratic principles. So, to an extent, the normative, constitutional state has some 'autonomy' (ibid.: 197). It is not dependent on Putin, cannot be got rid of by Putin, and is a resource that can be used against the administrative regime. Opposition calls to honour the constitution and the rule of law are a case in point. Another example would be Alexei Navalny's campaigns against corruption, which is clearly against the principles of the normative state. The result is that the 'dual state' requires constant fine-tuning. The imperatives of the normative state, particularly the need to hold regular elections, and the rule that the president can serve only two consecutive terms, mean that there are plenty of moments when the balance of the dual state can be upset. The balance between normative state and administrative regime is open to challenge at election time, and its stability depends on its being able to replicate itself across all of the electoral arenas – local, regional, parliamentary and presidential – that the normative state created by the constitution makes available.

One problem with the dual state idea as Sakwa described it is that it envisions change happening only in one direction: towards the supremacy of the normative state – in other words, towards democracy. The power of the normative state is latent within the dual state, stopping the administrative regime from supplanting it entirely. However, the normative state can be revived, and 'evolutionary gradualism in contemporary Russia could achieve the most revolutionary transformation in social relations and ultimately transform the quality of democracy' (Sakwa, 2010b: 203). The implication of this line of thinking is that the hollowing out of democracy, the compromise by the administrative regime that coexists with the normative state, can't really go any further. This is highly debatable; for many, the quality of Russian democracy would seem to have become worse since 2010 (when Sakwa was writing), and the sources of constitutional renewal in Russia seem weaker than ever.

Russia's system as neo-patrimonial

The ideas that have been put forward to describe the Russian system by area specialists are an improvement on the ideas about hybridity from comparative politics because they are sociologically richer: they take account of a broader array of factors. However, this advantage is somewhat lessened by the fact that they lay too much stress on stability in the current Russian political system. As we have seen, there has been change both across the post-Soviet period as a whole and in the shorter term, with Putin's return to the presidency in 2012 and the adoption of a populist cultural conservatism. In many ways, the literature that uses terms from comparative politics performs better at accounting for change, since it is able to see both the possibility for an expansion of authoritarianism and its weakening through electoral protest (Gel'man, 2014; 2015: 138–45). One possible way of bridging the gap between the Russianist versions and the comparative versions of hybridity might be to think of Russia's system as neo-patrimonial.

The concept of neo-patrimonialism

There is a growing literature on the post-Soviet political system as a version of patrimonialism, or neo-patrimonialism (Gel'man, 2016; Hale, 2010; Hanson, 2011; Isaacs, 2014; Lynch, 2005: 159–63; Whitmore, 2010). Neo-patrimonialism analyses how patrimonialism – personal claims to power, ties and relations – is combined with, and conflicted by, impersonal institutions, which have some existence independent of individual political actors. The latter are, first, a bureaucratic state machinery, the development of which pushes a part of the state towards more enduring hierarchies; and, second, impersonal market economic exchange, which adds additional channels to wealth to the personalized access to resources through the machinery of a state constructed around its leader(s). Rather than any particular institutional order, therefore, neo-patrimonialism describes a politico-economic system that is made up of conflicting modes of organization and domination and their legitimation (Erdmann and Engel, 2006). How and in what combination these conflicting modes of organization and domination and their justification are combined, and what leads to their conjunction, is a matter of material conditions and pressures but also of political choice and organization. This means that such systems can contain a wide range of personalized and formal institutions. Patronage and bureaucratic hierarchy exist alongside one another. Particularistic economic exchange, in which access to resources is influenced by personal ties and relational capital, coexists with impersonal market economic exchange and organization, where access to resources is more open and influenced by impersonal considerations.

Since it does not embody a particular set of institutional or organizational forms, neo-patrimonialism is best conceived as a space in which rulers try to ensure the continuity of their power (Robinson, 2017b). Figure 12.1 maps out the space that neo-patrimonialism occupies between personal and impersonal modes of political legitimation and between closed, personal access to economic wealth and more open, impersonal market forms. Neo-patrimonial polities may take different institutional forms within this

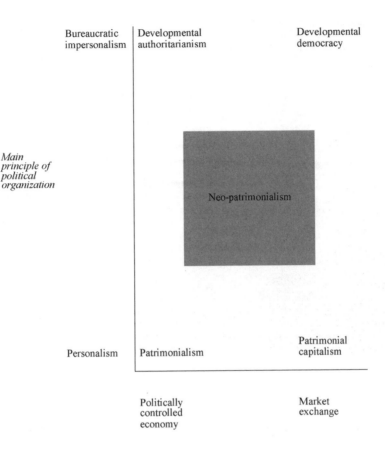

Bureaucratic
impersonalism

Developmental
authoritarianism

Developmental
democracy

*Main
principle of
political
organization*

Neo-patrimonialism

Personalism

Patrimonialism

Patrimonial
capitalism

Politically
controlled
economy

Market
exchange

Main principle of economic organization

Figure 12.1 *The neo-patrimonial space*

space according to their particular combination of different organizing and legitimating principles and modes of domination. What unites such systems is not any common institutional design but the fact that, first, the combination of personalism and impersonalism means that regime (essentially the rules that manage access to power) and state (the institutional locus of power) as forms of domination are not easily reconciled; and, second, and because of this, there is a high degree of uncertainty about the future. The rules concerning access to power – the regime – are essentially personalistic, although they may exist alongside what should be impersonal rules where there are political parties or some constitutional requirement for elections, thus complicating the consolidation of a stable regime. As we noted in chapter 1, a regime is consolidated and stable when elites achieve a set of rules concerning the access to power that they cannot change without

The cult of leadership: Putin, Lenin and Stalin impersonators outside Red Square

incurring a disproportionate cost to themselves. The existence of impersonal rules can lower the cost of trying to change how power can be accessed and by whom; such rules can create avenues for contesting who holds power and can provide opportunities to develop constituencies to support a challenge to personalism.

The resulting uncertainty over how power can be accessed and held on to is compounded by the fact that predominantly personalist politics exists alongside and is interwoven with larger administrative systems that have some of the features and functions of a modern bureaucratic state in a neo-patrimonial space. This brings up the problematic relationship between regime and state building that we discussed in chapter 1. Polities in the neo-patrimonial space should have some measure of state capacity that is supposed to provide welfare and security. It is a particular problem that regimes can be consolidated before levels of state capacity have been developed to meet these needs, and that regime maintenance constrains further development of state autonomy and capacity so that governance cannot mature (and in the case of Russia, provide post-communist recon-struction). Some measure of autonomy – separation of the state from the interests of elites – is necessary to develop welfare and security for a society as a whole rather than simply for elite groups. Developing state autonomy is therefore a constraint on elite groups and their ability to use resources both for private ends and to settle disputes within the regime. Both revenue accumulation and administration are needed for the provision of general welfare and security. Building state capacity also, therefore, constrains elites by claiming resources that they might otherwise be used to back regime consolidation, by weakening patronage and personalism.

This brings up the problems of political development that we discussed in chapter 1. If regime development happens before state development and constrains it, as it will in a neo-patrimonial system, will the regime be able to resist pressures for state development and functionality? Will a regime fall when these pressures become too great? Regime members may try to fix access to power and resources through agreements with one another. However, they cannot be certain that they can maintain these arrangements or the power bases that allow them to be made. In order to fulfil its functions, the state might encroach on these power bases – for example, to improve state revenues by curtailing corruption and attacking patronage networks. Uncertainty for regime members is heightened by the fact that they cannot always be clear what the motive is behind any encroachment on their arrangements. The interleaving of regime members and their clients through the administrative system means that it is hard to discern between a move to increase the functionality of the state and a power grab by some other elite group. Likewise, state officials interested in working to fulfil the state's functions cannot be sure that they will be able to do so without encountering some regime member's interests and opposition, that there will be the resources to complete their tasks, or that their actions won't be seen as hostile to some powerbroker.

Political development in a neo-patrimonial space is thus shaped by the difficulty of producing a functional relationship between regime and state and the high degree of uncertainty that this produces. Much of the literature on change and neo-patrimonialism is concerned with how the state–regime/ formal–informal tensions can lead to collapse and to regime change (for example, Bratton and Van de Walle, 1994). While this is the extreme end of change in neo-patrimonialism, we should not ignore the fact that polities in neo-patrimonial spaces are always struggling to manage the tensions that they contain. Such tension is, crudely, over, first, whether a regime can be consolidated through elite agreement and, second, whether it can develop enough state functionality, or be able to act as a substitute for the state, sufficient to provide for security and deal with pressures to deliver welfare (including through economic growth). The uncertainties that there will always be competing interests within the neo-patrimonial polity that will seek to push it towards one of the four corners of figure 12.1. Regime formation and its stability can contain these tensions by making the costs of acting to reduce uncertainty too high for a group, but over the longer term there also needs to be state functionality, or regime substitution for a functional state formation, to ensure stability and so that any exogenous shocks can be contained.

	Actors and motivation	Process	Conditions for 'successful move'
Movement towards patrimonialism	Leader and/ or elite faction sees possibility of supplanting other leaders and/or elite groups to become hegemonic; may be opportunistic or to resolve contest for power and achieve security of tenure.	Suppression or co-option of elite groups by core ruling group/leader; hollowing out of state and attenuation of market mechanisms in favour of personal political and economic control.	Low-level or containable demands on state from society so that the hollowing out of formal bureaucracy by personal rule doesn't create a societal backlash; private economic interests weakened so that they can be co-opted into personal rule or marginalized.
Movement towards patrimonial capitalism	Leader and/or elite faction seek economic advantage through economic liberalization; may be due to exogenous pressure and/or response to failure of economic management.	Economic management through state replaced by market mechanisms that operate only insofar as they do not gainsay elite interests; elite secures control of commanding heights of the economy and secures rents through politically sheltered private economic activity.	Low-level or containable demands on state from society and market so that the development of market in favour of elite does not create a societal backlash; contest over state resources as liberalization unfolds does not lead to unmanageable elite conflict.
Movement towards developmental authoritarianism	Leader and/or elite faction seek to force pace of economic development through increased bureaucratic control of economy; may be in response to state crisis/social pressure for growth.	Suppression of private economic activity and autonomy, in particular in areas such as investment, in favour of bureaucratic direction; politicized ('ideological') notion of development established as basis for bureaucratic autonomy from some elite interests.	Societal and elite demands for resources either through investment in favoured projects or welfare largely ignored by bureaucracy so that particularistic interests should be constrained; state develops capacity to control social and elite backlash against curbs on consumption required to fund development.

| Movement towards developmental democracy | Leader and/or elite faction seek to force pace of economic development through combination of bureaucratic management of the economy and private economic activity; may be in response to state crisis/social pressure for growth, likely to be backed by exogenous pressure. | Development of bureaucratic capacity and autonomy from most private elite interests; changing composition of elite as market empowers new actors; develop claim that administration of economy is through market rather than ideology. | Societal and elite demands for resources either through investment in favoured projects or welfare largely ignored by bureaucracy so that particularistic interests are constrained; state develops capacity to control social and elite backlash against changes in allocation of resources produced by marketization. |

Figure 12.2 *Exits from the neo-patrimonial space*

If a stable relationship between regime and state formation does not develop, it is an open question as to which of the forms of domination in neo-patrimonialism will shape its development. In the terms outlined in figure 12.1, the choice is roughly between moving up to the top of the figure, to a position where state dominates regime, or down to the bottom, where regime dominates state. If the former is the case, it may be possible for officials to reduce uncertainty so that the state can become 'developmental' – concerned with the provision of economic growth for a wider spectrum of society – rather than constrained by elite interests. If the latter, the result will be personalist political power and/or elite control over the market, which limits both economic distribution and the wider functionality of the state in favour of satisfying particular interests.

Movement in any direction is always possible – as are even contradictory movements – as a neo-patrimonial system tries to deal with pressures for change. External actors, such as international organizations, might, for example, assert pressure by insisting on greater respect for impersonal electoral rules or on the adoption and enforcement of policies (such as competition policies) that circumscribe elite rent-seeking. Similar pressures might come from within the polity as a result of elite conflict or social pressure, or because there is some need to develop state capacity (by building up revenue, for example) that requires some alteration in the relationship between patrimonial political structures and agents and the functional bureaucratic state. These pressures need to be managed so that they are not destructive of stability, or so that such destruction is handled in a way that enables a peaceable movement to one of the corners of figure 12.1. There will be leaders and factions who seek to maximize their patronage and personal powers at a cost to the wider state, and those who want to constrain particularistic interests to push development towards some political end or steered by market rationality so as to increase the state's functionality. There will also be social groups who support these leaders and their ideas in the hope that they might deliver economic growth, redistribution or opportunity.

Stability in a neo-patrimonial system requires that no groups or interests gain too much leverage to enact their project and move to one of the corners of figure 12.1. Figure 12.2 gives an abstracted overview of what forces might seek to move in which direction, what such a movement would entail, and what it might require minimally to be a successful movement to some form of developmental state, to some form of 'traditional' patrimonialism as originally described by Weber (1947: 622–49) (bottom left of figure 12.1), or to what Schlumberger (2008) has called patrimonial capitalism (bottom right of figure 12.1), where market instruments are adopted, usually because of external pressures, but the terms on which they work are set by local elites who subvert them to their material advantage.

Russia as a neo-patrimonial polity

We can map the developments of Russian politics since the end of the USSR as movements within the neo-patrimonial space. The collapse of the USSR marked the end of a form of developmental authoritarian polity. The CPSU had directed the economy politically, supposedly as an impersonal bureaucracy, but its status had been undermined by corruption and the networks of mutual protection established to shelter Soviet officials from punishment. By taking advantage of the demise of the USSR and gaining control of resources for their own use, Soviet officials moved Russia into a neo-patrimonial space as they substituted personal power for bureaucratic rule. They did this within what was formally a democratic system, one with an elected parliament and president. This established a tension between formal and informal politics.

The reforms of the early 1990s were an attempt to remove this tension by getting to the top-right corner of figure 12.1: the aim was to build a developmental democracy in which there was impersonalism in politics (the rule of law) and the economy (the rule of the market). But this failed because of opposition from vested interests, local elites and industrialists, who were keen to protect their personal power. This stymied state development and led to increasingly personalized forms of regime building. Formally, power was accessed through a constitutionally defined set of rules and institutions. But in practice these were undermined through personal deals between individuals and groups, such as those made by Yeltsin in co-opting elite factions into his administration, with the oligarchs over property, and with regional leaders over things such as local democracy and economic management. The process and conditions for exiting the neo-patrimonial space to developmental democracy as outlined in figure 12.2 were not completed or present. There was no separation of the bureaucracy from elite interests, and elite demands for resources could not be ignored. This meant that Russia remained stuck, with all of the instability that this entailed as elite groups competed for resources and influence.

It is a matter of debate as to how far Putin had a plan to escape the neo-patrimonial space when he came to power in 2000. Elite political management increased through the creation of United Russia and the limits put on regional autonomy. Because this was based on Putin's personal power and leadership status, it was impossible to increase the impersonalism that might have led to either developmental authoritarianism or democracy. There were elements of developmental authoritarianism in the greater control of the state over economic life under Putin, though it didn't develop into an economic plan for modernization under the state bureaucracy, since the rule of law was undermined by corruption. There was recognition of what needed to be done to improve the chances of developing a more functional state under Medvedev, but the push to develop state capacity and the rule of law didn't last. Some change of regional leaders took place, but they were torn between reforming local administration and securing the stability and electoral outcomes that Putin desired. The status quo was re-established when Putin returned to the presidency in 2012. This problem – Should the regime be strengthened or should administration be improved? – persists. In the end, and despite his strength as a leader, Putin has not forced change through but instead has used a variety of personal and impersonal mechanisms to secure regime stability.

The strengthening of the Putin regime does not mean that the place that Russia occupies in the neo-patrimonial space is a stable one. There are problems caused by the existence of constitutional political rules (Sakwa's 'normative state', the elections of competitive/electoral authoritarianism) alongside personalism and informality. This tension leads to protest over such things as electoral fraud and corruption from opposition groups and society. While this opposition has not as yet posed a danger to the regime, there are no guarantees that it will not erupt into something more threatening, especially if protest is badly handled. Poor protest management was a factor in the Arab Spring and in the overthrow of the Yanukovych regime at the EuroMaidan protest in Ukraine. There are also social expectations that the state will act as a protector and guarantor of common interests, security and economic well-being that have to be addressed and managed. This means that there are limits to how far the state can be diminished before its diminution becomes a threat to the stability of the regime. At some point the regime's abuses of power have to be reined in so that the state can function and accumulate the resources that it needs to function. We saw this in the 1990s, when Yeltsin was forced to take action against oligarchs who had propped up his regime to try to restore some fiscal health to the state.

Putin was more successful than Yeltsin at restoring some state capacity, particularly its ability to extract resources, but he was not able to build on his success because of the dangers of reform disturbing the regime on which his power rests. As a result, although Russia was able to cope with crisis after 2008, it was not able to develop new economic forces; it remains dependent on energy rents and has suffered economic recession and sluggish growth. Securing long-term state functionality remains a problem for Putin and his regime. Putin's answer to the problems of maintaining both state and regime has been to try to move the yardstick of state success from the economic to the more nebulous criteria of national sovereignty and civilizational strength. He can declare achievement in these areas rather than have to demonstrate it through the improvement of people's day-to-day lives. However, the declaration of success is not always convincing, as the demonstrations against corruption in 2017 have shown. Even Putin loyalists, such as the long-distance lorry drivers who took part in protests over road taxes, discount the regime's rhetoric when it impinges on their material fortunes. The instability that is part of being within a neo-patrimonial space remains, therefore, as a constant potential threat. The weakness of the Duma and of political parties, and the association through co-option of many political parties with the regime, means that there are few channels for society or state functionaries to push for reform and the development of state capacity. Reform has to come via the presidency and is affected by calculations about what it means for Putin's power. Even if reform proposals make it through the presidential filter there are no guarantees that they will address popular concerns, since policy may be blocked, subtly subverted or carried out in name only by any number of bureaucrats, local politicians and economic actors who see reform as a threat to their personal economic and political fortunes.

The idea of neo-patrimonialism as a space in which tensions between state and regime building pull the political system in various directions does not mean that we have to abandon ideas such as electoral authoritarianism completely. They can be integrated since they describe particular institutional problems that can exist within the neo-patrimonial space. The idea of tensions, and the fact that we can hypothesize about what needs to be done to resolve them, means that we have some way of making judgements about future development in Russia too. We can take the processes in figure 12.2 and see if they are being pursued through policy to try to move the country in any particular direction. Of course, more than one process might be followed, but that too is revealing, since it would lessen the prospects of escaping the neo-patrimonial space. We can take the conditions in figure 12.2 and use those as measures of whether or not processes/policies are having any success. And, finally, we have the possibility that there is no escape from the space, just collapse at some point in the future, followed by something else, or even a new form of neo-patrimonialism. Russia's difficulties imply that it is most likely that it will ricochet between different parts of the neo-patrimonial space for some time to come. However, Russia's weaknesses mean that we can never discount collapse. This is one reason why papers arguing that the end is nigh are a constant feature of Russian political analysis (for example, Monaghan, 2012; Petrov, 2016). Generally, such predictions are proven wrong. Getting to a point where collapse comes about is in many ways as difficult as getting to a point where the neo-patrimonial space can be exited. The fact that it doesn't take place, however, is no reason to reject ideas about the nature of Russian politics that highlight the country's many weaknesses.

Conclusion

Debates about what kind of political system Russia has are not going to be resolved by the arguments concerning neo-patrimonialism that we have just examined. However, the concept of neo-patrimonialism does show that classifications of the type of political system in Russia should try and account for what constitutes change and what its sources are. There is no point in characterizing a political system in a way that does not allow some means of analysing it across time, and descriptions of the political system in Russia need to consider both sources of stability and sources of instability. Russian studies, political science and international relations all suffered a shock when the USSR collapsed. This was because most of the descriptions of the USSR, and of the system of international relations of which it was a part, emphasized stability rather than looking for sources of change. The end of the USSR and the recent political history of Russia are object lessons on the need to keep the possibility of change in mind. The USSR disintegrated because it couldn't manage economic modernization without political reform, and political reform took forms that were destructive of the Soviet regime. Russia lurched from crisis to crisis under Yeltsin but defied expectations that crisis would last beyond that when Putin, helped by favourable economic circumstances and the weaknesses and foibles of his opponents, secured his regime and power and created a form of stability that has made him popular among ordinary Russians. This stability has been maintained through coercion, by corruption and electoral fraud, media manipulation and control over political competition. However, the reproduction of stability depends on Putin rather than on any firm institutional base. This makes it hard to see how the Russian political system can be stable in the longer term. Institutional bases for stability might emerge from within Putin's regime – if, for example, United Russia develops some greater role in controlling elite access to politics. Such a development would probably not facilitate democracy, but it could lead to a less personalist form of electoral authoritarianism that would keep Russia within the neo-patrimonial space. If no institutional sources of stability emerge, the most likely prospect is a return to something like the Yeltsin-era politics of conflict and crisis, in which elite groups fight for influence and a weak president tries to rein them in to stay in power. Democracy might eventually emerge from either Yeltsin-like chaos or from electoral authoritarianism as Russian society changes or as Russian politicians find that they cannot create stability except by compromising with each other. The emergence of democracy will be slow and tentative either way, and, while we wait for it, and wait for it to become stronger, we cannot be sure that it won't be pre-empted by something worse than what we currently have.

References

Allison, R. (2008) 'Russia resurgent? Moscow's campaign to "coerce Georgia to peace"', *International Affairs* 84(6): 1145–71.

Ambrosio, T. (2008) 'Catching the "Shanghai spirit": How the Shanghai Cooperation Organization promotes authoritarian norms in Central Asia', *Europe-Asia Studies* 60(8): 1321–44.

Ambrosio, T. (2009) *Authoritarian Backlash: Russian Resistance to Democratization in the Former Soviet Union*. Farnham: Ashgate.

Aris, S. (2009) 'The Shanghai Cooperation Organisation: "Tackling the three evils": A regional response to non-traditional security challenges or an anti-Western bloc?', *Europe-Asia Studies* 61(3): 457–82.

Åslund, A. (1989) *Gorbachev's Struggle for Economic Reform*. London: Pinter.

Åslund, A. (1995) 'The Case for Radical Reform', in L. Diamond and M. Plattner (eds), *Economic reform and Democracy*. Baltimore: Johns Hopkins University Press, pp. 74–85.

Asmus, R. (2010) *A Little War that Shook the World: Georgia, Russia, and the Future of the West*. Basingstoke: Palgrave Macmillan.

Atwal, M. and E. Bacon (2012) 'The youth movement Nashi: Contentious politics, civil society, and party politics', *East European Politics* 28(3): 256–66.

Bacon, E. and B. Renz, with J. Cooper (2006) *Securitising Russia: The Domestic Politics of Vladimir Putin*. Manchester: Manchester University Press.

Bahry, D. (2005) 'The new federalism and the paradoxes of regional sovereignty in Russia', *Comparative Politics* 37(2): 127–46.

Bahry, D. (2013) 'Making Autocracy Work? Russian Regional Politics under Putin', in W. M. Reisinger (ed.), *Russia's Regions and Comparative Subnational Politics*. London: Routledge, pp. 162–72.

Balzer, H. (2003) 'Managed pluralism: Vladimir Putin's emerging regime', *Post-Soviet Affairs* 19(3): 189–227.

Balzer, H. (2005) 'The Putin thesis and Russian energy policy', *Post-Soviet Affairs* 21(3): 210–25.

Barnes, A. (2006) *Owning Russia: The Struggle over Factories, Farms, and Power*. Ithaca, NY: Cornell University Press.

Baryshnikov, V. and R. Coalson (September 2016) 'Numbers don't lie: Statistics point to massive fraud in Russia's Duma vote, *Radio Free Europe/Radio Liberty*, www.rferl.org/a/ statistics-point-to-massive-fraud-russia-state-duma-elections/28002750.html.

Beissinger, M. (2002) *Nationalist Mobilization and the Collapse of the Soviet state*. New York: Cambridge University Press.

Belanovsky, S., M. Dmitriev, S. Misikhina and T. Omelchuk (2011) *Socio-economic Change and Political Transformation in Russia*. Moscow: Russian Presidential Academy of National Economy and Public Administration.

Biryukov, N. and V. Sergeyev (1997) *Russian Politics in Transition: Institutional Conflict in a Nascent Democracy*. Aldershot: Ashgate.

Blakkisrud, H. (2011) 'Medvedev's new governors', *Europe-Asia Studies* 63(3): 367–95.

Bol'shakov, I. (2012) 'The nonsystemic opposition', *Russian Politics and Law* 50(3): 82–92.

Bradshaw, M. J. and N. J. Lynn (1994) 'After the Soviet Union: The post-Soviet states in the world system', *Professional Geographer* 46(4): 439–49.

Bratton, M., and N. van de Walle (1994) 'Neopatrimonial regimes and political transitions in Africa', *World Politics* 46(4): 453–89.

Breslauer, G. (1999) 'Boris Yel'tsin as patriarch', *Post-Soviet Affairs* 15(2): 186–200.

Breslauer, G. (2002) *Gorbachev and Yeltsin as Leaders*. Cambridge: Cambridge University Press.

Brown, A. (2007) *Seven Years that Shook the World: Perestroika in Perspective*. Oxford: Oxford University Press.

Brudny, Y. M. (1993) 'The dynamics of "Democratic Russia", 1990–1993'. *Post-Soviet Affairs* 9(2): 141–70.

Bunce, V. (1985) 'The empire strikes back: the evolution of the Eastern bloc from a Soviet asset to a Soviet liability', *International Organization* 39(1): 1–46.

Bunce, V., and S. Wolchik (2011) *Defeating Authoritarian Leaders in Postcommunist Countries*. Cambridge: Cambridge University Press.

Chaisty, P. (2006) *Legislative Politics and Economic Power in Russia*. Basingstoke: Palgrave Macmillan.

Chaisty, P. (2012) 'The Federal Assembly and the Power Vertical', in G. Gill and J. Young (eds), *Routledge Handbook of Russian Politics and Society*. London: Routledge, pp. 92–101.

Chaisty, P. and S. Whitefield (2012) 'The effects of the global financial crisis on Russian political attitudes', *Post-Soviet Affairs* 28(2): 187–208.

Chaisty, P. and S. Whitefield (2013) 'Forward to democracy or back to authoritarianism? The attitudinal bases of mass support for the Russian election protests of 2011–2012', *Post-Soviet Affairs* 29(5): 387–403.

Chaisty, P., N. Cheeseman and T. Power (2014) 'Rethinking the "presidentialism debate": Conceptualising coalitional politics in cross-regional perspective', *Democratization* 21(1): 79–94.

Chebankova, E. (2007) 'Putin's struggle for federalism: structures, operation, and the commitment problem', *Europe-Asia Studies* 59(2): 279–302.

Cheterian, V. (2009) 'The August 2008 war in Georgia: from ethnic conflict to border wars', *Central Asian Survey* 28(2): 155–70.

Chryssogelos, A.-S. (2014) 'Vladimir Putin's popularity among populist parties in Europe illustrates the depth of the challenges facing European democracy', LSE blog, http://bit.ly/1oMUpbs.

Clark, W. A. (1998) 'Presidential Prefects in the Russian Provinces: Yeltsin's Regional Cadres Policy', in G. Gill (ed.), *Elites and Leadership in Russian Politics*. Basingstoke: Macmillan, pp. 24–51.

Colton, T. (1995) 'Superpresidentialism and Russia's backward state', *Post-Soviet Affairs* 11(2): 144–8.

Colton, T. J. (2000) *Transitional Citizens: Voters and What Influences Them in the New Russia*. Cambridge, MA: Harvard University Press.

Colton, T. J. (2008) *Yeltsin: A Life*. New York: Basic Books.

Connolly, R. (2009) 'Financial vulnerabilities in Russia', *Russian Analytical Digest* 65: 2–5.

Conradi, P. (2017) *Who Lost Russia? How the World Entered a New Cold War*. London: Oneworld.

Constitution (1977) *Constitution (Fundamental Law) of the Union of Soviet Socialist Republics*. Moscow: Novosti.

Cooper, J. (2006) 'Of BRICs and brains: comparing Russia with India, China, and other populous emerging economies', *Eurasian Geography and Economics* 47(3): 255–84.

Credit Suisse Research Institute (2013) *Global Wealth Report 2013*. Zurich: Credit Suisse AG.

Dannreuther, R. and L. March (2008) 'Chechnya: Has Moscow won?', *Survival* 50(4): 97–112.

Deyermond, R. (2012) 'Assessing the reset: Successes and failures in the Obama administration's Russia policy, 2009–2012', European Security 22(4): 500–23.

Dunlop, J. (1993) *The Rise of Russia and the Fall of the Soviet Empire*. Princeton, NJ: Princeton University Press.

Dunlop, J. (2012) *The Moscow Bombings of September 1999*. Stuttgart: ibidem.

Easter, G. (1997) 'Preference for presidentialism: Post-communist regime change in Russia and the NIS', *World Politics* 49(2): 184–211.

Easter, G. (2000) *Reconstructing the State: Personal Networks and Elite Identity in Soviet Russia*. Cambridge: Cambridge University Press.

Easter, G. (2012) *Capital, Coercion, and Postcommunist States*. Ithaca, NY: Cornell University Press.

Ekonomicheskaya ekspertnaya gruppa (2017) 'Ekonomicheskie obzory', www.eeg.ru/pages/186.

Enikolopov, R., M. Petrova and E. Zhuravskaya (2007) *Television and Political Persuasion in Young Democracies: Evidence from Russia*. Moscow: Centre for Economic and Financial Research at New Economic School working paper 112.

Enikolopov, R., V. Korovkin, M. Petrova, K. Sonin and A. Zakharov (2013) 'Field experiment estimate of electoral fraud in Russian parliamentary elections', *Proceedings of the National Academy of Sciences* 110(2): 448–52.

Erdmann, G. and Engel, U. (2006) *Neopatrimonialism Revisited – Beyond a Catch-all Concept*. Hamburg: German Institute of Global and Area Studies working paper 16.

Evangelista, M. (2002) *The Chechen Wars: Will Russia go the Way of the Soviet Union?* Washington, DC: Brookings Institution Press.

Evans, A. B. (2008) 'The first steps of Russia's Public Chamber: Representation or coordination?', *Demokratizatsiya* 16(4): 345–62.

Fainsod, M. (1963) *How Russia is Ruled*. Oxford: Oxford University Press.

Federal'naya sluzhba gosudarstvennoi statistiki (2013) *Rossiya v tsifrakh*. Moscow: Federal'naya sluzhba gosudarstvennoi statistiki.

Federal'naya sluzhba gosudarstvennoi statistiki (2017) 'Natsional'nie scheta', www.gks.ru/.

Fehér, F., A. Heller and G. Markus (1983) *Dictatorship Over Needs*. Oxford: Blackwell.

Fish, M. (1995) *Democracy from Scratch: Opposition and Regime in the new Russian Revolution*. Princeton, NJ: Princeton University Press.

Fish, M. (2000) 'The Executive Deception: Superpresidentialism and the Degradation of Russian Politics', in V. Sperling (ed.), *Building the Russian State: Institutional Quest for Democratic Governance*. Boulder, CO: Westview Press, pp. 177–92.

Fish, M. (2001) 'Democracy and Russian Politics', in Z. Barany and R. Moser (eds), *Russian Politics: Challenges of Democratization*. Cambridge: Cambridge University Press, pp. 215–54.

Fish, M. (2005) *Democracy Derailed in Russia*. Cambridge: Cambridge University Press.

Gaddy, C. and B. Ickes (2002) *Russia's Virtual Economy*. Washington, DC: Brookings Institution Press.

Gaddy, C. and B. Ickes (2010) 'Russia after the global financial crisis', *Eurasian Geography and Economics* 51(3): 281–311.

Gaidar, Y. (2007) *Collapse of an Empire: Lessons for Modern Russia*. Washington, DC: Brookings Institution Press.

Ganev, V. (2009) 'Postcommunist political capitalism: A Weberian interpretation', *Comparative Studies in Society and History* 51(3): 648–74.

Geddes, B., J. Wright and E. Frantz (2014) 'Autocratic breakdown and regime transitions: A new data set', *Perspectives on Politics* 12(2): 313–31.

Gel'man, V. (2000) 'Subnational Institutions in Contemporary Russia', in N. Robinson (ed.), *Institutions and Political Change in Russia*. Basingstoke: Palgrave Macmillan, pp. 85–105.

Gel'man, V. (2005) 'Political opposition in Russia: A dying species?' *Post-Soviet Affairs* 21(3): 226–46.

Gel'man, V. (2010) 'The Dynamics of Sub-national Authoritarianism: Russia in Comparative Perspective', in V. Gel'man and C. Ross (eds), *The Politics of Sub-national Authoritarianism in Russia*. Farnham: Ashgate, pp. 1–18.

Gel'man, V. (2011) 'Politics, Governance, and the Zigzags of the Power Vertical: Toward a Framework for Analyzing Russia's Local Regimes, in W. Reisinger (ed.), *Russia's Regions and Comparative Subnational Politics*. London: Routledge, pp. 25–39.

Gel'man, V. (2014) 'The rise and decline of electoral authoritarianism in Russia', *Demokratizatsiya* 22(4): 503–22.

Gel'man, V. (2015) *Authoritarian Russia: Analyzing Post-Soviet Regime Change*. Pittsburgh: University of Pittsburgh Press.

Gel'man, V. (2016) 'The vicious circle of post-Soviet neopatrimonialism in Russia', *Post-Soviet Affairs* 32(5): 455–73.

Gel'man, V. and G. Golosov (1998) 'Regional party system formation in Russia: The deviant case of Sverdlovsk oblast', *Journal of Communist Studies and Transition Politics* 14(1): 31–53.

Gel'man, V. and S. Ryzhenkov (2011) 'Local regimes, sub-national governance and the "power vertical" in contemporary Russia', *Europe-Asia Studies* 63(3): 449–65.

Gel'man, V. and O. Senatova (1995) 'Sub-national politics in Russia in the post-communist transition period: A view from Moscow', *Regional Politics and Policy* 5(2): 211–23.

Gel'man, V., O. Marganiya and D. Travin (2014) *Re-examining Economic and Political Reforms in Russia, 1985–2000: Generations, Ideas, and Changes*. Lanham, MD: Lexington Books.

Gerschenkron, A. (1962) *Economic Backwardness in Historical Perspective*. Cambridge, MA: Harvard University Press.

Gilbert, L. (2016) 'Crowding out civil society: State management of social organisations in Putin's Russia', *Europe-Asia Studies* 68(9): 1553–78.

Gill, G. (1990) *The Origins of the Stalinist Political System*. Cambridge: Cambridge University Press.

Gill, G. (1994) *The Collapse of a Single Party System: The Disintegration of the Communist Party of the Soviet Union*. Cambridge: Cambridge University Press.

GOLOS (2011) 'Statement of the GOLOS Association on the results of the elections of deputies for the State Duma, December 4, 2011', *Russian Analytical Digest* (106): 9–10.

Golosov, G. V. (2011a) 'The regional roots of electoral authoritarianism in Russia', *Europe-Asia Studies* 63(4): 623–39.

Golosov, G. V. (2011b) 'Russia's regional legislative elections, 2003–2007: Authoritarianism incorporated', *Europe-Asia Studies* 63(3): 397–414.

Golosov, G. V. (2012a) 'The 2012 political reform in Russia: The interplay of liberalizing concessions and authoritarian corrections', *Problems of Post-Communism* 59(6): 3–14.

Golosov, G. V. (2012b) 'Problems of the Russian electoral system', *Russian Politics and Law* 50(3): 18–39.

Golosov, G. V. (2014) 'The September 2013 regional elections in Russia: The worst of both worlds', *Regional and Federal Studies* 24(2): 229–41.

Golosov, G. V. (2017) 'Authoritarian learning in the development of Russia's electoral system', *Russian Politics* 2(2): 182–205.

Gorbachev, M. (1987) *Perestroika: New Thinking for Our Country and the World*. London: Collins.

Gorbachev, M. (1996) *Memoirs*. New York: Doubleday.

Goskomstat SSSR (1987) *SSSR v tsifrakh v 1987 godu*. Moscow: Finansy i Statistika.

Greene, S. (2013) 'Beyond Bolotnaia', *Problems of Post-Communism* 60(2): 40–52.

Greene, S. (2014) *Moscow in Movement: Power and Opposition in Putin's Russia*. Stanford, CA: Stanford University Press.

Guriev, S. and A. Rachinsky (2005) 'The role of oligarchs in Russian capitalism', *Journal of Economic Perspectives* 19(1): 131–50.

Gustafson, T. (1989) *Crisis Amid Plenty: The Politics of Soviet Energy under Brezhnev and Gorbachev*. Princeton, NJ: Princeton University Press.

Gustafson, T. (2012) *Wheel of Fortune: The Battle for Oil and Power in Russia*. Cambridge, MA: Harvard University Press.

Hale, H. E. (2004) 'The origins of United Russia and the Putin presidency: The role of contingency in party-system development', *Demokratizatsiya* 12(2): 169–94.

Hale, H. E. (2005) 'Regime cycles: Democracy, autocracy, and revolution in post-Soviet Eurasia', *World Politics* 58(1): 133–65.

Hale, H. E. (2006a) 'Democracy or autocracy on the march? The colored revolutions as normal dynamics of patronal presidentialism', *Communist and Post-Communist Studies* 39(3): 305–29.

Hale, H. E. (2006b) *Why not Parties in Russia? Democracy, Federalism, and the State*. Cambridge: Cambridge University Press.

Hale, H. E. (2010) 'Eurasian polities as hybrid regimes: The case of Putin's Russia', *Journal of Eurasian Studies* 1(1): 33–41.

Hale, H. E. (2015) *Patronal Politics: Eurasian Regime Dynamics in Comparative Perspective*. Cambridge: Cambridge University Press.

Hanson, P. (2007) 'The Russian economic puzzle: Going forwards, backwards or sideways?', *International Affairs* 83(5): 869–89.

Hanson, P. and E. Teague (2005) 'Big business and the state in Russia', *Europe-Asia Studies* 57(5): 657–80.

Hanson, S. E. (2007) 'The uncertain future of Russia's weak state authoritarianism', *East European Politics and Societies* 21(1): 67–81.

Hanson, S. E. (2011) 'Plebiscitarian patrimonialism in Putin's Russia', *Annals of the American Academy of Political and Social Science* 636(1): 32–48.

Harding, L. (2016) *A Very Expensive Poison: The Definitive Story of the Murder of Litvinenko and Russia's War with the West*. London: Guardian Books/Faber & Faber.

Hellman, J. (1998) 'Winners take all: The politics of partial reform in postcommunist transitions', *World Politics* 50(2): 203–34.

Henderson, K. and N. Robinson (1997) *Post-communist Politics*. London: Prentice Hall.

Hewett, E. (1988) *Reforming the Soviet Economy: Equality versus Efficiency*. Washington, DC: Brookings Institution Press.

Hill, R. and P. Frank (1986) *The Soviet Communist Party*. London: George Allen & Unwin.

Hoffman, E. and R. Laird (1982) *The Politics of Economic Modernization in the Soviet Union*. Ithaca, NY: Cornell University Press.

Holmes, L. (2008) 'Corruption and organised crime in Putin's Russia', *Europe-Asia Studies* 60(6): 1011–31.

Horowitz, D. (1990) 'Comparing democratic systems', *Journal of Democracy* 1(4): 73–9.

Horvarth, R. (2012) *Putin's Preventative Counter-revolution: Post-Soviet Authoritarianism and the Spectre of Velvet Revolution*. London: Routledge.

Hough, J. (1980) *Soviet Leadership in Transition*. Washington, DC: Brookings Institution Press.

Hough, J. and M. Fainsod (1979) *How the Soviet Union is Governed*. Cambridge, MA: Harvard University Press.

Hughes, J. (1996) 'Russia's federalization: Bilateral treaties add to confusion', *Transition* 2(19): 39–43.

Hughes, J. (2007) *Chechnya: From Nationalism to Jihad*. Philadelphia: University of Pennsylvania Press.

Huskey, E. (1995) 'The state-legal administration and the politics of redundancy', *Post-Soviet Affairs* 11(2): 115–43.

Huskey, E. (1999) *Presidential Power in Russia*. Armonk, NY: M. E. Sharpe.

Hutcheson, D. S. (2012) 'Party finance in Russia', *East European Politics* 28(3): 267–82.

Hutcheson, D. S. (2013) 'Party cartels beyond Western Europe: Evidence from Russia', *Party Politics* 19(6): 907–24.

Hyde, M. (2001) 'Putin's federal reforms and their implications for presidential power in Russia', *Europe-Asia Studies* 53(5): 719–43.

Isaacs, R. (2014) 'Neopatrimonialism and beyond: reassessing the formal and informal in the study of Central Asian politics', *Contemporary Politics* 20(2): 229–45.

Isaacs, R. and S. Whitmore (2014) 'The limited agency and life-cycles of personalized dominant parties in the post-Soviet space: The cases of United Russia and Nur Otan', *Democratization* 21(4): 699–721.

Johnson, J. (1997) 'Russia's emerging financial-industrial groups', *Post-Soviet Affairs* 13(4): 333–65.

Johnson, S. and H. Kroll (1991) 'Managerial strategies for spontaneous privatization', *Soviet Economy* 7(4): 281–316.

Jowitt, K. (1992) *New World Disorder: The Leninist Extinction*. Berkeley: University of California Press.

Judah, B. (2013) *Fragile Empire: How Russia Fell in and Out of Love with Vladimir Putin*. New Haven, CT: Yale University Press.

Keep, J. (1995) *Last of the Empires: A History of the Soviet Union, 1945–1991*. Oxford: Oxford University Press.

Kirkow, P. (1995) 'Regional warlordism in Russia: The case of Primorskii *krai*', *Europe-Asia Studies* 47(6): 923–47.

Kobak, D., S. Shpilkin and M. S. Pshenichnikov (2012) 'Statistical anomalies in 2011–2012 Russian elections revealed by 2D correlation analysis', http://arxiv.org/pdf/1205.0741v2.pdf.

Kolesnikov, A. (2013) 'Vladislav Surkov: ya byl ryadom s velikim chelovekom', *Russkii Pioneer*, 2 August, http://ruspioner.ru/honest/m/single/3718.

Konitzer, A. (2005) *Voting for Russia's Governors*. Washington, DC: Woodrow Wilson Center Press.

Kornai, J. (1992) *The Socialist System: The Political Economy of Communism*. Oxford: Clarendon Press.

Kotkin, S. (2001) *Armageddon Averted: The Soviet collapse, 1970–2000*. Oxford: Oxford University Press.

Kramer, M. (2009) 'The myth of a no-NATO-enlargement pledge to Russia', *Washington Quarterly* 32(2): 39–61.

Kristrol, W. and R. Kagan (1996) 'Toward a neo-Reaganite foreign policy', *Foreign Affairs* 75(4): 18–32.

Kropatcheva, E. (2016) 'Russia and the Collective Security Treaty Organisation: Multilateral policy or unilateral ambitions?', *Europe-Asia Studies* 68(9): 1526–52.

Kryshtanovskaya, O. (2008) 'The Russian elite in transition', *Journal of Communist Studies and Transition Politics* 24(4): 585–603.

Kubicek, P. (2009) 'The Commonwealth of Independent States: An example of failed regionalism?', *Review of International Studies* 35: 237–56.

Kuvaldin, V. (1998) 'Presidentsvo v kontekste rossiiskoi transformatsii', in L. Shevtsova (ed.), *Rossiya politicheskaya*. Moscow: Carnegie Endowment for International Peace, pp. 15–70.

Lassila, J. (2014) *The Quest for an Ideal Youth in Putin's Russia II: The Search for Distinctive Conformism in the Political Communication of Nashi, 2005–2009*. Stuttgart: ibidem.

Lassila, J. (2016) 'The Russian People's Front and Hybrid Governance Dilemma', in V. Gel'man (ed.), *Authoritarian modernization in Russia: ideas, institutions, and policies*. London: Routledge, pp. 95–112.

Laue, T. H. Von (1954) 'A secret memorandum of Sergei Witte on the industrialization of imperial Russia', *Journal of Modern History* 26(1): 60–74.

Ledeneva, A. (1998) *Russia's Economy of Favours: Blat, Networking and Informal Exchange*. Cambridge: Cambridge University Press.

Ledeneva, A. (2013) *Can Russia Modernise? Sistema, Power Networks and Informal Governance*. Cambridge: Cambridge University Press.

Lenin, V. (1949 [1902]) *What is to be Done? Burning Questions of our Movement*. Moscow: Progress Publishers.

Levada Tsentr (2010) 'Skolko politicheskikh partii neobkhodimo seichas Rossii?', www.levada.ru/archive/partii-i-obshchestvennye-organizatsii/skolko-politicheskikh-partii-neobkhodimo-seichas-rossi.

Levada Tsentr (2016) 'Oppozitsiya: neobxodimost', uznavaemost' i doverie', www.levada.ru/2016/03/14/oppozitsiya-neobhodimost-uznavaemost-i-doverie/.

Levitin, O. (2000) 'Inside Moscow's Kosovo muddle', *Survival* 42(1): 130–40.

Levitsky, S. and L. Way (2010) *Competitive Authoritarianism: Hybrid Regimes after the Cold War*. Cambridge: Cambridge University Press.

Linz, J. J. (1970) 'An Authoritarian Regime: The Case of Spain', in E. Allardt and S. Rokkan (eds), *Mass Politics: Studies in Political Sociology*. New York: Free Press.

Linz, J. J. (1990a) 'The perils of presidentialism', *Journal of Democracy* 1(1): 51–69.

Linz, J. J. (1990b) 'The virtues of parliamentarism', *Journal of Democracy* 1(4): 84–91.

Lo, B. (2002) *Russian Foreign Policy in the Post-Soviet era*. Basingstoke: Palgrave Macmillan.

Lo, B. (2008) *Axis of Convenience: Moscow, Beijing, and the New Geopolitics*. London: Royal Institute of International Affairs.

Lukinova, E., M. Myagkov and P. C. Ordeshook (2011) 'Metastasised fraud in Russia's 2008 presidential election', *Europe-Asia Studies* 63(4): 603–21.

Lynch, A. C. (2001) 'The realism of Russia's foreign policy', *Europe-Asia Studies* 53(1): 7–31.

Lynch, A. C. (2005) *How Russia is not Ruled: Reflections on Russia's Political Development*. Cambridge: Cambridge University Press.

McAllister, I. and S. White (2008a) 'Voting "against all" in postcommunist Russia', *Europe-Asia Studies* 60(1): 67–87.

McAllister, I. and S. White (2008b) '"It's the economy, comrade!" Parties and voters in the 2007 Russian *Duma* election', *Europe-Asia Studies* 60(6): 931–57.

McAuley, M. (1992) 'Politics, economics, and elite realignment in Russia: A regional perspective', *Soviet Economy* 8(1): 46–88.

McDaniel, T. (1991) *Autocracy, Modernization and Revolution in Russia and Iran*. Princeton, NJ: Princeton University Press.

McFaul, M. (2001a) *Russia's Unfinished Revolution: Political Change from Gorbachev to Putin*. Ithaca, NY: Cornell University Press.

McFaul, M. (2001b) 'Explaining party formation and nonformation in Russia: Actors, institutions, and chance', *Comparative Political Studies* 34(10): 1159–87.

McKinnon, R. (1993) *The Order of Economic Liberalization*. Baltimore: Johns Hopkins University Press.

Malcolm, N., A. Pravda, R. Allison and M. Light (1996) *Internal Factors in Russian Foreign Policy*. Oxford: Oxford University Press.

March, L. (2002) *The Communist Party in Post-Soviet Russia*. Manchester: Manchester University Press.

March, L. (2004) 'The Putin Paradigm and the Cowering of Russia's Communists', in C. Ross (ed.), *Russian Politics under Putin*. Manchester: Manchester University Press, pp. 53–75.

Marx, K., and F. Engels (1967 [1848]) *The Communist Manifesto*. Harmondsworth: Penguin.

Mearsheimer, J. J. (2014) 'Why the Ukraine crisis is the West's fault: The liberal delusions that provoked Putin', *Foreign Affairs* 93.

Medvedev, D. (2009a) 'Interview with Kommersant', 4 June, http://goo.gl/d4ziQ.

Medvedev, D. (2009b) 'Speech at Council of Legislators', 28 December, Federation Council, http://goo.gl/IeQbY.

Medvedev, D. (2009c) 'Rossiya, vpered!', http://kremlin.ru/news/5413.

Medvedev, D. (2010) 'Nasha demokratiya nesovershenna, my eto prekrasno ponimaem: zapis' v bloge Dmitriya Medvedeva posvyashchena razvitiyu Rossiiskoi politicheskoi sistemy', http://kremlin.ru/news/9599.

Ministry of Foreign Affairs (2000) 'The foreign policy concept of the Russian Federation', https://fas.org/nuke/guide/russia/doctrine/econcept.htm.

Ministry of Foreign Affairs (2008) 'The foreign policy concept of the Russian Federation', http://en.kremlin.ru/supplement/4116.

Ministry of Justice (2016) 'Spisok zaregistirovannikh politicheskikh partii', http://minjust.ru/nko/gosreg/partii/spisok.

Monagahan, A. C. (2012) *The End of the Putin era?* Carnegie Papers, July.

Morgan-Jones, E., and P. Schleiter (2004) 'Governmental change in a president-parliamentary regime: the case of Russia 1994–2003', *Post-Soviet Affairs* 20(2): 123–63.

Moser, R. (1998) 'The electoral effects of presidentialism in post-Soviet Russia', *Journal of Communist Studies and Transition Politics* 14(1–2): 54–75.

Moser, R. (2001) 'Executive-legislative Relations in Russia, 1991–1999', in Z. Barany and R. Moser (eds), *Russian Politics: Challenges of Democratization*. Cambridge: Cambridge University Press, pp. 64–102.

Moses, J. (2010) 'Russian local politics in the Putin–Medvedev era', *Europe-Asia Studies* 62(9): 1427–52.

Myagkov, M., P. Ordeshook and D. Shakin (2009) *The Forensics of Electoral Fraud: Russia and Ukraine*. Cambridge: Cambridge University Press.

Myant, M. and J. Drahokoupil (2011) *Transition Economies: Political Economy in Russia, Eastern Europe, and Central Asia*. London: John Wiley.

Nemtsov, B. (2009) 'Bankrotim oligarkhov – spasaem Rossiyu', *Yezhednevnii Zhurnal*, 18 February, www.ej.ru/?a=note&id=8825.

Newnham, R. (2011) 'Oil, carrots, and sticks: Russia's energy resources as a foreign policy tool', *Journal of Eurasian Studies* 2(2): 134–43.

North, D., J. Wallis and B. Weingast (2013) *Violence and Social Orders: A Conceptual Framework for Interpreting Recorded Human History*. Cambridge: Cambridge University Press.

Novokmet, F., T. Piketty and G. Zucman (2017) *From Soviets to Oligarchs: Inequality and Property in Russia, 1905–2016*, NBER Working Paper no. 23712.

Nygren, B. (2008) 'Putin's use of natural gas to reintegrate the CIS region', *Problems of Post-Communism* 55(4): 3–15.

Oates, S. (2013) *Revolution Stalled: The Political Limits of the Internet in the Post-Soviet Sphere*. Oxford: Oxford University Press.

Ó Beacháin, D. and A. Polese (eds) (2010) *Colour Revolutions in the Former Soviet Republics: Successes and Failures*. London: Routledge.

OECD (2006) *Economic Surveys: Russian Federation*. Paris: Organisation for Economic Co-operation and Development.

OECD (2009) *Economic Surveys: Russian Federation*. Paris: Organisation for Economic Co-operation and Development.

OECD (2011) *Economic Surveys: Russian Federation*. Paris: Organisation for Economic Co-operation and Development.

OECD (2014) *Economic Surveys: Russian Federation*. Paris: Organisation for Economic Co-operation and Development.

Okara, A. (2007) 'Sovereign democracy: A new Russian idea or a PR project?', *Russia in Global Affairs* 3.

O'Loughlin, J., G. Ó Tuathail and V. Kolossov (2004) 'A "risky westward turn"? Putin's 9-11 script and ordinary Russians', *Europe-Asia Studies* 56(1): 3–34.

Orttung, R. (2013) 'Navalny's campaign to be Moscow mayor', *Russian Analytical Digest* 136: 2–5.

Oversloot, H. (2007) 'Reordering the state (without changing the constitution): Russia under Putin's rule, 2000–2008', *Review of Central and East European Law* 32(1): 41–64.

Panfilova, E. A. (2016) 'Corruption Indices for Russian Regions', in C. Sampford, A. Shacklock, C. Connors and F. Galtung (eds), *Measuring Corruption*. London: Routledge, pp. 189–202.

Petrov, N. (2010) 'Regional governors under the dual power of Medvedev and Putin', *Journal of Communist Studies and Transition Politics* 26(2): 276–305.

Petrov, N. (2011) 'Who is Running Russia's Regions?', in V. Kononenko and A. Moshes (eds), *Russia as a Network State*. Basingstoke: Palgrave Macmillan, pp. 81–112.

Petrov, N. (2016) *Putin's Downfall: The Coming Crisis of the Russian Regime*. European Council on Foreign Relations, www.ecfr.eu/page/-/ECFR_166_PUTINS_DOWNFALL.pdf.

Philips, T. (2007) *Beslan: The Tragedy of School No. 1*. London: Granta.

Popov, V. (2014) *Mixed Fortunes: An Economic History of China, Russia, and the West*. Oxford: Oxford University Press.

Przeworski, A. (1986) 'Some Problems in the Study of the Transition to Democracy', in G. O'Donnell, P. C. Schmitter and L. Whitehead (eds), *Transitions Form Authoritarian Rule: Comparative Perspectives*. Baltimore: Johns Hopkins University Press, pp. 47–63.

Putin, V. (2000 [1999]) 'Russia at the Turn of the Millennium', in V. Putin, *First Person: An Astonishingly Frank Self-portrait by Russia's President*. London: Random House, pp. 209–19.

Putin, V. (2001) 'Annual address to the Federal Assembly of the Russian Federation', 3 April, http://en.kremlin.ru/events/president/transcripts/21216.

Putin, V. (2004) 'Obrashchenie Prezidenta Rossii Vladimira Putina, 4 sentyabrya 2004 goda', http://kremlin.ru/events/president/transcripts/22589.

Putin, V. (2007a) 'Vyderzhka iz stenograficheskogo otcheta c avtodorozhnikami, zanyatymi na stroitel'stve uchastka magistralu vokrug Krasnoyarska', http://archive.kremlin.ru/appears/2007/11/13/1900_type63374type82634_151504.shtml.

Putin, V. (2007b) 'Speech and the following discussion at the Munich Conference on Security Policy', 10 February, http://en.kremlin.ru/events/president/transcripts/24034.

Putin, V. (2008) 'Speech at expanded meeting of the State Council on Russia's development strategy through to 2020', *Johnson's Russia List* 29, 11 February.

Putin, V. (2012a) 'Russia: The ethnicity issue: Prime Minister Vladimir Putin's article for *Nezavisimaya gazeta*', 23 January, http://archive.premier.gov.ru/eng/events/news/17831.

Putin, V. (2012b) 'Rossiya i menyayushchiisya mir. Moskovskie novosti', 27 February, www.mn.ru/politics/78738.

Putin, V. (2012c) 'Vladimir Putin provyol zasedanie Soveta Bezopasnosti v rasshirennom sostave', http://kremlin.ru/transcripts/16328.

Putin, V. (2013a) 'Zasedanie mezhdunarodnogo diskussionnogo kluba "Valdai", 19 sentyabrya 2013 goda', at http://kremlin.ru/transcripts/19243.

Putin, V. (2013b) 'Poslanie Prezidenta Federal'nomu Sobraniyu, 12 dekabrya 2013 goda', http://news.kremlin.ru/transcripts/19825.

Putin, V. (2013c) 'Interv'yu Pervomu kanalu i agentsvu Assoshieyted Press, 4 sentyabrya 2013 goda', http://kremlin.ru/transcripts/19143.

Putin, V. (2013d) 'Interview for the documentary film *The Second Baptism of Rus*', 23 July, http://eng.kremlin.ru/transcripts/5747.

Putin, V. (2014a) 'Seliger 2014 National Youth Forum', http://en.kremlin.ru/events/president/news/46507.

Putin, V. (2014b) 'Obrashchenie Prezidenta Rossiiskoi Federatsiya', http://kremlin.ru/events/president/news/20603.

Putin, V. (2014c) 'Peterburgskii mezhdunarodnii ekonomicheskii forum', http://kremlin.ru/transcripts/21080.

Raskin, A. (2001) 'Television: Medium to Elect the President', in K. Nordenstreng, E. Vartanova and Y. Zassoursky (eds), *Russian Media Challenge*. Helsinki: Kikimora, pp. 93–114.

Reisinger, W. M. (ed.) (2013) *Russia's Regions and Comparative Subnational Politics*. London: Routledge.

Reisinger, W. M. and B. J. Moravski (2013) 'Deference or Governance? A Survival Analysis of Russia's Governors under Presidential Control', in W. M. Reisinger (ed.), *Russia's Regions and Comparative Subnational Politics*. London: Routledge, pp. 40–62.

Remington, T. F. (2001a) *The Russian Parliament: Institutional Evolution in a Transitional Regime, 1989–1999*. New Haven, CT: Yale University Press.

Remington, T. F. (2001b) 'Putin and the Duma', *Post-Soviet Affairs* 17(4): 285–308.

Renz, B. (2006) 'Putin's militocracy? An alternative interpretation of the role of "siloviki" in contemporary Russian politics', *Europe-Asia Studies* 58(6): 903–24.

Reuter, O. J. (2010) 'The politics of dominant party formation: United Russia and Russia's governors', *Europe-Asia Studies* 62(2): 293–327.

Reuter, O. J. (2013) 'Regional patrons and hegemonic party electoral performance in Russia', *Post-Soviet Affairs* 29(2): 101–35.

Reuter, O. J. and T. F. Remington (2009) 'Dominant party regimes and the commitment problem: the case of United Russia', *Comparative Political Studies* 42(4): 501–26.

Reuter, O. J. and G. B. Robertson (2012) 'Subnational appointments in authoritarian regimes: Evidence from Russian gubernatorial appointments', *Journal of Politics* 74(4): 1023–37.

Richter, J. (2009) 'Putin and the Public Chamber', *Post-Soviet Affairs* 25(1): 39–65.

Roberts, S. P. (2012a) *Putin's United Russia Party*. London: Routledge.

Roberts, S. P. (2012b) 'United Russia and the dominant-party framework: Understanding the Russian party of power in comparative perspective', *East European Politics* 28(3): 225–40.

Robertson, G. (2011) *The Politics of Protest in Hybrid Regimes: Managing Dissent in Post-communist Russia*. New York: Cambridge University Press.

Robertson, G. (2013) 'Protesting Putinism', *Problems of Post-Communism* 60(2): 11–23.

Robinson, N. (1992) 'Gorbachev and the place of the party in Soviet reform, 1985–91', *Soviet Studies* 44(3): 423–43.

Robinson, N. (1993) 'Parliamentary politics under Gorbachev: Opposition and the failure of socialist pluralism', *Journal of Communist Studies* 9(1): 91–108.

Robinson, N. (1995a) *Ideology and the Collapse of the Soviet System: A Critical History of Soviet Ideological Discourse*. Cheltenham: Edward Elgar.

Robinson, N. (1995b) 'Soviet ideological discourse and perestroika', *European Journal of Political Research* 27(2): 161–79.

Robinson, N. (1998) 'Classifying Russia's party system: the problem of "relevance" in a time of uncertainty', *Journal of Communist Studies and Transitional Politics* 14(1–2): 159–77.

Robinson, N. (1999a) 'Marxism, Communism and Post-communism', in A. Gamble, D. Marsh and T. Tant (eds), *Marxism and Social Science*. Basingstoke: Macmillan, pp. 302–19.

Robinson, N. (1999b) 'The global economy, reform and crisis in Russia', *Review of International Political Economy* 6(4): 531–64.

Robinson, N. (1999c) 'The CIS as an International Institution', in P. Heenan and M. Lamontagne (eds), *The CIS Handbook*. Chicago: Fitzroy Dearborn, pp. 16–27.

Robinson, N. (2000) 'The Presidency: The Politics of Institutional Chaos', in N. Robinson (ed.), *Institutions and Political Change in Russia*. Basingstoke: Palgrave Macmillan, pp. 11–40.

Robinson, N. (2001) 'The myth of equilibrium: Winner power, fiscal crisis and Russian economic reform', *Communist and Post-Communist Studies* 34(4): 423–46.

Robinson, N. (2002) *Russia: A State of Uncertainty*. London: Routledge.

Robinson, N. (2004) 'The Post-Soviet Space: The Soviet Successor States of the Commonwealth of Independent States', in A. Payne (ed.), *The New Regional Politics of Development*. Basingstoke: Palgrave Macmillan.

Robinson, N. (2008) *State, Regime and Russian Political Development*, Limerick Papers in Politics and Public Administration no. 3.

Robinson, N. (2009) 'August 1998 and the development of Russia's post-communist political economy', *Review of International Political Economy* 16(3): 433–55.

Robinson, N. (2011) 'Russian patrimonial capitalism and the international financial crisis', *Journal of Communist Studies and Transitional Politics* 27(3–4): 434–55.

Robinson, N. (2012) 'Institutional factors and Russian political parties: The changing needs of regime consolidation in a neo-patrimonial system', *East European Politics* 28(3): 298–309.

Robinson, N. (2013a) 'Economic and political hybridity: Patrimonial capitalism in the post-Soviet sphere', *Journal of Eurasian Studies* 4(2): 136–45.

Robinson, N. (2013b) 'The Contexts of Russia's Political Economy: Soviet Legacies and Post-Soviet Policies', in N. Robinson (ed.), *The political economy of Russia*. Lanham, MD: Rowman & Littlefield, pp. 15–50.

Robinson, N. (2013c) 'Russia's response to crisis: the paradox of success', *Europe-Asia Studies* 65(3): 450–72.

Robinson, N. (2017a) *Explaining Soviet collapse*. University of Limerick, Department of Politics and Public Administration, http://hdl.handle.net/10344/6121.

Robinson, N. (2017b) Russian neo-patrimonialism and Putin's "cultural turn"', *Europe-Asia Studies* 69(2): 348–66.

Robinson, N. and S. Milne (2017) 'Populism and political development in hybrid regimes: Russia and the development of official populism', *International Political Science Review* 38(4): 412–25.

Rose, R., W. Mishler and N. Munro (2006) *Russia Transformed: Developing Popular Reform for a New Regime*. Cambridge: Cambridge University Press.

Ross, C. (2002) *Federalism and Democratisation in Russia*. Manchester: Manchester University Press.

Ross, C. (2005) 'Federalism and electoral authoritarianism under Putin', *Demokratizatsiya* 13(5): 347–70.

Ross, C. (2010) 'Sub-national Elections and the Development of Semi-authoritarian Regimes in Russia', in V. Gel'man and C. Ross (eds), *The Politics of Sub-national Authoritarianism in Russia*. Farnham: Ashgate, pp. 171–90.

Ross, C. (2011) 'Regional elections and electoral authoritarianism in Russia', *Europe-Asia Studies* 63(4): 641–61.

Ross, C. (2012) 'Federalism and Defederalisation in Russia', in G. Gill and J. Young (eds), *Routledge Handbook of Russian Politics and society*. London: Routledge.

Ross, C. and R. Turovsky (2013) 'The representation of political and economic elites in the Russian Federation Council', *Demokratizatsiya* 21(1): 59–88.

Runciman, D. (2015) *The Confidence Trap: A History of Democracy in Crisis from World War I to the Present*. Princeton, NJ: Princeton University Press.

Russian Government (2009) 'Background material for the March 19, 2009, government meeting', http://government.ru/eng/docs/812/.

Rutland, P. (2003) 'Putin and the Oligarchs', in D. Herspring (ed.), *Putin's Russia: Past Imperfect, Future Uncertain*. Lanham, MD: Rowman & Littlefield.

Rutland, P. (2008) 'Putin's economic record: Is the oil boom sustainable?', *Europe-Asia Studies* 60(6): 1051–72.

Sakwa, R. (1995) 'The Russian elections of December 1993', *Europe-Asia Studies* 47(2): 195–227.

Sakwa, R. (1997) 'The regime system in Russia,' *Contemporary Politics* 3(1): 7–25.

Sakwa, R. (2004) 'Regime Change from Yeltsin to Putin: Normality, Normalcy or Normalisation?', in C. Ross (ed.), *Russian Politics under Putin*. Manchester: Manchester University Press, pp. 17–38.

Sakwa, R. (2005) 'The 2003–2004 Russian elections and prospects for democracy', *Europe-Asia Studies* 57(3): 369–98.

Sakwa, R. (2008) 'Putin and the oligarchs', *New Political Economy* 13(2): 185–91.

Sakwa, R. (2009) *The Quality of Freedom: Khodorkovsky, Putin, and the Yukos Affair*. Oxford: Oxford University Press.

Sakwa, R. (2010a) 'The dual state in Russia', *Post-Soviet Affairs* 26(3): 185–206.

Sakwa, R. (2010b) 'The revenge of the Caucasus: Chechenization and the dual state in Russia', *Nationalities Papers* 38(5): 601–22.

Sakwa, R. (2011) *The Crisis of Russian Democracy: The Dual State, Factionalism and the Medvedev Succession*. Cambridge: Cambridge University Press.

Sakwa, R. (2012) 'Systemic Stalemate: *Reiderstvo* and the Dual State', in N. Robinson (ed.), *The Political Economy of Russia*. Lanham, MD: Rowman & Littlefield, pp. 69–96.

Sakwa, R. (2013) 'Can Putinism solve its contradictions?', Open Democracy, 27 December, http://goo.gl/fqaLxr.

Sakwa, R. (2014) *Putin and the Oligarch: The Khodorkovsky–Yukos Affair*. London: I.B. Tauris.

Sakwa, R. and M. Webber (1999) 'The Commonwealth of Independent States, 1991–1998: Stagnation and survival', *Europe-Asia Studies* 51(3): 379–415.

Schedler, A. (2013) *The Politics of Uncertainty: Sustaining and Subverting Electoral Authoritarianism*. Oxford: Oxford University Press.

Schlumberger, O. (2008) 'Structural reform, economic order, and development: Patrimonial capitalism', *Review of International Political Economy* 15(4): 622–49.

Security Council (2009) 'Strategiya natsional'noi bezopastnosti Rossiisoi Federatsiu do 2020 goda', http://kremlin.ru/supplement/424.

Sharafutdinova, G. (2013) 'Gestalt switch in Russian federalism: The decline in regional power under Putin', *Comparative Politics* 45(3): 357–76.

Shearman, P. and M. Sussex (2000) 'Foreign Policy-making and Institutions', in N. Robinson (ed.), *Institutions and Political Change in Russia*. Basingstoke: Macmillan, pp. 151–72.

Shekhovtsov, A. (2017) *Russia and the Western Far Right: Tango Noir*. London: Routledge.

Shevchenko, I. (2004) *The Central Government of Russia: From Gorbachev to Putin*. Farnham: Ashgate.

Shevtsova, L. (2000) 'Can electoral autocracy survive?' *Journal of Democracy* 11(3): 36–8.

Shiraev, E., and V. Zubok (2000) *Anti-Americanism in Russia: from Stalin to Putin*. Basingstoke: Palgrave Macmillan.

Shlapentokh, V. (2006) 'Trust in public institutions in Russia: The lowest in the world', *Communist and Post-Communist Studies* 39(2): 153–74.

Shleifer, A., and D. Treisman (2000) *Without a Map: Political Tactics and Economic Reform in Russia*. Cambridge, MA: MIT Press.

Short Course (1941) *History of the Communist Party of the Soviet Union (Bolsheviks) (Short Course)*. Moscow: Foreign Languages Publishing House.

Sinitsina, I. (2009) *Experience in Implementing Social Benefits Monetization Reform in Russia*. Warsaw: Case Network Studies & Analyses.

Slider, D. (1994) 'Federalism, Discord, and Accommodation: Intergovernmental Relations in Post-Soviet Russia', in T. H. Friedgut and J. W. Hahn (eds), *Local Power and Post-Soviet Politics*. Armonk, NY: M. E. Sharpe, pp. 239–69.

Slider, D. (2010) 'How united is United Russia? Regional sources of intra-party conflict', *Journal of Communist Studies and Transition Politics* 26(2): 257–75.

Slider, D. (2012) 'Regional Governance', in G. Gill and J. Young (eds), *Routledge Handbook of Russian Politics and Society*. London: Routledge.

Slider, D. (2014) 'A Federal State?', in S. White, R. Sakwa and H. E. Hale (eds), *Developments in Russian Politics 8*. Basingstoke: Palgrave Macmillan, pp. 157–72.

Smith, M. and G. Timmins (2001) 'Russia, NATO and the EU in an era of enlargement: Vulnerability or Opportunity?', *Geopolitics* 6(1): 69–90.

Smyth, R. (2006) *Candidate Strategies and Electoral Competition in the Russian Federation: Democracy without Foundation*. New York: Cambridge University Press.

Soldatov, A. and I. Borogan (2015) *The Red Web: The Struggle between Russia's Digital Dictatorship and the New Online Revolutionaries*. New York: Public Affairs.

Solnick, S. (1998) *Stealing the State: Control and Collapse in Soviet Institutions*. Cambridge, MA: Harvard University Press.

Stalin, J. (1952 [1931]) 'O zadachakh khozyaistvennikov: rech' na pervoi Vsesoyuznoi konferentsii rabotnikov sotsialisticheskoi promyshlennosti, 4 fevralya 1931g', *Voprosy Leninizma*. Moscow: Gospolitizdat.

Stalin, J. (1952 [1934]) 'Otchetnii doklad XVII s''ezdu partii o rabote TsK VKP(b)', *Voprosy Leninizma*. Moscow: Gospolitizdat.

Stone, R. (2002) *Lending Credibility: The International Monetary Fund and the Post-communist Transition*. Princeton, NJ: Princeton University Press.

Tikhomirov, V. (1997) 'Capital flight from post-Soviet Russia', *Europe-Asia Studies* 49(4): 591–615.

Tikhomirov, V. (2000) *The Political Economy of Post-Soviet Russia*. Basingstoke: Macmillan.

Tolstrup, J. (2015) 'Black knights and elections in authoritarian regimes: Why and how Russia supports authoritarian incumbents in post-Soviet states', *European Journal of Political Research* 54(4): 673–90.

Tompson, W. (2005) 'Putin and the "Oligarchs": A Two-sided Commitment Problem', in A. Pravda (ed.), *Leading Russia: Putin in Perspective: Essays in Honour of Archie Brown*. Oxford: Oxford University Press, pp. 179–202.

Treisman, D. (1999) 'After Yeltsin comes … Yeltsin,' *Foreign Policy* no. 117: 74–86.

Treisman, D. (2011) 'Presidential popularity in a hybrid regime: Russia under Yeltsin and Putin', *American Journal of Political Science* 55(3): 590–609.

Troxel, T. (2003) *Parliamentary Power in Russia, 1994–2001: President vs Parliament.* Basingstoke: Palgrave Macmillan.

Tsygankov, A. P. (1997) 'From international institutionalism to revolutionary expansionism: The foreign policy discourse of contemporary Russia', *Mershon International Studies Review* 41(2): 247–68.

Tsygankov, A. P. (2009) *Russophobia: Anti-Russian Lobby and American Foreign Policy.* New York: Palgrave Macmillan.

Tsygankov, A. P. (2012) *Russia and the West from Alexander to Putin: Honor in International Relations.* Cambridge: Cambridge University Press.

Tsygankov, A. P. (2013) 'The Russia–NATO mistrust: Ethnophobia and the double expansion to contain "the Russian bear"', *Communist and Post-Communist Studies* 46(1): 179–88.

Tsygankov, A. P. (2015) 'Vladimir Putin's last stand: The sources of Russia's Ukraine policy', *Post-Soviet Affairs* 31(4): 279–303.

Urban, M. E. (1985) 'Conceptualizing political power in the USSR: Patterns of binding and bonding', *Studies in Comparative Communism* 18(4) 207–26.

Weber, M. (1947) *The Theory of Social and Economic Organization.* New York: Free Press.

White, A. C. (2016) 'Electoral fraud and electoral geography: United Russia strongholds in the 2007 and 2011 Russian parliamentary elections', *Europe-Asia Studies* 68(7): 1127–78.

White, D. (2006) *The Russian Democratic Party Yabloko: Opposition in a Managed Democracy.* Aldershot: Ashgate.

White, D. (2011) 'Dominant party systems: a framework for conceptualizing opposition strategies in Russia', *Democratization* 18(3): 655–81.

White, D. (2013) 'Taking it to the streets: Raising the costs of electoral authoritarianism in Russia', *Perspectives on European Politics and Society* 14(4): 582–98.

White, D. (2015) 'Political opposition in Russia: The challenges of mobilisation and the political–civil society nexus', *East European Politics* 31(3): 314–25.

White, S. (1996) *Russia goes Dry: Alcohol, State and Society.* Cambridge: Cambridge University Press.

White, S. and V. Feklyunina (2011) 'Russia's authoritarian elections: The view from below', *Europe-Asia Studies* 63(4): 579–602.

White, S. and I. McAllister (1996) 'The CPSU and its members: Between communism and post-communism', *British Journal of Political Science* 26(1): 105–22.

White, S., R. Rose and I. McAllister (1997) *How Russia Votes.* Chatham, NJ: Chatham House.

White, S., M. Wyman and S. Oates (1997) 'Parties and voters in the 1995 Russian Duma election', *Europe-Asia Studies* 49(5): 767–98.

Whitmore, S. (2010) 'Parliamentary oversight in Putin's neo-patrimonial state: Watchdogs or show-dogs?', *Europe-Asia Studies* 62(6): 999–1025.

Willerton, J. (1998) 'Post-Soviet Clientelist Norms at the Russian Federal Level', in G. Gill (ed.), *Elites and Leadership in Russian Politics.* Basingstoke: Macmillan, pp. 52–80.

Willerton, J. and A. Shulus (1995) 'Constructing a new political process: The hegemonic presidency and the legislature', *John Marshall Law Review* 28(4): 787–825.

Wilson, A. (2014) *Ukraine Crisis: What it Means for the West.* New Haven, CT: Yale University Press.

Wilson, K. (2006) 'Party-system development under Putin', *Post-Soviet Affairs* 22(4): 314–48.

Wilson, K. (2007) 'Party finance in Russia: Has the 2001 law "on political parties" made a difference?', *Europe-Asia Studies* 59(7): 1089–113.

Woodruff, D. (1999) *Money Unmade: Barter and the Fate of Russian Capitalism*. Ithaca, NY: Cornell University Press.

World Bank (2017a) 'Worldwide governance indicators', http://data.worldbank.org/data-catalog/worldwide-governance-indicators.

World Bank (2017b) 'Country data: Russia', http://data.worldbank.org/country/russian-federation.

World Bank (2017c) *Russia Economic Report 2017: From Recession to Recovery*. Washington, DC: World Bank.

Wyman, M., S. White, B. Miller and P. Heywood (1995) 'The place of "party" in post-communist Europe', *Party Politics* 1(4): 535–48.

Yakovlev, A. (2003) *Sumerki*. Moscow: Materik.

Yeltsin, B. (1994) *The View from the Kremlin*. London: HarperCollins.

Zabyelina, Y. (2017) 'Russia's Night Wolves motorcycle club: From 1%ers to political activists', *Trends in Organized Crime* 20: 1–15, https://doi.org/10.1007/s12117-017-9314-7.

Zamoyski, A. (2007) *Rites of Peace*. London: Harper Press.

Zimmerman, W. (2015) *Ruling Russia: Authoritarianism from the Revolution to Putin*. Princeton, NJ: Princeton University Press.

Index

Page numbers in *italics* refer to tables and figures